From Memory to Written Record

From Memory to Written Record

England, 1066—1307

M. T. Clanchy

Harvard University Press

Cambridge, Massachusetts

1979

For R. H. C. Davis my friend and teacher

Library of Congress Cataloging in Publication Data

Clanchy, M T
  From memory to written record, England, 1066-
1307.

    Bibliography: p.
    Includes index.
    1. England—Civilization—Medieval period,
1066-1485. 2. Illiteracy—England. 3. Culture
diffusion. I. Title.
DA185.C52   942.02   78-27528

ISBN 0-674-32510-9

Contents

Plates

Preface and acknowledgements

The title and subject of this book were suggested in my paper 'Remembering the Past and the Good Old Law', published in *History* (volume LV) in 1970. Since then I have benefited from discussing its themes with colleagues at the Medieval Society and the Historians' Discussion Group of the University of Glasgow and in other talks which I have given at the universities of Aberdeen, Dublin (UCD), Edinburgh, London (Institute of Historical Research), Manchester, Sheffield, and Stirling. I am grateful to all those who organized these talks or contributed to them. I also thank the University of Glasgow for travel grants and my fellow teachers of medieval history there for cooperating in a system of sabbatical leave which has enabled me to write. At an early stage I was encouraged by two scholars who have not lived to see this book: Max Gluckman helped me with anthropology and G. D. G. Hall with the history of law. From the confidence and enthusiasm of Mr John Davey, formerly of Edward Arnold Ltd, my ideas took publishable form.

In writing the book I have benefited from the comments of Dr Peter Davies, Professor Jack Goody, Dr Michael Richter, Mrs Felicity Riddy, Dr J. A. F. Thomson, Professor Ralph V. Turner and Mr C. P. Wormald, who have all read drafts of particular chapters. Mrs Katherine Thomson of the *Dictionary of Medieval Latin from British Sources* has advised me about the history of certain words, notably *rotulus*. The completed book was read in typescript by Dr C. H. Knowles and Professor S. E. Thorne. All these scholars have helped to eliminate errors and make positive improvements; they are not responsible for any of my mistakes.

In getting together the photographs for the plates I have had particular help from Miss Deborah Beevor, Mr Roger Custance, Miss Eleanor M. Garvey, Dr Edith Henderson and Mr Trevor Kaye. For permission to reproduce the plates I am indebted to: the Warden and Fellows of Winchester College (plate I); the British Library Board (plates II, III, IV, XI, XV); the Law School of Harvard University (plates V, VI, VII, XVI, XVII, XVIII, XIX); the Controller of Her Majesty's Stationery Office (plate VIII); the County Archivist of Berkshire (plates IX, X); the Houghton Library of Harvard University (plates XII, XIII); the Master and Fellows of Trinity College Cambridge (plate XIV).

Finally I wish to thank Miss Mary Brodie for typing, Mrs Glenna M. Satterthwaite for reading the proofs, and Miss Fay Sharman and the publishers.

University of Glasgow   M. T. Clanchy

Abbreviations

Anglo-Scottish Relations	*Anglo-Scottish Relations: Some Selected Documents* ed. E. L. G. Stones, reprint (1970).
Annales Monastici	*Annales Monastici* ed. H. R. Luard, Rolls Series XXXVI (1864–9).
Baronial Docs	*Documents of the Baronial Movement of Reform and Rebellion 1258–67* ed. R. F. Treharne and I. J. Sanders (1973).
Battle	*Chronicon Monasterio de Bello* ed. J. S. Brewer, Anglia Christiana Society (1846).
Becket Materials	*Materials for the History of Thomas Becket* ed. J. C. Robertson and J. B. Sheppard, Rolls Series LXXVII (1875–85).
Bennett & Smithers	*Early Middle English Verse and Prose* ed. J. A. W. Bennett and G. V. Smithers, 2nd edition (1968).
Berks. Eyre	*The Roll and Writ File of the Berkshire Eyre of 1248* ed. M. T. Clanchy, Selden Society XC (1973).
BIHR	*Bulletin of the Institute of Historical Research*
Bishop & Chaplais	*Facsimiles of English Royal Writs Presented to V. H. Galbraith* ed. T. A. M. Bishop and P. Chaplais (1957).
BJRL	*Bulletin of the John Rylands Library.*
BL MS	British Library (formerly British Museum) manuscript.
BM Facs	*Facsimiles of Royal and Other Charters in the British Museum* ed. G. F. Warner and H. G. Ellis I (1903).
Boase, *English Art*	T. S. R. Boase, *English Art 1100–1216* (1953).
Book of Fees	*The Book of Fees Commonly called Testa de Nevill* (1921–31).

Book of Prests	*Book of Prests of the King's Wardrobe for 1294–5 Presented to J. G. Edwards* ed. E. B. Fryde (1962).
Bracton	Henry de Bracton, *De Legibus et Consuetudinibus Angliae* ed. G. E. Woodbine (1915), reissued with translation and revisions by S. E. Thorne (1968–77).
CChR	*Calendar of Charter Rolls* (1903–27).
CClR	*Calendar of Close Rolls: Edward I* (1900–1908).
Chaplais, *Docs*	P. Chaplais, *English Royal Documents: King John – Henry VI* (1971).
Cheney, *Chanceries*	C. R. Cheney, *English Bishops' Chanceries, 1100–1250* (1950).
Cheney, *Notaries*	C. R. Cheney, *Notaries Public in England in the Thirteenth and Fourteenth Centuries* (1972).
Cheney, *Texts & Studies*	C. R. Cheney, *Medieval Texts and Studies* (1973).
Cheshire Facs	*Facsimiles of Early Cheshire Charters* ed. G. Barraclough, Lancashire and Cheshire Record Society (1957).
Clanchy, '*Moderni*'	M. T. Clanchy, '*Moderni* in Medieval Education and Government in England', *Speculum* L (1975), pp. 671–88.
Clanchy, 'Remembering'	M. T. Clanchy, 'Remembering the Past and the Good Old Law', *History* LV (1970), pp. 165–76.
CLibR	*Calendar of Liberate Rolls: Henry III* (1917–64).
ClR	*Close Rolls: Henry III* (1902–38).
Court Baron	*The Court Baron* ed. F. W. Maitland and W. P. Baildon, Selden Society IV (1890).
CPatR	*Calendar of Patent Rolls* (1891–).
CuriaRR	*Curia Regis Rolls* (1923–).
Curtius, *European Lit.*	E. R. Curtius, *European Literature and the Latin Middle Ages* trans. W. R. Trask (1953).
Dialogus	*Dialogus de Scaccario* ed. C. Johnson (1950).
Duggan, *Decretals*	C. Duggan, *Twelfth-Century Decretal Collections and their Importance in English History,* University of London Historical Studies XII (1963).
Eadmer, *Historia*	*Eadmeri Historia Novorum in Anglia* ed. M. Rule, Rolls Series LXXXI (1884).
Eadmer, *Vita*	*The Life of St Anselm by Eadmer* ed. R. W. Southern (1962).

EHR	*English Historical Review*
English Library	*The English Library before 1700* ed. F. Wormald and C. E. Wright (1958).
Essays to Poole	*Essays in History Presented to R. L. Poole* ed. H. W. C. Davis (1927).
Fleta	*Fleta Commentarius Juris Anglicani* ed. H. G. Richardson and G. O. Sayles, Selden Society LXXII (1953), LXXXIX (1972).
Foedera	*Foedera etc. or T. Rymer's Foedera* ed. A. Clark *et al.*, Record Commissioners' publications, I-III (1816–30).
Galbraith, 'Literacy'	V. H. Galbraith, 'The Literacy of the Medieval English Kings',*Proceedings of the British Academy* XXI (1935), pp. 201–38.
Galbraith, *Studies*	V. H. Galbraith, *Studies in the Public Records* (1948).
Gervase	*The Historical Works of Gervase of Canterbury* ed. W. Stubbs, Rolls Series LXXIII (1879–80).
Giraldus	*Giraldi Cambrensis Opera* ed. J. S. Brewer *et al.*, Rolls Series XXI (1861–91).
Glanvill	*The Treatise on the Laws and Customs of the Realm of England Commonly Called Glanvill* ed. G. D. G. Hall (1965).
Goody, *Literacy*	*Literacy in Traditional Societies* ed. J. Goody (1968).
Gransden, *Historical Writing*	A. Gransden, *Historical Writing in England c.550–1307* (1974).
HMSO	Her Majesty's Stationery Office publications.
JMH	*Journal of Medieval History.*
Jocelin	*The Chronicle of Jocelin of Brakelond* ed. H. E. Butler (1949).
Kauffmann, *Romanesque MSS*	C. M. Kauffmann, *Romanesque Manuscripts 1066–1190* (1975).
Ker, *English MSS*	N. R. Ker, *English Manuscripts in the Century after the Norman Conquest* (1960).
Legge, *Anglo-Norman*	M. D. Legge, *Anglo-Norman Literature and its Background* (1963).
Matthew Paris	*Matthaei Parisiensis Chronica Majora* ed. H. R. Luard, Rolls Series LVII (1872–84).
MM for Stenton	*A Medieval Miscellany for D. M. Stenton* ed. P. M. Barnes and C. F. Slade, Pipe Roll Society new series XXXVI (1960).
Monasticon	W. Dugdale, *Monasticon Anglicanum* ed. J. Caley *et al.*, (1817–30).
Mowbray Charters	*Charters of the Honour of Mowbray* ed. D. E. Greenway (1972).

Northants. Facs	*Facsimiles of Early Charters from Northamptonshire Collections* ed. F. M. Stenton, Northamptonshire Record Society IV (1930).
Orderic	Orderic Vitalis, *Historia Ecclesiastica* ed. M. Chibnall (1969–).
Oxford Facs	*Facsimiles of Early Charters in Oxford Muniment Rooms* ed. H. E. Salter (1929).
P & M	F. Pollock and F. W. Maitland, *The History of English Law before the Time of Edward I,* 2nd edition (1898).
Parkes, 'Literacy'	M. B. Parkes, 'The Literacy of the Laity' in *The Medieval World* ed. D. Daiches and A. Thorlby (1973), pp. 555–77.
Patrologiae	*Patrologiae: Cursus Completus Series Latina* ed. J. P. Migne (1844–73).
PRO	Public Record Office.
PRS	Pipe Roll Society publications (1884–).
R & S	H. G. Richardson and G. O. Sayles, *The Governance of Medieval England from the Conquest to Magna Carta* (1963).
Ramsey	*Chronicon Abbatiae Rameseiensis* ed. W. D. Macray, Rolls Series LXXXIII (1886).
RC	Record Commissioners' publications (1805–48).
Richardson, *Jewry*	H. G. Richardson, *The English Jewry under Angevin Kings* (1960).
Rot. Lit. Claus.	*Rotuli Litterarum Clausarum 1204–27,* ed. T. D. Hardy (1833–44).
Rot. Lit. Pat.	*Rotuli Litterarum Patentium 1201–16,* ed. T. D. Hardy (1835).
RRA-N	*Regesta Regum Anglo-Normannorum 1066–1154,* ed. H. W. C. Davis, J. Johnson, H. A. Cronne and R. H. C. Davis (4 vols, 1913–69).
RS	Rolls Series: *Rerum Britannicarum Medii Aevi Scriptores* (1858–97).
S.	Society serial publications.
SCCKB	*Select Cases in the Court of King's Bench under Edward I* ed. G. O. Sayles, Selden Society LV (1936) LVII (1938) LVIII (1939).
SCPWW	*Select cases of Procedure without Writ under Henry III* ed. H. G. Richardson and G. O. Sayles, Selden Society LX (1941).
Smalley, *Historians*	B. Smalley, *Historians in the Middle Ages* (1974).
Smalley, *The Bible*	B. Smalley, *The Study of the Bible in the Middle Ages,* 2nd edition (1952).

Southern, *Medieval Humanism*	R. W. Southern, *Medieval Humanism and Other Studies* (1970).
SPC	*Select Pleas of the Crown* ed. F. W. Maitland, Selden Society I (1887).
SS	Selden Society publications (1887–).
Statutes	*Statutes of the Realm* ed. A. Luders *et al.*, Record Commissioners' publications, I (1810).
Stenton, *Feudalism*	F. M. Stenton, *The First Century of English Feudalism 1066–1166*, 2nd edition (1961).
Stenton, *Justice*	D. M. Stenton, *English Justice between the Norman Conquest and the Great Charter* (1965).
Stubbs, *Charters*	*Select Charters* ed. W. Stubbs, 9th edition, ed. H. W. C. Davis (1913).
Study of Medieval Records	*The Study of Medieval Records: Essays in Honour of K. Major* ed. D. A. Bullough and R. L. Storey (1971).
Thompson, *Literacy*	J. W. Thompson, *The Literacy of the Laity in the Middle Ages* University of California Publications in Education IX (1939).
TRHS	*Transactions of the Royal Historical Society.*
Van Caenegem, *Writs*	*Royal Writs in England from the Conquest to Glanvill* ed. R. C. van Caenegem, Selden Society LXXVII (1959).
VCH	*Victoria History of the Counties of England.*
Walter Map	*De Nugis Curialium* ed. M. R. James, Anecdota Oxoniensa, Medieval and Modern series XIV (1914).
Walter of Henley	*Walter of Henley and Other Treatises on Estate Management and Accounting* ed. D. Oschinsky (1971).
Wattenbach, *Schriftwesen*	W. Wattenbach, *Das Schriftwesen im Mittelalter,* 3rd edition (1896).
WiltsRS	Wiltshire Record Society publications, formerly Wiltshire Archaeological and Natural History Society.

Introduction

This book is about the uses of literacy in the Middle Ages. It concentrates on England in the two and a half centuries from 1066 to 1307 (from the Norman Conquest to the death of Edward I) because these years constitute a distinctive period in the development of literate ways of thinking and of doing business. In the eleventh century literate modes were still unusual, whereas in the thirteenth century they became normal among the rulers. This formative stage in the history of literacy has received less attention from scholars than the invention of printing in the later Middle Ages, although it is no less important. Printing succeeded because a literate public already existed; that public originated in the twelfth and thirteenth centuries. Writing was not new in 1066, of course, either in England or elsewhere. In the royal monasteries of Anglo-Saxon England, as in other parts of Europe, an original literate culture had been created which was distinguished especially by its illuminated manuscripts of parchment. From these royal and monastic roots new uses and forms of writing proliferated in the twelfth and thirteenth centuries and took shapes which would last for generations.

The particular argument of this book is that this growth in the uses of literacy is indicated by, and was perhaps primarily a consequence of, the production and retention of records on an unprecedented scale (unprecedented, that is, in England). The difference between Anglo-Saxon and thirteenth-century England in this respect is marked. From Anglo-Saxon England about 2,000 charters and writs (including originals and copies and an indefinite number of forgeries) survive. From thirteenth-century England, on the other hand, tens of thousands of such charters and writs survive; this estimate is no more precise because the documents have never been systematically counted. How many documents once existed (as distinct from how many now survive), either in the Anglo-Saxon period or in the thirteenth century, is a matter for conjecture and inevitably therefore for different opinions. An estimate further on in this book suggests that eight million charters may have been written in the thirteenth century alone for smallholders and serfs.[1]

The increase was not merely in numbers of parchments, but in the

---

[1] See pp. 34–5 below.

spread of literate modes both territorially and socially. By the reign of
Edward I royal or seignorial writs reached every bailiff and village in
England, making writing familiar throughout the countryside. Similarly the use of charters as titles to property made its way down the
social hierarchy – from the royal court and monasteries (in the eleventh
century and earlier) to secular clerks and knights (in the twelfth century), reaching the laity in general by the reign of Edward I. This is not
to say that everyone could read and write by 1307, but that by that time
literate modes were familiar even to serfs, who used charters for conveying property to each other and whose rights and obligations were beginning to be regularly recorded in manorial rolls. Those who used writing
participated in literacy, even if they had not mastered the skills of a
clerk. One measure of this change is the possession of a seal or *signum*,
which entitled a person to sign his name. In Edward the Confessor's
reign only the king is known to have possessed one for authenticating
documents, whereas in Edward I's reign even serfs were required by
statute to have them.[2]

The book is arranged in two parts. The first part describes the making
of records, because their gradual accumulation in archives and their
distribution throughout the country prepared and fertilized the ground
in which literacy could germinate. Through the spread of record-
making the practice of using writing for ordinary secular business, as
distinct from using it exceptionally for solemn religious or royal purposes, became first familiar and then established as a habit. Among the
laity, or more specifically among knights and country gentry in the first
instance, confidence in written record was neither immediate nor automatic. Trust in writing and understanding of what it could – and could
not – achieve developed from growing familiarity with documents.

The second part of the book therefore describes the growth of a literate
mentality. It traces the halting acceptance of literate modes by the
rulers, both clerical and lay. The use of writing for business purposes
was almost as unfamiliar to many monks in the twelfth century and
earlier (except in the great houses under royal patronage) as it was to
knights and laity. Elementary rules of business, such as the need to
write dates on letters, were only learned with difficulty because they
raised novel questions about the writer's place in the temporal order.
Forgery was consequently rife. Despite the increasing use of documents
(both authentic and forged) traditional oral procedures, such as the
preference for reading aloud rather than scanning a text silently with
the eye, persisted through the Middle Ages and beyond. There were also
special problems to be overcome in England, such as the variety and
different status of the languages in use after the Norman Conquest.

Outside the king's court and great monastic houses, property rights
and all other knowledge of the past had traditionally and customarily
been held in the living memory. When historical information was
needed, local communities resorted not to books and charters but to the

[2] See ch. 2, n. 24 and ch. 7, nn. 39–40 below.

oral wisdom of their elders and remembrancers. Even where books and charters existed, they were rarely consulted at first, apparently because habits of doing so took time to develop. Unwritten customary law – and lore – had been the norm in the eleventh century and earlier in England, as in all communities where literacy is restricted or unknown. Nevertheless two centuries later, by Edward I's reign, the king's attorneys were arguing in many of the *quo warranto* prosecutions against the magnates that the only sufficient warrant for a privilege was a written one and that in the form of a specific statement in a charter. Memory, whether individual or collective, if unsupported by clear written evidence, was ruled out of court. As written titles had only come into common use relatively recently and as few charters were sufficiently exact, the *quo warranto* prosecutions threatened to disfranchise nearly all the magnates. Although the *quo warranto* cases were rapidly suspended in the 1290s and the king's government had to concede that tenure 'from time out of mind' was a legitimate claim, the principle had been established for the future that property rights depended generally on writings and not on the oral recollections of old wise men. Hence the title of this book, *From Memory to Written Record*, refers to this shift in ways of thinking and acting, which made its mark between the Norman Conquest and the reign of Edward I.

The title is a variation of H. J. Chaytor's classic, *From Script to Print* (first published in 1945), which described the differences between the manuscript culture of the Middle Ages and the print culture of the Renaissance. Acknowledging its debt to Chaytor, *From Memory to Written Record* takes a step behind the conditions he described to the time when even important information was usually held in the memory alone and not in script of any sort. The shift from habitually memorizing things to writing them down and keeping records was necessarily prior to the shift from script to print, and was as profound a change in its effects on the individual intellect and on society. Literacy is also approached here from a different point of view from Chaytor. Whereas he was chiefly concerned with vernacular and literary works, this book (while not excluding literature) is primarily based on Latin business documents and legal records. The development of literacy from and for practical purposes of day-to-day business, rather than creative literature, is the theme of *From Memory to Written Record*.

A change as obvious as the growing number of records has not gone unnoticed by historians. V. H. Galbraith in particular has stated the general argument in various forms, for example:

> Early society is ordered and governed by oral tradition. . . . Then there is a long twilight of transition, during which the written record encroaches more and more upon the sphere of custom. In this way the volume of written evidence available steadily increases until we reach a time – *not I think earlier than the thirteenth century* – when most of society's major activities find some sort of written record. More, however, is at stake than the mere volume of

evidence. As documents grow more plentiful their whole meaning changes.[3]

Although this book differs from Galbraith in its interpretation of particular documents, its general aim is to build upon his work and extend it from the growth of 'public' records (that is, the documents of the king's government) to all types of writing, and from the writings themselves to the people they affected. Twentieth-century scholars of medieval England tend to be specialists in particular types of writing, because the records are so large and complex, whereas medieval makers and users of documents would have seen less significance in such distinctions as public and private, royal and ecclesiastical, or historical and literary. Essential as they are for specialized study, these distinctions can obscure the breadth and unity of medieval experience.

This book necessarily therefore draws throughout on the expertise of other scholars and consistently uses a selective method, which needs explaining and perhaps also justifying. First of all, because it is an axiom of the argument that the number of documents markedly increased in the period 1066–1307, no single scholar can claim to have studied them all or even most in detail. This book proceeds by citing a limited number of examples, often in detail, in order to illustrate a series of propositions. These citations (many of which have been noted by previous authors in other contexts) have been selected from a large body of material; they aim to be typical or particularly significant.

An additional principle of presentation which needs explaining is that, although this book is solely concerned with the making of manuscripts, it generally cites printed editions of texts rather than the manuscripts themselves. Even where manuscripts are referred to, the reader is normally directed to a facsimile and not to the original document. This procedure has been adopted because much of the argument is novel and some readers will wish to pursue or verify translated citations or references as readily as possible. While admiring manuscript culture and trying to convey to the reader its special qualities, every author must acknowledge the advantages which printing has brought to scholars by making uniform texts available in multiple copies. Furthermore, generalizations cannot often be made directly from medieval manuscripts, because each one usually requires detailed study and presentation by an editor (to establish the best text, assess the date, identify persons and so on) before it can be adequately understood. Editing texts and generalizing from them in books like this one are different endeavours.

Although this book makes few original observations about particular manuscripts, it is intended to provide a new general survey of the medieval documents of England in the period it concerns. Chapter 3 on

---

[3] *Studies*, p. 26 (my emphasis). This argument was first put forward by Galbraith in 1935, 'Literacy', pp. 204–6, and finally in 1962: 'At the very outset of the thirteenth century, with the beginnings of the official archives preserved in the Public Record Office, we pass from a customary and largely oral society to an age of record', *The Historian at Work*, p. 3.

'Types of Record', for example, or chapter 6 on 'Languages of Record' aim to describe their subjects comprehensively though far from exhaustively. Such broad treatment is made necessary by the book's prevailing theme of literacy developing over time across many types of writing activity. This treatment has the added incidental advantage of bringing together areas of scholarship which are normally kept apart. Thus chapter 6 discusses all written languages used in England at the time (Latin, French, English and Hebrew in approximate order of frequency), whereas scholars often specialize in one language only. Likewise chapter 3 includes scholastic texts and works of literature as well as charters and rolls. The inevitable superficiality of this approach is counterbalanced, in theory at least, by the range of discussion achieved.

The purpose of concentrating on one place, England, and on a well defined period, the years from 1066 to 1307, is to make the subject manageable. More general studies of literacy, particularly by anthropologists, have emphasized both the diversity of forms which literacy can take and the common recurrent features which distinguish all literate cultures from non-literate ones.[4] Descriptions of the development of literacy in particular places and periods (as in this book), on the other hand, provide a variety of readers with sufficiently detailed information to draw reliable conclusions for their own purposes. The shift from memory to written record, which occurred in England in the twelfth and thirteenth centuries, was not restricted to England although it is most evident there. It was a western European phenomenon, as the graph at page 44 suggests, which compares the number of letters extant from the chanceries of England, France and the papacy between c.1066 and c.1200. Comparable graphs could be drawn to show the growth of documentation in the medieval kingdoms of the Spains and of Sicily, or in Germany and the Italian city states, although the sources of information are more fragmentary in these instances. It is probable, moreover, that the letter writing energies of the papacy, from the reign of Gregory VII (1073–85) onwards, set new standards of documentation – both in output and quality – which compelled secular governments to follow suit.

In the period 1066–1307 England was peculiarly open to continental influences because the monarchy was controlled first by the Normans, secondly by the Angevins and then in the thirteenth century by the Poitevin and other southern favourites of King John and Henry III. Edward I likewise was a ruler of European stature and interests. Nevertheless this combination of influences created in England over the twelfth and thirteenth centuries an amalgam of Anglo-Saxon, French and Latin culture which is a distinct entity rather than a mere accumulation of parts. Although English experience of literacy was far from being unique or self-contained, it presents itself as a relatively coherent whole in the period 1066–1307 because the country was dominated by a

[4] Goody, *Literacy* and *The Domestication of the Savage Mind* (1977). J. Vachek, *Written Language*, Janua Linguarum, Series Critica XIV (1973), advances comparable arguments from linguistic analysis.

centralizing royal bureaucracy. Even though the day-to-day power and importance of the royal government has been exaggerated by 'public' record-oriented historians, it has left a formidable reminder of its manifold activities in the hundreds of thousands of parchments now preserved in the Public Record Office in Chancery Lane. William the Conqueror's Domesday survey at the beginning of the period and Edward I's *quo warranto* prosecutions at the end were both countrywide enquiries, which aimed to record the most important rights of the king and his feudatories in writing. Nothing on this scale survives from any other European state. The Emperor Frederick II conducted a comparable survey in the kingdom of Sicily in the 1220s, but its details are now lost.

No inquiry by any medieval government ever exceeded in scope and detail the survey inaugurated by Edward I in March 1279, which immediately preceded the *quo warranto* prosecutions. Commissioners in each county were instructed to list by name and have written down in books all villages and hamlets and every type of tenement whatsoever, whether of the rich or the poor, and whether royal or otherwise.[5] The stated purpose of this survey was to settle questions of ownership once and for all. The returns have only survived in their original form from a handful of counties in the south Midlands (much of Oxfordshire, Huntingdonshire and Cambridgeshire and parts of Bedfordshire and Buckinghamshire) and they vary in their attention to detail.[6] Some exceed the commissioners' instructions and list every serf by name, while others are very brief. It may be more than a coincidence that the area producing extant returns lies on a line between the university towns of Oxford and Cambridge.[7] Only there perhaps were a sufficient number of clerks found to make the survey. Students, who had learned to note down their masters' lectures, could apply this expertise to the king's business. If this hypothesis is correct, it looks as if the survey of 1279 was too ambitious even for Edward I. Only in the clerkly area of Oxford and Cambridge was literacy sufficiently widespread to fulfil his aims. Unlike the Domesday survey of two centuries earlier, the survey of 1279 excited little comment among chroniclers. They were by then perhaps long accustomed, and even weary, of the monarchy's preoccupation with making surveys and lists, especially when 'no advantage came of it' (in the opinion of the Dunstable chronicler).[8] The numerous surveys of Edward I's reign suggest that the bureaucracy's appetite for information exceeded its capacity to digest it. Making lists was in danger of becoming a substitute for action.

---

[5] Commission in *Patent Rolls*, 1272–81, p. 343; *Foedera* I, part ii, p. 567; *Rotuli Hundredorum*, RC, II, p. ix.

[6] Most of the returns are printed in *Rotuli Hundredorum* II, pp. 321–877. They are analysed by E. A. Kosminsky, *Studies in the Agrarian History of England in the Thirteenth Century* (1956), pp. 7–46.

[7] W. Urry, *Canterbury under the Angevin Kings* (1967), p. 3.

[8] *Annales Monastici* III, p. 263. H. M. Cam, *The Hundred and the Hundred Rolls* (1930), p. 240. I owe the elucidation of this reference to Professor E. L. G. Stones.

It is possible that Englishmen became exceptionally conscious of records as a direct consequence of the Norman Conquest. Making records is initially a product of distrust rather than social progress. By making Domesday Book William the Conqueror set his shameful mark on the humiliated people, and even on their domestic animals, in the opinion of the *Anglo-Saxon Chronicle*.[9] The harsh exactitude of Norman and Angevin officials, with their writs and pipe rolls, caused churchmen and ultimately even laymen to keep records of their own. Thus it has been calculated that out of 971 papal decretal letters of the twelfth century whose destination is known, 434 went to England.[10] This statistic does not mean that the papal *curia* expended nearly half its energies on English business, but that English recipients were more careful to preserve papal letters than clergy in other European states. Similarly of 27 early collections of decretals compiled by canon lawyers in Europe as a whole, 15 are English.[11] The history of record-making and literacy in England merits separate study, provided it is understood that medieval England was part of Europe and not an island in the cultural sense.

A difference between this book and some previous studies of records by historians is that it tries to avoid being prejudiced in favour of literacy. Writing gives the historian his materials and it is consequently understandable that he has tended to see it as a measure of progress. Furthermore, literate techniques are so necessary to twentieth-century western society, and education in them is so fundamental a part of the modern individual's experience that it is difficult to avoid assuming that literacy is an essential mark of civilization. By contrast, anthropological studies of non-literate societies in the third world and sociological studies of deprived urban proleteriats in the west both suggest that literacy in itself is primarily a technology. It has different effects according to circumstances and is not a civilizing force in itself, although there is a relationship between national minimal literacy averages and the mastery of modern industrial technology.[12] Identifying literacy as a 'technology of the intellect,' J. Goody has given examples of how 'writing is not a monolithic entity, an undifferentiated skill; its potentialities depend upon the kind of system that obtains in any particular society.'[13]

For medievalists a warning was sounded in the 1950s by the Hungarian paleographer, I. Hajnal: 'It is constantly worth asking whether we are right in wishing to contrast at any price spoken language and written language as agents of civilization, considering the first as an obstacle to progress and the second as its active promoter.'[14] An example of what Hajnal warned against appears in a recent history of English

[9] See ch. 1, n. 26 below.

[10] Van Caenegem, *Writs*, p. 366, n. 5.

[11] Duggan, *Decretals*, pp. 66, 124.

[12] C. M. Cipolla, *Literacy and Development in the West* (1969), is an introduction to modern mass literacy.

[13] Goody, *Literacy*, p. 3, cf. pp. 11ff, 198ff.

[14] *L'Enseignement de l'écriture aux universités médiévales* ed. L. Mezey (2nd edn, Budapest, 1959), p. 20.

education. Its otherwise excellent summary of the period 1066–1307 concludes:

> Over the past two centuries literacy and education had certainly grown in extent and also become more secularized: England was far more civilized as a result. The vast rural majority, however, still passed their lives in mental confinement, limited by their own experiences in a small circumscribed world ruled by village custom and popularized religion.[15]

The first sentence equates literacy with education and the growth of literacy with the extension of civilization. The second sentence assumes that literacy was the only medium for communicating educative ideas. As they have left few records, not much can be known about the culture and mental experience of medieval peasants. It is argued in chapter 7 of this book that, judging even by the criterion of understanding Latin, peasants may have had knowledge without formal schooling. Whether a little Latin made them or anyone else more educated, in the broad sense of understanding and mastering one's environment, is a matter of opinion.

Reliance on literacy can be narrowing, since it restricts communication to those who have learned its techniques. Although scholars benefit from the resources of documents which literacy makes available, there is little sociological evidence to suggest that a minimal ability to read and write has released proleteriats in modern societies from mental confinement. Whether a larger proportion of the population of England pass their lives 'in a small circumscribed world' now or in the year 1000 is a matter for conjecture only, as the evidence is sparse and diverse. It is possible – though debatable – that technologies of communication much more recent than literacy, notably television, broaden people's minds because they can be assimilated by everyone who can see and hear, just as speech and gesture were mastered before literate modes took root.

This book is not intended, however, as a general essay on modes of communication, although like all historical works it is a product of its own time and of contemporary interests. The recent proliferation of non-literate forms of communication like television and of electronic and photographic systems of storing and retrieving information may teach the historian to put his books and documents into perspective. The technology based on Greek and Roman alphabetic script, which has dominated European culture for more than two thousand years in its classical (papyrus), medieval (parchment) and modern (printed paper) forms, may be entering its final century. The development of written record in medieval England or elsewhere was not a simple or irreversible advance in some march of progress and civilization, but it was a change of profound historical importance. This book aims to recover a little of what was lost by the growth of literacy as well as indicating what was gained.

[15] J. Lawson and H. Silver, *A Social History of Education in England* (1973), p. 39. The authors have been influenced by H. S. Bennett, *Life on the English Manor* (1937), p. 34.

Part I

The Making of Records

1

Memories and myths of the Norman Conquest

Once the conquest of 1066 was achieved, King William 'decided to bring the conquered people under the rule of written law'. He therefore had a codification drawn up of Mercian, Dane and Wessex law and, 'to give the finishing touch to all his forethought', Domesday Book was made so that 'every man might be content with his own rights, and not encroach unpunished on those of others.' This version of events, making William the Conqueror responsible for the transition from memory to written record, is preserved in an oral tradition told by Henry of Blois, King Stephen's brother, to Richard Fitz Neal who recorded it in the *Dialogue of the Exchequer* around 1179.[1] As Henry was bishop of Winchester, he may have been transmitting an authentic local tradition emanating from the treasury at Winchester where Domesday Book had originally been kept. Like many legends, Henry's story oversimplifies details and shortens the time-scale in order to convey a fundamental and probably widespread belief. The Norman Conquest did mark a new start in the making of records and Domesday Book was its most awesome precedent.

Having accepted Henry's story, however, as a valuable opinion, it is immediately necessary to add provisos to it. For if the story were taken literally and whole, at least in the form in which Fitz Neal gives it, it could be misleading. Obviously, for a start, Domesday Book did not succeed in recording everyone's rights between its covers. Nor in the century after it was made was it frequently used to settle questions about such rights, although William the Conqueror may have hoped that it would be. More open to misunderstanding, though less obviously misleading, is the association of Domesday Book with law codes and the proposition that William the Conqueror 'decided to bring the conquered people under the rule of written law'. The Latin phrase for 'written law' here is *juri scripto legibusque*, which recalls the *jus* and *lex* of Roman jurisprudence. Fitz Neal, rather than the original tradition, may have associated William the Conqueror specifically with Roman law, since it was a fashionable academic subject in Fitz Neal's time. By presenting William as a maker of literate law, Fitz Neal was associating him with the emperors of antiquity and bringing England into the international fraternity of jurisprudence. The original tradition may simply have said

[1] *Dialogus*, p. 63.

that William, because he was a conqueror, aimed to put the laws and everyone's rights into writing so that there could be no further dispute about them.

Across a broader time-span, the idea of William the Conqueror replacing the uncertainties of memory and the spoken word by definitive written law is both illuminating and open to misinterpretation at one and the same time. The idea implies that nothing of importance had been written down before 1066 and also that William the Conqueror's records were decisive for the future. Neither implication is acceptable in that form. Important as his achievements were in the development of literate ways of doing business, it would be a misunderstanding of William the Conqueror's administration either to undervalue his debt to the Anglo-Saxon past or to exaggerate his contribution to later forms of medieval government. Like other historical legends, the story of William the Conqueror bringing the people under the rule of written law achieves its dramatic effect by minimizing both the past and the future. In historical fact England already had literate traditions extending back for centuries and conversely non-literate habits and methods of proof persisted in unexpected quarters for generations after the Norman Conquest. Bringing the people under the rule of written law, in the broad sense of decisively and irrevocably extending the uses of writing, needs more precise definition and description.

By way of introduction, the rest of this chapter therefore first looks back at the Anglo-Saxon writing and then moves forward via Domesday Book to the *quo warranto* proceedings of Edward I. Separated by two centuries, Domesday Book and the *quo warranto* proceedings mark the two most ambitious attempts in medieval England to reduce government and property-holding to writing. The fact that such attempts needed repeating makes it clear that no sudden and single venture could succeed. Literate modes could not be imposed by royal decree.

Anglo-Saxon uses of writing

A reassessment of the place of Anglo-Saxon documents in the development of literacy requires a book on its own instead of a preamble to this one. Nothing less than a book would be adequate, since the period is long and the documents, though relatively few, are diverse and difficult. What follows is no more than an indication by a non-specialist of those areas of the subject which bear particularly on the situation at the time of the Norman Conquest. A possible misconception to clear away at the outset is any assumption that the Normans had greater expertise in writing than the Anglo-Saxons. On the whole, Norman administrators probably had less experience than Anglo-Saxon ones of written records and the Normans before 1066 had not shown such a consistent interest as the Anglo-Saxons in recording their history and institutions in literate forms. There was nothing in Normandy comparable with the *Anglo-Saxon Chronicle* and the law codes. The Englishman Orderic Vitalis says that his fellow monks of St Evroul in Normandy 'shrank from bending their minds to the task of composing or writing down their traditions. So in the end I, who came here from the remote parts of Mercia as a ten-year-old boy [in 1085] have endeavoured to commit to writing an account of the deeds of the Normans for Normans to read.'[2] Although Orderic exaggerated his originality, as there already were histories of the Norman dukes, the general idea that Englishmen showed the Normans the usefulness of writing has much to commend it.

Nevertheless a Norman innovation, which may have contributed to the belief that William the Conqueror introduced Roman *jus scriptum*, was the replacement of Old English by Latin as the language of royal writs. This was not an immediate change in 1066, but was probably a consequence of appointing Normans and other foreigners to bishoprics and abbacies.[3] Latin made quick progress because it was the written language with which William's clerks (in both the ecclesiastical and modern sense), from Archbishop Lanfranc of Canterbury downwards, were most familiar. In the eyes of contemporaries on the European continent Latin was the only language of record; a person unfamiliar with it was illiterate. In this frame of mind the foreigners made a fresh start in assembling theological libraries for monasteries and cathedrals, both by gifts of books (like those made by Lanfranc to Canterbury and William of St Carilef to Durham) and by making new manuscripts. 'The century after the Norman Conquest . . . is the greatest in the history of English book production.'[4] In the new books, moreover, less emphasis was put on the illustrations and more on the text than was usual in Anglo-Saxon manuscripts.[5]

In increasing the use of Latin writing the Norman Conquest brought England into the mainstream of medieval literate communication. At the same time, in the short term, the Conquest may have caused a reduction in literacy (in the modern sense of being able to read and write the language one speaks), because it divorced writing further from everyday speech. Although Old English in its standard written form was itself an archaic and learned language by 1066, it was obviously nearer to the vernacular than Latin. In these paradoxes the difficulties of assessing the effects of the Norman Conquest can be appreciated.

Even greater difficulties arise in estimating how much writing was done in pre-Conquest England and for what purposes. To take the question 'How much?' first of all. An estimate of the extent of writing activity in medieval states is best approached through documents like writs and charters, rather than books, as documents are more widely distributed and they can be attributed to specific persons and times. A disadvantage of estimating by documents, however, is that single sheets of parchment are less likely than books to have survived for a thousand years. Some ephemeral memoranda were probably thrown away as soon as their usefulness was expended. Admitting these disadvantages, the

[2] Orderic, bk v, ch. 1, vol. iii, p. 4.
[3] See pp. 165–6 below.
[4] Ker, *English MSS*, p. 1. See also M. Gibson, *Lanfranc of Bec* (1978), pp. 178–81.
[5] C. R. Dodwell, *The Canterbury School of Illumination* (1954), pp. 17, 26, 32.

number of writs and charters extant (in either originals or copies) is the best measure of writing activity available, inadequate though it is.

From Anglo-Saxon England rather less than 2,000 writs and charters survive. P. H. Sawyer's list, which includes copies as well as originals and also lost and incomplete texts, numbers 1,875 items.[6] To this for our purposes should be added a number of purely ecclesiastical documents and a small but significant group of miscellaneous memoranda, such as one concerning levies of men for warships.[7] Conversely an indefinite number, even of the documents listed by Sawyer, are forgeries made after 1066. The number is indefinite because scholars' criteria for deciding questions of authenticity inevitably differ. For example, of the 164 documents written in the name of Edward the Confessor, 44 are likely to be spurious and there are doubts about a further 56.[8] Over all, the majority (1,163 items) of the documents listed by Sawyer are grants and declarations made in the names of kings and the next largest group are grants by bishops (165 items). About half of all the documents listed purport to date from the century immediately preceding the Norman Conquest, and it is among these also that forgery after the Conquest is the more likely.

The 2,000 or so writs and charters extant from Anglo-Saxon England are a small number compared with those extant from the period 1066–1307 and particularly from the thirteenth century. A single collection (which is not the largest) of mainly thirteenth-century charters, the so-called *Registrum Antiquissimum* of Lincoln cathedral, numbers 2,980 items in the printed edition.[9] A single session of the royal justices in eyre in an average-sized county in Edward I's reign used about 500 membranes of parchment and produced more than 2,000 documents in four or five weeks.[10] Although statistics can mislead – and medieval statistics above all – comparisons of numbers are important because an axiom of this book is that the permanent growth of literacy is related to the growth of documents.

The incalculable question, which becomes progressively harder yet more important to answer the further back one goes in time, is what relation documents now extant bear to the numbers originally made. What proportion of the original whole are the 2,000 or so Anglo-Saxon writs and charters? The conjectures made in answer to this question for late Anglo-Saxon England are necessarily so large that there will never be agreement about them. Recent examples of such conjectures appear in two lectures given to the Royal Historical Society in 1974. In the first J. Campbell draws attention to miscellaneous memoranda in Old English, such as the one already mentioned concerning levies of men for

[6] *Anglo-Saxon Charters* (1968). For a general introduction see N. Brooks, 'Anglo-Saxon Charters: the Work of the Last Twenty Years' in *Anglo-Saxon England* ed. P. Clemoes (1974) III, pp. 211–31.

[7] *Anglo-Saxon Charters* ed. A. J. Robertson (2nd edn, 1956), no. lxxii.

[8] See ch. 9, n. 66 below.

[9] Ed. C. W. Foster and K. Major, Lincoln Record S. (12 vols, 1931–73).

[10] See ch. 4, n. 26 below.

warships, and suggests that they are 'survivors from a much larger number' and that their existence is one reason for thinking that there was 'a considerable degree of lay literacy' in late Anglo-Saxon England.[11] In the second lecture S. Harvey restates her contention that the Anglo-Saxon government had documents in its treasury upon which Domesday Book was based.[12] The conjecture which both lectures have in common is that many documents in Old English were lost after the Norman Conquest, because the Normans preferred Latin and also because many writs and memoranda may have been ephemeral in purpose in the first place.

The possibility that the Normans dispersed archives of documents and destroyed an extensive literate culture in Old English cannot be excluded, although in some monasteries the Conquest may have had the reverse effect as the English monks laboured to justify their practices and cults to the conquerors. Eadmer of Canterbury describes in the 1090s how he sees 'men of the present age anxiously trying to find out about the actions of their predecessors . . . yet they cannot for all their pains succeed in doing as they would wish because the elusive scarcity of documents [*scriptorum inopia fugax*] has buried them in oblivion.'[13] Even explicit mentions like this of lack of documents could be interpreted as signs of Norman destructiveness, despite William the Conqueror's claim to be the lawful successor of Edward the Confessor.

It is difficult to assess the implications of lost documents. Whereas Campbell argues for 'a considerable degree of lay literacy', C. P. Wormald reasserts that 'the traditional view of restricted literacy is substantially valid for the whole early English period.'[14] Harvey's contention is as controversial. She states that 'chroniclers and cartulary-makers have long told us explicitly of the earlier treasury documents and how the Domesday survey using them as its *exemplar* sought additional and extraordinary material.'[15] The chronicle to which she refers is that of Abingdon abbey and the cartulary is Heming's. A preliminary difficulty is that the words translated as 'documents' or 'records' in this context are *scriptura* in the Abingdon text and *cartula* in Heming's. These words are more likely to be feminine singular forms than neuter plural ones, in which case the Abingdon chronicler refers not to 'the records [*scriptura*] of the royal treasury' but to an individual 'writing,' and Heming likewise not to 'documents' but to an individual 'little charter' [*cartula*]. The difference between singular and plural is important when the quantity of documents is at issue. The texts which both the Abingdon chronicler and Heming cite in this context are connected

---

[11] 'Observations on English Government from the Tenth Century to the Twelfth Century', *TRHS* 5th series XXV (1975), p. 42.

[12] 'Domesday Book and Anglo-Norman Governance', *ibid*. p. 175.

[13] *Historia Novorum in Anglia* ed. M. Rule, RS LXXXI (1884), p. 1. R. W. Southern describes the monks' search for documents after the Norman Conquest, 'The Sense of the Past', *TRHS* 5th series XXIII (1973), pp. 247ff.

[14] 'The Uses of Literacy in Anglo-Saxon England and its Neighbours', *TRHS* 5th series XXVII (1977), p. 113.

[15] See n. 12 above.

with the Domesday survey. Whether they are earlier or later than Domesday Book is not explicitly stated.

The Abingdon *scriptura* is a list of the abbot's hundreds and hides in Berkshire, which accord with entries in Domesday Book concerning the time of Edward the Confessor.[16] In origin this *scriptura* might be any one of the following:

1 a memorandum extracted from Domesday Book itself;
2 one of the records made at the time of the Domesday survey, from which Domesday Book was compiled;
3 a record made in Edward the Confessor's reign and subsequently used in the compilation of Domesday Book.

Harvey prefers the third alternative, though the others are also possibilities, as the Domesday survey collected information concerning the time of Edward the Confessor and it kept these preliminary records in royal treasuries. The Abingdon chronicler's reference to 'another book of the royal treasury of the time of King William' does not exclude the possibility that the *scriptura* was extracted from Domesday Book, as the text cited from this other book contains details not included in Domesday.[17] The sense seems to be that both the *scriptura* and the other book were made in the time of King William. Heming's cartulary likewise refers to records in the treasury of King William *senior* (in other words, William the Conqueror) and not to pre-Conquest documents. In his use of the word *exemplar* Heming is not referring to a documentary precedent for the Domesday survey, as Harvey suggests, but to an 'exemplification' or confirmatory transcript of some evidence concerning Oswaldslaw hundred. In this purely local context he is explaining that 'as confirmation of this business, an exemplification of it is written down in an authentic charter of the king, which is preserved with the descriptions of the whole of England in the royal treasury.'[18] The 'descriptions' mentioned here are most probably the preliminary records produced by the Domesday survey, from which the book itself was compiled. These alternative interpretations illustrate the difficulties of distinguishing between references to pre- and post-Conquest documents and they also suggest that the case for the existence of earlier treasury documents has been overstated.[19]

Administrative documents were certainly used in late Anglo-Saxon England, since a few copies of them still exist. Whether there were once

[16] Text ed. D. C. Douglas, 'Some Early Surveys from the Abbey of Abingdon,' *EHR* XLIV (1929), p. 623.

[17] D. C. Douglas (*ibid.*, p. 619, n. 2) notes differences between this text and Domesday's, whereas Dr Harvey ('Domesday Book', p. 176) suggests that it is an extract 'from Domesday itself'.

[18] 'ad hujus rei confirmationen exemplar ejus in autentica regis cartula, ut predixi, scriptum est, que in thesaura regali cum totius Anglie descriptionibus conservatur,' *Hemingi Chartularium Ecclesie Wigorniensis* ed. T. Hearne (1723) I, p. 288. V. H. Galbraith, *Domesday Book: its Place in Administrative History* (1974), p. 110.

[19] Charters and title-deeds were kept, for example, in the royal *haligdom* (see ch. 5, nn. 37–9 below), but a treasury archive of taxation lists is a different matter.

enough to be kept systematically in archives and to be commonplaces of business are still matters for conjecture. If there had once been many more documents, the forms of those surviving should be stereotyped (as is the case with thirteenth-century charters and writs) because bureaucratic routines would develop. The Anglo-Saxon sealed writ, with its economy of expression, comes closest to such standards. V. H. Galbraith has been the protagonist of the argument that the sealed writ goes back to Alfred's reign or earlier, and that 'long before the Norman Conquest the Saxon kings had a secretariat of their own, and the first great step had been taken towards bureaucratic government.'[20] But P. Chaplais interprets the Alfredian evidence differently and points out that 'no seal impression or trace of sealing of any kind prior to the Confessor's reign has been found', although that is not evidence that none ever existed.[21] The sealed writ is certainly pre-Conquest, but it may have been introduced no earlier than Cnut's reign; whether Anglo-Saxon writs usually carried seals authenticating them before the reign of Edward the Confessor cannot be definitely decided. Chaplais is likewise sceptical about whether the Anglo-Saxon kings had a secretariat of their own; as late as Edward the Confessor's reign the organization of the secretariat 'is a matter for speculation'.[22] Royal scribes are occasionally named and the consistent wording of writs suggests established drafting rules, yet at least one authentic writ of Edward the Confessor can be shown to have been produced in the *scriptorium* of Westminster abbey. Nevertheless by that reign sealing probably took place in a royal office; to that extent at least there was a chancery.

Whatever view is taken of the state of the evidence, it cannot warrant Galbraith's assertion that by the tenth century in the administration of England 'the whole structure was articulated by the royal writ.'[23] It is debatable whether bureaucracy had developed as far as that by 1150, yet alone 950. Certainly the Anglo-Saxon vernacular writ, as it existed in the reign of Edward the Confessor, was the root from which later varieties of royal charters and letters grew, but the forms had to be changed before the writ could articulate the whole structure of government. From William I's reign, but not earlier, writs were used for giving instructions (injunctions) to named individuals.[24] Similarly the practice of keeping sealed writs as title-deeds, 'one of the most important phases in the general change-over from an oral procedure to a written one', was still in the process of happening in William I's reign.[25] Differences of opinion are therefore as large about the purposes for which Anglo-Saxon documents were made as they are about the numbers which once existed. It seems unlikely that England was governed by a bureaucracy using documents in its routine procedures before 1066.

[20] *Studies*, p. 36. Cf. Galbraith, 'Literacy', p. 218.

[21] Bishop & Chaplais p. xii.

[22] *ibid*. For recent work on the Anglo-Saxon 'chancery' see Wormald, 'The Uses of Literacy', p. 111, n. 69.

[23] *Studies*, p. 36.

[24] Chaplais, *Docs*, p. 5, n. 4. Cf. ch. 5, n. 16 below.

[25] Bishop & Chaplais, p. xi.

The uses of Domesday Book

The chief reason for suggesting that Anglo-Saxon government had not already brought the people 'under the rule of written law', in the sense of ruling through a bureaucracy, is that even the Norman conquerors did not succeed in doing this. The effects of Domesday Book are easy to exaggerate because it impressed contemporaries so much. In a well known passage the *Anglo-Saxon Chronicle* says that King William had the investigation made so narrowly 'that there was no single hide nor virgate of land, nor indeed – it is a shame to relate but it seemed no shame to him to do – one ox or one cow nor one pig which was there left out and not put down in his record.'[26] This description obviously exaggerates in order to emphasize the frightening – and shameful – thoroughness of the Domesday survey. Similarly Fitz Neal explained a century later that the book had been called *Domesdei* 'by the natives' because it seemed to them like the Last Judgment described in Revelation.[27] The tremendous image of Christ in majesty, seated as a judge holding the book of the Scriptures or laws, would have been familiar to anyone entering a Romanesque church, either sculpted over the doorway or as a mural painting within.[28]

Fitz Neal is explaining that by his time Domesday Book was of symbolic rather than practical importance: 'That is why we have called the book *The Book of Judgment*, not because it contains decisions on various difficult points, but because its decisions like those of the Last Judgment are unalterable.'[29] For Fitz Neal Domesday Book was a majestic and unchangeable memorial of the Norman Conquest. The earliest copies of it likewise suggest that its function was symbolic rather than practical. Two multi-coloured editions were made: one in the twelfth century (the manuscript called *Herefordshire Domesday*) and another in the thirteenth (the Exchequer Breviate), the most elegant manuscript ever produced by the royal administration.[30] But the Breviate was of no practical value because it omitted all details of land use. *Herefordshire Domesday* has some marginal notes updating it, making it more useful than the Breviate, yet even here the work is left uncompleted. Embellished like liturgical texts, these manuscripts reinforce the idea that Domesday Book was seen as a sacred book of judgment.[31]

[26] *The Anglo-Saxon Chronicle: a Revised Translation* ed. D. Whitelock *et al.* (1961), pp. 161–2.

[27] *Dialogus*, p. 64. Revelation, ch. xiii, verse 8.

[28] Romanesque tympana of Christ in majesty survive at Rochester and Barfreston (Boase, *English Art*, plate 68) and an earlier sculpture at Barnack (D. Talbot Rice, *English Art, 871–1100* (1952), plate 19a). From the second quarter of the twelfth century portions of a mural survive at Canterbury (Boase, *English Art*, plate 25) and a miniature, prefacing a commentary on Revelation, in a Durham MS. (Kauffmann, *Romanesque MSS*, plate 129).

[29] *Dialogus* p. 64. This argument is expanded at ch. 5, nn. 19–21 below.

[30] Balliol College Oxford MS. 350 and PRO Exchequer E. 36/284.

[31] I differ here from V. H Galbraith, *Domesday Book* (1974), pp. 106ff. See also p. 228 below.

A surprising fact about Domesday Book is that it seems to have been used so rarely in the two centuries after it was made. There are only ten references extant specifically to the use of information connected with Domesday Book between the time it was made and the death of Henry I in 1135.[32] Nor do most of these references unequivocally refer to the book as such, but to writs (*breves*) or charters (*carte*). These writs or charters are probably the same as the 'descriptions of the whole of England in the royal treasury', which Heming mentions in his cartulary.[33] As a consequence of the Domesday survey the king's government therefore possessed, perhaps for the first time, not only a great book but an archive of writings to which it could refer.[34] Nevertheless this archive was not carefully kept, as it disappears without trace. It is last mentioned by Henry of Huntingdon (writing probably in the early 1130s), who says that the information of the Domesday survey had all been written in 'charters' (*carte*), which were brought to William the Conqueror and 'are kept deposited in treasuries up to the present day'.[35] The disappearance of these treasuries of documents is an argument in favour of the hypothesis that earlier Anglo-Saxon archives had likewise vanished. But it also suggests that even in the middle of the twelfth century government had not yet developed to the point where archives were progressively accumulated.

After Henry I's reign there is no further evidence of Domesday Book being searched for specific information (although fair copies were made of it, as already mentioned) until a plea roll of 1221 notes: 'Remember to search Domesday for the bishop.'[36] Even this reference suggests that it was private litigants, rather than royal officials, who first realized that the book might be used to their advantage. In the 1250s, however, Henry III and his favourites begin to refer to it. In 1256 the king used it to show that the men of Cheshire were obliged to pay for repairing the bridge at Chester.[37] Three years later Peter of Savoy had Domesday Book cited in Parliament to prove that Witley in Surrey was not ancient demense of the crown from before the Conquest, as his tenants alleged, because it had been held then by Earl Godwin and not by the king; Peter was therefore entitled to increase the rent.[38] Proving ancient demesne became a routine use of Domesday Book in Edward I's reign. For example, in a case in 1306 one counsel asks: 'Are we ancient demesne or not?' and another replies: 'We will send to the Exchequer to search in Domesday.'[39] Two generations earlier counsel's question would have been answered, not by searching Domesday Book, but by asking a jury of

---

[32] *Herefordshire Domesday* ed. V. H. Galbraith and J. Tait, PRS new series xxv (1950), pp. xxv–xxvii sets out these references conveniently.

[33] See n. 18 above.

[34] See ch. 5, n. 18 below.

[35] *Historia Anglorum* ed. T. Arnold, RS lxxiv (1879), p. 207.

[36] *CuriaRR* x, p. 68. Galbraith, *Studies*, pp. 119–20.

[37] *CLibR* iv, p. 282.

[38] *SPCWW*, p. 92, no. 76. *VCH Surrey* iii, p. 63. R. S. Hoyt, *The Royal Demense in English Constitutional History* (1950), pp. 175–7.

[39] *Year Books of 34–5 Edward I* ed. A. J. Horwood, RS xxxi (1879), p. 311.

twelve knights to give oral testimony; there are numerous instances of the latter procedure in the plea rolls of Henry III's reign.[40] This change in the method of obtaining information – from hearing the testimony of reliable local men to looking up a book kept by the Exchequer – is one indicator of the transition from memory to written record. Once the new procedure has become familiar, that is, from the last quarter of the thirteenth century, relevant extracts from Domesday Book were copied into numerous cartularies and registers.

Two centuries thus elapsed before Domesday Book became a record which was regularly consulted or valued for its contents. Why was this so? One answer is that such a book would only have been of limited use at any time. It was founded on a misconception of how to use writing in administration. The Normans seem to have been so impressed by the way written record, in the form of charters, gave apparent durability to their individual acts that they assumed that a big book would give similar permanence to the government of the whole of England. A document could indeed make time stand still, in the sense that it could pass on a record of an event to remote posterity, but it could not prevent change. In Domesday Book lords and serfs, animals and ploughs, mills and streams, all stand in arrested motion like clockwork automata when the mechanism fails. But historical change has a self-sustaining momentum; not even William the Conqueror could prevent change, and so Domesday Book soon went out of date. Its only practical use was to answer questions about archaisms like ancient demesne. The qualities which make it an unrivalled historical record for us today detracted from its usefulness to medieval administrators.

Another answer to the question why Domesday Book took so long to be consulted is that it was too precocious. In the twelfth century a mythology seems to have grown up around it. The educated believed that it had brought the people under the rule of written law and 'the natives' compared it with the Last Judgment. Both the educated and the natives were more accustomed to writings in the form of symbolic and sacred books than to business documents for mundane use. Practical questions were answered by oral testimony and not by reference to documents. Only gradually, as documents began to accumulate, did habits of consulting them and ultimately of depending on them become established. Domesday Book began to be consulted regularly in Edward I's reign and no earlier because dependence on records in general only became at all regular at that time. Through this change Domesday Book ultimately became a useful but limited work of reference instead of an awesome relic like a Gospel book.

Although Domesday Book had not brought the people under the rule of written law in any specific sense, it had associated writing with royal power in a novel and unforgettable way. Of course there were precedents for it, from imperial Rome and the Carolingian polyptychs, but there is no firm evidence that anything of the sort had been attempted

[40] E.g. *Berks. Eyre*, nos. 388, 596.

before in England. The organization which had made the Domesday survey possible was Anglo-Saxon – the grouping of local communities into shires, hundreds and vills; the practice of juries giving solemn oral testimony which was binding on their communities. The Norman novelty lay in using this organization to compile a written record which reflected the efficiency of Anglo-Saxon government. The unique event of the Conquest produced a unique document. Nevertheless, because Domesday Book was unique in scale and purpose, it could not itself form the first document in a continuing series. Bureaucracy begins with the pipe rolls of the twelfth-century Exchequer rather than with Domesday Book.[41]

Edward I's 'quo warranto' proceedings and the Earl Warenne

Even in Edward I's reign documentary methods of proof were not as firmly established as his lawyers assumed in the *quo warranto* proceedings. The story of the Earl Warenne exhibiting a sword from the Norman Conquest instead of a charter before Edward's judges, saying 'This is my warrant!', shows that old oral traditions and attitudes persisted despite Domesday Book and the immeasurably greater increase in documentation in the thirteenth century. Some historians have found the Warenne story as unacceptable as Edward's judges may have done, because it seems so primitive and ill-founded by literate standards of proof. Thus it was removed in 1913 from the canon of Bishop Stubbs's *Select Charters*, which used to be the bible of history students.[42] The story is certainly inaccurate in details, but it has a value comparable with the myths Fitz Neal recorded a century earlier about the Norman Conquest and written law. Myth is not necessarily the 'purely fictitious narrative' of a dictionary definition. In oral tradition it can be a formulation of fundamental belief and experience handed down in a memorable way. The Warenne story recalls a non-literate tradition of the Norman Conquest and, if examined as an evocation of dying oral culture, it indicates better than more formal records the change of attitudes which had occurred since the coming of the Normans.

The story appears in one version of the chronicle of Walter of Guisborough and runs as follows:

> The king disturbed some of the great men of the land through his judges wanting to know by what warrant [*quo warranto*] they held their lands, and if they did not have a good warrant, he immediately seized their lands. Among the rest, the Earl Warenne was called before the king's judges. Asked by what warrant he held, he produced in their midst an ancient and rusty sword and said: 'Look at this, my lords, this is my warrant! For my ancestors came with William the Bastard and conquered their lands with the sword, and

[41] See ch. 5, n. 22 below.
[42] The reasons for removing the story are discussed by H. M. Cam, *Liberties and Communities in Medieval England* (1944), pp. 176–7 and G. T. Lapsley, *Crown, Community and Parliament* (1951), pp. 35–62.

by the sword I will defend them from anyone intending to seize them. The king did not conquer and subject the land by himself, but our forebears were sharers and partners with him.'[43]

Historians have rightly pointed out that the story contains inaccuracies and inconsistencies. Edward I's *quo warranto* prosecutions did not demand warrants for 'lands' but for franchises or privileged jurisdictions. Nor were the magnates' lands seized by the king, as he was not powerful enough to do that. Nor is there evidence from other records that the Earl Warenne protested in these terms, although he was harassed by *quo warranto* prosecutions. Moreover, the story is attributed to a different earl, Gilbert de Clare of Gloucester, in another version of this chronicle and in the best version it does not appear at all. The story also oversimplifies the conduct of judicial proceedings in Edward I's reign. An earl had learned counsel to advise him and to speak on his behalf. Warenne would have known not to threaten royal judges in open court and that a rusty sword was not going to help his cause at law, since claims without charters were inadmissible in many *quo warranto* cases.

At first sight so many inaccuracies suggest that the Warenne story is worthless for serious historical purposes. At best it is a popular legend; it is certainly not a precise account of legal proceedings. Nevertheless it is important and useful precisely because it does seem to be a popular legend. At the heart of the story is a memory which allegedly went back to the Norman Conquest and an archaic method of proof, the exhibition of the rusty sword, which had been superseded in Edward I's courts by written evidence and book-learned law. The story seems to be a desperate reassertion of the primacy of oral tradition over recorded history and of non-literate forms of proof over Edward I's lawyers and their demands for charters. Although Warenne's assertions were inadmissible at common law, they had generations of tradition behind them and they probably still commanded wide sympathy. Despite its inaccuracy of detail and the inevitable scarcity of evidence about non-literate beliefs, the heart of the Warenne story can be shown to be credible.

To consider first the memory of the Norman Conquest. The claim that an earl like Warenne was entitled to privileges by right of conquest was certainly circulating at the time of the *quo warranto* proceedings, as it is explicitly contradicted by a royal attorney in 1286 in an action against the earl of Hereford.[44] One justification for this claim was the notion that the earls (*comites*) were the descendants of the companions (*comites*) of William the Conqueror. Similarly the larger idea inherent in the Warenne story, that the descendants of the Norman conquerors were living memorials of that conquest, regardless of whether they had documents to prove it, was certainly a century old. In about 1175 the chief justiciar, Richard de Lucy, recommended Henry II to confirm the charters of Battle abbey (which were recent forgeries in fact) because

[43] *The Chronicle of Walter of Guisborough* ed. H. Rothwell, Camden S. 3rd series LXXXIX (1957), p. 216.
[44] D. W. Sutherland, *Quo Warranto Proceedings in the Reign of Edward I* (1963), p. 83.

'even if all charters perished, we should all still be its charters, since we are enfeoffed from the conquest made at Battle.'[45] Richard meant that the king's companions should be Battle's testimonials because the abbey had been founded in thanksgiving for the victory at Hastings.

In emphasizing conquest the Warenne story may also be recalling a more general and ancient belief among the medieval nobility. That warriors were superior to writers and to all their works seems to have been part of the traditional ideology of the barbarians, who had conquered the Roman empire and replaced the constraining written law of Rome by flexible oral custom. Matthew Paris had recorded one formulation of this idea in a declaration allegedly made by some of the French baronage against the clergy in 1247. They declared that 'all of us, the king's chief men, perceive by applying our minds that the kingdom was not won by written law, nor by the arrogance of clerks, but by the sweat of war.'[46] To the Normans in particular, who were usurpers wherever they triumphed – whether in France, England, Italy or Syria – the righteousness of conquest was part of a mythology.[47]

The most interesting part of the Warenne story is not the justification of conquest, however, for that is quite common in medieval political ideas, but his alleged production of an 'ancient and rusty sword' which purported to be the very sword used by the first Earl Warenne at the Norman Conquest. Whether this relic was authentic and whether it ever was shown to Edward I's judges are features of the story which cannot be verified. It is possible that such a revered weapon might have been kept and it is also possible that the earl might have shown it to the judges on some occasion less formal than a session of the court considering his case. Although at first sight the story suggests that Warenne was threatening the court with his sword, closer scrutiny shows that he was enunciating a familiar theory of conquest and supporting it by the most appropriate type of evidence, the symbolic instrument of conquest. The sword was rusty; it was a relic, not a practical weapon.

The use of objects, including swords, as props in the theatre of memory was recommended in medieval academic treatises, since 'the remembrance of things is held by the images, as though they were letters.'[48] At a less exalted level it had been usual practice, before charters became common, to preserve the memory of a title to property in the object which had symbolized the conveyance. The earl of the story was producing something different, yet comparable, in the sword which symbolized his family's acquisition of their lands. To emphasize the importance of personal mementoes in evidence of title, an earlier Earl Warenne in a gift to Lewes priory in 1147 had given it possession by the hairs of his head; these, together with his brother's, were cut off before the altar by

[45] *Battle*, p. 165. Battle abbey's forgeries are referred to at ch. 9, n. 64 below.
[46] Matthew Paris IV, p. 593. Matthew attributes this declaration to the influence of the Emperor Frederick II.
[47] R. H. C. Davis, *The Normans and their Myth* (1976). In general see D. W. Sutherland, 'Conquest and Law' in *Post Scripta: Essays etc. In Honour of G. Post* ed. J. R. Strayer and D. E. Queller, *Studia Gratiana* XV (1972), pp. 33–51.
[48] F. Yates, *The Art of Memory* (1966), p. 64 (citing Martianus Capella).

Henry of Blois, bishop of Winchester.[49] Such symbolic objects were retained by the beneficiary, but they have rarely survived because their significance could easily be lost when it depended on oral transmission only. Among recorded examples of such objects accompanying gifts of land are a cup given to Durham cathedral in *c*.1066 by Copsi, earl of Northumberland, which (according to a Durham author writing in *c*.1100) 'is preserved in the church and retains the memory of that deed for ever'; a gold and ruby ring given to St Paul's cathedral in the first half of the twelfth century by Osbert de Camera, which was affixed to his charter; a staff cut 'from the land' concerned and given to Ramsey abbey in 1121–2 by Wulfget, 'which we still have' (according to the Ramsey chronicler writing in *c*.1170).[50] Although specific records like these of such objects are rare, the practice was presumably common-place. A comparable practice survives to the present day in the giving of wedding rings.

There was nothing necessarily unusual, then, in the Earl Warenne possessing a symbolic memento of the Norman Conquest, nor in objects serving as evidence of title to property. More strange was the form of the earl's symbol, a sword, and the allegation that he produced it before the king's judges. At least from the beginning of the thirteenth century, and probably from Henry II's reign, the king's court had refused to take cognizance of symbolic mementoes other than seals. Furthermore, it would certainly not have considered any object to be a sufficient title to a franchise unless it were supported by a charter. Instances of objects other than sealed writings being produced as evidence of title in royal courts are consequently very rare.

One interesting case made its way on to the royal records in 1213, however, when a litigant objected to the prior of Durham producing a charter against him, which 'is not made according to the custom of the realm nor is there a seal on it, but a certain knife which can be put on or taken off'.[51] This charter (one half of a chirograph in fact, dated 1148) is still preserved at Durham and from it hangs a knife with a polished haft of horn and a broken rusty blade.[52] This knife could indeed be easily 'put on or taken off', as it is attached by a strip of parchment which is threaded through a hole in the haft and then tied. Judging by the numbers of references to them in charters, knives like this were favour-ite symbols of conveyances in the Anglo-Norman period, although they have seldom survived.[53] It is possible that many charters of the twelfth century, which have empty parchment strips hanging from them, were

[49] *BM Facs*, no. 25. *Early Yorkshire Charters: the Honour of Warenne* ed. C. T. Clay (1949) VIII, p. 84.

[50] *Symeonis Monachi Opera Omnia* ed. T. Arnold, RS LXXV (1882) I, p. 97. W. Dugdale, *The History of St Paul's Cathedral* ed. H. Ellis (1818), p. 6. *Ramsey*, p. 246, no. 264.

[51] *CuriaRR* VII, p. 39. The word for 'knife' in this text is *cnipulus*, not *ompulus*; I am grateful to Mr R. E. Latham for this correction.

[52] Illustrated in black and white (actual size) by K. Major, 'Blyborough Charters' in *MM for Stenton*, plate xv, and in colour (reduced size) by C. J. Stranks, *Durham Cathedral* (1976), p. 21.

[53] P & M II, p. 88. See also ch. 5, nn. 42–3 and ch. 8, nn. 9, 20 below.

originally authenticated by knives rather than seals. Most exceptional is a charter dated 1151 for St Denys priory near Southampton with two parallel slits in it, through which the blade of the donor's symbolic knife was once fixed to the parchment.[54]

Although knives were common enough, a sword is unusual as a symbol of title despite its being the most obvious symbol of knightly and secular power. A knight's oath at his inauguration was made by his placing a sword on an altar, just as other symbolic objects were placed in conveyances of property. Justifying this practice, John of Salisbury argued that this symbolic gesture by a knight was valid without any form of words in writing, such as a bishop or abbot needed at his profession, for 'who would demand of a non-literate [*illitteratus*], whose duty is to know arms rather than letters, that he should make a lettered profession?'[55] When Thomas de Muschamps became a monk at Durham, probably shortly before his death in c. 1130, he invested St Cuthbert and the monks with the estate of Hetherslaw by his sword offered on an altar. In this instance investiture by sword was the symbol, not of the beginning of a knightly career, but of its ending.

In presenting his sword to the monks of Durham priory, Thomas de Muschamps laid down his arms and offered up his worldly goods in one symbolic gesture. Nevertheless this gesture did not prove as memorable as it should have done. Unlike the Earl Warenne, Durham priory neglected to keep the sword. Record of it survives only because the monks were obliged to get writs from King Stephen and Henry II, when Thomas's heirs repeatedly refused to surrender Hetherslaw.[56] In pursuit of this claim Absalom, the prior from 1154–8, wrote a public letter to the sheriff of Northumberland insisting that he and another monk had actually witnessed the investiture with the sword two or three decades earlier.[57] Ironically the day for settling this claim was fixed by Stephen of Bulmer, whose uniquely inscribed and labelled carving knife (recording an agreement with Lindisfarne) is now preserved as a title deed at Durham.[58] Although Durham priory apparently failed in this claim and Thomas's sword was not kept, this dispute at least provides an instance, comparable with the Earl Warenne's, of a title to property depending on the evidence of a sword.

There are, moreover, at least two English examples of early medieval swords being kept as symbolic mementoes. The better known is the Conyers falchion, which is exhibited in Durham cathedral museum.[59] This sword was the symbol by which the head of the Conyers family held the manor of Sockburn from the bishop of Durham. Each head of the

[54] *BM Facs*, no. 32.
[55] *Policraticus*, bk vi, ch. 10, ed. C. C. J. Webb (1909) II p. 25.
[56] J. Raine, *The History and Antiquities of North Durham* (1852), appendix, p. 141. *RRA-N* III (1968), p. 92, no. 257.
[57] 'et per gladium suum eundem sanctum beatum scilicet Cuthbertum investisse', Raine, *North Durham*, appendix, p. 141.
[58] See ch. 8, no. 20 below.
[59] Illustrated by G. F. Laking, *A Record of European Arms and Armour* (1920) I, pp. 128–9. See also *VCH Yorkshire North Riding* I, p. 450.

family was obliged up to 1860 to show the sword to the bishop as evidence of title. Although this is a parallel with Warenne's sword, a problem is that the falchion does not seem to be the original weapon, as it dates from no earlier than the thirteenth century and has been associated (by the heraldry on its pommel) with Richard of Cornwall, the brother of Henry III. A closer parallel with Warenne is a sword (no longer existing), which was kept in the royal treasury 'to this day' according to the Ramsey chronicler writing in c. 1170.[60] It was preserved 'as evidence of God's bounty and the royal victory' over the Scots by King Athelstan at Brunanburh in 937. St Odo of Canterbury had miraculously provided it, when Athelstan's own sword had slipped from its scabbard. The Ramsey chronicler is careful, however, to report this story with a cautious note, 'as is said'.

Closer in time to the Warenne story and perhaps for that reason a closer parallel is Edward I's use of the symbolism of arms and armour in a letter to the pope in 1301.[61] This letter put forward a battery of arguments, from both myth and recent history, to justify English overlordship in Scotland. Boniface VIII had argued in 1299 that Scotland belonged to the Roman church from ancient times and he challenged Edward to produce his titles and muniments.[62] Edward was thus obliged in effect to state by what warrant he claimed jurisdiction over Scotland, just as two decades earlier he had required magnates like the Earl Warenne to show warrants for their jurisdictions. Although Edward made it clear at the outset that he did not consider himself bound to answer the pope in this case, his lengthy explanation concedes that an answer was necessary. Placed in a similar situation to his magnates a little earlier, though with many more documents at his disposal, Edward and his advisers resorted to arguments from myth and symbolism almost as readily as the earl in the Warenne story.

Unlike the Earl Warenne, however, Edward did not possess an ancient sword as a symbol of conquest. Athelstan's miraculous sword, which the Ramsey chronicler had mentioned a century earlier, had either got lost or the chronicler may have been mistaken in his original information. Nevertheless Edward did attempt to compensate for not having Athelstan's sword by referring to a fissure in a rock near Dunbar, which had allegedly been made by a miraculous sword blow from Athelstan. This blow had been facilitated by the intervention of St John of Beverley (not St Odo of Canterbury this time) and, according to Edward's letter to the pope, 'may still be seen as an evident sign of this event'.[63] Edward had also a more recent and convincing argument from arms. After King William the Lion was taken prisoner by the English in 1174 he had offered his helmet, lance and saddle on the altar of York minster as tokens of subjection, 'and they are kept and preserved in that church up to the present day.'[64]

These comparisons between the Warenne story and other sources suggest that it would not have appeared as peculiar or incredible to

[60] *Ramsey*, p. 16. [61] *Anglo-Scottish Relations*, pp. 96–117.
[62] *ibid*. p. 87. [63] *ibid*. p. 99. [64] *ibid*. p. 102.

people in *c*.1300 as it has to some twentieth-century historians. The descendants of the Norman conquerors, particularly the earls, probably did believe in a right of conquest. Physical objects, especially knives, were kept as titles to property. Although the use of swords as mementoes is rare in England at least, the sword was the archetypal symbol of knightly as distinct from clerkly authority. Titles to authority or property could not always be proved by producing charters or citing precedents in writing. To justify English claims in Scotland Edward I's government had to resort to myth and physical symbols just as the earl did in the Warenne story. Taken together, these fragmentary details help to reconstruct ways of thinking and remembering which were widespread before the coming of written records. The growth of literacy did not occur in a cultural vacuum. It replaced non-literate ways, which seemed equally natural to those who were accustomed to them. The most difficult initial problem in the history of literacy is appreciating what preceded it.

A paradox of the Warenne story is that, although it is ill-founded by literate standards of proof, it is essentially more truthful than some of the pleadings based on charters which were duly recorded in the official rolls of the *quo warranto* proceedings. In producing an ancient sword instead of a charter as his title from the Norman Conquest, the earl showed greater historical awareness than an abbot who produced a charter of William the Conqueror. Many – perhaps most – charters of Edward the Confessor or William the Conqueror circulating in the thirteenth century were forgeries, including even those of Battle abbey founded by William himself, because title-deeds had been the exception rather than the rule in the eleventh century.[65] If Edward I's lawyers in the *quo warranto* proceedings had persisted in demanding titles in writing from 1066 or even earlier, using the argument that 'time does not run against the king', nearly all owners of property in England would have been disfranchised.[66] In 1290 by the *quo warranto* statute a compromise was made.[67] In subsequent case law the king was understood to have conceded that documentary proof would not be required henceforward from any date earlier than the accession of Richard I in 1189. The last decade of the twelfth century was a realistic date from which to expect written titles, as tenure by charter among the tenants-in-chief at least was beginning to be normal by then.

In the 1290s the earl of the Warenne story could therefore return his 'ancient and rusty sword' to its scabbard for all time, as it was now a mere historical oddity instead of being a living relic transmitting memory to future generations. 'Legal memory', that artificial memory which depended primarily on documentary proof and not on mementoes or mortal oral testimony, had been arbitrarily set at 1189 and remained there for the rest of the Middle Ages. This is the context within which

[65] Forgery is discussed at ch. 9 below.
[66] Sutherland, *Quo Warranto Proceedings*, p. 14. Clanchy, 'Remembering', p. 174 and *Moderni*, p. 688.
[67] Sutherland, *Quo Warranto Proceedings*, pp. 91–110. See also p. 123 below.

this book aims to trace the shift from memory to written record between the Norman Conquest and the reign of Edward I. William the Conqueror had not brought the people under the rule of written law. Nor was Domesday Book the last judgment; rather, it was a symbolic new start. By contrast two centuries later, in the last decades of Edward I's reign, when the Earl Warenne allegedly produced his ancestral sword as testimony of the Norman Conquest, his claim (assuming that something like it was made) went unrecorded in the official rolls of the king's court because it was irrelevant. By then the province of myth and hearsay was the only appropriate place for a story which claimed priority for memory over written record in the king's court.

The growth of reliance on writing has been a continuing process without a precise beginning or end. In England it had started long before 1066 with Roman inscriptions and Anglo-Saxon charters and would go on for centuries after 1307. This book concentrates on the two and a half centuries from 1066 to 1307 because it argues that these are the years in which the use of writing first became normal for government business and titles to property. This change is marked by the increasing number of documents which were kept and by growing indications that landowners were themselves becoming literate. The difference between the uses of writing in 1066 and 1307 has been introduced in this chapter by comparing myths about the effects of the Norman Conquest, because myths can convey pre-literate beliefs.

In the twelfth century, when charters were still uncommon and bureaucracy had scarcely begun, William the Conqueror was credited with the impossible and therefore heroic feat of having made a definitive book of judgment by which to govern the conquered people. A century or more later the idea of bringing the people under written law had come closer to reality, with the expansion of royal and seignorial bureaucracies and the use of charters even by some serfs. Popular legend reacted then with the story of the Earl Warenne, who is committed to the equally heroic task of halting the *quo warranto* proceedings with his rusty sword. The Norman Conquest, which was identified with the threat of written record in the twelfth century, had become by 1307 in the Warenne story a symbol of the good old days of simple and forceful memory. Magnates like Warenne could indeed curtail the king's political power and they maintained a tradition of doing so from Magna Carta onwards, but they could not stop the advance of writing into more and more areas of ordinary life because that was caused by the massing of documents in archives and the spread of literate skills over the country.

2

The proliferation of documents

In 1170 Master David of London wrote from France to an unnamed agent in England, giving him directions about the safekeeping of his correspondence.[1] The year before David had been a representative at the papal *curia* of Henry II and Gilbert Foliot, bishop of London, against Thomas Becket. As a consequence he had earned an annuity of £20 (paid partly by the king and partly by Foliot) and the enmity of Becket. The controversy had become so fierce in the last few months of Becket's life that David took steps to safeguard this new pension. He explained to his agent in England that he had obtained from Henry II two charters, one confirming the king's portion and the other Foliot's obligation. As Henry II's eldest son, Henry the Young King, had just been crowned, David also obtained a letter close from Henry II, commanding the Young King to issue similar charters for him.

The two royal charters, and the letter close promising two more, only safeguarded the principle of David's pension. In addition he needed writs detailing how the payments were to be made. The king's bailiff in Godalming, Ranulf de Broc, was therefore ordered in another royal letter close to pay David £15 a year at specified intervals. This letter, David explained, was intended to save him having to apply for a new royal writ to the bailiff every time he required payment. A similar letter was sent to the bishop of London concerning the remaining £5 of the pension. To ensure that the bishop was not charged twice, another royal writ had to be issued ordering the sheriffs of Middlesex not to exact the £5 from the bishop in future. Likewise the Exchequer (which accounted with the sheriffs) was instructed to allow the £15 from Ranulf de Broc and the £5 from the bishop, so that Ranulf and the bishop would not have to apply for writs acquitting them each time. Settling how David's pension was to be paid had therefore necessitated letters to various levels of the king's bureaucratic hierarchy ranging from the bailiff, Ranulf, up to the barons of the Exchequer. By these means David had acquired a series of 'standing orders' so that the payments due to him would be authorized automatically in future.

David was still not satisfied. 'To be on the safe side', he wrote, 'so that

[1] Z. N. Brooke, 'The Register of Master David of London' in *Essays to Poole*, p. 240. *Memoranda Roll 1 John* ed. H. G. Richardson, PRS new series xxi (1943), pp. lxxx–lxxxi.

they cannot malign me, I have had sealed [by the Chancery] a transcript of that [writ to the Exchequer] and a transcript of the one which is to be sent to Ranulf.' David told his agent 'to keep these with my charters'; he was evidently rapidly acquiring an archive of his own. Even so, neither the king's letters nor the transcripts allayed his anxieties entirely. As an added precaution, he got two of the king's confidential ministers, Richard of Ilchester and Geoffrey Ridel, to write on his behalf to William St John and Thomas the Sealer (who were probably officers of the chief justiciar in England) 'so that things may be made to run expeditiously'. After all these letters, David had the temerity to conclude his instructions to the agent by telling him that he had not been able to obtain the one writ which the agent wanted for himself, because he did not wish to trouble the king with trifles when Henry was so worried about Becket.

To sum up, the documents which David needed to safeguard his pension comprised two charters from Henry II, two charters from the Young King and a letter close to the Young King; writs to Ranulf de Broc, the bishop of London, the sheriffs of Middlesex and the barons of the Exchequer; official transcripts of two of these writs; two letters from ministers to officials in England. Altogether eleven royal documents were to be produced and two letters from ministers. These letters would in their turn have created other correspondence. David had also, of course, to get the letter written to his agent and to keep the copy of it, which was preserved in his register and hence retained for posterity.

Master David's letter explains better than many generalizations how records proliferated, and it suggests the point this process had reached at the time of Becket's death, a century after the Norman Conquest. In England, with its extraordinarily centralized monarchy, the principal producer of documents was the king's government. Many, perhaps most, of the letters produced were written within the organization to other royal officials. The letters to the bailiff, the sheriffs and the Exchequer, and those from Richard of Ilchester and Geoffrey Ridel, illustrate this in Master David's case. Behind any solemn royal charter now extant there once existed numerous ancillary documents – petitions, drafts, transcripts, writs to officials, letters to other interested parties, and correspondence among the officials themselves 'so that things may be made to run expeditiously'. As the king moved continually from place to place within England, and often across the Channel as well (particularly in Henry II's case), he communicated with many of his officials by letters. Almost any royal order required some sort of writ to, or from, the Exchequer in London; the purpose of Master David's 'standing orders' was to reduce the repetitious issue of writs of this sort.

Moreover, all these officials had to be cajoled and encouraged by offerings and fees to produce the necessary documents. One advantage enjoyed by royal clerks was that they were not expected to make such offerings to each other and could therefore get the documents they needed free of charge, thus further enlarging the number of documents produced. On one occasion at Henry II's court, Thurstan, the king's steward, complained to Henry that Adam of Yarmouth, the spigurnel (the sealer of writs), had refused to seal a writ for him for nothing. It emerged that Adam felt aggrieved because Thurstan had not let him have two cakes when he was entertaining guests; Adam had refused to seal the writ in retaliation. The king resolved the dispute by making Adam sit down, with the writ and his seal, while Thurstan offered him two cakes on bended knee. This little piece of gossip, from Walter Map's *Courtiers' Trifles,*[2] illustrates how the king himself could get involved in the pettiest disputes within his household and the discretion his bureaucrats had to dispense or withhold favours. The proliferation of documents meant that government became more dependent on literates; it did not make it any less arbitrary or capricious.

In Walter Map's story and Master David's letter it is evident that the initiative for obtaining the writs came from the beneficiaries and not from the bureaucracy itself. David was anxious to provide against every conceivable mishap; so he took the trouble to obtain transcripts for himself, writs to other officials, and letters from persons of influence to expedite his business. Once the bureaucratic machine had taken shape, over-anxious users encouraged it to grow progressively more complex and extensive. On the other hand, neither Thurstan, the king's steward, nor David are entirely typical in their attitudes, as both were connected with the royal court and would consequently have had a special knowledge of, and interest in, forms of documentary proof. David had also attended the schools of Paris and Bologna, which would have made him literate in every sense of the word. By 1170 the king's government was much more dependent on documents than a century earlier, but it was still relatively primitive. It would be wrong to assume that the whole of England was bureaucratically controlled in Henry II's reign.

Documents at village level

A century later, however, by Edward I's reign, the use of documents had extended down to village level. The English *Song of the Husbandman* (probably dating from the early fourteenth century) depicts the beadles collecting taxes from the peasants, 'the men on the earth' (*men upo mold*), by the authority of an Exchequer writ. The beadles say: 'You are written in my list, as you know very well' (*Thou art writen y my writ that thou wel wost*).[3] The beadles may not have been exaggerating. The statute of Exeter of 1285 had required local bailiffs to supply the king's commissioners with the names, written down in a roll, of every village, half-village and hamlet within franchises as well as in the kingdom as a whole.[4] Furthermore, from at least the 1270s, seignorial stewards and bailiffs were meant to have written on rolls the names of all males (excluding clerics) over the age of 12; these lists were read out twice a year when the sheriff or the franchise-holder visited the locality for the view of frankpledge.[5] In theory at least Edward I's government thus had

[2] Walter Map, bk v, ch. vi, p. 242.
[3] *The Political Songs of England* ed. T. Wright, Camden S. 1st series VI (1839), p. 151.
[4] *Statutes*, p. 210.   [5] *Court Baron*, pp. 68–9.

access to lists of every place of habitation, however small, and of every man, however lowly his status.

By 1300 beadles and their like were accustomed to making lists; or rather, that was the practice recommended by writers of treatises on estate management in Edward I's reign. *Husbandry* recommends the bailiff in the autumn to list everything that remains on the manor, such as tools and horsehoes, great and small, so that he will know what to buy for the coming year.[6] The same book mentions in passing, as if it were a commonplace, *la respounse del issue de let* – the record of yields of milk from the cows.[7] Such a record may have been a notched wooden tally, and not a parchment. Even so, it shows that some manorial bailiffs and reeves used records, other than their memories, for day-to-day management. The editor of these treatises, D. Oschinsky, argues that 'it was probably within their power to write symbolic signs and figures', but she does not think that a reeve or his agents could read or write Latin.[8] Nevertheless one of the treatises, *Seneschaucy*, assumes that the bailiff or reeve can read (in French, if not in Latin), as it warns him to admit no one and hand over nothing from the manor to any person whatsoever 'without the warrant of a writ' under pain of repaying the loss from his own purse.[9] If the bailiff or reeve were unable to read such warrants when they were delivered to him, he would soon have been out of pocket. It is impossible to know how many farms in England in 1300 were administered with the degree of bureaucratic efficiency laid down in the rule books. At the least, however, the leading men in villages must have considered wooden tallies a commonplace and been familiar with written warrants in Edward I's reign.

Even in Henry III's reign the lowest class in society, vagrants, were expected to carry written testimonials of their trustworthiness. Thus in Essex in 1248 five men from as far afield as Barnard Castle and Canterbury, after being acquitted of theft, were forbidden to return to the county unless they brought with them 'their testimonial of trustworthiness'.[10] That a written document is referred to here, rather than oral testimony, is suggested by two cases from Sussex in 1261–2. In one Robert de Parys of Battle, who had been arrested as a horse thief, obtained the bailiff of Grinstead's permission to go away and fetch a testimonial of his trustworthiness, but he never returned.[11]

The other case from Sussex is more explicit about the testimonial being in writing. William of Badgeworth (in Gloucestershire) sued Peter de Turvill, the bailiff of the honour of Bramber (in Sussex), for wrongful imprisonment and grievous bodily harm. William's story, which was upheld by a special jury, was that he had come to Sussex to

---

[6] *Walter of Henley*, p. 436.   [7] *ibid*. p. 430.   [8] *ibid*. p. 223.

[9] 'sanz garant de bref', *ibid*, p. 292. Parkes, 'Literacy', pp. 559–60 argues that reeves could read and write.

[10] 'warrantum suum de fidelitate', PRO JUST/1/232, m. 3. I owe this and the references immediately following to Dr H. R. T. Summerson, whose knowledge of the crown pleas MSS of Henry III is unrivalled.

[11] JUST/1/912A, m. 40.

visit a relative when he was arrested by Peter on suspicion of theft. He asked Peter's permission to return to Badgeworth to obtain 'letters testifying to his trustworthiness' from his lord's court.[12] William was duly issued at his manorial court with a letter, sealed by the bailiff and suitors of Badgeworth, testifying that he was a trustworthy man. He then returned to Sussex and presented his letter to Peter in the honourial court at Bramber, but Peter reacted by imprisoning him in a dungeon and only released him because he was at death's door. Although this case shows that William's letter failed to protect him (initially at least), it also suggests that the sending of such letters between seignorial courts was a routine procedure. The bailiffs who had the letters written, the suitors or members of the court who sealed them, and the recipients who benefited from them, must all have been sufficiently familiar with writing to understand the import of a letter. Indeed William – mistakenly as it turned out – had such confidence in his letter that he thought it would save him from a dungeon when he returned to Sussex.

Comparable with testimonials of trustworthiness are the warrants of lawful purchase which accompanied sales of livestock. In Kent in 1241 John le Keche and others were acquitted of stealing oxen, but the jury noted that they had bought the animals foolishly and 'without the warrant that they could have had'.[13] That a written warrant was meant is made clear by a case from Oxford in 1258 in which a receipt (in the form of a letter patent) for the purchase of a horse is mentioned.[14] Similarly in 1292 a plaintiff told the king's justices that he had been deprived of a letter issued in the name of Hereford corporation, stating that he was searching for a stolen horse.[15] The conclusion to draw from such evidence is that by the second half of the thirteenth century it was imprudent for anybody to wander far from his own village without some form of identification in writing, both for himself and for anything in his possession. Medieval society's savage laws against strangers and vagrants may have been a forceful promoter of literacy in the countryside.

Given these facts, it comes as no surprise to find that by 1300 some serfs or villeins used documents. If they wished to advance themselves or provide for younger sons or daughters, they had to imitate their betters and exploit written procedures. A Latin poem written in c.1276 describes, from a hostile point of view, the efforts of the people of Stoughton to sue their lord, the abbot of Leicester. One of the rustics says: 'I will go to the king, I will bow to the king, I will hand him the case in writing' (*Ad regem vadam, coram rege cadam, causam scriptam sibi tradam*).[16] But these wretches, who had hoped to be *magistri* ('masters' in both the academic and the social sense), were quickly overawed by a smooth advocate at the king's court and returned weeping and empty-

---

[12] 'litteras testimoniales de fidelitate', JUST/1/911, m. 8.

[13] JUST/1/359, m. 29 (Dartford).

[14] KB/26/158, m. 8 (*Coram Rege*).

[15] *Select Bills in Eyre* ed. W. C. Bolland, SS xxx (1914), p. 35, no. 55.

[16] R. H. Hilton, 'A Thirteenth-Century Poem on Disputed Villein Services', *EHR* LVI (1941), p. 95.

handed. In this case the serfs had achieved nothing with their document and were treated almost as a band of rebels. Occasionally, however, individuals were more successful. An action in the King's Bench twenty years later concerned a certain John son of Robert of Estgate, whose grandmother had been a serf of Robert de Mortimer.[17] Robert of Estgate had (according to the plea roll) 'subsequently increased in goods and by his trading improved himself so much' that he acquired lands by charters from the Mortimers. Robert is thus a real instance of that stereotype, the peasant of servile origins who bettered himself by trade. The charters from the Mortimers were intended to give documentary reinforcement to his eminent status.

The legality of serfs acquiring or conveying property by charters is complex. In the case just mentioned Robert had been obliged to surrender his charters to William de Mortimer, his lord, who argued on those grounds that Robert was his villein; but John, Robert's son, claimed to be a freeman and was adjudged to be so. Similarly the Peterborough abbey cartulary, entitled *Cartae Nativorum*, can be interpreted in contrary senses.[18] 'Natives' or 'serfs' charters' might imply that these were illegal documents, which had consequently been surrendered to the lord, the abbot of Peterborough, just as Robert had surrendered his charters to William de Mortimer; if that is so, Peterborough abbey made a record of the charters because they concerned its own property. Conversely the title *Cartae Nativorum* might suggest that charters made by serfs were a legal commonplace; they were recorded in the cartulary to reinforce their validity, just as private charters of greater men were sometimes enrolled in the royal archives for further security. The former hypothesis, that the documents had been surrendered to Peterborough because serfs had no legal title by charter, is the more likely.

Whether or not the serfs who made these charters had a legal right to do so, the existence of the Peterborough documents (even in cartulary copies) demonstrates that in the latter half of the thirteenth century small properties were being conveyed by peasants using writing. Whether the persons and properties concerned were technically free or unfree, these charters are a landmark in the development of written record. There are, for example, 15 *cartae nativorum* from the village of Tinwell in Rutland; seven of these charters concern half acres of land, another five one acre each, and the remaining three the rent and sale of some houses.[19] If in many parts of England, as is probable, and not just on the Peterborough abbey estates, single acres and half acres were being conveyed by charter by 1300, the number of peasants' charters produced amounts to hundreds of thousands or even millions. Supposing that on average one charter was produced for each acre of arable once in the thirteenth century, the number of charters made would total at least

[17] *SCCKB* III, pp. 47–9.

[18] Ed. C. N. L. Brooke and M. M. Postan, Northamptonshire Record S. xx (1960). Cf. E. King, *Peterborough Abbey* (1973), ch. 6.

[19] *Cartae Nativorum*, pp. 131–6, nos. 397–411.

eight million.[20] It is very unlikely of course that a charter was made for every acre, even of arable. On the other hand, the *Cartae Nativorum* show that numerous documents concerned less than one acre and the same land might be rented or conveyed more than once in the century. Attempted partitions and short-term conveyances must have been common, because the population and hence the pressure on land had reached a peak by 1300. It seems reasonable to conclude that at least hundreds of thousands, and perhaps millions, of peasants' charters were made, although those who made them were the more prosperous small-holders and in that sense were not typical serfs (see the charter of William Benedict, plate VI).

Unlike papal or royal letters for the great monastic houses, peasants' charters would not have been kept when they went out of date; because the legal status of the charters was dubious, peasants did not make cartularies, and such small and fragile documents would have been difficult to preserve anyway. Nevertheless a few actual charters (as distinct from copies like those in the *Cartae Nativorum*), undoubtedly concerning unfree tenures, have been found and more are likely to come to light. R. H. Hilton describes a lease (dating from *c.*1230) between Gloucester abbey and a widow, Emma, who was to perform ploughing and other duties in addition to paying a money rent.[21] Even if she were not of servile status herself, some of the services prescribed are those of an unfree tenement. Her charter is in the form of a bipartite chirograph, which implies theoretical equality between the contracting parties, Emma and the abbot. The abbey's half of the chirograph (the extant half) is authenticated, as was required, by Emma's seal, which bears her name and a cross as a central device.

The possessor of a seal was necessarily a person familiar with docu-ments and entitled to participate in their use. The metal matrix of a seal like Emma's would not have been made to use once only. Even if it were massproduced by casting and sold ready made with a blank space around the border, as is possible, the owner's name had still to be engraved by hand. The name made the seal unique and hence legally valid. Possession of a seal thus implied that its owner could read his own name, as well as being prepared to authenticate documents with the impress of his 'signature'. Emma's chirograph therefore demonstrates that a holder of unfree land, even a woman (albeit a widow), might 'sign' a document as early as 1230. From the same date or earlier there survives a chirograph (illustrated on the endpapers of this book), made by the earl of Chester and Lincoln with the men of Freiston and Butter wick in Lincolnshire, which bears the seals of at least fifty of the men.[22] Most of these men were probably not technically serfs, but they were certainly smallholders.

[20] R. Lennard, *Rural England, 1086–1135* (1959), p. 393 estimates the arable acreage (excluding the northern counties and Middlesex) in 1086 at 7·2 million at least. Popula-tion and land-use had undoubtedly increased since then.

[21] R. H. Hilton, *The English Peasantry in the Later Middle Ages* (1975), p. 153.

[22] PRO Ancient Deeds LS 270, illustrated in H. Jenkinson, *Guide to Seals in the PRO* (2nd edn, 1968), plate ii.

In Henry II's reign his chief justiciar, Richard de Lucy, had smiled contemptuously when Gilbert de Balliol had mentioned a seal, saying: 'It was not formerly the custom for every petty knight to have a seal, which befits only kings and important people.'[23] Yet a century later not only knights, but some of the smallest property-owners had seals. So far from opposing this development, the statute of Exeter of 1285 actually required 'bondsmen' to have seals to authenticate their written evidence, when they served on inquests for which there were insufficient freemen.[24] The government was prepared to overlook the distinction between freeman and serf when it found it inconvenient. On the other hand, as with the surrender of serfs' charters, some lords attempted to enforce that distinction rigidly. In 1295 the customary tenants of Bromham in Wiltshire were fined 100 shillings 'because they made a common seal in contempt of the lord', the abbot of Battle.[25] Seals for individuals may have been tolerated more readily; a communal seal suggested an organized association against the lord. Perhaps too Battle abbey pursued a consistent policy against seals, as it was an abbot of Battle, Richard de Lucy's brother, whom Gilbert de Balliol had been opposing a century earlier. Despite the objections of some lords, seals like charters were probably possessed by the majority of landowners, however small their holdings, by 1300. The possession of any type of seal implied that its owner considered himself to be of sufficient status to use and understand documents, even if this were an aspiration rather than a reality.

The chronology of charter making

By the latter half of the thirteenth century charters and documents were evidently a commonplace in England. Although in legal theory it was not essential to have a charter to validate a conveyance of property, Bracton shows that the ceremony of livery of seisin (which had traditionally given legality to the conveyance) had itself become dependent on documentary evidence. He explains that the donor may make the livery through an agent, provided the agent has a procuratorial letter or writ from the donor, together with his charter, so that it may be said that the agent 'had both a writ and a charter'. Bracton records this phrase, 'he hadde bothe writ and chartre', in English.[26] This is exceptional at such an early date (perhaps as early as 1230); it suggests that documentary evidence had become sufficiently familiar to enter into everyday speech. Similarly the word *fet* in Anglo-Norman or *factum* in Latin, translated as a 'deed', comes to have its modern meaning of a 'title-deed' or charter from the late thirteenth century.[27] A 'deed' was no longer the

---

[23] *Battle*, p. 108.

[24] *Statutes*, p. 210. Cf. ch. 7, n. 39 below.

[25] G. C. Homans, *English Villagers of the Thirteenth Century* (1941), p. 332.

[26] Bracton, fo 40, vol. ii, p. 125. Whether the livery was made by the donor or his agent, the ceremony still required the conveyance of an object symbolizing the gift; see ch. 8, nn. 23–4 below.

[27] P & M II, p. 220, n. 1.

physical act of conveyance, symbolized by a turf from the land and livery of seisin; instead it was a sealed document which the donor made.

Giovanni di Bologna, a notary on Archbishop Pecham's staff from 1279, would not have agreed with the generalization that documents were commonly used in England in Edward I's reign. He wrote: 'Italians, like cautious men, want to have a public instrument for practically every contract they enter into; but the English are just the opposite, and an instrument is very rarely asked for unless it is essential.'[28] Compared with Italy, and Bologna in particular whose university specialized in legal and business training, it was doubtless true that the English produced fewer documents. But Giovanni exaggerates the discrepancy between Italian and English practice. By the statute of merchants of 1285 every important town in England was obliged to have a clerk to enrol recognizances of debt in duplicate and write out bills of obligation authenticated by a royal seal.[29] The making of this statute might suggest that written contracts had not been the practice hitherto, but in fact this legislation amended existing rules rather than introducing something entirely new. Even if the notion that an Englishman's word is his bond was already in existence, it was an established rule of the common law at the time Giovanni was writing that the only type of enforceable contract was one expressed in a sealed document; the sealing and delivery of the parchment made the contract. As early as 1235 a plea was adjudged to be void because the plaintiff did not produce either a charter or a chirograph; moreover, the clerk recording this plea originally wrote that the covenant itself was void, though he subsequently corrected *convencio* to *loquela* (a plea).[30] Being a notary, Giovanni may have not considered a contract under seal to be a valid public instrument, because it required no notarial authentication. Self-interest or ignorance may have led him to discount the importance of charters and chirographs in England, where anyone possessing a seal was considered competent to authenticate his own written acts.

It is true nevertheless that compared with Italy, and with later centuries, England in 1300 was not universally document-minded. Yet the point had been reached by then where charters and written instructions penetrated to every village. Giovanni di Bologna was generalizing from the great cities of northern Italy and comparing their merchants with English ones. If the use of documents in the countryside in Italy and England were compared, English peasants, particularly in the open fenlands where the *Cartae Nativorum* were made, were probably as familiar with writing as their counterparts in the plains of Lombardy. Moreover, comparisons need to be made not only across Europe, but across the centuries. Viewed chronologically, England was remarkably document-minded in 1300 compared with the situation in 1100. In the twelfth and thirteenth centuries, as far as titles to property among

---

[28] *Summa* ed. L. Rockinger (1863), p. 604, trans. Cheney, *Notaries*, p. 135.

[29] *Statutes*, p. 99. T. F. T. Plucknett, *Legislation of Edward I* (1949), pp. 138–44. Cf. ch. 9, n. 52 below.

[30] *CuriaRR* xv, p. 345, no. 1365. P & M ii, pp. 219–20.

laymen were concerned in particular, the balance in England had shifted from memory to written record.

To generalize, in the eleventh century laymen of all classes and many religions gave and received tenancies often without any kind of documentary evidence.[31] In the twelfth century magnates used documents occasionally and they and the gentry made gifts for religious houses by charter because the monks wanted this. In the thirteenth century laymen began to convey property to each other by charter; in the latter half of the century this practice extended below the gentry class to some peasants. Laymen used documents among themselves as a matter of habit only when they became sufficiently familiar with literate modes to trust them. By 1300 even serfs, the more prosperous ones at least, were familiar with documents. These generalizations do not necessitate everybody being able to read by 1300, still less to write. Clerks did the writing throughout the Middle Ages; most of the reading was likewise done by them, as the custom was to read out loud. By these means laymen of all classes, who remained technically illiterate, could participate in the use of documents and were encouraged to do business with charters (see plates I, V and VI).

To these generalizations the bookland of the Anglo-Saxon past is the most obvious exception. Bookland was exceptional by definition, as it created a privileged status in land by virtue of the grant of a 'landbook' or charter. It is difficult to judge how widespread bookland had been or to assess its effects on the growth of literacy among laymen. As with other questions about the uses of writing before the Norman Conquest (which are discussed in chapter 1), there is room for conjecture and therefore for controversy. For Maitland, bookland was 'an alien, ecclesiastical institution, from which few inferences can be drawn', whereas Stenton argued that the granting of bookland to royal thegns shows that 'the conception of the chartered landholder who is not a churchman was well established before the end of the ninth century.'[32] Although bookland had the theoretical potential to create a class of chartered tenants, both clerical and lay, it seems to have declined in importance in the century preceding the Norman Conquest instead of increasing. This may have been because the landbook itself was too unauthentic a form of document ever to have served as an adequate foundation for literate business.[33] Whatever the cause of the decline of bookland, written titles to property make a new start after the Norman Conquest on the basis of the autographed diploma and the sealed writ (see plate I).

Another exception to the generalization that in the eleventh century laymen gave tenancies without any kind of documentary evidence is a writ in the name of Geoffrey de Mandeville, which purports to date from

[31] J. C. Holt, 'Politics and Property in Early Medieval England', *Past and Present* LVII (1972), p. 38.

[32] P & M II, p. 87; cf. *ibid*. I, p. 60. F. M. Stenton, *The Latin Charters of the Anglo-Saxon Period* (1955), p. 63.

[33] As argued by Galbraith, 'Literacy', p. 217 and *Studies*, p. 32.

the reign of William the Conqueror or William Rufus. In this writ
Geoffrey orders Edric, his reeve, and the men of Waltham in Berkshire
to take nothing from Hurley priory without a *documentum* from the
prior.[34] (Hurley was a daughter house, which Geoffrey had endowed, of
Westminster abbey.) At first sight such an order suggests that
documentary authority was common on the estates of Norman barons,
whose officials like Edric were accustomed to receiving letters. But this
interpretation is almost certainly mistaken. Firstly, the word *documentum* most probably means an oral instruction rather than a writing.
Furthermore, the writ itself may be a forgery of the mid-twelfth century, as Westminster abbey produced a revised version of Geoffrey's
foundation charter for Hurley (together with other audacious forgeries) at that time.[35] Whether forged or not, Geoffrey's writ to Edric
is not what it appears to be, namely a letter from one of William the
Conqueror's barons to his reeve, as it was almost certainly written by
and in the interests of Westminster abbey. The real purpose of such a
document was not to convey information to Edric, but to serve as evidence of Hurley's exemption from the authority of Waltham.

One way of investigating how extensively documents were used at the
beginning of the twelfth century is to examine the extant charter collections of magnates in Henry I's reign. Even at this exalted level of society
few charters (including writs and less formal letters) seem to have been
made, and the majority of these derived from religious houses. Although
the numbers are too small to be significant as statistics, they do indicate
a common pattern. Information about four magnates, whose charters and
other letters have been collected by modern editors and can therefore be
counted with confidence, is tabulated below:[36]

Charters issued by magnates of Henry I

	Year of coming of age etc.	Year of death	Number of active years	Number of charters	Charters per year
Miles, earl of Hereford	*c.* 1121	1143	22	10	.45
Nigel d' Aubigny	*c.* 1107	1129	22	17	.77
Robert, earl of Gloucester	*c.* 1113	1147	34	17	.50
Roger 'le Poer'	1101	1139	38	31	.82

[34] J. Armitage Robinson, *Gilbert Crispin, Abbot of Westminster* (1911), p. 135, no. 7.

[35] P. Chaplais, 'The Original Charters of Herbert and Gervase Abbots of Westminster' in
MM for Stenton, pp. 97–8, 105–8.

[36] 'Earldom of Hereford Charters' ed. D. Walker, *Camden Miscellany* Camden S. 4th
series XXII (1964), pp. 13–16. *Mowbray Charters*, pp. 5–19. *Earldom of Gloucester Charters* ed. R. B. Patterson 1 (1973). E. J. Kealey, *Roger of Salisbury* (1972), pp. 228–71.
The statistics have been compiled by me and are not the responsibility of the editors
cited.

Robert, earl of Gloucester, was Henry I's bastard son whom 'philosophy educated in the liberal arts.'[37] The other three magnates were among the new men whom Henry had 'raised from the dust';[38] Miles was the constable, Nigel succeeded to the Mowbray honour in the north, and Roger was at first chancellor and then chief justiciar. All four men were therefore products of the educated court of Henry I and would have been unusually familiar with documents. Yet the table shows that they each issued in their own names less than one charter per year, if extant documents are taken as the criterion.

Obviously more charters once existed; references have been found for example to another 26 grants made by Robert, earl of Gloucester.[39] If these are added to his 17 extant charters, Robert issued 1.27 charters per year on average. Charters, whether extant or lost, comprised only a small proportion of the total number of documents issued. Master David of London's correspondence shows how many ancillary documents might accompany a royal charter. Figures based on the output of Henry I's scribes (which are discussed more fully below) suggest that the number of extant charters might be multiplied by 100 in order to estimate the total output of documents. Assuming a similar pattern for magnates, which is probably overestimating their output, the number of documents issued each year by the four men tabulated would be 45 by Miles, 77 by Nigel, 50 by Robert, and 82 by Roger. On that assumption, the conclusion is that such men wrote one or two letters a week.

At first sight it is hard to believe that these magnates wrote so few letters. It is true that Roger was described as 'almost illiterate' by William of Newburgh;[40] but he at least produced more documents than Robert, who was said by William of Malmesbury to have drunk such 'a full draught of the knowledge of letters' that he readily understood a papal bull.[41] Literacy concerned being learned in Latin and would not directly relate to an interest in issuing charters. Neither Roger's alleged lack of learning nor Robert's abundance of it necessarily invalidate the figures tabulated. The most reasonable inference to draw is that the figures are substantially accurate, as the average number of extant charters issued per year correlates quite well between the four magnates at 0.63.

Some editors of twelfth-century charters have argued that magnates possessed organized writing offices or chanceries. But the variety of hands and drafting styles in extant charters suggests that documents were usually written by the beneficiaries themselves, if they were religious houses, or by which ever chaplain or scribe was available. Haphazard methods are understandable if only one or two letters had to be written on average each week. Even bishops in England did not

[37] *The Historia Regum Britanniae of Geoffrey of Monmouth* ed. A. Griscom (1929), pp. 219–20.
[38] Southern, *Medieval Humanism*, pp. 212ff.
[39] *Earldom of Gloucester Charters*, pp. 169–75.
[40] 'fere illitteratus', *Chronicles* ed. R. Howlett, RS LXXXII (1884), I, p. 36. For the meaning of *illitteratus* see ch. 7, n. 26 below.
[41] *Historia Novella* ed. K. R. Potter (1955), p. 23.

develop organized writing offices until *c.*1200; a generation or two earlier their letters, like those of other magnates, indicate a variety of scribal practices.[42] Great men certainly employed clerics in their households on a regular basis, but that had been so for centuries; household clergy performed a variety of religious and learned functions, among which writing had always been one, though it was not yet done on a specialized and regular basis.[43]

The output of royal documents

In twelfth-century England only the king possessed permanently organized writing facilities, under the ultimate supervision of the chancellor, and even these were somewhat makeshift and of recent origin. Only the Exchequer, created by Henry I, had a stable existence. 'What is the Exchequer?' asked Gerald of Wales. 'It is the seat of the public treasury in England, a sort of square table at London, where royal dues are collected and accounted for.'[44] Its receipts on inscribed wooden tallies and audited accounts on great rolls of parchment, the pipe rolls, absorbed most of the record-making energies of the government, as they required numerous ancillary documents like the writs Master David of London had to obtain to ensure that his pension was paid. As David's correspondence also illustrates, there had in practice to be more than one writing office, because the Exchequer remained static while the king perambulated. A clerk in charge of the *scriptorium* sat at the Exchequer table and was responsible for finding and supervising the scribes who wrote the chancellor's roll and the writs and summonses. 'These duties,' commented Fitz Neal in the *Dialogue of the Exchequer*, 'need but few words to explain, but demand almost endless labour, as those know who have learned by experience.'[45]

How many scribes laboured in this way, and how many documents they wrote, are matters for conjecture. As far as personnel are concerned, the problem is that some scribes or clerks performed duties as chaplains in the royal household as well as acting as writers.[46] Moreover, there were different grades of clerk; some simply wrote and copied, while others (the predecessors of the Chancery Masters) composed and dictated the letters. Nor were all the king's letters produced in his *scriptorium*: royal charters, just like seignorial ones, might be written by the beneficiaries' clerks (see plate III) or by a scribe casually employed. T. A. M. Bishop has demonstrated that four charters of Henry II for Lincoln, written in a professional cursive hand which palceographers would once have called a distinctively Chancery style, were in

[42] Cheney, *Chanceries*, pp. 55–6.

[43] I differ here from R. B. Patterson, *Earldom of Gloucester Charters*, p. 26, who argues that the earls had a bureaucracy although they lacked the organization which could be called a chancery (p. 30): and from D. E. Greenway, *Mowbray Charters*, p. lxvi, who suggests that the Mowbrays had a chancery in the second half of the twelfth century.

[44] Giraldus III, p. 28.   [45] *Dialogus*, p. 26.

[46] T. A. M. Bishop, *Scriptores Regis* (1961), pp. 23–4.

fact written by a scribe of the bishop of Lincoln.[47] Of the 750 or so royal charters extant in originals from the twelfth century, only 450 can be shown to have been written by identifiably royal scribes.[48]

Consequently estimates vary of the size and nature of the writing facilities which later became known as the Chancery. One of Becket's biographers, William Fitz Stephen, described him when chancellor in 1158 as having 52 clerks in his service.[49] Bishop, on the other hand, has identified the hands of 16 royal scribes in the period 1155–8, but only four of these can be shown to have been regularly employed.[50] The discrepancy between these estimates is not as great as it appears. Fitz Stephen's figure of 52 included the clerks of Becket's entourage and those who dealt with vacant benefices and other ecclesiastical business. Bishop's number, on the other hand, is confined to scribes (that is, it does not include all clerks) and to those whose handwriting is still extant. As Bishop points out, surviving royal charters cannot give a reliable estimate of the output of the Chancery, because 'it was not simply with the object of parting with the lands and rights of the crown that Henry II maintained a Chancery writing staff.'[51]

An increasing number of executive orders to bailiffs and sheriffs and so on, concerning daily administration, were put in writing. The volume of writs generated by the Exchequer alone was considerable. The earliest pipe roll, that for 1130, refers to the issue of nearly 300 *brevia* authorizing expenditure.[52] These *brevia* comprise only one class of letter; the figure of 300 should probably be multiplied by 10 or 20 to estimate the average total output per year of royal letters of all sorts (charters, precepts, warrants, requests for information and so on) in Henry I's reign. Suppose the multiple of 15 is taken (as the mean between 10 and 20), then $300 \times 15 = 4,500$ letters produced each year. Bishop estimates that Henry I employed at least four scribes in c. 1130.[53] In that case each scribe wrote an average of 1,125 letters a year, or three letters each day. Three letters a day may not seem the 'almost endless labour' which Fitz Neal described later in the century, but three is an average for every day of the year and each letter had to be free from errors. The average number of charters extant (in originals or copies) per year from Henry I's reign is 41.[54] That figure may therefore need to be multiplied by 100 or more to appreciate the total output of royal letters each year. In other words, about one per cent of the original output has survived.

It must be emphasized that the estimates in the preceding paragraph are largely conjectural. Their purpose is to provide a context for specific numbers concerning the output of royal documents, which are set out in the graph at p. 44 and in the table appended to this chapter. The graph compares the number of letters extant on average per year of reign (in

[47] *ibid.* pp. 9, 14. Cf. ch. 4, n. 50 below.   [48] *ibid.* p. 3, 11.
[49] *Becket Materials* III, p. 29.   [50] Bishop, *Scriptores Regis*, p. 30.
[51] *ibid.* p. 32.   [52] *ibid.* p. 32.   [53] *ibid.* p. 30.
[54] The number is based on *RRA-N* as computed by A. Murray, 'Pope Gregory VII and his Letters', *Traditio* XXII (1966), p. 166, n. 46.

originals or copies, but excluding forgeries as far as possible) issued by the kings of England and France and the popes between the time of the Norman Conquest and the reign of Henry II. The table (appendix pp. 58–59) shows the average weekly consumption of sealing wax by Henry III's Chancery over nearly half a century between 1226 and 1271; it will be argued that the amount of wax used correlates with the number of letters sealed. Both the graph and the table therefore indicate a marked and relatively steady increase in the number of documents issued over the years. The numbers rise 'in a sort of geometrical progression',[55] doubling every two or three decades: for the reign of William Rufus an average of 15 documents per year are extant; for Henry I 41; for Henry II about 115. In the thirteenth century the Chancery's consumption of wax increased even faster, as the figures below (which are averaged and summarized from the table at pp. 58–9 indicate:

Sealing wax used by the Chancery

Approximately 5 year intervals	*Amount of wax per week (in lb)*
1226–30	3.63
1230–33	4.03
1237–40	4.78
1242–45	7.58
1245–46	8.56
1250–54	7.86
1255–60	13.02
1260–65	20.31
1265–71	31.90

Although the numbers in both the graph and the table contain anomalies and uncertainties and are not acceptable as true statistics, at the level of generalization over decades and centuries they demonstrate how the mass of documents increased. No statistics from the twelfth and thirteenth centuries can be expected to do much more than indicate general trends.

The graph makes no claim to use hitherto unnoticed information, as it is based on printed lists and summaries.[56] The figures available are sparse and imprecise, because royal documents in this period do not usually specify the year in which they were made. The number of documents issued by each ruler per year has therefore been averaged over the whole of his reign; in the case of the papacy only pontificates of 8 years or more have been included. The number of documents extant are

[55] Galbraith, *Studies*, p. 57.

[56] For England, from William I to Stephen, the numbers are those computed by A. Murray (n. 54 above); for Henry II's reign the estimate of a total of 3,500–4,500 originals and copies has been taken at the mean of 4,000 to give an annual average of 115; this estimate derives from Bishop, *Scriptores Regis*, p. 3, as computed by Van Caenegem, *Writs*, p. 4. For France, the totals (including mentions of *acta* as well as extant copies) are those of R. Fawtier, *The Capetian Kings of France* trans. L. Butler and R. J. Adam (1962), p. 8. For the papacy, the numbers are based on P. Jaffé, *Regesta Pontificum Romanorum* (1882); cf. R. W. Southern, *Western Society and the Church in the Middle Ages* (1970), p. 109 and A. Murray (n. 54 above).

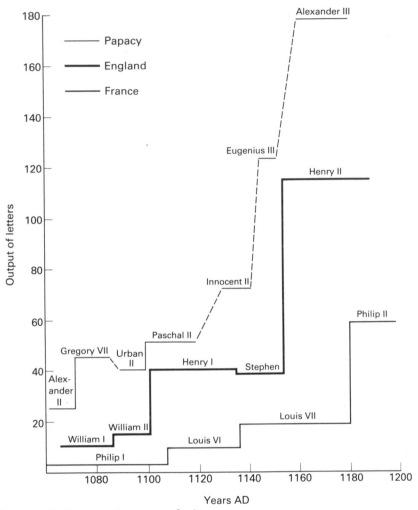

Number of letters extant per year of reign

not of course the same as the total number produced; it has already been suggested that those extant for England might be multiplied by 100 in order to estimate the number which once existed. It is known similarly that Pope Alexander III must have issued many more letters than survive.[57] The popes and the kings of France are included in the graph for comparison and in order to show that the increasing use of documents was a general trend in western Europe. Two other increases in the period 1060–1180 also need to be taken into consideration: the population of western Europe may have doubled and the number of monastic houses multiplied at least tenfold. As many, perhaps most, royal and papal letters concerned monasteries and were preserved by

[57] Duggan, *Decretals*, pp. 120–21, 144–5.

them, monastic expansion may be the greatest single cause of the increasing number of documents up to *c.*1200.

In thirteenth-century Europe too the number of documents continued to increase fast. The average number of letters extant per year for the pontificate of Innocent III (1198–1215) is 280, whereas for Innocent IV (1243–54) it is 730. By the end of the century Boniface VIII (1294–1303) is estimated to have issued 50,000 letters a year.[58] Similarly more than 15,000 letters are known of Philip the Fair of France (1285–1314), compared with the 2,500 of Philip Augustus (1180–1223).[59] Registration of copies of letters by the senders means that comparisons of numbers between the twelfth century and the thirteenth are not very significant, however, as more record survives of the dispatch of letters from *c.*1200 onwards by the rulers of England, France and the papacy.

The table (appendix, pp. 58–9), showing the amount of sealing wax used by Henry III's Chancery, is intended to be a surer way of measuring the output of documents in the thirteenth century than counting extant letters. Although many letters were registered in the Chancery rolls from John's reign onwards, numerous routine documents (common law writs are the best example) were not enrolled. The weight of wax used should therefore give a better indication of the total volume of documents than either the Chancery rolls or extant writs and charters. It must be emphasized, however, that the figures concern the Chancery only; wax used by the Exchequer was accounted for separately and only its cost, and not its weight, was recorded. Because the Chancery had to account to the Exchequer, its records specify the weight used as well as the cost. This careful accounting has left the historian with a constant measure to apply over the years, whereas the cost alone is insignificant because of fluctuations. It is true that different quantities of wax were used for sealing various types of document (for instance, charters were authenticated by the great seal, whereas some letters close bore the privy seal), but there is no reason to think that on average either more or less wax was used per document in the 1220s than in the 1260s.

It is not possible, however, to enumerate how many documents were sealed with each pound of wax, mainly because it cannot be established whether common law writs were sealed with the whole great seal or only a portion of it. Although weight cannot be converted into a specific number of parchments, it is reasonable to assume that a rise in the weight of wax indicates a commensurate increase in the sum total of documents issued. Despite not being able to quantify the number of parchments, these figures have the advantage over all others that they were compiled at the time by an official, the keeper of the hanaper. Some allowance must be made for the honesty or efficiency of the official concerned, but at least the historian does not have to estimate an indefinite number of lost or unrecorded documents.

The figures derive from the liberate rolls which record authorizations

---

[58] R. Fawtier's estimate, reported by C. H. Lawrence in *History* lviii (1973), p. 429, reviewing W. Ullmann, *A Short History of the Papacy*.

[59] Fawtier, *The Capetian Kings*, p. 9, n. 2.

for payments from the treasury, in this case to the spigurnels (sealers) or serjeants of the chapel royal 'for sealing the king's writs'. The average weight of wax used per week has been calculated throughout by dividing the weights recorded in the rolls by the number of whole weeks concerned. The years 1226–71 have been selected because the liberate rolls for these years are published, which makes it possible to verify the data. Anomalies in the figures suggest that they are generally accurate. The relatively low weights for June 1253–February 1254 and for July 1262–November 1262 may be accounted for by Henry III's absence in France at about these times. Conversely the exceptionally high weight of 31·69 lb per week for the period from October 1261 to January 1262 coincides with the apogee of Henry III's reassertion of power over the barons in the struggle with Simon de Montfort. More wax may have been required to summon the king's followers, issue safe-conducts and pardons, confirm titles to property, and so on. An anomaly which cannot be readily explained, however, is the low figure of 8·15 lb per week for the first half of 1259, as this was the period of legislative and reforming activity by the barons; perhaps ordinary government business was curtailed by reform.

Documents and bureaucracy

By and large, both the graph of letters extant and the table of wax used suggest that the number of documents increased progressively, only being temporarily affected by political crises. In the graph the civil war of Stephen's reign shows a small recession, yet the numbers of letters are more than double those of William Rufus's time. Similarly the volume of wax used in Henry III's Chancery does not usually correlate with the frequent political crises in the years concerned, despite the exceptions discussed in the preceding paragraph. The weight of wax used, 17·1 lb per week, in the months of de Montfort's dominance between the battles of Lewes (May 1264) and Evesham (August 1265), is similar to the 16·87 lb used per week in the last months of Henry's personal rule before the parliament at Oxford in June 1258. Both king and barons depended on documents in order to assert their authority.

The increasing mass of royal documents tended to enlarge and stratify the bureaucracy which produced them. The origin and early development of English government departments has been described by numerous constitutional and administrative historians over the last century and does not require general repetition here. There was obviously a close connexion between the growth in numbers of documents and of the functionaries who made them. This is best illustrated by a story, told by Fitz Neal in the *Dialogue of the Exchequer*, which can be taken to stand as typical. Fitz Neal describes how Henry II employed Master Thomas Brown, who had been the secretary of Roger II of Sicily, to keep a watching brief in the king's interests over the administration. In this capacity Brown made a roll 'of the laws of the realm and the secrets of the king'.[60] To make this roll Brown needed a scribe to sit at the Exchequer table. But his scribe could not be fitted on to the writers' bench at the Exchequer because it was already occupied (from right to left) by the treasurer, the treasurer's scribe (who wrote the pipe roll), the chancellor's scribe (who copied from the treasurer's scribe and made the chancellor's roll), the chancellor's clerk (who supervised the chancellor's scribe) and the clerk of the constabulary.[61] Brown's scribe was therefore given a place higher up, where he could make his copy over the treasurer's scribe shoulder. As the pupil in the *Dialogue* comments, the scribe must have been 'lynx-eyed to avoid mistakes'.

This story, together with the numbers cited in the graph and the table, leave the impression that the proliferation of documents and functionaries was inexorable and almost subject to some mathematical law. Nevertheless there are significant exceptions to the rule that documents steadily multiplied. Even Fitz Neal's story about Thomas Brown's scribe can be interpreted in a contrary sense. After Brown's death or retiral in *c.* 1180 the copy of the pipe roll which he had kept was discontinued, though his scribe may have stayed at the Exchequer as the earliest king's remembrancer.

A clearer instance of the bureaucracy being first enlarged and then curtailed appears in Fitz Neal's remarks about another of Henry II's confidants, Richard of Ilchester, archdeacon of Poitiers, who sat on another side of the Exchequer table. Richard's duties were to supervise the making of the rolls and to stop the treasurer from falling asleep.[62] As we have seen, Master David of London had hoped to expedite his business by getting a letter addressed to him. Richard introduced a system of keeping a copy of every summons sent to a sheriff in order to prevent him from altering it: 'so, when the sheriff was sitting at his account and the chancellor's clerk was reading the summons, the archdeacon's clerk, with his eye on the copy, watched him to see that he made no mistake.'[63] By this means a check was kept on both the chancellor's clerk and the sheriff. 'But', Fitz Neal continues, 'as time went on, and the number of debtors enormously increased, so that a whole skin of parchment was scarcely long enough for a single summons, the number of names and the labour involved proved overpowering.' The roll of summonses was therefore abolished. As Fitz Neal points out, it had not really been necessary in the first place, as all the debts summoned were already recorded on the pipe roll. This anecdote illustrates the speed at which record-making increased: the lists of debtors had become enormous within a decade or so; but it also shows that the advance of bureaucracy could, occasionally at least, be stopped. The formation of the royal bureaucracy was thus a complex process of experiment and makeshift; although the net result, when averaged over decades, was a constant increase in the production of documents.

[60] *Dialogus*, p. 35.
[61] *ibid*. p. 18 and diagram of the seating arrangements at p. xlii.
[62] *ibid*. p. 27.   [63] *ibid*. pp. 74–5.

The work of Hubert Walter

From the point of view of posterity – by looking, that is, at documents which have survived – the most decisive increase in production occurred within a decade or so on either side of 1200. The earliest extant series of plea rolls, feet of fines, and Chancery enrolments of outgoing letters begin at this time. These are the years in which Archbishop Hubert Walter held office, first as chief justiciar (1193–8) of Richard I and then as chancellor (1199–1205) of King John. Whether Hubert invented all these types of record, or whether some had existed earlier but did not survive, are matters for conjecture. An explicit instance of deliberate record-making by Hubert is the earliest tripartite final concord, dated 15 July 1195. The document is endorsed:

> This is the first chirograph that was made in the king's court in the form of three chirographs, according to the command of his lordship of Canterbury [Hubert Walter] and other barons of the king, to the end that by this form a record can be made to be passed to the treasurer to put in the treasury.[64]

The reference to Hubert's responsibility for the innovation is reinforced by his brother, Theobald, being the plaintiff whom this chirograph concerns. The purpose of the third copy (which was the novelty), or 'foot of the fine', is explicitly stated to be 'to the end that by this form (*per illam formam*) a record' might be deposited in the treasury. Keeping a third copy was not entirely novel, however, as the practice had Anglo-Saxon precedents and within living memory Henry II had personally insisted in 1164 that a third copy of the chirograph recording the controversial Constitutions of Clarendon should be put 'in the royal archives.'[65]

Although there were precedents for Hubert Walter's action, the importance of the feet of fines should not be underestimated. For the first time a form of record had been deliberately inaugurated as a continuing series for archival purposes. Furthermore the feet of fines gave private individuals the opportunity to have transactions kept on permanent record in the royal treasury. What had in the past been exceptional practice now became the rule; that is the principle underlying many of Hubert's bureaucratic reforms. Although the king's government already made regular records for its own purposes, it had not normally extended its archival facilities to private individuals. A few non-royal conveyances of property were enrolled in the pipe rolls and the *Cartae Antiquae* before 1195; but, unlike the feet of fines, this practice was neither systematic nor regular.[66] The use of feet of fines was of course confined to the more prosperous landowners, who were

---

[64] *Feet of Fines: Henry II and Richard I*, PRS XVII (1894), p. 21. P & M II, pp. 97–100. C. R. Cheney, *Hubert Walter* (1967), p. 96.

[65] 'in regum archivis', *Becket Materials* III, p. 288 (Herbert of Bosham, bk iii, ch. 29). See also ch. 3, n. 20 below.

[66] *Cartae Antiquae* ed. L. Landon, PRS new series XVII (1939), p. XV.

able to pay the fees and take the risks of litigating in the king's court. Hubert Walter could not, and probably did not intend to, benefit everybody. Nevertheless the extent to which these documents became widespread among landowners within a few years is indicated by a concord made at Westminster on 29 October 1198 between William de Bruce of Annandale and Adam of Carlisle concerning eight ploughgates in Lockerbie.[67] Lockerbie was (and is) in Scotland, though the fine was filed with those from Northumberland.

The success of the feet of fines archive may have been the cause which encouraged the government to enrol copies of royal letters during Hubert Walter's chancellorship. These rolls form three main series – the charter, close and patent rolls, extant from the first, second and third years of John's reign respectively.[68] Like the feet of fines, the Chancery rolls benefited private individuals, who paid fees to have their royal grants recorded in them.[69] Had such rolls existed in Henry II's time, for example, Master David of London would have been able to have the various royal letters he obtained recorded there. These rolls also served the government as an official register. In 1201 (the second year of the extant charter rolls) Jocelin of Brakelond records that King John ordered an inquiry to be made 'through his register about what sort of charter' he had given the monks of Ely because the monks of Bury disputed its terms.[70] The contentious passage was duly found, as it still can be in the charter rolls, and letters protecting Bury were issued. The immediate consequence of this, however, was an armed raid by Bury on Ely and not a peaceful settlement.[71] Similarly, many years later, Henry III wrote to Pope Gregory X in 1272 assuring him that some letters patent, which the prior of Christ Church Canterbury was exhibiting in a lawsuit at the Roman *curia*, were a forgery because 'no such letters can issue from our court unless they have first been registered [and] we have had our register searched about this case with the utmost care and diligence, and nothing whatsoever is to be found in it about the aforesaid letters.'[72] In fact the king was mistaken, as these letters had been enrolled in the patent rolls in November 1265.[73] It was easier to make records than to use them efficiently.

The twelfth century had been a great period of making documents, the thirteenth was the century of keeping them. From the viewpoint of the historian today, the formation of an archive seems an obvious and essential step, once documents were produced in any quantity. To medieval governments, however, neither the urgency nor the usefulness of archives would have appeared as compelling. Copying outgoing

[67] *Feet of Fines 10 Richard I*, PRS XXIV (1900), pp. 53–4. G. W. S. Barrow, *The Kingdom of the Scots* (1973), p. 114.

[68] Chaplais, *Docs*, p. 4, n. 1.

[69] H. G. Richardson, *Memoranda Roll 1 John*, pp. xxxv–li, argues that collection of fees was the sole purpose of instituting enrolments.

[70] 'per registrum suum cuiusmodo cartam,' Jocelin, p. 133, cf. pp. 157–60.

[71] *Rotuli Chartarum*, RC (1837), p. 91. Jocelin, pp. 133–4.

[72] *Diplomatic Documents* ed. P. Chaplais, HMSO (1964), p. 304, no. 434.

[73] *CPatR* 1258–66, pp. 496–7.

letters on to rolls was an immense labour, as Fitz Neal's anecdote about the fate of Richard of Ilchester's attempt to enrol the Exchequer summonses illustrates. Hubert Walter was not necessarily the inventor of the principle of enrolling outgoing charters or of filing incoming documents (returned writs, feet of fines and so on) on leather thongs, but he did create the principles of organization which made continuous royal archives possible.

It would be rash to assume that such archives brought a return of information to the government which balanced the worry and expense of making them. Like Domesday Book, the Chancery and judicial rolls and writ files benefited remote posterity rather than contemporaries, since they provide minutely detailed information about the countryside and people of England as viewed by the king's government. The making of such records is an indicator of the efficiency of the government rather than its cause. They are a notable step in the transition from memory to written record because documents created more documents in their own image, not because they made for more effective government in themselves. The two examples cited in the preceding paragraph, of King John consulting his 'register' in 1201 and Henry III in 1272, suggest that the information provided, even when it was correct, did not help to keep the peace. The royal archives constituted a vast potential source of information, which could not be thoroughly consulted in the medieval period itself. Historians today are better equipped to search the rolls than the king's clerks were in the thirteenth century.

The creation of these central government archives (still extant in the Public Record Office in Chancery Lane) during Hubert Walter's years of office has been frequently described and has therefore been summarily treated here. Just as important in the proliferation of documents at the time was Hubert's effect on local government, although very few local records survive from this early period. Within his first year of office as chief justiciar, in the instructions for the justices' visitation in September 1194, he instituted coroners in each county including a clerk; from this order stemmed the coroners' rolls.[74] From 1202 and 1203 comes the earliest evidence of the coroner's rolls being used to check oral testimony in county courts. In the Lincolnshire justices' visitation of 1202 the county was fined £200 because their oral 'record' differed from that of the coroners' rolls.[75] Likewise in Staffordshire in 1203 the county court and the coroners 'recorded' that Simon Pring had not been outlawed, whereas the rolls of the coroners (as distinct from their persons) and of the sheriff showed that he had. In the judgment against the county court and the coroners preference was accorded to the written records.[76]

Hubert Walter's instructions for the justices' visitation in September

[74] Stubbs, *Charters*, p. 254, no. 20. Some written records of crown pleas had been made before 1194, R. F. Hunnisett, 'The Origins of the Office of Coroner', *TRHS* 5th series VIII (1958), p. 97, n. 4.

[75] *SPC*, p. 16, no. 38. See pp. 56–7 below concerning oral 'record'.

[76] *ibid*. p. 28, no. 62.

1194 also provided the first public local archives and official writers. The purpose of this legislation was to regulate loans made by the Jews.[77] Neither moneylenders' bonds nor royal intervention in Jewish business were novelties in themselves; what was new was the establishment of archives and supervised writing facilities on a regular basis. It was ruled that *all* debts and pledges of the Jews were to be put in writing: loans were to be made in designated places only, where two scribes (financed by fees) would be provided and supervised by a clerk appointed by the king's commissioners, William of Sainte-Mère-Eglise and William of Chimillé. The documents recording the loans were to be written in the form of bipartite chirographs: one part would be kept by the Jew and the other deposited in a communal archive (*in arca communi*) or public chest, with three sealed locks, whose keys were kept by the Jews, the Christians and the royal commissioners respectively. As if this were not sufficient security, the commissioners' clerk was also to keep in a roll up-to-date transcripts of all the chirographs in the chest; furthermore a roll of receipts of money by the Jews was to be kept in triplicate. These regulations were not all immediately enforced, but within two decades 17 towns (mainly county towns) had archives of this sort.[78]

By these means the principles of producing authenticated documents, retaining them in archives and transcribing copies on to rolls for ready reference spread from the royal Chancery and Exchequer to provincial centres. It may not be a coincidence that the earliest extant borough records, the Leicester guild rolls of 1196, survive from this period, although Leicester itself was not a Jewish centre.[79] The king's government was not in this instance primarily concerned with promoting record-making as such, but with taxing the Jews and their transactions as thoroughly as possible. Taxation had been the king's main motive for making records, certainly since the institution of the Exchequer at the beginning of the twelfth century and probably since Domesday Book.

The same principles, of making multiple records in the localities for taxation purposes, received their greatest extension in the plans for the carucage of 1198, which was required to finance Richard I's war against Philip Augustus in Normandy. This tax on every plough team necessitated making a survey of how many teams there were in each village. Such a survey was not novel in itself; as in the Domesday inquest, 'all these things were to be reduced to writing' (*in scriptum redigebantur*).[80] The innovation lay in requiring rolls to be made in quadruplicate. In each county a clerk and a knight were to act as collectors. Each was to have a copy of the carucage roll; a third copy was to be kept by the sheriff and a fourth by the baronial steward, whose lord's land was involved. Thus of these four rolls, only one was to be kept by a clerk; the three others were in the hands of laymen.

[77] Stubbs, *Charters*, p. 256. Cf. ch. 5, n. 104 below.

[78] Richardson, *Jewry*, pp. 14–19.

[79] The earliest borough records are listed by G. H. Martin in *TRHS* 5th series XIII (1963), p. 129. Cf. ch. 3, n. 59 below.

[80] Stubbs, *Charters*, p. 249.

If these regulations had been enforced, every baronial steward would have possessed a list of his lord's plough teams, which comprised his basic resources in men and animals. Familiarity with documents, if not literacy itself, would have been compulsorily extended to knights and barons and their officers by legislation. It is doubtful, however, whether all these rolls were made, as Hubert Walter resigned from the chief justiciarship in the summer of 1198 at his own insistence (according to Richard I) because of 'the intolerable burden of work and his own incapacity'.[81] Perhaps the difficulties in making England a more documented kingdom had temporarily overwhelmed him. Yet he returned to record-making within a year as King John's chancellor.

Much of this chapter has emphasized the role of the king's government in the production and proliferation of documents. The main reason for this emphasis is that royal administration is the best documented, and therefore the most measurable, example of the production of records in medieval England. Moreover, there is every reason to think that the king was by far the largest producer of documents at the time, as well as having the best archives to transmit them to posterity. In England, from the time of William the Conqueror's Domesday Book and Henry I's Exchequer onwards, it was not the church or churchmen as such who were the principle promoters of the documentary habit but the king's clerks. Although such men were technically clerics, they usually put the interests of the king before those of the church as an institution. Thomas Becket, chancellor and archbishop, is the most notable exception to this rule. More typical is Hubert Walter. 'Where did the archbishop come from?' asked Gerald of Wales in his denunciation of Hubert at the papal *curia* in 1199. 'From the Exchequer. . . . This was the academy, this was the school, in which he had already grown old, from which he was called to all the grades of his [ecclesiastical] dignities, like nearly all the English bishops.'[82]

Hubert was no theologian, nor probably even a canon lawyer; there is no real evidence that he was a graduate of Bologna.[83] *Illiteratus* (in the opinion of an unfriendly chronicler), or 'only indifferently endowed with book-learning' according to a more charitable estimate,[84] he had been brought up in the household of his kinsman, Ranulf de Glanvill, who became the chief justiciar. Both Hubert and Ranulf have been credited with the authorship in *c.*1187 of the legal treatise *Glanvill*, whose prologue regrets the impossibility of reducing the laws of England entirely to writing because of the ignorance of scribes and the confusion of the sources.[85] If either Hubert or Ranulf were accepted as the author, it would be possible to see where Hubert derived an ambition to put so much into documentary form. In that case the Jewish archives of 1194,

[81] *Foedera* I, part 1, p. 71.
[82] Giraldus III, p. 28. Cheney, *Hubert Walter*, p. 4.
[83] C. R. Cheney, 'Hubert Walter and Bologna', *Bulletin of Medieval Canon Law*, new series II (1972), pp. 81–4.
[84] Cheney, *Hubert Walter*, p. 181, n. 2 and p. 164, n. 2. See also ch. 7, nn. 22, 80 below.
[85] Glanvill, p. 3. Attributions of authorship are discussed at pp. xxxi–iii. See also J. C. Russell, 'Ranulf de Glanville', *Speculum* XLV (1970), pp. 69–79.

the feet of fines of 1195, the rolls of plough teams of 1198, and the Chancery rolls of 1200 were all products of a consistent purpose in making records, pursued by Hubert throughout his years of office.

The Exchequer may well have been Hubert's school, as Gerald of Wales alleged, although he probably only came to it when he was grown up. As a member of the chief justiciar's household, Hubert could have learned about making records from the acknowledged experts, Richard of Ilchester and Richard Fitz Neal. The earliest known reference to Hubert 'surnamed Walter' is as a witness to a charter in c.1181, where his name accompanies those of the two Richards and of Glanvill.[86] Richard of Ilchester's innovations in record-making have already been mentioned.[87] Richard Fitz Neal, as author of the *Dialogue of the Exchequer*, had shown his aptitude for instructing by question and answer and his delight in the technicalities of documents. 'Master', asks his pupil, 'why do you not teach others that knowledge of the Exchequer for which you are famous, and put it into writing lest it should die with you?'[88] Even in that question the concern for putting as much as possible into writing is evident. The making of records was a difficult and technical business, not requiring book-learning nor academic training as such, but instruction by those with practical experience. Fitz Neal claimed to teach 'useful things' (*utilia*), not the 'clever things' (*subtilia*) of the university masters.[89] Hubert became the legatee of all this expertise and put it to more ambitious uses. The proliferation of documents was a European and a continuing phenonomen, yet if it were to be associated in England with one man, he would be Hubert Walter.

Royal influence on other records

From the king's government first the bishops and then other magnates learned how to make records. The bishops of Winchester, who were the earliest barons to keep systematic accounts in their pipe rolls (extant from 1208), imitated the methods used in the Exchequer.[90] This is not surprising, as the bishops between 1174 and 1238 were successively Richard of Ilchester (Henry II's watchdog at the Exchequer), Godfrey de Lucy (a royal justice and son of a chief justiciar) and Peter des Roches (King John's and Henry III's financial expert). Godfrey de Lucy, another candidate for the authorship of *Glanvill*,[91] was also the first bishop to date his letters systematically; the idea came from the royal Chancery, although the form of dating derived from the papal one.[92]

Conversely when bishops began to keep registers of their own, probably after the Lateran Council of 1215, the idea derived from the church, but the form of the first English registers is royal. The earliest are those

[86] *Cartae Antiquae* ed. J. Conway Davies. PRS new series XXXIII (1957), p. 56. Cheney, *Hubert Walter*, p. 19.
[87] See nn. 62–3 above.   [88] *Dialogus*, p. 5.
[89] Clanchy, *'Moderni'*, p. 678.
[90] *Walter of Henley*, p. 224. Cf. ch. 3, n. 46 below.
[91] Glanvill, p. xxxiii, n. 2.   [92] Cheney, *Chanceries*, p. 87.

made at Lincoln (starting before 1217) and York (starting in 1225).[93] Although the structure of the earliest registers is experimental and inconsistent, the documents are predominantly arranged in the format of royal Chancery rolls, that is, the parchments are stitched together head to tail to produce a long scroll. Episcopal and papal registers on the European continent, on the other hand, are usually in the form of books, as are bishops' registers in England by the latter half of the thirteenth century. In other words, the English bishops began by imitating the king's Chancery and only brought their registers into line with ecclesiastical practice elsewhere after fifty years or more.

The initiators of registers in roll format at Lincoln and York were both former royal Chancery officials, who had seen – and probably assisted in inaugurating – the system of Chancery enrolments in the early years of John's reign. Hugh of Wells, bishop of Lincoln (1209–35), described himself as 'formerly chancellor of King John'.[94] Walter de Gray, archbishop of York (1214–55) had been the first chancellor to ensure, in 1205, that his appointment to the chancellorship was itself recorded in a royal charter.[95] Former employment in the royal Chancery did not by itself guarantee that a bishop would produce a register. Hugh's brother, Jocelin, bishop of Bath and Wells (1206–42), was a Chancery official who does not seem to have made one.[96] Nevertheless this negative does not affect the validity of the general proposition that bishop's records follow the lead of the royal Exchequer and Chancery.

The instance of Jocelin of Wells, who did not make a register, suggests that it is worth noticing how slowly the practice of keeping registers spread among the dioceses. Before 1250, outside Lincoln and York, no other bishop kept a register except possibly William de Ralegh, bishop of Winchester (1244–50), who likewise emanated from the king's court where he had been the principal royal justice.[97] Judging from registers known, the lead given by the great dioceses of Lincoln and York was not immediately followed. Perhaps smaller dioceses did not have the same need to keep a check on appointments of clergy through a register. The table opposite shows the dates of the earliest registers, either still extant (E) or mentioned (M) in a medieval source, for each diocese.[98]

Apart from indicating that it took a century for every English diocese to institute a register, the table confirms the generalizations underlying this chapter – that documentation did not become usual outside the king's court until the latter half of the thirteenth century, and that the reign of Edward I was the period when record-making became really extensive.

[93] *ibid.* pp. 104–5. D. Smith, 'The Rolls of Hugh of Wells', *BIHR* XLV (1972), pp. 168–70, argues that the Lincoln register may have been started in 1214.

[94] Cheney, *Chanceries*, p. 107, n. 1.

[95] *Foedera* I, part i, p. 93.

[96] S. Painter, *The Reign of King John* (1949), pp. 79–80.

[97] Cheney, *Chanceries*, p. 149 argues that it is unlikely that Ralegh kept a register.

[98] Based on *ibid.* pp. 147–9.

Earliest bishops' registers

before 1217	Lincoln	E
1225	York	E
1251–74	Rochester	M
1257–80	Exeter	E
1258–95	Coventry & Lichfield	M
1264–6	Bath & Wells	E
1266–80	Winchester	M
1268–1302	Worcester	E
1271–84	Salisbury	M
1275–82	Hereford	E
1279–92	Canterbury	E
1283–1311	Durham	M
1288–1305	Chichester	M
1292–1324	Carlisle	E
1299–1325	Norwich	E
1304–13	London	E
1316–37	Ely	M

There is a time-lag of a generation or more between a form of documentation being developed and its finding general acceptance. Not even the bishops, the most highly educated group of barons with their close connexions with the king's court and their general knowledge of the universities and papal practice, hastened to make records. It is possible that they deliberately refrained from making registers, because they knew better than the king's clerks that records of this sort did not bring in a profitable return of information. Lists of churches in the diocese, showing their values and the names of the patrons and incumbents, were already kept by some bishops in a *matricula* or *scrutinium*, which was easier to consult, though less detailed, than a register.[99] But there is no evidence that bishops thought about record-making as disinterestedly as that. The most academic, conscientious and efficient bishop of the thirteenth century, Robert Grosseteste of Lincoln (1235–53), was among the first to keep a register.[100] Registers were by no means the only type of record made or kept by bishops. Nevertheless they are the best measure of the rate of episcopal record-making because they are summaries of other documents, deliberately made for future reference.

While bishops were slow to make records, when compared with the king's government, lay barons and knights were inert. They too, however, imitated royal methods and found themselves increasingly involved in the king's business, which meant using documents. An early example of imitation by a baron of a royal writ is the letter sent in c. 1130 by Richard Fitz Gilbert of Clare to one of his tenants, ordering him to restore a tithe to Stoke priory in Suffolk.[101] The letter concludes with a

[99] *ibid.* pp. 110–19. See also ch. 3, n. 55 below.
[100] *Rotuli Roberti Grosseteste* ed. F. N. Davis, Canterbury and York S. x (1913) or Lincoln Record S. xi (1914).
[101] Stenton, *Feudalism*, pp. 75, 269.

warning: 'And if you do not so, Adam, my steward, is swiftly going to do it, so that I hear no plaint for want of right.' The phraseology echoes that of royal writs of right, as in a letter of Henry I protecting Ramsey abbey:[102] 'And if you do not do so, Ralf Basset is going to have it done, so that I hear no plaint about it for want of right.'

If the two passages are compared in the original Latin, the similarities and differences are more obvious. Richard Fitz Gilbert's clerk wrote: 'Et si tu non facis, Adam dapifer meus faciat cito, ut non audiam clamorem penuria recti.' Whereas Henry I's clerk wrote: 'Et nisi feceris, Radulphus Basset faciat fieri, ne audiam inde clamorem pro penuria recti.' The sense and the principle words are the same in both passages. Fitz Gilbert's clerk made some minor variations, either out of ignorance (his Latin is not so neat), or because he wanted to avoid direct imitation. It is not suggested that he copied this particular writ of Henry I's, but something very similar. A baron like Fitz Gilbert would have received such royal writs himself, admonishing him to do right to his tenants. Understandably he paid the king the compliment of imitation, when he gave similar warnings one step further down the feudal hierarchy.

The initiative in using documents came from the king and gradually made its way down the social scale – to most barons by 1200, to knights by 1250, to peasants by 1300. The proliferation of documents is regulated by this time-scale. In the words of Maitland, 'the *carta*, the written agreement, the seal, these are aristocratic forms; gradually they make their way downwards and pervade the whole community; but they begin at the top.'[103] After documents begin to be extensively used, there is still a further delay before they are systematically kept in archives and registered for future reference. The king's government set an increasingly fast pace in the production of records, which left even the higher clergy, who had traditionally been the writing experts, far behind.

A final illustration of the way the proliferation of royal documents disseminated literate modes is found in the change in the meaning of the word 'record' itself. In the twelfth century to 'record' something meant to bear oral witness, not to produce a document. Thus in the civil war of Stephen's reign the earls of Gloucester and Hereford made a treaty in the form of sealed letters; yet both parties also named witnesses, who were 'to make legal record [*recordationem*] of this agreement in court if necessary.[104] The spoken work was the legally valid record and was superior to any document. Likewise in Henry II's reign Glanvill's treatise provides the text of a writ which orders a sheriff to have a plea 'recorded' (*recordari*) in his county court, and then he is to convey this 'record' (*recordum*) to the king's court by four knights.[105] It is evident that the knights convey the record orally, as the parties to the plea

[102] Van Caenegem, *Writs*, p. 418, no. 12.
[103] *Court Baron*, p. 116.
[104] *Earldom of Gloucester Charters*, pp. 95–6, no. 95. Cf. ch. 8, n. 32 below.
[105] Bk viii, ch. 10, p. 102. Cf. *Dialogus*, p. 116, where 'recordatio comitatus' is used in a similar context.

are ordered to come to 'hear the record'. We have already seen instances from 1202 to 1203 of such an oral record being found to conflict with written records, and examples appear in the earliest plea rolls of sheriff and knights having to make a record in the king's court in this way.[106]

Fifty years later, however, by the time Bracton's legal treatise was taking its final shape, the procedure for making a record of this type requires the seals of the sheriff and of the coroners, which are obviously to be attached to a letter.[107] No longer are four knights required, but only two, as their word is now of secondary importance. This change, from an oral to a predominantly written procedure, appears to have occurred in John's reign. In a case in 1214 the sheriff of Cornwall is ordered to have a record of his county court at Westminster 'by four knights who were present at that record and by his sealed letters'. In other words, this instruction combines elements of Glanvill's and Bracton's procedures; in fact two knights appeared at Westminster, instead of four, similarly presaging Bracton's procedure.[108] The clearest instance of how 'record' now meant a document occurs in a similar case in 1227.[109] Four knights from the Essex county court appeared at Westminster and 'brought the record and judgment, expressed in writing, under this form'. Details of the case then follow, which have evidently been copied down by the clerk compiling the plea roll from the document handed in to the court by knights, as he does not note everything, but says that the rest 'is more fully contained in the record'.

Knights who bore record to Westminster, orally in the twelfth century and by letters in the thirteenth, became familiar with literate modes and learned the ways of the king's court. From such men the king increasingly drew his local officials – sheriffs, coroners, escheators and so on. The most important consequence of the proliferation of documents was that it prepared the gentry, the country-keeping knights, for literacy. Documents had to precede widening literacy. They had to have increased by accumulation in central archives and extensive distribution over the country before understanding of them became widespread in the shires. The gentry were not going to learn to read until documents were available and necessary. Necessity and availability also made for easy familiarity with writing, and from familiarity stemmed confidence in literate ways of doing business. Traditionally, literate modes had been the preserve of clerics and rulers. It took time, combined with a massive increase in the number of documents, to change traditional habits. The purpose of charting the increasing number of documents in this chapter has not been as an end in itself, but because that was the foundation on which any permanent extension of literacy had to stand.

[106] See nn. 75–6 above. *CuriaRR* I, pp. 44, 66; II, pp. 260, 296.
[107] Bracton, fo 149b, vol. ii, p. 423.
[108] *CuriaRR* VII, p. 169.
[109] *Bracton's Note Book* ed. F. W. Maitland (1887) II, pp. 195–8, no. 243. Cf. the parallel text (with variants) *CuriaRR* XIII, pp. 16–17, no. 77.

Appendix

Weight of wax used in sealing Chancery writs, 1226–71

Source: *CLibR* I–VI. Up to 22 May 1250 enrolments are made at intervals of about 3–4 months, but they do not specify the period covered; this has been estimated in the table below from the dates of preceding enrolments. From 22 May 1250 enrolments specify the period in dates expressed by saints' days and regnal years; these dates have been modernized. Enrolments are missing or incomplete for those years omitted from the table.

Volume and page nos.	Period covered	Weight of wax (in lb)	Number of weeks	Amount of wax used per week (in lb)
I: 16, 38, 44, 52, 65	18 Dec. 1226 – 29 Jan. 1228	183	58	3.15
I: 69, 78, 86, 100, 111, 115	29 Jan. 1228 – 20 Jan. 1229	158	51	3.09
I: 120, 127, 132, 138, 140, 145, 155, 162	20 Jan. 1229 – 24 Jan. 1230	242.5	52	4.66
I: 166, 175, 184	24 Jan. 1230 – 12 July 1230	89.5	24	3.72
I: 204, 215, 222, 226, 234, 239	23 Jan. 1233 – 20 Oct. 1233	169.5	39	4.35
I: 260, 274, 285, 297, 308, 314	22 Jan. 1237 – 20 Feb. 1238	245	55	4.45
I: 375, 391, 395, 421, 445	8 Jan. 1239 – 1 Feb. 1240	281	55	5.11
II: 120, 137, 149, 171, 177	8 March 1242 – 27 April 1243	425	59	7.2
II: 232, 241, 265, 285	3 Feb. 1244 – 17 Jan. 1245	398	50	7.96
II: 312; III: 16	17 Jan. 1245 – 16 Dec. 1245	428	48	8.91
III: 59, 89	16 Dec. 1245 – 25 Oct. 1246	362	44	8.22
III: 385	22 May 1250 – 26 Oct. 1251	510	74	6.89
IV: 105	26 Oct. 1251 – 2 Feb. 1253	606	66	9.18
IV: 143	2 Feb. 1253 – 29 June 1253	181	21	8.62
IV: 159	29 June 1253 – 24 Feb. 1254	142	33	4.3
IV: 256	6 Jan. 1255 – 20 Nov. 1255	464	45	10.31
IV: 353	20 Nov. 1255 – 13 Jan. 1257	700	60	11.67
IV: 400	13 Jan. 1257 – 25 Oct. 1257	570	39	14.61
VI: 269	25 Oct. 1257 – 9 June 1258	540	32	16.87
IV: 448	9 June 1258 – 22 Jan. 1259	520	33	15.75
IV: 469	22 Jan. 1259 – 27 July 1259	220	27	8.15

Volume and page nos.	Period covered	Weight of wax (in lb)	Number of weeks	Amount of wax used per week (in lb)
iv: 486	27 July 1259 – 3 Nov. 1259	170	14	12.14
iv: 532	3 Nov. 1259– 15 Oct. 1260	584	49	11.92
v: 33	13 [sic] Oct. 1260– 15 May 1261	455	31	14.67
v: 59	15 May 1261– 13 Oct. 1261	450	22	20.96
v: 73	13 Oct. 1261 – 14 Jan. 1262	412	13	31.69
v: 96	14 Jan. 1262 – 9 June 1262	457	22	20.77
v: 116	13 July 1262 – 2 Nov. 1262	196	16	12.25
vi: 277	19 Jan. 1263 – 29 May 1263	412	19	21.69
v: 130	5 June 1263 – 30 Jan. 1264	793	34	23.32
v: 155	29 May 1264 – 5 Jan. 1265	530	31	17.1
v: 182	5 Jan. 1265 – 20 Oct. 1265	791	41	19.29
v: 295	29 Sept. 1265 – 18 Oct. 1267	1611	107	15.06
vi: 50	18 Oct. 1267 – 18 Oct. 1268	1831	52	35.21
vi: 131	18 Oct. 1268 – 6 May 1269	1786	28	63.78
vi: 160	6 May 1270 [sic] – 2 Feb. 1271	995	38	26.18

3

Types of record

To appreciate the significance of the great increase in record-making in the twelfth and thirteenth centuries some scheme, classifying documents into different types, needs to be borne in mind. The elementary scheme suggested in this chapter is not intended to do more than provide an introduction to English medieval documents in this period by taking a general view over the whole area of writing activity.[1] The different classes of document proposed are not entirely mutually exclusive, nor do the examples given exhaust the variety of documents which exist. One consequence of the massive increase in the number of documents is that no individual historian today can claim to have seen all, or even most, of the evidence. Modern scholars tend to be experts in particular categories of document, such as monastic charters or royal writs or illuminated Bibles. Within these categories further specialization takes place: monastic charters from particular periods or regions are studied for instance, because the documents are so numerous and varied. Professional scholarship is necessarily based on Adam Smith's principle of the division of labour.

The variety of writings

An educated Englishman in the thirteenth century, by contrast, would have become familiar with a variety of writings over his lifetime – charters to safeguard his landed property, royal writs for litigation, homilies for devotion, romances for entertainment, and so on. Among the 40 or so volumes which Guy de Beauchamp, earl of Warwick, gave by charter to Bordesley abbey in 1306 are books of the Bible, meditations and saints' lives, romances and histories, a book of physic and one of surgery, a child's primer, an encyclopedia, and 'a little red book in which are contained many diverse things'.[2] All the books are described as

[1] The best concise survey of the records is G. R. Elton, *The Sources of History: England 1200–1640* (1969). The richest anthology of typical documents in English translation is *English Historical Documents* II *1042–1189* ed. D. C. Douglas and G. W. Greenaway (1953); III *1189–1327* ed. H. Rothwell (1975).

[2] M. Blaess, 'L'abbaye de Bordesley et les Livres de Guy de Beauchamp', *Romania* LXXVIII (1957), pp. 511–18.

'romances', meaning that they are in French and not Latin. A step down the social scale, the Northamptonshire gentleman, Henry de Bray of Harlestone, copied out with his own hand in Latin at the age of 52 (in 1322) a compilation for the instruction of his heirs containing a general description of the world, a more detailed description of England (its counties, bishoprics, kings and Cinque Ports), extracts from Domesday Book and other royal records, information about Northamptonshire feudal and local government, a list of his own tenants, the dimensions of Harlestone common field and the village, a table of measures, records of his expenses, and numerous copies of documents concerning his property.[3] Both Guy's charter listing books and Henry's estate book are exceptional survivals. Most of the nobility and gentry were not so careful with their documents; but they would all have come across, even if they did not possess, a comparable variety of written records during their lives.

The experience of medieval writers and makers of records cuts across the lines dividing knowledge which scholars draw today. Although writers became gradually more specialized as the demand for documents increased, in the twelfth century and earlier they tended to perform a variety of functions. One of Thomas Becket's biographers, William Fitz Stephen, describes how he was a draftsman in his chancery, a subdeacon in his chapel, a reader in his law court, and on occasions a judge.[4] In the chancery he would have been familiar with letters and literary style, in the chapel with liturgical books, and in the law court with records of pleas. Becket himself had started his career as an accountant to a London merchant and was also described as a 'clerk and accountant' of the sheriffs of London.[5] He thus had experience of financial and civic record-making before he went into Archbishop Theobald's service and thence into the king's. In the thirteenth century Matthew Paris, who was the scribe and illustrator of most of his own works, wrote the chronicles for which he is famous in Latin prose, but he also composed lives of English saints in French verse for aristocratic ladies.[6] In addition he had a very competent knowledge of charters and royal writs (which he cites verbatim), Latin verse, heraldry, cartography, and an interest in natural science. His exceptionally varied activities emphasize the difficulty of classifying medieval writings too strictly into types.

Even single works of Matthew's defy exclusive classification. His best known book, the *Chronica Majora*, is in part a history copied from other sources (Matthew performed here the role of editor and scribe) and in part a contemporary monastic chronicle composed by himself. It is also an illustrated book of lively caricatures probably intended to entertain, a cartulary of documents (in the *Liber Additamentorum*), an atlas (each

---

[3] *The Estate Book of Henry de Bray* ed. D. Willis, Camden S. 3rd series XXVII (1916). Cf. nn. 92, 93 below concerning laymen's cartularies.

[4] *Becket Materials* III, p. 1.

[5] *ibid*. II, p. 361; III, p. 14.

[6] R. Vaughan, *Matthew Paris* (1958), pp. 168–81.

volume was originally prefaced with maps and itineraries), and an heraldic reference book. Matthew included in it, moreover, his famous drawing from life of the elephant given by St Louis to Henry III in 1255 (together with a discourse on elephants) and the beautiful painting of the Virgin and Child, with himself kneeling at her feet, which prefaces the final part of the chronicle.[7] In Matthew's mind history, literature, art and science were not separate realms of knowledge.

The works of Matthew Paris are an exceptional instance of a typical characteristic of medieval writings. Documents and books in manuscript tend to depart from standard forms and to contain a diversity of subject matter because there is no printing press automatically imposing uniformity. In the layout and content of their works writers and scribes aimed at the elegance which results from regularity and consistency, but personal idiosyncrasies and interests inevitably remained prominent in writings produced entirely by hand. Moreover, it is often impossible with medieval books to give an adequate single classification to an individual volume, as a modern librarian does, because a variety of works are frequently bound between the same covers. Guy de Beauchamp's 'little red book' containing many diverse things is an example of the problem. Miscellanies of this sort often reflected the interests of the compiler or owner of the book. The diverse contents had unity in his own experience and needs, rather than in any external scheme of things. An excellent introduction to the variety of works bound together into books in the thirteenth century is Oschinsky's descriptive list of the manuscripts containing treatises on accountancy and estate management.[8] For example, MS. 17 includes (among other items) parliamentary statutes, cooking recipes, a lapidary (a discourse on precious stones), a glossary of measures, and treatises on management. Similarly MS. 68 contains Walter of Henley's treatise on husbandry, together with Walter of Bibbesworth's poem to aid learning French, a moral poem (*La desputaisen du cors et de l'âme*), proverbs, a brief encyclopedia called *L'image du monde*, and other works. Diverse as these subjects might appear to a modern scholar, they could all have been of interest or use to a country gentleman like Henry de Bray.

Even illuminated manuscripts, which look as if they were made exclusively for their magnificent paintings, might be seen in other ways. When in the 1180s Henry II arbitrarily gave the Winchester Bible to the ascetic St Hugh for his Charterhouse at Witham, the Carthusians were delighted because 'the correctness of the text pleased them especially, even more than the delicacy of the penmanship and the general beauty of the work.'[9] There is likewise the remarkable case of the Sherborne abbey manuscript which is partly a cartulary of documents concerning a lawsuit in 1145 and partly an illuminated missal for use at

---

[7] *ibid.* plates xvi, xix, xxi, frontispiece.

[8] *Walter of Henley*, pp. 11–50. Cf. Parkes, 'Literacy', p. 562.

[9] *The Life of St Hugh of Lincoln* ed. D. L. Douie and H. Farmer (1961) I, p. 86. It is possible that the work here referred to is not the Winchester Bible (Kauffmann, *Romanesque MSS*, no. 83), but another Bible (*ibid.* no. 82) from Winchester.

the altar in Holy Week.[10] But enough has now been said to indicate the variety of medieval documents. Exceptions such as those described above make it all the more necessary to formulate some general rules of classification.

The most fundamental distinction to make is between primary and secondary records. A charter extant in its original form as a single piece of parchment (preferably with the seal still attached) is a primary record, whereas a copy of that charter in a monastic cartulary or in the royal Charter rolls is a secondary record. By this classification original charters, writs, chirographs, wills, court rolls, ministers' accounts and so on are primary records; whereas chronicles, cartularies, the Chancery rolls, Domesday Book and similar surveys are secondary records because they are compiled from other sources. In this sense too most medieval books, from copies of the Bible downwards, are secondary because they were made from exemplars. This distinction between primary and secondary does not readily apply in all cases. Thus the parts of Matthew Paris's chronicles which he himself composed and wrote are essentially primary records, whereas many original charters and court rolls may have been compiled from drafts which were thrown away and in that sense they too are secondary records. If this latter assumption is universally applied, however, all extant medieval documents become secondary records, which is absurd.

Taken generally, the distinction between primary and secondary is applicable and useful, because it emphasizes the difference between documents in their original form and copies or edited versions of them, whether medieval or modern. Primary and secondary records usually differ too in their format. Primary records are most often single sheets of parchment or a small stitched gathering, whereas secondary records are made up into rolls or bound books. The format of the records has affected their chance of survival over the centuries. The great majority of primary documents have been lost, because they consisted of single sheets of parchment, whereas registers and books survive in relative abundance. One purpose of copying documents into registers in the Middle Ages was to ensure that their texts did survive. To keep classifications simple, this chapter only discusses records made on parchment. Writings on paper, wood, fabric, metal and so on are discussed in the next chapter; the most common English non-parchment records were tally sticks (see plate VIII) like those used in the Exchequer.

Statements issued by individuals

The primary records most commonly met with are letters of one sort or another. They are here collectively described as 'statements issued by individuals' because the generic term 'letters' is ambiguous and can mislead. A variety of descriptive terms for such written statements were used in the Middle Ages, such as *breve, carta, chirographum* and *litterae* itself. These terms were not used with strict consistency or uniformity,

[10] See ch. 5, n. 36 below.

nor are they mutually exclusive. Nevertheless they can be adapted to create definitions which distinguish documents by their function with a fair degree of precision.

Charters

Working on this principle, a charter is a public letter issued by a donor recording a title to property (see plates I, V and VI). Charters are frequently therefore addressed to the general public – to 'those whom the present writing shall reach' or to 'all who shall hear and see this charter'. As the general public was the same as the Christian community, the donor sometimes addressed 'all the sons of Holy Church' or 'all the faithful in Christ' or 'cleric and lay'. Additionally or alternatively, he might particularize and address 'his constables and stewards and barons and all his men and friends, French and English, of Yorkshire'. All the above examples are taken from the charters of Roger de Mowbray, who died in 1188.[11] What the donor did not do in a charter was to address the beneficiary exclusively, because the charter itself was given to the beneficiary (and sometimes written by him) and served as a kind of open testimonial. Addresses have such a variety of forms primarily because standardization became usual only in the thirteenth century, when charters were issued in tens of thousands. The charter form is much older than the Norman Conquest; the main change which occurred thereafter is that their texts and format at last became stereotyped owing primarily to the increase in numbers.[12]

In practice a charter might concern any form of property, although rights over land were by far the most common conveyances in a primarily agricultural community. Of other gifts, we have already seen that Guy de Beauchamp listed books in a charter in 1306. A few years earlier John de Camoys had conveyed his wife, Margaret, with her goods and chattels to Sir William Paynel by a charter, insisting that he did this of his own free will. The ordinary formulas for conveying land, 'I have given and granted, released and quitclaimed', are used in this charter. The details survive because Margaret and William attempted to claim dower from John's lands and the case came before Parliament in 1300–1302.[13]

The amount of detail in which a conveyance is described varies according to the nature of the property, the date it was made, and the mutual trust between the parties. A later charter describing the same property might be more specific. For example, in 1209 or earlier William Blanch granted (among other lands in Ewell near Epsom) half an acre in Dunfurlong. When Gilbert son of Osbert obtained a confirmation of this

[11] *Mowbray Charters*, nos. 31, 347, 20, 167, 166, 380. Cf. ch. 8, n. 2 below.

[12] Cheney, *Chanceries*, ch. 3, describes the development of standardized forms in charters over the period 1100–1250. A good introductory collection of texts (with English translations) is *Transcripts of Charters Relating to Gilbertine Houses* ed. F. M. Stenton, Lincoln Record S. XVIII (1922). Cf. ch. 8, n. 6 below, and ch. 9, nn. 1–2 below.

[13] *Rotuli Parliamentorum* (1783) I, p. 146. P & M II, pp. 395–6.

grant from William Blanch's heir, John, in the 1230s, the new charter defined the half acre in Dunfurlong more exactly as that lying 'between the land of John Skinner and of William Cupping'.[14] In this more precise description may be seen the influence of Gilbert's brother-in-law, Walter of Merton, the future chancellor who was already a royal clerk. Some attempts at definition were more amateur. A crudely written charter of the late twelfth century, issued by Jordan of Cheadle, describes the land he is giving as extending 'in length from a certain oak towards Hedislethe, which has been uprooted there' up to another point.[15] Jordan's contemporaries in the village would have known where this particular oak used to stand, but not the general public, present and future, to whom the charter is addressed. Occasionally the specifications in a charter can evoke a whole landscape. This is an extract from a grant of land at Lambrigg (near Kendal) in the Lake District, describing the boundaries in *c.* 1210:

> then by Sti Coleman up to the nearest pile of stones which is towards the north under the head of Langescaghe, and then rising beyond Langescaghe up to the little valley which is next to the upper head of Lickegile, then out across the head of Lickegile by the middle of the moor . . . [and so on].[16]

Chirographs

Rather similar in function to charters, though different in format, are chirographs. A chirograph recorded an agreement between two parties. The agreement might concern almost anything – matters of state, a conveyance of land, a marriage settlement, or the repayment of a loan of money to a Jew. Unlike a charter, each of the parties received a copy of the agreement, usually authenticated by the seal of the other party (see plate VII). The method is described in detail, probably because it was still relatively unfamiliar, in an agreement made before papal judges delegate between the prior of Luffield and John, vicar of Towcester, in *c.* 1215:

> This composition is reduced into a duplicate writing, made in the form of chirograph, of which writing [*scriptura*] the prior of Luffield is to have one document [*scriptum*] sealed with the seals of the judges and of John, while John is to have the other document sealed with the seals of the judges and of the prior.[17]

The document was thus written out in duplicate and then cut in half. Across the line of the cut, before it was made, was written in capital

---

[14] *Fitznell's Cartulary* ed. C. A. F. Meekings, Surrey Record S. XXVI (1968), nos. 57, 62, cf. p. lxii.

[15] *Cheshire Facs*, no. 14.

[16] *Northants Facs*, no. liii.

[17] *Luffield Priory Charters* ed. G. R. Elvey, part i, Buckinghamshire Record S. XV (1968) or Northamptonshire Record S. XXII (1968), p. 71, no. 68. The novelty lay in the method of sealing and not in the chirographic format itself, which dated from the 9th century or earlier, B. Bischoff, *Mittelalterliche Studien* (1966) I, p. 118.

letters a formula such as JUSTUS DOMINUS ET JUSTICIAS (an extract from Psalms XI, 7) or the word CHIROGRAPHUM (see plate VII).[18] Forgery of one part could thus be checked by aligning the severed formula with its counterpart. As a further precaution, the cut was often made by a wavy or indented line, instead of a straight one. This practice grew so common in the later Middle Ages that chirographs became generally known as 'indentures'.

The text of a chirograph might be drafted in the form of a letter to all and sundry (like a charter), or it might be a memorandum recording that this is the covenant or final concord which has been made, at such and such a court or place, in the presence of certain persons who are named. The making of a chirograph might conclude an actual dispute between the parties, or alternatively the chirographic form was often used for amicable conveyances, because it had the advantage over an ordinary charter that both donor and beneficiary received a copy and these copies could be checked against each other. The first official records of proceedings in the king's court, extant as originals, are halves of chirographs recording agreements made in 1176 and 1182,[19] the former cut straight and the latter indented. Moreover, some chirographs were made in triplicate: the two parties each received a copy and the third copy was deposited in an archive for safekeeping. This had been an Anglo-Saxon practice, which was revived (using a different format) by Hubert Walter when he introduced royal feet of fines in 1195.[20] The practice was extended to ecclesiastical records by an interpretation of canon 38 of the Fourth Lateran Council in 1215.[21]

Like other documentary forms, the chirograph made its way down the social scale. At the top it was the standard form for international treaties, of which the earliest extant exemplars are four Anglo-Flemish alliances made in the twelfth century.[22] Likewise in times of civil war magnates used chirographs to record alliances. Extant examples are two treaties made in Stephen's reign, one between the earls of Chester and Leicester and the other between the earls of Gloucester and Hereford.[23] Similarly the war between King John and his barons was concluded by a chirograph beginning, 'This is the covenant made between Lord John, king of England, for the one part, and Robert Fitz Walter, marshal of the army of God and of the holy church in England [and other named barons] on the other.'[24] This treaty immediately preceded Magna Carta itself, which was issued in the form of an ordinary charter, presumably in order to emphasize that it was a free gift by the king and not a compromised agreement. Nevertheless when Magna

[18] L. C. Hector, *The Handwriting of English Documents* (1958), plate iii.

[19] *BM Facs*, nos. 55, 63.

[20] All three parts of a royal chirograph (date 1272) are illustrated by C. Johnson and H. Jenkinson, *English Court Hand* (1915) II, plate xviib. See also ch. 2, n. 65 above.

[21] Cheney, *Chanceries*, p. 132.

[22] P. Chaplais, 'English Diplomatic Documents' in *Study of Medieval Records*, p. 23, n. 6.

[23] Stenton, *Feudalism*, pp. 25ff, 286–8. *Earldom of Gloucester Charters* ed. R. B. Patterson (1973), plate xiv, or ed. R. H. C. Davis in *MM for Stenton*, plate xi.

[24] J. C. Holt, *Magna Carta* (1965), p. 342, plate v.

Carta was reissued in 1218 by the regent, William Marshal, it too was drawn up *in modum chirographi*.[25] At the other end of the political and social scale, we have already discussed the chirograph which the widow, Emma, made with the abbot of Gloucester in *c*. 1230 concerning ploughing and other servile duties.[26] The chirograph was a most versatile, and therefore a very common, type of document; but it is unusual for more than one of the original parts to survive to the present day.

Certificates

In addition to charters and chirographs, public statements by individuals were issued in the form of recognizances, testimonials, notifications, wills, sealed memoranda and similar records. For convenience these miscellaneous documents are here called certificates. They are often similar in form to charters, but they do not exclusively concern gifts of property. The following extract from a testimonial by Miles earl of Hereford, probably issued shortly before he died in 1143, is exceptional in its subject matter but typical in its form:

> Miles earl of Hereford to all his friends, French and English, of England and of Wales, greeting. You are to know that this Folebarba is my jester and my man. So I entreat all my friends that they look after him, lest harm happen to him. And if anyone does him good for love of me, I will know how to thank him.[27]

Folebarba (? Funny Beard) was perhaps apprehensive of being parted from his master and hoped that this certificate of the earl's affection would help him; whether it did or not is unknown – jesters inevitably made enemies.

By far the commonest form of certificates were recognizances concerning the payment of money debts. The earliest moneylender's bonds extant in England are eight documents from the coffers of the financier, William Cade, whose archives came into the possession of the crown on his death in *c*. 1166. The documents are brief and take the form of undertakings by persons named to stand surety for others, or themselves make payments to Cade or his son, Ernulf, at specified dates.[28] Documents classed here as certificates are so varied that it would be impossible to describe all types. Sometimes there is no convincing explanation as to why a particular record was ever made or preserved. Richard of Anstey's account of the protracted delays he experienced in the lawsuit he prosecuted between 1158 and 1163 has been described in numerous general histories of the period.[29] Yet why Richard made this memorandum is unclear. It begins like a solemn charter or prayer by invoking the

[25] *Annales Monastici* II, p. 290 (Waverley Annals). Galbraith, *Studies*, p. 13.
[26] See ch. 2, n. 21 above.
[27] 'Earldom of Hereford Charters' ed. D. Walker, *Camden Miscellany* Camden S. 4th series XXII (1964), p. 15, no. 7. This document also confirms a gift of land to Folebarba.
[28] See ch. 9, n. 23 below. For Jewish moneylenders' bonds see ch. 6, nn. 17–21 below.
[29] P. M. Barnes, 'The Anstey Case' in *MM for Stenton* pp. 1–23.

Trinity, but it is not addressed to anyone, nor does it ask for anything or give it; it simply records his expenses and how and when they were incurred. Another form of certificate which must have been common by Edward I's reign were the testimonials which served as warrants identifying persons or their goods when moving about the country.[30]

Letters

The documents considered so far are not 'letters' in the modern sense of missives. Charters, chirographs and certificates were not usually sent by the writer to a recipient who is addressed in the document; instead they were addressed to the public and handed to the beneficiary at the time they were written. They were primarily intended to be records rather than communications. The habit of sending missives, conveying ephemeral information about day-to-day matters, developed slowly because writing in Latin was too formal a medium. 'Letters' (*litterae*) were appropriate for 'literature' to pass on to posterity; the spoken word of messengers sufficed for conveying the ordinary business of the day. The finest letters were composed and kept as examples of style and were not necessarily sent to their addressees. In the first half of the twelfth century the art of writing such elaborate yet intimate letters reached a peak in the collections of St Bernard, Peter the Venerable, and Abelard and Heloise. This type of correspondence was exemplified in England in the latter half of the century in the letter collections of John of Salisbury and Gilbert Foliot. The best single example is John's letter to Peter abbot of Celle in c. 1159 recalling their friendship.[31] It is often impossible to establish whether letters in anthologies like these are authentic missives; they may be literary essays, propaganda pieces, or even forgeries, as has been alleged of the correspondence between Abelard and Heloise.

In the thirteenth century more mundane letters begin to survive, which are actual missives although they are less intimate. An example are the letters written to Ralf Nevill, bishop of Chichester (1224–44), by his steward in Sussex, Simon of Senlis. These concern the management of the farms, the doings of the local clergy, arrangements for visits, requests for favours, and so on. They evoke without effort a picture of country life which a rhetorician could not have bettered, yet they have survived only because Ralf was the chancellor and Simon's letters became mixed in with the royal archives.[32]

[30] See ch. 2, nn. 9–15 above.
[31] *Letters* ed. W. J. Millor *et al.* (1955) I, pp. 183–4. In general see A. Morey and C. N. L. Brooke, *Gilbert Foliot and his Letters* (1965), ch. 2 and G. Constable, *Letters and Letter Collections* (1976).
[32] Some have been published: in English translation by W. H. Blaauw, *Sussex Archaeological Collections* III (1850), pp. 45–73; in Latin by W. W. Shirley, *Royal Letters: Henry III* XXVII (1862), I and II, and J. Boussard in *Révue Historique* CLXXVI (1935), pp. 226–7. In this collection there are also evocative letters to Nevill from other persons, e.g. Hector, *The Handwriting of English Documents*, plate vi(a).

Writs

Letters first become common in England, not in the form of correspondence between individuals, but as 'writs' (*brevia*). Writs have a brevity and directness of style which contrasts with the elaboration of explicitly personal letters; as a result they can sometimes reveal more of individual attitudes. 'If we have given our peace even to a dog, it should be inviolably preserved', King John wrote in 1203 to the Londoners when reproving them for molesting the Jews.[33] The term 'writ' is used in this classification exclusively to mean a written command given by one person to another. The most frequent issuer of writs was the king, as in this example by Henry I: 'Henry, king of the English, to the abbot of Ramsey, greeting. I forbid you to do Hugh Oilard anything but right, no matter what writ might be produced. Witness: the chancellor. At Gloucester.'[34]

It is debatable whether a writ in this form is a real missive directed by the sender to the addressee. The writs of Henry I are letters patent (see plates II–IV); this means that they were open documents, which were handed to the beneficiaries at the time they were made, like charters. In the writ cited above, it was up to Hugh Oilard, the beneficiary, to show the document to the abbot of Ramsey as evidence of the king's intervention in his case. The king took no further steps to ensure that the writ reached the abbot unchanged, nor did he require the abbot to reply to him directly. The phrase, 'no matter what writ might be produced', demonstrates that writs were already being issued in some numbers, but it also suggests that the king had no knowledge of what happened to them. If he were not ordinarily responsible for dispatching them, his ignorance is understandable.

Real missives were introduced by Henry II in the form of letters close. A letter close was sealed on the tie that kept it rolled up, so that it could be opened only by the addressee (whose name was written on the loose end of the tie) breaking the seal.[35] Henry II also made many writs 'returnable'; this meant that the addressee, usually a sheriff, was instructed to produce the writ at a subsequent time and place, most often before a royal justice.[36] A method had therefore been devised of sending confidential instructions in writing and of checking on whether these writs were obeyed. Likewise in Henry II's reign writs begin to take common forms, both for administration (for instance the writs of summons used by the Exchequer) and for litigation. Writs in common form, available for purchase, were the framework of Henry II's legal reforms, based on the principle that no one need answer for his freehold without a royal writ.[37] Henry II had thus created a system which could potentially massproduce documents from a few stereotypes in a formulary. As a

[33] *Rot. Lit. Pat.*, p. 33.

[34] Van Caenegem, *Writs*, p. 420, no. 17. Cf. R. C. van Caenegem, *The Birth of the English Common Law* (1973), p. 37.

[35] Chaplais, *Docs*, pp. 7–9, plate 25d.

[36] Stenton, *Justice*, pp. 32–3.

[37] Glanvill, bk xii, ch. 25, p. 148. Cf. ch. 8, n. 90 below.

result, from his reign onwards the number of royal writs being issued increased very fast. Making writs returnable also ensured that the documents themselves came back to the royal archives. The earliest group of writs close now extant are common law writs issued by the chief justiciar in 1199,[38] although two writs of 'liberate' (concerning payments from the treasury) survive from Henry II's reign.[39]

This discussion has concentrated on royal writs because they set the pattern and are by far the most common. Royal practice was imitated by the magnates and by officials in the counties; we have already seen an example of a writ sent by a baron, Richard Fitz Gilbert, to his steward in c. 1130;[40] similarly, writs sent by sheriffs to their bailiffs are extant from about a century later.[41] In due course writs generated other letters and memoranda in the form of replies to their demands and written plaints and petitions to the king for redress; replies to royal writs (returns of inquests) are extant in originals from Henry III's reign and petitions from Edward I's.[42]

Memoranda kept by institutions

Most of the documents so far described, particularly charters and chirographs, could serve as memoranda and were kept as such by the persons they benefited. Such documents differ, however, from the type of memoranda which were systematically compiled, usually by institutions, as a record of past practice for their own future guidance. Court rolls, financial accounts, cartularies and chronicles cannot be classed as single 'statements issued by individuals', because they usually form part of an accumulating series of records compiled by an authority. Although in the light of hindsight compiling memoranda seems an obvious step once the idea of writing for posterity in charters had become familiar, there is a time-lag of a century or more between the two activities. It is probable that the only type of cumulative written record used at all widely by the Anglo-Saxons was the chronicle. A century after the Norman Conquest the one continuous series of memoranda kept by the crown were the Exchequer pipe rolls; numerous additional types of Exchequer record were, however, created in Henry II's reign, for instance rolls of receipts[43] and the rolls made by Richard of Ilchester and Thomas Brown.[44] Judging by documents extant, cumulative non-financial record-keeping by the crown began during Hubert Walter's years of office between 1193 and 1205; the plea rolls of the royal

[38] The earliest writ files are listed in *Berks. Eyre*, pp. xci–xcii.
[39] Chaplais, *Docs*, p. 10, nn. 1, 3.
[40] See ch. 2, n. 101 above.
[41] Listed in *Berks. Eyre*, pp. cv–cvii. See ch. 8, n. 91 below.
[42] *Guide to the Contents of the PRO*, HMSO (1963) I, pp. 27–8 (Inquisitions), 190 (Ancient Petitions).
[43] A facsimile of the receipt roll for Michaelmas term 1185 has been published by H. Hall (1899). The earliest receipt rolls are described and listed by H. Jenkinson in *Archaeologia* LXXIV (1925), pp. 298, 327–8.
[44] See. ch. 2, nn. 60, 63 above.

courts, the coroners' and sheriffs' rolls in the counties, feet of fines, the Chancery rolls of outgoing letters, all start or are first unequivocally referred to at this time.[45]

Financial accounts

Outside the king's court, making cumulative memoranda got under way in the thirteenth century. Seignorial accounts belatedly followed the lead of the Exchequer, the earliest extant series being the pipe rolls of the bishops of Winchester starting in 1208.[46] These rolls record receipts (in money, crops and livestock) and expenditure on the bishop's manors in detail. They are so orderly that they must have been based on drafts or preliminary accounts in writing submitted by each bailiff. Although the earliest Winchester rolls draw up balances of receipts and expenditure, they do not aim to show profit and loss as such, but to act as a check against the bishop being cheated by his ministers. The king's Exchequer provided a model for collecting revenues rather than for running a business. The earliest records calculating the profits of manors are the Christ Church Canterbury accounts of 1224–5.[47] Manorial accounts of any sort remain very rare until the latter half of the thirteenth century and the majority of those extant were produced by the greater monasteries. Lay lords undoubtedly also possessed ministers' accounts, as some survive by chance in the Public Record Office when estates were forfeited to the crown; an example are the records of Adam of Stratton, an Exchequer official and financier, who was put on trial for corruption in 1289.[48] In addition to manorial accounts, accounts of the separate departmental heads in the great religious houses, the obedientiaries, begin to be extant from the 1260s; among these are the earliest non-royal household accounts.[49] Similarly Merton College at Oxford has accounts of its administrative officers from 1277.[50] The accounts of towns follow a similar pattern to manors; the earliest continuous series are the Shrewsbury rolls of accounts of 1256 which were cast at weekly intervals.[51]

The most remarkable early accounts are the household rolls made in 1265 for Eleanor, countess of Leicester, the sister of Henry III and wife of

[45] See pp. 48–53 above.

[46] The two earliest Winchester rolls are edited by H. Hall (1903) and N. R. Holt (1964). Cf. ch. 2, n. 90 above. The best introductions to manorial documents are J. Z. Titow, *English Rural Society, 1200–1350* (1969) and *Manorial Records of Cuxham, Oxfordshire* ed. P. D. A. Harvey, Oxfordshire Record S. L (1976).

[47] E. Stone, 'Profit and Loss Accountancy at Norwich Cathedral Priory', *TRHS* 5th series XII (1902), p. 27.

[48] *Accounts and Surveys of the Wiltshire Lands of Adam de Stratton* ed. M. W. Farr, WiltsRS XIV (1959).

[49] Early rolls are discussed in *Compotus Rolls of the Priory of Worcester* ed. J. M. Wilson and C. Gordon, Worcestershire Historical S. (1908), p. ix and H. W. Saunders, *An Introduction to the Obedientiary and Manor Rolls of Norwich Cathedral Priory* (1930), p. 21.

[50] *The Early Rolls of Merton College Oxford* ed. J. R. L. Highfield (1964).

[51] G. H. Martin, 'The English Borough in the 13th Century', *TRHS* 5th series XXII (1963), pp. 136–7.

Simon de Montfort (see plate XI). These record her expenditure, mainly for the supply of food and drink, under different departmental headings such as the kitchen and the marshalcy of the stables. The entries are made in a variety of cursive hands, which suggests that they were compiled by the week or fortnight. Furthermore they specify the expenditure of each day separately and thus comprise a kind of diary of expenditure. The rolls cover the period 19 February to 29 August, the latter date being nearly a month after Simon's death at the battle of Evesham. As the accounts are set out in a regular form, these rolls are evidently not the first of their kind, although they are the earliest to survive. Perhaps Eleanor retained these ones because they concerned the last weeks of Simon's life. Their chance survival suggests that by the middle of the thirteenth century many magnates' households, both clerical and lay, were keeping daily accounts of expenditure in writing on parchment. But because such records concerned petty expenditure only, they must usually have been treated as ephemeral and thrown away. The most commonplace records are the least likely to survive.

Surveys and rentals

Extant financial accounts of the thirteenth century raise the question of what type of records preceded them. Obviously the great monastic estates made some financial records before 1200. Payments (both made and received) were probably recorded on tally sticks from early in the twelfth century, although there was no conception at that time of keeping a continuous series of financial memoranda to guide the steward of an estate. A landlord in the twelfth century obtained an overall view of his property, not from account rolls, but from a survey. The typical survey was not part of an accumulating series of records, as it was made *ab initio* by the incoming lord. Jocelin of Brakelond describes how Abbot Samson conducted such a survey:

> At his order a general description [*descriptio generalis*] was made in each hundred of leets and suits, hidages and corn dues, payments of hens, and other customs, revenues and expenses, which had hitherto been largely conceded by the farmers; and he had all these things set down in writing, so that within four years from his election [in 1182] there was not one who could deceive him concerning the revenues of the abbey to a single pennyworth, and this although he had not received anything in writing from his predecessors concerning the administration of the abbey, save for one small sheet containing the names of the knights of St Edmund, the names of the manors and the rent due from each farm. Now this book, in which were also recorded the debts which he had paid off, Samson called his *kalendarium*, and he consulted it almost every day, as though he could see therein the image of his own efficiency as in a mirror.[52]

[52] Jocelin, p. 29.

Samson called his survey a *kalendarium* because in classical Latin that word had meant a list of debts due at the kalends of each month.[53] Surveys and rentals of this sort, summarizing in writing the revenues due to a lord, became increasingly common. Jocelin refers in the citation above to an earlier list made at Bury St Edmunds, whose size he minimizes, as Abbot Baldwin's *Book of Feoffments* (dating from early in the twelfth century), is still extant.

The precedent for all such surveys, great and small, was Domesday Book, which had likewise been called a *descriptio*.[54] Judging by surveys known, the decade 1180–90 when Samson made his *kalendarium*, was the most productive period: from these years came the royal Assize of Arms and the *rotuli de dominabus* (lists of marriageable ladies), and enquiries conducted by Durham and St Paul's cathedrals, Glastonbury abbey, and the Knights Templar; likewise the earliest known bishop's *matricula* or *scrutinium*, that of Baldwin of Worcester, dates from this decade.[55] A remarkably detailed survey was made by Christ Church priory at Canterbury in *c*.1200. Set out in four columns, it lists each tenant, the amount of his annual rent, the date when payment is due, and the whereabouts and dimensions of the tenements. For example, the first entry describes the land of the sister of Roger son of Hamel as lying 'behind the wall of our almonry; its breadth northwards 26 feet; length from the street westwards 110 feet'.[56] In recording the dimensions of individual tenements the priory hoped perhaps to settle boundary disputes by referring to the precise evidence of writing instead of the partial recollections of neighbours.

In the thirteenth century the practice of making surveys in writing extended beyond the royal government and great religious houses to landlords in general. In the rules for estate management, composed for the countess of Lincoln in the 1240s, Robert Grosseteste recommends an incoming landlord to make a survey of his revenues in triplicate; just as Abbot Samson had consulted his *kalendarium* almost every day, Grosseteste recommends the countess to 'keep this roll by you and often look at it.'[57] In addition to serving as rentals for estates, such surveys were the basis of systematic taxation: notable early examples are the royal subsidy assessments of 1225, Wallingford's rolls of tradesmen of 1227 and 1230 (see plates IX and X), and the well documented valuation of the English church (diocese by diocese) for the papal tenth of 1254.[58]

---

[53] A copy (dating from *c*.1230) of Samson's *kalendarium* is extant, ed. R. H. C. Davis, Camden S. 3rd series LXXXIV (1954). This text suggests that Jocelin exaggerated the scope of Samson's survey, as it had not been completed by 1190.

[54] V. H. Galbraith, *Domesday Book* (1974), ch. 5, discusses Abbot Baldwin's *Book of Feoffments* and other early surveys.

[55] B. A. Lees lists the surveys in *Records of the Templars in England: the Inquest of 1185* (1935), p. xxix. For Bishop Baldwin's *matricula* see Cheney, *Chanceries*, pp. 115–16. A bishop's *matricula* differed from his *registrum*, see ch. 2, n. 99 above.

[56] W. Urry, *Canterbury under the Angevin Kings* (1967), p. 249 and map 2b, sheet 3. For the layout of this MS. see *ibid*. frontispiece.

[57] *Walter of Henley*, p. 388.

[58] C. Johnson and H. Jenkinson, *English Court Hand* (1915), plates xiia, xiib (subsidy

Impressive though surveys are as pioneers of written record and as historical documents, they cannot have been as useful to landlords as annual accounts because they soon went out of date. All surveys shared with Domesday Book the characteristic of being symbols of efficiency and authority rather than its reality.

Legal records

In courts, lists and books of rules are generally earlier than systematic memoranda of particular cases, just as surveys and rentals precede financial accounts. Thus in boroughs the oldest records, apart from the charters constituting them, are lists of guildsmen forming the corporation and custumals summarizing municipal bye-laws. Leicester's guild rolls begin in 1196;[59] they are the oldest series of memoranda now extant made outside the king's court or a monastery. Northampton has a custumal of similar date, although it is not in its original form.[60] The most remarkable early custumal is a roll in French made for Exeter, which was probably compiled in the 1230s by the town clerk, John Baubi.[61] The borough court's rolls of pleas are usually of later date: 'the court's official memory still reposed in the heads of its *probi homines* [responsible men] when the guild began to commit its lists of names, fines, and vats of ale to parchment';[62] exceptionally early are the rolls of the Wallingford burghmoot which begin in 1231–2.

The records of the king's court follow a comparable pattern, with lists and rulebooks preceding enrolments of actual litigation. Notes of pecuniary penalties (oblations, fines, amercements) are listed in the pipe rolls of the exchequer from Henry I's reign and separate rolls of amercements were kept in Henry II's reign. Likewise from late in Henry II's reign comes Glanvill's treatise 'on the laws and customs of England', which is essentially a custumal for the king's court summarizing its most common rules in writing, as the author explains in his prologue.[63] Rolls of pleas, on the other hand, are not extant until 1194; they were perhaps an innovation made by Hubert Walter soon after he became chief justiciar in 1193.[64] In ecclesiastical courts the interval between writing down rules and recording cases appears to be longer. The classic textbook, Gratian's, was composed in *c*.1140. The first English diocesan

---

assessments). Wallingford's roll of 1227 is illustrated at plate ix below. The church valuation of 1254 is ed. W. E. Lunt, *The Valuation of Norwich* (1926).

[59] Martin, 'The English Borough', pp. 129, 132–3. Cf. ch. 2, n. 79 above and ch. 9, n. 30 below.

[60] G. H. Martin, 'The Origins of Borough Records', *Journal of the Society of Archivists* II (1960–64), p. 152.

[61] *The Anglo-Norman Custumal of Exeter* ed. J. W. Schopp (1925). This edition has complete facsimiles.

[62] Martin, 'The Origins of Borough Records', pp. 153, 149.

[63] Glanvill, p. 3.

[64] R & S, pp. 185, n. 6, 214, argue that plea rolls were kept as early as 1176, but they do not distinguish between plea rolls and the amercement rolls mentioned in *Dialogus*, pp. 70, 77.

statutes are those of Archbishop Stephen Langton in c. 1213–14 and half
a dozen dioceses have statutes earlier than 1230, whereas ecclesiastical
rolls of suits and act books are not extant with regularity until the very
end of the thirteenth century.[65] But in this instance extant records are
misleading, as ecclesiastical cases were usually recorded in chirographs
in triplicate (for the judge and the two parties), instead of being enrolled,
and consequently have not survived as well as rolls.[66]

The pattern of making memoranda in local courts other than
boroughs – hundred and manor courts for example – is less clear. Their
records are more scattered and relatively few are extant, because local
lordships have not had such a continuous institutional life as boroughs
or the king's government. As in other courts, keeping lists of names
seems to have preceded making records of proceedings. Thus Jocelin of
Brakelond describes the bailiffs of the sacrist and cellarer of Bury St
Edmunds enrolling men in frankpledge each year as early as 1200,
whereas the first hundred court rolls date from the 1260s and they
survive from no more than a dozen places before 1300.[67] Similarly the
earliest manor court rolls come from the 1240s and it is unlikely that
any earlier ones will be found.[68] Even plea rolls from county courts are
extraordinarily rare, considering the court's importance as the principal and regular assembly of each shire. The only county court rolls
extant from the thirteenth century are some from Cheshire (beginning
in 1259), which are exceptional anyway because the earldom of Chester
was a privileged jurisdiction.[69] As in the development of the king's court,
lists of fines from county courts are more common at first than records of
pleas.[70]

Local court rolls become more common towards the end of the thirteenth century, but they remain rare compared with the plea rolls of the
king's court, which exist in multiple copies in Edward I's reign. Similarly among cities and boroughs, only eleven possess extant records of
any type earlier than Edward I's accession, although that figure doubles
by the time of his death.[71] On the other hand, treatises written for
baronial stewards in the 1260s and 1270s assume that court rolls are

[65] C. R. Cheney, 'The Earliest English Diocesan Statutes', *EHR* LXXV (1960), p. 29. Rolls
and act books are listed by R. H. Helmholz, *Marriage Litigation in Medieval England*
(1974), pp. 233–5.

[66] See above nn. 17, 21. J. E. Sayers, *Papal Judge Delegates in the Province of Canterbury*
(1971), pp. 243–51.

[67] Jocelin, p. 102. H. M. Cam, *The Hundred and the Hundred Rolls* (1930), p. 286.

[68] *Select Pleas in Manorial Courts* ed. F. W. Maitland, SS II (1888), pp. xii–xiii. W. O.
Ault argues that manorial rolls probably began no earlier than the 1240s, *Post Scripta:
Essays etc. in Honour of G. Post* ed. J. R. Strayer and D. E. Queller, *Studia Gratiana* XV
(1972), pp. 511–18. The survey of manorial records directed by Professor R. H. Hilton has
likewise not found any court rolls earlier than those known to Maitland and Ault (letter
from Hilton to me in February 1978).

[69] *Calendar of County Court, City Court, and Eyre Rolls of Chester* ed. R. Stewart-Brown,
Chetham S. new series LXXXIV (1925), pp. 1–34. R. C. Palmer discusses early county court
records in *EHR* XCI (1976), p. 777.

[70] W. A. Morris, *The Early English County Court* (1926), pp. 197–230, prints miscellaneous records of this type dating from 1258–64.

[71] Martin, 'The English Borough', p. 128.

kept: the *Court Baron* has the bailiff say to the steward, 'By my faith, see here all that for which you ask written down in this roll' and John of Oxford's treatise advises the bailiff's clerk 'to note down everything that is done in the court as it occurs'.[72] Even if every clerk made a roll, he certainly did not note down everything. Local court rolls are usually laconic. Their main purpose was to record the names of litigants and suitors attending the court and of persons who had been fined; they do not often give details either of the facts or of the law involved in particular cases. Such rolls derived their form from lists and often they are little more than that.

Year Books

Contrasting with the rigorously summarized local court rolls are the Year Books, which merit attention because they are the largest and most detailed collection of dialogue made in the Middle Ages. They are reports of court cases, beginning in the reign of Edward I, which purport to record the actual words (translated into French or Latin) of litigants, their counsel and the judges for the benefit of law students and practitioners.[73] The Year Books' practice of recording dialogue seems to have emanated from law reporters in London and not from the king's clerks. The earliest instance of such reporting occurs in London's Latin record of the royal justices' visitation of the City in 1244. Certain cases are recorded twice, first in reported speech, as is usual in plea rolls, and then again in dialogue form using the first person. For example, Alfred de Pinchbeck sued John de Coudres, a former sheriff, for wrongful imprisonment. The plea roll records in formal and general terms Alfred's complaint and John's defence that Alfred had resisted arrest and refused to find a pledge for good behaviour.[74] In the alternative version of this case, however, more circumstantial details are given: it explains that Alfred's family had been imprisoned at Newgate because a Jew had accused him of killing the Jew's wife; when Alfred returned from King's Lynn fair, John, the sheriff, had demanded a pledge from him because of this charge. The alternative version then records John's cross-examination by the justices in direct speech:

> The justices said: 'For what cause did you exact a pledge from Alfred, whereas he was not in the City when the Jewess was allegedly killed?'
> John said: 'I asked him for a pledge and when he drew his knife, I seized his hand with the knife, for which cause I imprisoned him.'
> The justices said: 'You had no cause to exact a pledge from Alfred.'[75]

[72] *Court Baron*, pp. 58, 72.
[73] T. F. T. Plucknett, *Early English Legal Literature* (1958), ch. vi.
[74] *The London Eyre of 1244* ed. H. M. Chew and M. Weinbaum, London Record S. VI (1970), p. 77, no. 190.
[75] *ibid.* p. 134, no. 345. Cf. p. 163 below.

This version thus explains the facts of the case and the points of law involved by recording the justices' questions and comments, whereas the official plea roll is concerned only to note the procedural stages of the case in due form. This comparison between alternative versions of the same case illustrates the paradox, familiar to historians, that unofficial records are often more informative and factual than the formal texts made by professional clerks. Although formal legal records are the largest group of medieval documents extant, they are not as thorough as their orderly appearance suggests.

This description of memoranda-making has proceeded mainly by referring to the earliest extant exemplars of various types of record and it leads to the general conclusion that outside the king's court the main series of memoranda started in the thirteenth century. Although great monastic houses had made surveys and rentals in the twelfth century and the royal Exchequer kept pipe rolls from the reign of Henry I, communal and seignorial court rolls and financial accounts are products of the thirteenth century; they were almost certainly not made before the 1190s. There are, however, two obvious objections to generalizing in this way. Firstly, the earliest records extant are not necessarily the earliest records made. For example, a Cheshire chirograph of 1228 refers to 'the authentic roll of our lord the earl' (of Chester) which preserves memory and record, whereas the earliest roll of any sort now extant from Cheshire is a plea roll from 1259.[76] The roll referred to in 1228, the 'Domesday' roll which registered covenants, existed as late as 1580 when extracts were copied from it. It was probably the first of its kind, however, as it started with a poem explaining that its 'holy page' would ensure that the agreements enrolled in it were kept.[77] Secondly and conversely, a record surviving from an early date may have always been unique and did not necessarily form part of a cumulative series of memoranda; estate surveys from the twelfth century for example, like Abbot Samson's *kalendarium*, were intended to be unique.

To sum up, the general impression left by the evidence, taking account of references to documents now lost as well as those that survive, is that the habit of making and keeping records of proceedings in continuous series stemmed from the king's court at the end of the twelfth century and took another century to spread across the country. Hazarding a guess, manors which did not belong to the king or to ecclesiastical magnates probably only began, as a rule, to have financial accounts and court rolls in Edward I's reign.

Chronicles

One type of cumulative memorial, the chronicle, had far older origins. Not all chroniclers were monks: Ralf de Diceto and Roger of Howden were secular clerics and Arnold Fitz Thedmar, the probable author of

---

[76] *Cheshire Facs*, p. 48. Cf. n. 69 above.
[77] R. Stewart-Brown, 'The Domesday Roll of Chester', *EHR* xxxvii (1922), p. 496.

the London chronicle, was a layman.[78] Nevertheless the typical chronicle was monastic and had its origins in the Benedictine preoccupation with the careful regulation of time. The typical monastic chronicler distinguished his function from that of the historian: 'The historian proceeds diffusely and elegantly, whereas the chronicler proceeds simply, gradually and briefly', Gervase of Canterbury explained in c.1188.[79] 'The chronicler computes years *Anno Domini* and months and kalends and briefly describes the actions of kings and princes which occurred at those times; he also commemorates events, portents and wonders. There are many, however, writing chronicles or annals who exceed their limits.'[80] Because Gervase intended to remain a humble chronicler, he insists that he wants 'to compile rather than to write' and explains that he does not write for a public library, but for his own monastic family at Christ Church Canterbury.[81] The typical chronicle was thus a dated series of events recorded for the guidance of a monastic house; it was not an interpretation of the past presented to the public by a historian. Paradoxically, but understandably, the greatest monastic chroniclers, like Matthew Paris or Gervase himself, went far beyond these narrow limits.

The chronicle is thus an unstylish production, concerned with the matter rather than the manner of presentation, and 'added to year by year and therefore composed by various people'.[82] The writer of this description, an anonymous monastic annalist of the thirteenth century associated with Winchester, advises the composer of a chronicle to see that there is always a sheet attached to the book, on which may be noted in pencil the deaths of illustrious men and other memoranda whenever the news comes to hand. At the end of each year the monk 'who has been appointed to the task, and not just anyone who so wishes, should write out briefly and succinctly in the body of the book what he thinks truest and best to be passed down to the notice of posterity'.[83] That such notes were commonly kept is suggested by John of Salisbury's statement about sixty years earlier that he had seen in the archives of churches 'notes of memorable things', which would help future writers even where chronicles were unavailable.[84]

Twentieth-century historians have often distinguished between chronicle sources, which they consider biased and unreliable, and official records (such as the Chancery rolls) which they prefer. Yet the best chronicles were the official records of the monastic houses which produced them and were treated as such on occasions by the royal government. When Matthew Paris attended the ceremonies in 1247 for the Feast of Edward the Confessor, Henry III ordered him from the throne in

---

[78] Gransden, *Historical Writing*, pp. 509ff.

[79] Gervase, I, p. 87. V. H. Galbraith, *Historical Research in the Middle Ages* (1951), p. 2.

[80] Gervase I, pp. 87–8.

[81] 'compilare potius quam scribere cupio,' *ibid.* p. 89.

[82] *Annales Monastici* IV, p. 355.

[83] *ibid.* Cf. Cheney, *Texts & Studies*, p. 224. Gransden, *Historical Writing* pp. 319–20.

[84] 'rerum memorabilium subnotationes,' *Historia Pontificalis* ed. M. Chibnall (1956), p. 2.

Westminster Hall 'to write an accurate and full account of all these things and commit them indelibly to notable writing in a book, so that their memory shall in no way be lost to posterity'.[85] The king evidently knew that Matthew was writing a chronicle and invited him to dinner. Similarly when Edward I looked for historical precedents to support his claims in Scotland in 1291, he turned first to monastic chronicles and not to the royal archives. At the same time he sent monasteries information about his claims and ordered them 'to be noted in your chronicles as a perpetual memorial of the business'.[86] In Edward's time the monastic chronicle was the most ancient, but still the most secure and productive form of record in existence.

Cartularies

Like chronicles, these are monastic in origin. Heming, a monk of Worcester who composed much of the earliest cartulary extant, describes his purpose:

> I, Heming the monk, have composed this little book concerning the possessions of this our monastery, so that it may be clear to our posterity which and how many possessions in land pertain to the endowment of this monastery for the sustenance of the monks, the servants of God; or rather which [possessions] ought by right [to be ours], although we have been unjustly dispossessed of them by force and fraud.[87]

A cartulary was thus a collection of title-deeds copied into a register for greater security. Unlike chronicles, cartularies do not have ancient origins in England. They were products of the insecurity brought about by the Norman Conquest and the civil war of Stephen's reign, combined with greater competition between monastic houses to acquire and retain lands, which resulted from the increase in the number of monasteries in the twelfth and thirteenth centuries. Thus the compiler of Ramsey abbey's *Book of Benefactors* explains in c.1170 that the abbey had lost almost everything in the 'dark and gloomy days' of King Stephen, both from attacks from enemies and domestic disputes, 'and so we have collected together in one volume our chirographs and the charters of our privileges . . . as a warning for future ages and to instruct our readers.'[88] This compiler also translated the abbey's pre-Conquest documents from English into Latin to make them more acceptable. Apart from convenience and greater security, another advantage of copying records into a cartulary was that they could be modernized and improved, or even forged.

[85] Matthew Paris IV, pp. 644–5. Vaughan, *Matthew Paris*, pp. 3–4.
[86] Bartholomew de Cotton, *Historia Anglicana* ed. H. R. Luard, RS XVI (1859), p. 182. Cf. E. L. G. Stones, 'The Appeal to History in Anglo-Scottish Relations', *Archives* IX (1969), pp. 12ff.
[87] N. R. Ker, 'Heming's Cartulary' in *Studies in Medieval History Presented to F. M. Powicke* (1948), p. 63.
[88] *Ramsey*, p. 4. Gransden, *Historical Writing*, pp. 279–80.

The first portion of Heming's cartulary was not composed by him, but dates from a generation before the Norman Conquest; Heming made his portion towards the end of the eleventh century. The only other cartulary extant from the eleventh century, the Oswald cartulary, also emanates from Worcester. It is therefore probable that the cartulary form in England was created at Worcester in the generation before the Norman Conquest and brought to fruition by Heming as a consequence of the Conquest. English monks in the great Benedictine houses aimed to justify and explain their heritage to the Norman masters.[89] There may even be a direct connexion between Heming's cartulary and the Normans, as V. H. Galbraith has suggested that Samson of Bayeux, the bishop of Worcester in Heming's time, had been the compiler of Domesday Book.[90] The next oldest cartulary extant is the Rochester book *Textus Roffensis*, again from an ancient monastic house, which dates from c. 1125. No more than half a dozen cartularies are earlier than 1150 and fewer than thirty earlier than 1200.[91] Like other series of memoranda (excepting chronicles and royal Exchequer records), cartulary-making became firmly established, not in the twelfth century, but in the thirteenth. In this century the practice spread from monasteries to laymen, although lay cartularies from the thirteenth century are very rare.[92] They seem to have been particularly prevalent in Northamptonshire; from there come Richard Hotot's estate book (see plate XV), Ralf Basset's roll, and the Braybrooke cartulary.[93] Richard Hotot was probably a brother of William Hotot, abbot of Peterborough (1246–9); so he could have learned about the importance of keeping documents from the abbot. In 1322 another Northamptonshire gentleman, Henry de Bray, actually wrote his own cartulary, as we have already seen.[94]

Registers

In the medieval period the commonest term for a cartulary was a *registrum*. The rolls of the Chancery were likewise described as a *registrum*[95] and so was Domesday Book on one occasion.[96] This wide definition of 'register' is useful, as all these records shared the common characteristic of being edited collections, in books or rolls, which had been compiled from primary sources from separate pieces of parchment. Moreover, some of the works described as cartularies in the preceding

[89] R. W. Southern, 'The Sense of the Past,' *TRHS* 5th series XXIII (1973), pp. 247–50.
[90] *Domesday Book*, pp. 50–51.
[91] Ker, *English MSS*, p. 20. G. R. C. Davis, *Medieval Cartularies of Great Britain* (1958), p. xi.
[92] The earliest is the cartulary of the Constable family of Flamborough (dating from the 1200s), Davis, *Medieval Cartularies*, no. 1224.
[93] *ibid.* nos. 1256, 1188A, 1206. Richard Hotot's book has now been acquired by the British Library (Add. MS. 54228), cf. E. King, 'Large and Small Landowners in Thirteenth-Century England', *Past and Present* XLVII (1970), pp. 39–43.
[94] See n. 3 above.   [95] See ch. 2, nn. 70, 72 above.
[96] Galbraith, *Domesday Book*, p. 105, n. 2.

paragraphs do not exclusively concern charters: the estate books of Richard Hotot and Henry de Bray were intended as general reference books for their families and are not narrowly legalistic. Once the idea of copying documents into books for greater security and convenience became familiar, the practice took many forms. For instance, the royal Exchequer made registers in books, like a monastic house, to provide fair copies and guides to its records and to note down miscellanea. The oldest of these Exchequer remembrance books (Domesday Book excepted) are the Red Book and the Black Book, which were compiled in the 1230s.[97] The one most commonly used by scholars today is *The Book of Fees*, containing surveys of feudal tenures between 1198 and 1293. A note on its flyleaf, probably written at the time it was compiled in 1302, reminds the user that the book is a register and not a primary source: 'Remember that this book was composed and compiled from several official inquests . . . and therefore the contents of this book is to be used for evidence here in the Exchequer and not for the record.'[98] Registers like this were guides; they did not have the authority of the original documents themselves, which were the authentic official records.

On the other hand, another class of registers were treated as official records. These were the registers which recorded copies of outgoing documents, as distinct from monastic cartularies and Exchequer remembrance books which recorded documents in the compiler's possession. The greatest series of registers of outgoing documents are the Chancery rolls of royal letters, beginning in the first three years of John's reign; the Charter roll is described as a register as early as 1201.[99] Another well known series are the bishops' registers (starting in 1217 or a little earlier), which were modelled on the Chancery rolls.[100] Even earlier than the Chancery rolls are the provisions Hubert Walter had made in 1194 for registering Jewish chirographs of loans and receipts on rolls in designated centres throughout England.[101] The earliest local register of recognizances of debt which is extant, however, is London's *Liber A* beginning in 1276.[102] London also has early rolls of registered wills (beginning in 1258), and some title-deeds are enrolled in the court of Husting rolls (beginning in 1252).[103]

The practice of registering deeds of title in towns probably followed the lead of the Chancery rolls, although it could have derived from monastic practice. The earl of Chester's Domesday roll 'which preserves memory and record' is the earliest known of such registers, but it is now lost.[104] The oldest municipal register extant is a roll from Wallingford, made in 1231–2.[105] This roll is of particular interest because it appears to be a record of conveyances of small properties (houses, rents, market

---

[97] Described in *Dialogus*, pp. xi–xii. [98] *Book of Fees* I, p. xx.
[99] See ch. 2, nn. 68, 70 above. [100] See ch. 2, nn. 93–100 above.
[101] See ch. 2, n. 78 above. [102] Ed. R. L. Sharpe (1899).
[103] *Calendar of Wills Proved and Enrolled in the Court of Husting* ed. R. L. Sharpe (1889) I, p. xxiv.
[104] See nn. 76, 77 above.
[105] G. H. Martin, 'The Registration of Deeds of Title in the Medieval Borough' in *Study of Medieval Records*, pp. 155–6.

stalls and so on), which had been made orally in the borough court without charters. The next oldest Wallingford register, made in 1252–3, seems by contrast to be a summary of charters.[106] It looks as if in the twenty years between 1232 and 1252 the habit of conveying property in writing had become established among the Wallingford burghers.

Learned and literary works

The increasing number of documents issued and memoranda compiled in the twelfth and thirteenth centuries is matched by a substantial upsurge in the production of 'books', in the general modern sense of learned and literary works. Yet medieval books were essentially different from modern ones because they were manuscripts. Consequently the total numbers are small by modern standards and counting them is of useful but only limited value, since individual manuscript volumes are not uniform objects like printed books. Making approximate estimates from contemporary catalogues, Durham cathedral library had about 490 volumes in the twelfth century, Rochester cathedral about 241 in 1202, and Christ Church Canterbury about 1300 volumes in the catalogue of Prior Henry of Eastry (1285–1311).[107] These estimates are subject to every kind of qualification, because the makers of medieval library catalogues were not primarily concerned with counting their stock. The earliest Durham catalogue (from which the estimate of 490 volumes has been derived) illustrates the difficulties of counting, as various items are described as being in a certain number of 'books' (*libri*) or 'sets' (*paria*) or 'parts' (*particuli*) or 'quires' (*quaterniones*). Furthermore, books varied so much in size and in the layout of each page that the number of volumes gives little indication of the amount of reading material available. In general, however, library catalogues show that many more books were acquired in the twelfth and thirteenth centuries, as they often list new acquisitions from particular persons.

Individuals likewise possessed few books by modern standards. Robert Grosseteste, the greatest English scholar and bishop of the thirteenth century, perhaps had about 90; Master John of Foxton, who sold his books on Scripture to Lincoln cathedral library in *c.*1235, possessed about 34 volumes on that subject; Master Peter of Peckham, a lawyer, had 18 books in a coffer when he died in 1293; Guy de Beauchamp, earl of Warwick, gave away about 40 books in 1306.[108] The limitations of such fragmentary information are obvious. An inexplicable exception to the rule that neither individuals nor institutions had

---

[106] *ibid.* pp. 156–7.

[107] *Catalogi Veteres Librorum Ecclesiae Cathedralis Dunelm*, Surtees S. VII (1838), pp. 1–10. The dated catalogue from Rochester, ed. W. B. Rye, is printed in *Archaelogia Cantiana* III (1860), pp. 54ff. The size of Christ Church library is estimated by F. Wormald, 'The Monastic Library' in *English Library*, p. 22, cf. plate 10. For library catalogues see also ch. 5, nn. 55–7 below.

[108] R. W. Hunt, 'The Library of Robert Grosseteste' in *Robert Grosseteste* ed. D. A. Callus (1955), pp. 127–9 (Grosseteste and Foxton). *SCCKB* I, p. clxiv (Peckham). See n. 2 above (Beauchamp).

many books is a court case from Worcestershire in 1221, in which the toll collector of Wychbold was alleged to have impounded 'two carts which bore the books of Richard, dean of Worcester'.[109] Two carts suggests a large number of books, but whether they all belonged to Richard and where they were being taken is not specified.

Library catalogues are more informative about the types of books kept than about numbers; but there are difficulties here too, as some catalogues only list some of their books (those kept in particular places for example) and items specified can be difficult to identify because many books had no uniform titles. The library of Bury St Edmunds, which can be reconstructed with confidence for the twelfth century, indicates the main categories of books.[110] It was largely built up – by gift and purchase and by copying in the *scriptorium* – by one abbot, Anselm, between 1121 and 1148. By the end of the twelfth century Bury possessed bibles and liturgical books, texts of the main Church Fathers (largely added by Abbot Anselm), pagan Latin classics, histories both English (for example, Bede and the *Anglo-Saxon Chronicle*) and European (for example, Paul the Deacon and the *Gesta Francorum*), 'modern' (that is, twelfth-century) scholastic textbooks in divinity and law, and some 'modern' Latin literature such as the poems of Walter of Châtillon.

It would not be profitable to list in greater detail here the various books used and made in England between 1066 and 1307, as that would involve an extended essay on medieval learning and literature in Latin, Hebrew, French and English. Instead, a few main types will be alluded to briefly. Unlike some of the forms of documents and memoranda already discussed in this chapter, books were not a novelty at the time of the Norman Conquest, nor is the format of the book unfamiliar to the modern reader. Although books were no novelty, they do seem to have been a rarity in late Anglo-Saxon England. Or at least the prelates appointed by the Normans considered the libraries they found to be so inadequate that they restocked them on an unprecedented scale.[111] Abbot Anselm's work at Bury is an example of what was done in the main cathedrals and abbeys. Nor were the principal texts which were acquired or made in the century after the Norman Conquest new in themselves: they were the Bible, the Church Fathers, the pagan Latin classics, all works hallowed by antiquity. Scribes and illuminators wrote more accurate texts and embellished them in new ways, but they did not alter their essentials. These classics continued to be the foundation of any medieval library.

Alongside these relatively few perennials, planted by the sages of antiquity (whether Jewish, Christian or pagan), there were growing up numerous recent books by lesser men. These latter works were lesser in

---

[109] *Rolls of the Justices in Eyre for Lincolnshire and Worcestershire* ed. D. M. Stenton, SS LIII (1934), p. 574, no. 1167. King John likewise had a library large enough to transport in carts: see ch. 5, n. 63 below.

[110] R. M. Thomson, 'The Library of Bury St Edmunds in the Eleventh and Twelfth Centuries', *Speculum* XLVII (1972), pp. 617–45.

[111] See ch. 1, nn. 4–5 above.

dignity, but not necessarily in length; the *Ormulum*, a series of homilies on the Gospels in the Missal composed in *c*.1200, numbers 20,512 short lines in Middle English in its extant form, which is perhaps one eighth of the original.[112] Furthermore, as John of Salisbury commented in *c*.1150 (quoting Bernard of Chartres), 'modern' authors are dwarfs, but they stand on the shoulders of the giant sages of antiquity and so see more and further than their predecessors.[113] This confident attitude, combined with widening literacy caused by the dissemination of documents of all kinds in the twelfth century, produced a growing number of newly composed writings as well as further copies of the classics, both pagan and Christian. These new works are of two principal sorts. Firstly, there are the productions of the schoolmen, which aimed to cope with the increasing mass of written material by providing guides to it (in Latin) in logically organized treatises: the *Summa Theologiae* of Thomas Aquinas (composed in *c*.1260) is the best known of such texts. Secondly, there are the very varied works composed for the book-reading or book-using public, both cleric and lay, in Latin, French and English – poems, songs, histories, romances, saints' lives, sermons, and so on.

Learned works

Taking the writings of the schoolmen first, the typical scholastic book is in the form either of a *glossa* or of a *summa*; both took definite shape in the twelfth century and aimed to cope with the increasing number of documents. The *glossa*, the 'gloss' around a text, is discussed with reference to the layout of the page in the next chapter. The *summa* is explained here. Robert of Melun, an Englishman by birth and bishop of Hereford (1163–7), defined a *summa* both as 'a concise encyclopedia of instances' and 'a compendious collection of instances'.[114] The prototype was Abelard's *Sic et Non* (composed in the 1130s), which aimed to cut through the 'mass of words' presented to divinity students by bringing together selected contradictory quotations under headings and subheadings.[115] Although many *summae* juxtaposed contradictory texts in this way, the essence of the genre was that it comprised a selection of texts organized in accordance with a logical scheme. Likewise although many *summae* contained explanatory commentaries, at the basis of the *summa* form were the quotations cited from authorities; Abelard's *Sic et Non* had no commentary apart from a prologue.

Long before the twelfth century rhetoricians had collected quotations, particularly from classical authors, into anthologies called *florilegia* (bunches of flowers) and this practice continued. As well as using such anthologies himself, Gerald of Wales presented his *Gemma Ecclesias-*

[112] Ed. R. M. White and R. Holt (1878).

[113] *Metalogicon* bk iii, ch. 4, ed. C. C. J. Webb (1929), p. 136. Clanchy, *'Moderni'*, p. 676.

[114] 'singulorum brevis comprehensio', 'singulorum compendiosa collectio', M. D. Chenu, *Nature, Man and Society in the Twelfth Century* trans. J. Taylor and L. K. Little (1968), p. 298.

[115] Prologue to *Sic et Non* ed. B. B. Boyer and R. McKeon (1976), p. 89.

tica (written in *c.*1197) as a kind of *florilegium* selected from the 'mass of words': 'I am like one who with much labour extracts precious gems from the innumerable sands of the seashore, or one who, walking through spacious gardens, plucks the useful and virtuous from among the worthless and fruitless plants, separating the lilies and roses from the nettles and brambles.'[116] Such an anthology differed from a *summa* in its function: the *florilegium* provided verbal ornament to garnish a composition, whereas the *summa* invited its readers to examine the citations critically. The *florilegium* stemmed from the ancient arts of grammar and rhetoric, whereas the *summa* stemmed from 'modern' logic and dialectic.

Within the general class of *summae* there were numerous species, theological and legal textbooks being the most common. Bracton presented his treatise on English law, which was contemporary with Aquinas's *Summa Theologiae*, as a *summa*:

> I, Henry de Bracton, to instruct the lesser judges, if no one else, have turned my mind to the former judgments of just men, examining diligently their decisions . . . and have compiled whatever I found therein worthy of note into one *summa*, organized by titles and paragraphs, without prejudice to any other opinion, and committed to memory forever by the aid of writing.[117]

Bracton's description epitomizes the main elements of a *summa*: it is compiled for instruction; it is a selection of authoritative statements; it is organized systematically. Similarly Fleta, who composed a legal treatise a generation after Bracton, explains in his prologue why it will be useful:

> To many who are in a hurry and many who are unlearned, a compendium in a brief volume of the justices' judgments may be very necessary, so that an inquirer does not have to turn over a mass of books and chapters, when he will find what he is looking for without trouble, brought together here in a brief space.[118]

A *summa* was a sort of highly organized and selective register, which aimed to instruct a wider public than one monastic house like a cartulary, or one government department like an Exchequer remembrance book. If a *summa* is defined as broadly as that, the genre includes a variety of formularies and treatises which instruct by citing examples in how to conduct law courts, draft charters, cast financial accounts, manage estates, and so on.[119] In a sense too the collections of papal decretals and parliamentary statutes (see plates XVI, XVII and XVIII)

---

[116] Giraldus II, p. 6. Cf. A. A. Goddu and R. H. Rouse, 'Gerald of Wales and the *Florilegium Angelicum*', *Speculum* LII (1977), pp. 489–90.

[117] Bracton, fo 1a, vol. ii. p. 19.

[118] Fleta, p. 3. Fleta's claims echo the *Decretum* of Ivo of Chartres and the *Libri Sententiarum* of Peter Lombard: U. T. Holmes, 'Transitions in European Education' in *Twelfth-Century Europe and the Foundations of Modern Society* ed. M. Clagett *et al.* (1966), pp. 26–7.

[119] Such treatises are discussed by Oschinsky, *Walter of Henley*, pp. 3–74, 225–57.

which lawyers used were *summae*.[120] Compiling *summae* was a reaction to the proliferation of documents and books in the twelfth and thirteenth centuries; they were intended as a guide through the maze, although sometimes they added to the confusion.

Literary works

The very varied works written for, or used by, the general reader in this period are not characterized by a single dominant type like the *summa*. Old works continued to be read, particularly the pagan Latin classics, and new ones were created, in Latin and Hebrew verse and prose, and in the vernacular languages of French and English. Ideally, from the point of view of making and using documents, all works available in England in whatever language and whatever their provenance are relevant. But generalization about what was read is made difficult by the emphasis of modern scholarship, which usually concentrates on one of the languages only and is concerned primarily with linguistic development or critical assessment of newly created literature. An educated layman in 1300, by contrast, like Henry de Bray, was probably familiar with some writing in three literary languages (Latin, French and English) and did not necessarily care whether the sermons, songs and tales he heard or read were new or old.

Scholarship in England has tended to concentrate on medieval literary works in inverse proportion to their frequency. Latin was the commonest literary language in the period 1066–1307, yet the use of Latin in England has never been comprehensively surveyed. English, on the other hand, which was the least used literary language (apart from Hebrew), has been intensively studied. French has fared much better than Latin, but not as well as English. Consequently the use of Latin works in medieval England is too large and unstudied a subject to summarize in a few pages, whereas summaries of writings in English and French are unnecessary, as excellent introductions to them already exist.[121] As interim introductions to Latin works, there are discussions of the Twelfth-Century Renaissance and of medieval Latin in Europe as a whole:[122] there are also surveys of particular types of writing in England, notably history and biography.[123] Most importantly, the basic materials for what was read have been listed in N. R. Ker's *Medieval Libraries of Great Britain: a List of Surviving Books*.[124]

[120] Duggan, *Decretals*. For parliamentary statutes see ch. 4, n. 73 below.

[121] R. M. Wilson, *Early Middle English Literature* (3rd edn, 1968). Legge, *Anglo-Norman. The Catalogue of Romances in the British Museum* ed. H. L. D. Ward and J. A. Herbert (3 vols, 1883–1910) lists non-Latin saints' lives and other devotional works as well as romances and poems.

[122] Introductions in English are: C. H. Haskins, *The Renaissance of the Twelfth Century* (1927); Curtius, *European Lit.*; Wilson, *Early Middle English Literature*, ch. 2 ('The Anglo-Latin Background'). See also *Editing Medieval Texts: English, French and Latin Written in England* ed. A. G. Rigg (1977).

[123] Gransden, *Historical Writing*. R. W. Southern, 'Aspects of the European Tradition of Historical Writing', *TRHS* 5th series XX–XXIII (1970–73). Smalley, *Historians*.

[124] 2nd edn (1964).

Although this chapter has aimed to describe the main types of manuscript made in the period 1066–1307, and not to prescribe rules, some general conclusions about the development of documentary forms in England can be drawn. Many of the forms were ancient. The charter, the chirograph and the rhetorician's letter had been used by the Anglo-Saxons and derived from the traditions of the late Roman empire. Similarly, skills in writing and illuminating books and ensuring that posterity had a record of the past had been the preoccupation of monks for half a millennium before the Norman Conquest. What was new after 1066 was the increase in the number of documents made and the gradual extension of literate modes to more people and diverse activities. As a result old forms, like the charter and the chirograph, became stereotyped in the thirteenth century because numbers imposed standardization. The form of the letter itself, which had been used hitherto mostly as an open declaration or a literary device, became with Henry II's letters close an actual missive sent from one person to another.

The increase in the number of documents in circulation encouraged institutions to organize and record those which most concerned them in cartularies and registers, both of documents received and of documents sent out. The habit of making an accumulating series of memoranda year by year, of which the chronicle had been the forerunner, was extended first to financial accounting and then to the proceedings of law courts, from the king's court downwards. Memoranda as such were not new; the novelty consisted in annually accumulating series.

Likewise books as such were not new: the Bible, the Church Fathers and the pagan classics were the heritage of antiquity, preserved and lovingly illuminated by monks. Innovation came from the schoolmen of the twelfth century, who provided in the *summa* a tool for cutting through the increasing mass of written words. Contrasting with the uniformity and order which the schoolmen attempted to impose on documents are the variety of literary works produced in Latin, particularly during the Twelfth-Century Renaissance, and in French and English from the latter half of the twelfth century onwards. In the eleventh century and earlier making documents in England had been largely the prerogative of monks. In the twelfth and thirteenth centuries schoolmen and secular clerics successfully challenged this tradition. Monks and schoolmen between them created and wrote nearly all the types of document described in this chapter. Thereafter, however, the initiative lay neither with monks nor with schoolmen, who wrote in Latin, but with those who wrote in vernacular languages for a gradually enlarging public.

4

The technology of writing

The materials of which records have been made, and the methods used to transform words into symbols appropriate to those materials, have varied considerably.[1] In the Inca empire knotted cords of different colours and lengths, the *quipu*, recalled numbers and chronology and even allegedly the names and qualities of past rulers. In ancient Mesopotamia information was inscribed in clay and baked into bricks to form a durable archive. Parchment was the principal writing material in medieval Europe. Illuminated manuscripts, like the Bury and Winchester Bibles from twelfth-century England, epitomize the achievments of the Middle Ages as much as great churches in stone. Like stone, parchment was a durable material which demanded of its users an awareness of form and a consciousness of posterity. More ephemeral and less awesome writing surfaces were also used in the Middle Ages: birch bark in Novgorodan Russia, papyrus in pre-Norman Sicily and Italy, hazel wood in the English Exchequer for tally sticks, and most commonly wax tablets for making notes or drafts.

The combination of skills required to produce these diverse artefacts of written record, ranging in medieval Europe from the expertise of the tanner and the tally-cutter to that of the book illuminator and the master in the schools, constitute a technology. A particular technology of writing shapes and defines the uses of literacy in a region or culture, just as other products, such as cloth or metalwork, depend for their forms on their technology of manufacture. For example, because it was more difficult to write with a quill on parchment than it is with a modern ballpoint on paper, writing was considered a special skill in the Middle Ages which was not automatically coupled with the ability to read. Hence it is an anachronism, arising from a failure to appreciate technological differences, to apply modern criteria of literacy to the medieval past. A medieval historian has to be as aware of the technology of manuscripts, as a historian of nineteenth-century Europe is of industrial processes.

[1] For a general introduction see I. J. Gelb, *A Study of Writing* (2nd edn, 1963) and for the Middle Ages see J. Stiennon, *Paléographie du Moyen Age* (1973). The fundamental works on medieval writing techniques are A. Giry, *Manuel de diplomatique* (1894) and Wattenbach, *Schriftwesen*.

There was not, however, in the twelfth and thirteenth centuries a technological revolution in the means of production of writings comparable with the introduction of the codex (or book) format and of parchment in the late Roman empire or with the invention of printing in the Renaissance. The closest the twelfth and thirteenth centuries came to such technological innovation was in the increasing use of seals, since they were a precursor of printing and an accelerator of bureaucracy (as argued in chapter 9 below); but seals were not a medieval invention in themselves. Instead, the suitability of traditional materials and methods was tested by the increasing demand for documents and they were consequently modified and adapted. Thus a new style of script, the cursive, was created in the twelfth century to enable scribes to write faster. New layouts were designed for greater clarity, like the glossed scholastic text, or for greater convenience, like the pocket-sized Bibles made in the thirteenth century. To cope with the problem of keeping records, the king's government experimented with different formats of rolls. Although these changes are technical and detailed, they are fundamental to understanding the increasing use of written record, because the extension of literacy depended on the mastery of available writing techniques.

Medieval methods of writing have been most frequently discussed in the context of paleography and diplomatic, particularly in works which instruct the student in how to read manuscripts and to establish their provenance and authenticity. This chapter inevitably covers some of the same ground, but with a different emphasis, as it considers documents primarily as manufactured objects and concentrates on how their makers in England reacted to the demand to produce records on an unprecedented scale. As existing methods were adapted, rather than revolutionized, our discussion begins with the scribe in his traditional posture.

The scribe and his materials

The scribe sitting at his desk is depicted in numerous manuscripts in the guise of the author writing the book which is being copied. In place of the venerable author, most commonly one of the Four Evangelists, some scribes and illuminators of the twelfth century began to have themselves depicted in this way. The most remarkable example of the practice is the full-page portrait of Eadwine, monk of Christ Church Canterbury, whose picture has an inscription round the frame declaring him to be 'the prince of writers' whose praise and fame will not die.[2] Eadwine sits in the conventional pose (apart from facing to the left instead of to the right), with a quill pen in his right hand and a penknife in his left, on

---

[2] 'scriptorum princeps ego; nec obitura deinceps laus mea, nec fama. . . .' This inscription, in the form of a riddle in verse, is compared with other self-descriptions of scribes by Wattenbach, *Schriftwesen*, p. 505. The full text is given by C. R. Dodwell, *The Canterbury School of Illumination* (1954), p. 36. Eadwine's portrait has often been published, e.g. *ibid.* plate 23 and Kauffmann, *Romanesque MSS*, plate 187. Eadwine's work is illustrated at plate XIV below.

an elaborately carved upright chair, leaning towards a high writing desk draped with a cloth, on which is a book open at a blank page. In another unusual full-page portrait, contemporary with Eadwine's but this time of the author, Laurence prior of Durham (1149–54) sits at a desk which is shown as a folding extension of the chair, projecting out from its arms.[3]

Verbal portraits of the scribe indicate much the same features. These are found in lexicons, like Alexander Neckham's *De Nominibus Utensalium* (composed at the end of the twelfth century), which describe everyday things. A work derived from Neckham begins its picture of the scribe as follows: 'A writer of books [*librarius*], who is commonly called a scribe [*scriptor*], should have a chair with projecting arms for holding the board upon which the quire of parchment is to be placed.'[4] This work then describes the tools required for preparing the parchment – the knife or razor for scraping it, the pumice for cleaning and smoothing it, and the boar or goat's tooth for polishing the surface to stop the ink running. Then there are the tools for ruling the lines – the stylus, the pencil, the straight ruler, the plumb line, and the awl for pricking holes to mark the beginnings of the lines. Finally there is the writing equipment itself – the quill pens and penknife, the inkhorn, and the various coloured inks. This description also includes the importance of adequate heat and good light for writing, although the hot coals recommended seem mainly intended for drying the ink on damp days rather than keeping the scribe himself warm. There are some indications that in monasteries writing was a seasonal activity. Orderic Vitalis, the English historian of the Normans, says at the end of one of his books (which he penned himself) that he is so numbed by the winter cold that he is going to finish his book at this point and will relate what he has omitted when the spring returns.[5]

Writing was certainly seen as an act of endurance in which 'the whole body labours.'[6] As such, it was an appropriate theme for sermons and homilies in monasteries. A twelfth-century sermon copied into a Durham manuscript exhorts its hearers to consider how they may become scribes of the Lord, writing with the pen of memory on the parchment of a pure conscience, which has been scraped by the knife of divine fear, smoothed by the pumice of heavenly desires, and whitened by the chalk of holy thoughts (the chalk is a detail which Neckham's lexicon omits).[7] The metaphors extend the theme still further: the ruler

[3] Boase, *English Art*, plate 53a. Bertram prior of Durham (1189–1212), on the other hand, is depicted on his seal reading or writing at a lectern, *ibid*. p. 288 and plate 93d. See also *English Library*, plate 6b and Kauffmann, *Romanesque MSS*, plate 215.

[4] C. H. Haskins, *Studies in the History of Medieval Science* (1924), p. 361. Cf. *A Volume of Vocabularies* ed. T. Wright (1857) I, pp. 116–17. Descriptions of scribes' equipment are collected by Wattenbach, *Schriftwesen*, pp. 207–61.

[5] Orderic, bk iv, vol. ii, pp. 360–61. Cf. n. 9 below.

[6] Wattenbach, *Schriftwesen*, p. 495. Cf. ch. 8, n. 71 below.

[7] R. A. B. Mynors, *Durham Cathedral MSS* (1939), p. 9. Comparable metaphorical descriptions are cited by Wattenbach, *Schriftwesen*, pp. 208–9 and Curtius, *European Lit.*, pp. 318–19.

is the will of God, the bifurcated knib of the pen is the joint love of God and our neighbour, the different coloured inks are heavenly grace, and the exemplar is the life of our Redeemer.

Obviously neither visual nor verbal portraits of the scribe are drawn directly from life in all their details, as they formed part of a conventional repertoire. Since one of the functions of a lexicon like the *De Nominibus Utensalium* was to enlarge the reader's vocabulary, it tends to exaggerate the amount of equipment the scribe requires in order to present as many unfamiliar words as possible. The average scribe did not presumably sit in an elaborate chair at an elegantly draped desk; nor did he normally write on the blank pages of a bound book, as in Eadwine's portrait, but on a folded quire of parchment. Moreover, the classic portraits of the scribe are monastic in origin. They describe the traditional copyist, who wrote beautiful liturgical books from an exemplar at an even pace. In the twelfth century a new type of scribe, less worthy of a dignified portrait, came to the fore. He was the secular clerk, who rapidly wrote letters and official records from dictation. The 'scribbler' and 'petty clerk', who fawned around the king's Chancery in the thirteenth century (the description is Henry III's),[8] had little in common with Eadwine, 'the prince of writers'.

The most important equipment of the twelfth-century writer who composed for himself or wrote from dictation, as distinct from the copyist, was not the parchment book depicted in conventional portraits of scribes, but the writing tablets on which he noted down his drafts. The tablets were ordinarily made of wood, overlaid with coloured wax, and often folded into a diptych which could be worn on a belt. When something needed noting down, the diptych was opened, thus exposing the waxed surfaces which were written on with a stylus. A story by Orderic Vitalis illustrates their use. He was visited by Anthony, a monk of Winchester, who showed him a copy of a life of St William. Orderic wished to have a copy too, 'but in truth, since the bearer was in haste to depart, and the winter cold prevented me from writing, I made a full and accurate abbreviation on tablets, and now I shall endeavour to entrust it summarily to parchment.'[9] This story incidentally illustrates again how writing with a pen on parchment, as distinct from making notes with a stylus on wax, was a seasonal activity for Orderic.

It seems to have been common practice for monastic authors to write on wax and then have a fair copy made on parchment. Eadmer describes the difficulties St Anselm had in writing the *Proslogion*, because the tablets on which it was written were first lost and then shattered, perhaps by diabolical intervention.[10] That wax was the normal medium for writing in the twelfth century is also indicated by other saints' biographies. The author of the life of Christina of Markyate remarks how he could not pollute 'the wax by writing' how scandalously the cleric

---

[8] 'scriptitor,' 'clericulus', Matthew Paris v, p. 374.

[9] Orderic, bk vi, ch. 3, vol. iii, p. 218. References to wax tablets are collected by Wattenbach, *Schriftwesen*, pp. 51–89.

[10] Eadmer, *Vita*, pp. 30–31. Cf. ch. 8, n. 81 below.

had behaved who had been commended to Christina as her companion by Thurstan, archbishop of York.[11] On his deathbed in 1200 St Hugh dreamed that the great pear tree in his garden at Lincoln had fallen to the ground and he was worried about the waste of its timber, 'for so many diptychs could be cut from it that there would be more than enough for the scholastic studies of the whole of England and France.'[12]

In the thirteenth century pieces of parchment were used for notes, either as a substitute for wax tablets or in addition to them. Such notes are occasionally referred to in the royal plea rolls.[13] Making notes on parchment had also been a practice of Robert Grosseteste. This is known because dispute arose about which of his works were authentic. The regent-master of the Franciscans stated that Grosseteste had made some marginal notes in manuscripts because 'when some noteworthy thought occurred to him, he wrote it down there so that it should not escape his memory, just as he also wrote many slips of parchment [*cedulas*] which are not all authoritative.'[14] This statement suggests that Grosseteste was not accustomed to using wax tablets for his notes and drafts, although undue reliance should not be put on an argument from silence. The practice of making memoranda, whether on wax or parchment, contradicts the common assumption that medieval people had such good memories that they required no notes. Once they were literate, they had the same needs as a modern writer. Drafts on wax or slips of parchment are the equivalent of a modern author's original manuscript, while the parchment text is comparable to a fair copy by a professional typist.

Before discussing parchment, a few words need to be said about paper. The earliest paper documents extant in England are a register from King's Lynn beginning in 1307 and another from Lyme Regis in 1309.[15] London described its registers of apprentices, citizens, and debts as the 'paper' or 'papers' of the Chamber of Guildhall in 1300 (and perhaps as early as 1275), but its extant records from this period are in fact made of parchment.[16] Paper occurs first in seaports because it was imported. In the long term its principal advantages over parchment were that it was easier to write on and potentially cheaper. The most significant fact about paper in England in the period up to 1307 is that it was scarcely known. Consequently parchment became established for centuries to come as the appropriate material for all the most formal records, because they took shape in the twelfth and thirteenth centuries.

The commonest word for parchment was *membrana*, simply meaning animal skin. In northern Europe the skins normally used were those of cattle and sheep. The finest parchment was vellum, made of calf skin.

[11] *The Life of Christina of Markyate* ed. C. H. Talbot (1959), p. 114.
[12] *The Life of St Hugh of Lincoln* ed. D. L. Douie and H. Farmer (1961) II, p. 209.
[13] C. T. Flower, *Introduction to the Curia Regis Rolls*, SS LXII (1943), pp. 9, 271.
[14] R. W. Hunt, 'The Library of Robert Grosseteste' in *Robert Grosseteste* ed. D. A. Callus (1955), p. 127. Cf. n. 54 below.
[15] G. S. Ivy, 'The Bibliography of the MS Book' in *English Library*, p. 36.
[16] *Calendar of Early Mayor's Court Rolls* ed. A. H. Thomas (1924), pp. 87, 163, 170. *Chronicles of Edward I and Edward II* ed. W. Stubbs, RS LXXVI (1882) I, p. 86.

Thus to make the great Bury Bible in the time of Abbot Anselm (1121–48), Hervey, the sacrist, obtained parchment from Scotland (perhaps meaning Ireland) because he could not find calf skins locally which suited the illuminator, Master Hugh.[17] Sheep skin was the usual material for royal records, both because it was cheaper and because, according to the *Dialogue of the Exchequer*, it is not easy to make an erasure on sheep skin without it showing plainly.[18] Once parchment has been scraped and prepared for writing on, it is usually impossible to tell what species of animal skin is being used.

It is frequently assumed that parchment was rare and expensive and that its high cost obstructed the spread of literacy. Such an assumption fails to distinguish between the finest parchments, required for illuminated manuscripts like the Bury Bible, and cheaper varieties. It is also necessary to take into account the relative cost of other items, such as the scribe's time, the cost of ink and binding materials, and (in the case of letter-writing) the cost of sealing wax and delivery. These costs in their turn need to be related to the general cost of living. As no detailed study has been made along these lines, only a few indicative facts will be cited here. When Henry II asked St Hugh how much money he needed to build up a library for the new Charterhouse at Witham, Hugh replied that one silver mark would be enough for a long time.[19] The king smiled at this, saying, 'What heavy demands you make on us', and gave him 10 marks. As Adam of Eynsham, Hugh's biographer, wished to emphasize the saint's modesty, he may have minimized his requirements; even so, Adam's story assumes that 10 marks (£6 13s. 4d.) would have bought a large amount of parchment.

At the time Adam wrote this biography, the Exchequer was keeping accounts of its running costs. Although these records do not survive in complete series and some of the sums are fixed charges, which went back to Henry II's time or earlier, they do supply sufficient information to sample the relative costs of different stages in the production of documents in the 1220s and 1230s.[20] Parchment was charged for at a fixed rate of 10 shillings a year. As this sum was already customary when Fitz Neal wrote the *Dialogue of the Exchequer*, it does not indicate the real cost; but in some terms varying supplementary charges, ranging between 20 and 40 shillings a year, are recorded which presumably do indicate actual expenditure on parchment. Compared with these sums, one scribe in 1222, Robert of Bassingbourn, was paid 3s. 2d. for 10 days work 'while he wrote summonses' and the customary charge for scribes was 5 pence per day each.[21] Similarly in Easter term of the same year the nightwatchman and lighting cost the customary 12 shillings (1½ pence per night) and the rushes on the floor 3s. 5d. Ink was also a notable

[17] *Memorials of St Edmunds Abbey* ed. T. Arnold, RS xcvi (1890), ii, p. 290. Gransden, *Historical Writing*, p. 395.

[18] *Dialogus*, p. 31.

[19] *The Life of St Hugh of Lincoln* i, p. 85.

[20] What follows derives from *CLibR* vi, appendix i, pp. 240–84, and *Dialogus*, pp. 12–13, 31.

[21] *CLibR* vi, no. 2163.

expense, which increased in a constant ratio with the expenditure on parchment. In Fitz Neal's time 2 shillings a year had been allowed for it, that is, one fifth of the cost of parchment; by the 1220s 3 shillings a year was being allowed and by the 1230s 40 pence for the half year.[22] The cost of sealing the writs was likewise high (about 12 pence for 30 writs on average), although this sum may include the sealer's charge as well as the cost of the wax (about 7 pence per pound). An even greater expense was delivering writs to their destinations (more than 2 pence per writ in the 1220s); on 11 July 1226 the charge for carrying 6 writs to sheriffs in various counties was 3s. 6d.[23]

These figures are not presented as statistics of real expenditure, but as an indication of relative costs. As far as materials were concerned, parchment seems to have been rather cheap. Ink and sealing wax were surprisingly expensive, although all materials were relatively cheap compared with the customary charges for labour of both the unskilled, like the nightwatchman, and the skilled scribes at 5 pence per day. If parchment cost the Exchequer at the most about 50 shillings a year in the 1220s and 1230s, that is the equivalent of 4 silver marks, a negligible sum considering that the standard rate for a single fine or oblation in the king's court was ½ mark. Like Henry II, Henry III might have smiled at the suggestion that a few marks for parchment was a heavy burden on his revenues.

It does not follow from the proposition that parchment was relatively cheap that the finished product, the manuscript, was commensurately so; but the high costs of manuscripts arose primarily from their being produced by hand and not from the initial cost of animal skins. In the last decades of the thirteenth century the obediantaries' accounts of some monasteries are sufficiently detailed to distinguish between the cost of writing materials and labour costs. Like the Exchequer records, these accounts suggest that even the finest parchment was cheaper than the scribe's time. For example, at Norwich cathedral priory in 1288 12 dozen skins of vellum cost 17s. 5d., whereas the scribes were paid 20s. 5d.; similarly in 1296 12 dozen calf skins cost £2 1s. 6d., while the scribes writing the book for which they were ordered were paid £3 6s. 10d.[24] These costs are far higher than the Exchequer's expenditure on parchment at the beginning of the century, but they are for vellum not sheep skin, and the average price of cattle (and hence of their hides) had increased by about a third since the 1220s.

The initial cost of parchment depended on the availability of animal skins. The assumption that they were scarce can be examined by relating the demand for parchment to the animal population. Although there is insufficient data to make estimates on a national scale, a sample follows which relates the number of animals in two localities at different

[22] *Dialogus*, p. 12. *CLibR* VI, nos. 2169, 2259.
[23] *CLibR* VI, no. 2180.
[24] H. W. Saunders, *An Introduction to the Obedientary and Manor Rolls of Norwich Cathedral Priory* (1930), pp. 107, 180. The sum of £3 6s. 10d. may be an overestimate, as it includes miscellanea.

dates in the thirteenth century to an estimate of the amount of parchment used by the king's justices when they visited those localities. On the basis of tax returns M. M. Postan has estimated that there were 14,988 sheep and 2,645 cows and calves in a group of 23 villages in south Wiltshire in 1225, and 17,059 sheep and 4,298 cows and calves in the 33 villages of Blackbourne hundred in Suffolk in 1283.[25] At the same time the king's justices and their litigants were probably the largest single consumers of parchment. When they visited a county the size of Wiltshire of Suffolk for a solemn eyre, they and the litigants would have used, on a generous average estimate, 300 membranes of parchment for their rolls and another 200 for ancillary documents.[26] At first sight 500 membranes seems a large amount of parchment, yet 500 sheep skins comprise the flocks of 32 taxable households in south Wiltshire in 1225 or 38 in Blackbourne hundred in 1283. In Wiltshire the number of households cited comprises about three quarters of a village and in Suffolk just under one village.

These figures are not given to suggest that 500 sheep were slaughtered whenever the king's justices appeared on the scene, although large quantities of meat and corn were consumed by their entourages on these visitations, but to show that relatively few sheep skins were required for parchment even by the king's justices. The sheep of one village or less, even in a predominantly arable area like Suffolk, could supply a county's requirements. The large number of animals kept in England, particularly sheep for wool production, may have made parchment cheaper there than elsewhere. But that is a guess, as sheep skins were used for numerous purposes and the provenance of parchment is rarely specified. In general the evidence does not suggest that institutions considered parchment an expense inhibiting the production of documents, although examples can be found of individual writers making economies.

Apart from parchment the most important material for making records, as distinct from ephemeral drafts written on wax, was wood. In Michaelmas term 1224 the Exchequer spent 5 shillings on rods for tallies at the same time as it spent 4 shillings on parchment.[27] Tallies were used as receipts for money or other items rendered, such as bags of corn at a mill, and also as records of obligations to make payments.[28] The appropriate sums were shown on the tally by notches of differing widths, depths, and intervals (see plate VIII). Like a chirograph, the English tally was a bipartite record. When the notches had been cut on the stick,

[25] *Essays in Medieval Agriculture* (1973), pp. 227, 229.

[26] This estimate is based on 5 judges each having a roll of 60 membranes, another 100 membranes being used for about 1,000 original and judicial writs and jury panels, and another 100 for final concords, *veredicta* etc. For the range of eyre records see *Berks. Eyre*, p. xvii.

[27] *CLibR* VI, no. 2169. The 5s. was a customary charge, *Dialogus*, p. 12. There were also in 1224 the costs of leather for filing the tallies (9d.) and of 'a big sack' to keep them in (14d.).

[28] What follows is based on H. Jenkinson, 'Exchequer Tallies', *Archaeologia* LXII (1911), pp. 367–80, and 'Medieval Tallies, Public and Private,' *Archaeologia* LXXIV (1925), pp. 289–353. M. M. Postan, *Medieval Trade and Finance* (1973), pp. 32–3. P & M II, p. 215.

to the satisfaction of both renderer and receiver, the tally was split down its length so that each party had the same record. The interlocking halves were intended to act as a check against forgery. Although the numbers on the tally were cut with a knife, the names and business of the parties it concerned were written in script in ink (see plate VIII). Some tallies also bore seals like charters. Tallies were not a primitive survival from the preliterate past, but a sophisticated and practical record of numbers. They were more convenient to keep and store than parchments, less complex to make, and no easier to forge. They were the foundation and origin of the royal financial system of the twelfth century and were widely adopted by private accountants in the thirteenth, who described in detail how they should be cut, just as Fitz Neal had done in the *Dialogue of the Exchequer*.[29]

Of the millions of medieval tallies made, only a few hundred survive. In 1834 the Exchequer tallies stored at Westminster were burned after the passing of the statute abolishing the Receipt of the Exchequer. The fire accidentally spread to the Houses of Parliament and thus brilliantly symbolized the abolition of the *ancien régime* and the triumph of 'reform'. The burning of the tally sticks has further ironies for the historian, because at the same time the Record Commissioners were publishing in lavish volumes with spurious Latin titles the earliest medieval records in parchment, like the Chancery rolls of King John. The Commissioners would not have dreamed of burning Domesday Book or the Chancery rolls, yet the earliest records of the Exchequer were deliberately destroyed because they were in a medium, wood, which was too uncouth for scholars to appreciate.

Wax, parchment and wood were the commonest documentary materials in medieval England. In addition to them, inscriptions were of course made on other materials, notably on stone, metal, bone and fabric. Such inscriptions are too varied and scattered to discuss in detail here. The lettering of those that were cut and painted on stone monumental slabs and sculptures, or engraved and enamelled on brasses, seals, swords, rings, cups and so on were probably designed by scribes. Their users presumably understood the significance of the Latin inscriptions, even if that were the limit of their literacy. Everyone would have seen inscriptions, or at least symbolic letters, on vestments and sacred images and utensils in churches. Similarly the Bayeux Tapestry, with its simple captions in Latin (HIC HAROLD REX INTERFECTUS EST, for example), assumes an audience in which someone could read. Coins are a special case. Because they were the medium in which lettering circulated most extensively among the population as a whole, their inscriptions were made by a form of massproduction. The lettering was not individually engraved on to the dies in accordance with a scribe's design; instead the letters were formed in sections by moneyers using punches of different shapes.[30] Coins were

[29] *Walter of Henley*, pp. 222–4, 460–61. *Dialogus*, pp. 22–4.
[30] G. C. Brooke, *A Catalogue of English Coins in the BM: The Norman Kings* (1916) I, pp. xlii–xliii.

the only form of writing which remained unaffected by the Norman Conquest; even a century later in Henry II's reign archaic lettering was still in evidence.[31]

Committing words to writing

The commonest way of committing words to writing was by dictating to a scribe. 'Reading and dictating' were ordinarily coupled together, not 'reading and writing';[32] the skill of writing a letter in proper form was the 'art of dictation' (*ars dictaminis*), a branch of rhetoric. Writing was distinguished from composition because putting a pen to parchment was an art in itself. Even when an author declares that he is writing something, he may in fact be using the term metaphorically. Thus John of Salisbury remarks in a letter to Peter, abbot of Celle, in c. 1159: 'While I was writing this [*scriberem*], the secretary was moved to laughter by the greeting at the head of the letter.'[33] His secretary (*notarius*) was presumably penning the letter and not John himself; he was evidently not a mere copyist, as he told John that the greeting was ridiculous and advised him against mixing his metaphors. Occasionally manuscripts depict the author of the work dictating to the scribe. A picture which may be of English provenance showing Peter of Poitiers dictating his *Compendium Historie* to a scribe is illustrated at plate XII. Certainly of English provenance are a miniature (dating from c. 1130) of Josephus dictating his history of the Jewish wars to the scribe, Samuel, and a drawing (attributed to Matthew Paris) of Plato dictating to Socrates.[34]

Exceptions to the rule that authors dictated their works are usually monks, as distinct from secular clerics. Monks wrote more of their own works because they were expected to be humble and also because some had training in a *scriptorium*. We have already seen that St Anselm wrote his own draft of the *Proslogion* on wax tablets and Eadmer, his biographer, wrote in the same way.[35] As well as writing his own draft Eadmer also penned his own fair copy on to parchment, as did the greatest monastic historians, Orderic Vitalis, William of Malmesbury and Matthew Paris.[36] By and large, however, the role of the composer (*dictator*) was kept distinct from that of the scribe (*scriptor*). 'The scribe must be careful not to write anything of his own in the roll', Fitz Neal advises in the *Dialogue of the Exchequer*, 'but only what the treasurer has instructed by dictation.'[37] Some scribes, like Eadwine, were supreme artists in calligraphy and presumably considered themselves superior to composers or clerks who wrote from dictation, whereas others were copyists who scarcely understood the exemplar in front of them.[38]

[31] D. F. Allen, *A Catalogue: Henry II: Cross and Crosslets Type* (1951), pp. xxxv–vi.

[32] 'legere vel dictare', Orderic, bk iii, vol. ii, p. 2. See ch. 8, n. 82 below.

[33] *Letters* ed. W. J. Millor *et al.* (1955) i, p. 183.

[34] Kauffmann, *Romanesque MSS*, plate 118. P. Brieger, *English Art, 1216–1307* (1957), plate 43a.

[35] See n. 10 above and ch. 8, n. 81 below.   [36] See ch. 8, n. 80 below.

[37] *Dialogus*, p. 31.   [38] See p. 181 below.

The style of the script depended on a variety of circumstances: the scribe's ability, the region and period in which he was working, the type of document being written, and whether the scribe was copying from an exemplar or writing from dictation. Thus Norman and English hands can be distinguished in the generation after the Conquest, as can Romanesque and Gothic by the last decades of the twelfth century.[39] Like other art forms, handwriting in England came under French influence. From the point of view of making records, the most important development was the emergence of cursive scripts in the twelfth century and their establishment in the thirteenth as the characteristic hands for writing business documents. Contemporaries, as well as modern paleographers, distinguish between the symmetrical and closely written 'book hand', which is the predecessor of the blackletter script of the earliest printed books, and 'court hand' or cursive, which is freer and more fluent. (Plates III, V, XIV and XVIII illustrate book hands of varying dates and types, while plates IV, VI, XVI and XVII illustrate court or cursive hands.) The medieval term for book hand was *textus*, which is more appropriate as *textus* literally means a 'weave'. Thus an inventory of books in the royal treasury in *c.* 1300 describes one book of transcripts as being written *in grosso texto* (in a large or heavy weave), whereas another is *sub manu curiali* (in court hand).[40]

Gerald of Wales tells an anecdote from a century earlier which indicates a similar distinction.[41] One of his rival claimants to the bishopric of St David's, the abbot of St Dogmael, was given a reading test by the papal judges delegate. They asked the abbot to read the letter from Innocent III commissioning them to examine him. His counsel objected that it was not fair to test him on a writing of that kind, which he was not used to, and suggested church books instead. So a missal was brought 'with a large and legible script', but the abbot would not read this either. Despite the abbot's refusal, and presumed inability, to read at all, Gerald's story shows that contemporaries were already aware of the difference between the familiar book hand of a missal and the novel court hand of a papal letter.

Contemporaries also make clear that different scripts were appropriate for different kinds of document. Alexander Neckham describes three styles, one for business documents, another for books, and a third for glosses and marginalia.[42] The glossing hand, for writing commentaries around texts, was an intermediate style between the weighty book hand and the cursive court hand (see plate XIV). Further specialized scripts become apparent in the thirteenth century, particularly among royal clerks, who developed distinctive variations of court hand for pipe rolls, Chancery enrolments, and so on. The good scribe did not

[39] Ker, *English MSS*, pp. 22–7 (Norman and English), 2–3 (Romanesque and Gothic).
[40] Chaplais, *Docs*, p. 50.
[41] Giraldus III, p. 234. Gerald gives the text of Innocent III's letter, *ibid*. pp. 68–9. Gerald's reliability is discussed at ch. 7, nn. 103–4 below.
[42] 'De Nominibus Utensalium' in *A Volume of Vocabularies*, p. 117. Cf. U. T. Holmes, *Daily Living in the Twelfth Century* (1952), p. 70.

therefore aim to write in a unique style distinctive to himself, like a modern writer, but to have command of a variety of scripts appropriate to different functions and occasions. 'Many writers who form a good and competent script for quires [that is, for copying books]', says one treatise, 'do not know how to adjust their hand for writing letters [in the sense of correspondence].'[43]

Because the competent scribe could write in a variety of styles, attributions of manuscripts to particular writers on stylistic grounds alone are peculiarly difficult and tend towards anachronism. Just as medieval writers did not usually aim at absolute uniformity in the spelling of proper names and the use of capital letters and punctuation, they likewise varied their scripts. For example, two charters for Robert Mauduit, King John's chamberlain, are both explicitly stated to have been written by Louis, clerk of Rockingham, as he adds the words 'who wrote this charter' after his name in the list of witnesses.[44] Yet the two charters differ so much, quite gratuitously, in their scripts and conventions that only the most expert paleographer would have attributed them to the same scribe. Louis even varied the way he wrote his own name, as the idea of a distinctive signature was unfamiliar in England, where the authenticity of a document depended upon seals and the word of named witnesses.

Some paleographers have attempted to create a more rigid classification of scripts than the documents warrant. Early cursive or court hands have suffered in particular, when they have been described as 'chancery hands'. The assumption behind this term is that cursive script was taught by writing masters in chancery schools. Because there is no evidence in England for the existence of such masters or schools, and little enough for organized chanceries before the last quarter of the twelfth century, some paleographers have relied on dogmatic assertions. For example, the script of Bodleian MS. Savile 21, which is alleged to be that of Robert Grosseteste, has been analysed in two paleographical textbooks. In one the script is described as the type dominant in the chancery of Lincoln cathedral,[45] whereas in the other it is said to have been obviously learned in a chancery school but is too unclear to have satisfied any chancellor.[46] In fact it is not known where Grosseteste learned to write, nor is this writing necessarily his.[47] Other authentic exemplars of Grosseteste's handwriting do exist, however, which demonstrate that he, like other university masters, wrote in a fast cursive script.

To explain the emergence and similarity of such cursive scripts the Hungarian paleographer, I. Hajnal, has advanced an alternative

[43] Conrad of Mure, 'Summa de Arte Prosandi' in *Briefsteller und Formelbücher* ed. L. Rockinger (1863) I, p. 439. Wattenbach, *Schriftwesen*, p. 297.

[44] *Northants. Facs*, plates viii and x. T. A. M. Bishop illustrates the varied handwriting of one royal scribe, see n. 50 below.

[45] N. Denholm-Young, *Handwriting in England and Wales* (1954), plate 11.

[46] S. Harrison Thomson, *Latin Bookhands of the Later Middle Ages* (1969), plate 89.

[47] Hunt, 'The Library of Robert Grosseteste', pp. 133–4.

hypothesis to that of masters teaching in chancery schools.[48] He suggests that writing was taught in the cathedral schools and emerging universities as part of the *ars dictaminis*. Although this hypothesis is difficult to prove, Hajnal at least explains why university masters like Grosseteste wrote a cursive script. Hajnal's hypothesis also places the clerks who wrote charters and business documents in a new perspective, as it implies that many of them were university graduates or 'wandering scholars' who had at least attended a first year course. Writing Latin from dictation was a difficult business, which required a technique different from that of monastic scribes who copied from an exemplar. University students would certainly have acquired this technique, even if it were not specifically taught, in order to write up the lectures they heard. It is possible to point to examples of university graduates, like Becket, who started their careers as secretaries, whereas an English writer trained in a chancery school has yet to be found.[49]

The most careful study of the origin of cursive script in England is T. A. M. Bishop's analysis of twelfth-century royal charters and writs. He shows that these documents were not written in a distinctly royal chancery hand, since one scribe might use a variety of forms and conversely the same scripts were used outside the royal Chancery.[50] He suggests that the cursive forms, which emerge early in the twelfth century, 'are simply the miniscule forms adapted, by the various habits of individual scribes, for the purpose of writing quickly. . . . The cursive is the result of licence, not discipline; it is evidence not of a common training but of something simpler and historically more interesting: a common pressure of urgent business.'[51] Bishop thus rejects the necessity for instruction by writing masters, whether in a chancery or a university school, and argues instead that cursive is a spontaneous development resulting from the proliferation of documents. (Plates II and IV illustrate the development of cursive hands among the scribes of Henry I and King Stephen.)

Accepting Bishop's analysis, the cursive is simply a quicker way of writing and was therefore used wherever speed was important. Hence it became the speciality of those writing offices, like the royal Chancery, which produced the most documents. Cursive was appropriately called 'court hand' by contemporaries because most rapid writing was done by courts, not because it was taught in courts or chanceries. It was not so much the distinctive mark of an official, as a practical way of getting through the business. It is consequently neither surprising, nor a contradiction in terms, to find cursive script being used for writing books from the latter half of the thirteenth century (see plates XVI and XVII). It was quicker, and therefore cheaper, and more familiar to laymen and to

[48] *L'Enseignement de l'écriture aux universités médiévales* ed. L. Mezey (2nd edn, Budapest, 1959).

[49] See ch. 3, n. 5 above and ch. 7, n. 59 below.

[50] *Scriptores Regis* (1961), plate v (the varied handwriting of Scribe xiii) and pp. 9, 14 (Lincoln charters). Similar suggestions had been made by Cheney, *Chanceries*, p. 54. Cf. ch. 2, nn. 47, 48 above.

[51] *Scriptores Regis*, p. 13, cf. pp. 6–7.

those clergy who saw more of business documents than of liturgical books. Some cursive features can even be seen in earlier books, most remarkably in the manuscript in Middle English, *Vices and Virtues*, dating from *c.*1200.[52] Cursive script is thus a product of the shift from memory to written record: the demand was no longer primarily for elaborately copied monastic books, but for documents written economically yet legibly. Saving the scribe's time was a paramount consideration, because labour costs were the principal element in the price of a manuscript. Fine manuscripts written in book hand continued to be produced, however, until they succumbed in the sixteenth century to the joint attack of printing and the destruction of monasticism.

In the conventions used for abbreviating, punctuating, and making alterations or corrections, scribes in this period made minor modifications rather than any major innovation like the cursive script.[53] A great deal of care was taken to check manuscripts for errors. Some readers emended texts as they read them.[54] In cathedrals it was the duty of such officials as the chancellor and the precentor to correct the books in their charge; at Salisbury the income from a virgate of land was assigned to this specific purpose.[55] In the Exchequer, where errors literally meant money, Fitz Neal describes the elaborate provisions for establishing accurate texts.[56] Similarly in the Chancery the senior clerks were supposed to check the writs before they were sealed, having regard to their form (*ratio*), script (*littera*), wording (*dictio*) and spelling (*silliba*).[57] Despite these checks errors in documents, as distinct from books, are quite common, particularly in the royal plea rolls. Even in the spelling of place names, where diversity was tolerated, there were rules. In the Cambridgeshire justices' visitation of 1286 one defendant objected to the plaintiff's writ because it spelt the village of Harston 'Hardlestone scilicet cum *d*';[58] so the plaintiff had to obtain another writ without the offending *d* in the middle.

An important aspect of medieval handwriting, which has not been systematically studied, is bad writing. In particular, incompetently written charters are quite common in the twelfth century and can still be found in the thirteenth (see plate VI). G. Barraclough's facsimiles of Cheshire charters provide good examples.[59] A charter for Poulton abbey in *c.*1146 is written on an irregularly shaped piece of parchment in a shaky hand which cannot keep the lines straight. The last witness, who

[52] C. E. Wright, *English Vernacular Hands* (1960), plate 3. M. B. Parkes, *English Cursive Book Hands* (1969) and Parkes, 'Literacy', p. 563.

[53] In general see L. C. Hector, *The Handwriting of English Documents* (1958), chs. iii and iv and Ker, *English MSS*, ch. vi.

[54] Robert Grosseteste ed. D. A. Callus (1955), frontispiece, illustrates marginal notes and amendments by Grosseteste. References to the correction of scribal errors are collected by Wattenbach, *Schriftwesen*, pp. 317–44.

[55] *Lincoln Cathedral Statutes* ed. H. Bradshaw and C. Wordsworth (1892) I, pp. 284–5. *Register of St Osmund* ed. W. H. Rich-Jones, RS LXXVIII (1883), I, p. 224.

[56] *Dialogus* pp. 18, 28–9, 31, 74, 126.

[57] Fleta, bk ii, ch. 13, p. 125.

[58] *Liber Memorandorum Ecclesie de Bernewelle* ed. J. W. Clark (1907), pp. 155–6.

[59] *Cheshire Facs*, nos. 1, 4(1), 14.

has his name prominently in the centre of the document, is called 'Willelmus Spuens Mendacium'. Judging from the position of this name, 'William Vomiting Falsehood' was presumably the writer; the significance of the name is anybody's guess. The charter of Humfrey, lord of Bunbury, dating from 30 years later, is likewise written in a peculiar script and contains divergent spellings of common Latin words, such as *humagium* for 'homage', *harabilis* for 'arable', and *testebus* instead of *testibus* for 'witnesses'. Equally striking is the charter of Jordan of Cheadle, which was written by Roger the Chaplain, who seems to have been having trouble with his pen and decides in the second line to increase the size of his script. This charter also contains the naive drafting error of describing the boundaries of the land in relation to 'a certain oak which has been uprooted'.[60]

Eccentrically written books, as distinct from charters, are very rare because the scribe of a book was not writing just an occasional page. The strangest book, from the point of view of physical appearance, is the *Ormulum*, which is a series of homilies on the Gospels in Middle English verse. The book was probably penned, as well as being composed, over an extended period around 1200 by Orm himself, who was an Augustinian canon. He writes in an exceptionally large and heavy hand on irregularly shaped pieces of parchment, sometimes of rough quality.[61] Towards the end of the book the script becomes crowded and occasionally runs from one column into the other, with extra words fitted in vertically as well, as if the writer was preoccupied with saving parchment. Although Orm's book has an unprofessional appearance, it is obviously not the product of an illiterate. Writing in English, he had few models to follow and may not have considered appearances important anyway. His book may reflect the ideal of the Augustinian canons of teaching the Gospel in simplicity and poverty.

The problem raised by divergent and amateur documents is what kind of training and practice their writers had. It is often assumed that in the country writing was done by a local monk or clerk who was an expert. But there was little common training in writing or anything else for either monks or secular clergy before about 1200. Monasteries with great *scriptoria*, like Christ Church Canterbury, were exceptional. Not many clerks in the twelfth century could have had experience either of a cathedral school or university or of an organized writing office. By the thirteenth century, on the other hand, average standards of writing improve, presumably because more clerks were getting an appropriate education. At first many monks and secular clergy would have been unfamiliar with business documents like charters, even if they knew a little about books. Had Orm written a charter, he would no doubt have made it look as if it were produced by a semi-literate, which would be a false inference. Perhaps badly written documents principally indicate the difficulties of writing well and emphasize the professional standards

---

[60] See ch. 3, n. 15 above.

[61] J. E. Turville-Petre, 'Studies in the *Ormulum* MS', *Journal of English and Germanic Philology* XLVI (1947), pp. 1–27. Cf. Wright, *English Vernacular Hands*, plate 2.

of the majority of books and charters. To explain how such elegance and consistency were achieved in the majority of local documents remains an outstanding and probably insoluble problem, comparable with explaining how country churches were designed and built as micro-cosms of the great cathedrals.

Layout and format

The commonest sign of an amateur writer is bad layout (see plates I and VI), as the clarity of the message conveyed by the script is enhanced or obscured by this. The incompetently written charters already described all have irregularities of layout. In the twelfth century and earlier some scribes of charters were understandably more accustomed to writing books. This is revealed not only by their book hands, but by their layout. One of Westminster abbey's writs of Edward the Confessor, written just before the Norman Conquest, appears to be the lower portion of a previously ruled leaf of parchment, presumably intended for a book.[62] Similarly a charter of Henry de Portu, dating from 1120–30, is written on a book-sized folio in two columns.[63] The writer was evidently uncertain about this layout and takes his text across the central space, the two columns being used only to make it easier to write in straight lines. Richard Fitz Neal in the *Dialogue of the Exchequer* is as concerned with good layout as he is with other details of office procedure. He was evidently interested in layout as an art form, as he describes a history he claims to have written himself, entitled *Tricolumnis*, because it was arranged in three columns dealing with ecclesiastical, royal and miscel-laneous business respectively.[64] Tabulation by columns, distinguishing different types of subject matter, was a novelty at the time. Thus another contemporary (possibly Gervase of Canterbury) carefully explains the three-column layout he had devised for his *Mappa Mundi*, which was not a representation of the earth's surface, but a gazetteer of religious houses:

> Note that our page is divided as if into three columns. The first column contains the dignities of places, that is, archbishoprics, bishoprics, abbacies and priories. The second lists the names of the places and the saint to whom the church is dedicated. The third shows to which order and habit, and to which mother church, the inmates belong.[65]

This first attempt at a comprehensive list of religious houses was a consequence of the recent increase in their numbers combined with the growing fashion for making surveys and memoranda in writing.

Fitz Neal describes the correct layout for an Exchequer pipe roll, giving details (which can be verified from extant rolls) of how the lines

---

[62] Bishop & Chaplais, plate xxiiib.   [63] *Oxford Facs*, no. 14.

[64] *Dialogus*, p. 27. This history may have been an aspiration of Fitz Neal's rather than a reality.

[65] Gervase II, pp. 417–18.

should be ruled and the headings spaced out.[66] When describing how the name of the sheriff of each county should be engrossed at the head of the enrolment, Fitz Neal used the term *depingitur* (literally, 'depicted') instead of *scribitur* ('written'). The connexion with painting implied by this term is appropriate, as more elaborate letters were used for headings and in some manuscripts they were picked out in red, that is, in rubrics. The use of colour was functional, as well as being an embellishment, because it helped the reader to find his place, as prologues to manuscripts point out. The author of Ramsey abbey's *Book of Benefactors* explains that he has inserted rubrics 'for the notice of readers'; similarly the Barnwell priory register exhorts the diligent reader to use its list of rubrics.[67] The functional use of rubrics, and the elegant layout of headings and paragraphs as a whole, is nowhere better exemplified than in the larger volume of Domesday Book.[68] In manuscripts, as in medieval art in general, function and use went together.

The most elaborate layouts are found in the works of the glossators of the Bible and of Roman and canon law; the glossed Psalter of Eadwine is illustrated as an example of layout at plate XIV. The gloss took definite shape in the twelfth century and grew out of the practice of lecturers and students making explanatory notes in spare space around the texts they studied. A gloss was sometimes written between the lines of the text (an interlinear gloss) as well as in the margins. By the thirteenth century some manuscripts have around their outer borders a gloss on the gloss.[69] A special type of script, which was economical of space but quick to write, was sometimes used for glosses, as has already been mentioned.[70] The successive series of glosses around a central text show, like tree rings, the proliferation of written record over generations of scholars. Whereas the gloss's scholastic companion, the *summa*, aimed to cut through the mass of words to the original core, the gloss did the reverse, as the commentaries swamp the main text.[71] As examples of precise yet elaborate calligraphy, however, medieval glossed books have no rivals. They show how the technology of writing was refined in the twelfth century to meet new needs.

Turning from the layout to the format of the finished writing, changes in both the size and shape of manuscripts occurred. In general the average size of documents and books got smaller. This generalization does not imply that large charters and books were no longer produced, but only that they were no longer typical. In the latter half of the thirteenth century books of smaller size, using a more compressed script and written on thinner parchment, become relatively common.[72] One such volume could contain the texts of three or four volumes of the preceding century. Books of the Bible, students' textbooks and other

---

[66] *Dialogus*, p. 29, cf. pp. 104–5. See the facsimiles of twelfth-century pipe rolls (for the years 1130, 1156, 1167) in C. Johnson and H. Jenkinson, *English Court Hand* (1915) II, plates iva, vb, viii.

[67] *Ramsey*, p. 65. *Liber Memorandorum Ecclesie de Bernewelle*, p. 20.

[68] See ch. 8, n. 122 below.   [69] Duggan, *Decretals*, plate viii.

[70] See n. 42 above.   [71] Smalley, *The Bible*, plate i.

[72] Hunt, 'The Library of Robert Grosseteste', p. 121.

manuals (for instance, collections of English parliamentary statutes) were produced in formats small enough (15cm × 12cm or less) to be carried in the pocket (see plate XVI).[73] It has been suggested that the friars were the force behind the demand for more portable books because they had to move from place to place, yet they were also expected, the Dominicans in particular, to be well read.[74] Students likewise required relatively cheap and portable books. But portability and economy are not a complete explanation for small books, as some of them are elaborately ornamented; illuminated Bibles are among the works most frequently produced in pocket-sized formats.[75]

The basic explanation for books getting smaller is that they were gradually changing their function. The traditional large books were intended to be placed on lecterns and displayed or read aloud in monastic communities. The new smaller formats were designed for individual private study, if they were academic books, or meditation, if they were religious. Although the techniques had been developed for making small books by 1300, the extent of this change should not be exaggerated. Individuals still had few books of any size and reading aloud persisted. Nevertheless, as part of the shift from memory to written record, the emphasis in production had moved by 1300 from large liturgical folios to small intelligible manuals.

In the shapes of documents, as distinct from books, greater numbers likewise brought a reduction in average size and increasing standardization. This is most evident in episcopal charters, where by 1200 scribes almost invariably write on the longer way of an oblong parchment, whereas in the first half of the twelfth century many charters are written on the shorter way. C. R. Cheney summarizes these changes: 'For a century after 1100 we shall see a steady movement from a diplomatically crude to a finished type, from a spacious and extravagant to a small and economical format, from a normal book hand to a businesslike and distinctive charter hand.'[76] The twelfth century was the period when many forms of business document 'took shape', shapes they would retain into the sixteenth century and beyond.

Rolls or books?

In the format of royal documents the most far-reaching change was the use of rolls instead of books.[77] Rolls are so familiar to any medievalist who has worked in the Public Record Office that their existence tends to be taken for granted. Yet there is no evidence that rolls were made by the

[73] Harvard Law Library has a good collection of early pocket books of English statutes: MSS 56–9, 173–5.
[74] C. H. Talbot, 'The Universities and the Medieval Library' in *English Library*, pp. 76–7.
[75] D. Diringer, *The Illuminated Book* (2nd edn, 1967), p. 267.
[76] *Chanceries*, p. 51. Long charters of the first half of the twelfth century are illustrated in *Charters of Norwich Cathedral Priory* ed. B. Dodwell, PRS new series XL (1974), plate iii.
[77] In general see Wattenbach, *Schriftwesen*, pp. 105–74.

royal government before the twelfth century and, in the forms they took, they are peculiar to England. Continental governments, from the papacy downwards, kept their most important records in the form of books not rolls. Consequently when William the Conqueror undertook his *descriptio* of the conquered land, the results were compiled for posterity in volumes, 'Domesday Book', not in rolls. Although some of the preliminary drafts for Domesday Book may possibly have been stitched together into rolls, they were described vaguely as *breves* or *carte* and not as rolls.[78] A special Latin word for the record in roll format came into vogue in the twelfth century at the earliest: it was a *rotulus*.

This word seems to have been brought into general use by Fitz Neal's *Dialogue of the Exchequer*. He describes a variety of types of roll – 'rolls of the treasury' or 'great annual rolls of accounts' (that is, the pipe rolls), 'rolls of the chancery', 'rolls of receipts', the 'lesser rolls of the itinerant justices', and others.[79] To Fitz Neal and his colleagues working in the Exchequer in the 1170s the roll or *rotulus* was evidently a commonplace. Nevertheless the general public were probably unfamiliar both with the name and the thing until Fitz Neal's book made the secrets of the Exchequer plain to his readers. His purpose, he explained in his prologue, was to reveal hidden treasure or the treasury (the Latin *thesaurus* means both 'treasure' and 'treasury') in ordinary language, 'even though it is permissible to invent new terms'.[80] Fitz Neal may not have been aware that *rotulus* was a new term, as it could have been part of the jargon of the Exchequer since his boyhood when his father had been the treasurer of Henry I. Rolls had certainly been made then, as Fitz Neal refers to 'the old annual rolls of that king' and furthermore much of the pipe roll for the fiscal year ending Michaelmas 1130 is still extant.[81]

The novelty of the roll in the twelfth century, outside the Exchequer that is, is suggested by the variety of forms the word takes. Fitz Neal's form, *rotulus*, took time to establish itself as the norm. A certificate confirming acquittance from paying Danegeld, dated the eighth year of Henry II's reign (1162), states that the acquittance was written down at the Exchequer 'in the roll' (*in rollo*).[82] As this statement can be checked with the extant pipe roll and as the acquittance is one of a series of written privileges obtained by Ralf of Caen, who is described by Henry II as 'my clerk', the form *rollus* must have been acceptable in official circles in the 1160s. Early in the thirteenth century, on the other hand, Jocelin of Brakelond uses a feminine form, *rolla*, to describe a bailiff's roll and also to describe 'the great roll of Winchester'.[83] The latter description is strange, as the context shows that this 'great roll' is

[78] For the Domesday drafts see ch. 1, nn. 32–5 above. For early meanings of *breve* see nn. 86–7 below.

[79] *Dialogus*, pp. 17, 62, 70.   [80] *ibid.* pp. 5, 6. Cf. n. 85 below.

[81] *ibid.* p. 42; cf. ch. 5, n. 22 below. *Magnum Rotulum Scaccarii de Anno 31 Henry I* ed. J. Hunter, RC (1835).

[82] *The Registrum Antiquissimum of the Cathedral Church of Lincoln* ed. C. W. Foster, Lincoln Record S. xxvii (1931), I, p. 73, no. 120.

[83] Jocelin, pp. 101, 46. Concerning this bailiff's roll see ch. 3, n. 67 above.

Domesday Book. Perhaps Jocelin did not know that Domesday was in the form of a book, or alternatively *rolla* may have meant for him any sort of formal record. Some years earlier, in the 1180s, Alan prior of Christ Church Canterbury had likewise referred to the 'roll of Winchester', using another variant, *rotula*. Although the context is obscure, this reference may also be to Domesday Book, since Alan was arguing that the muniments and privileges of the whole English church would be subverted if they had to accord with 'that roll' (*rotulam illam*).[84] An alternative possibility is that Alan was referring to a pipe roll or some other form of Exchequer record kept at Winchester.

These rare and scattered references suggest that until the thirteenth century writers were uncertain about how a roll should be described in Latin and some of them may also have been unclear about what a roll really was in the royal bureaucratic sense. The royal records were not available for public inspection then as they are now. A sheriff answering at the Exchequer would certainly have seen the clerks writing things down, but he would not necessarily have understood how the rolls were compiled until Fitz Neal revealed these 'holy mysteries' in his book.[85] Fitz Neal implies moreover that confusion about the nomenclature of the rolls had existed even in the Exchequer itself, as he remarks at one point that the 'so called exaction roll' (*rotulus qui exactorius dicitur*) is also named *breve de firmis*.[86] The word *breve* (originally associated with 'abbreviation') came to mean a writ or short letter, as distinct from a roll, in the course of the twelfth century. It is possible that the 'exaction roll', which listed the sheriffs' farms, may have been the oldest written record used in the Exchequer and had been called a *breve* before the word *rotulus* came into vogue. Monastic obituary rolls in the late eleventh and early twelfth centuries were likewise sometimes described as *brevia* or *breves*.[87]

An apparent exception to the rule that the word *rotulus* only came into general use in Fitz Neal's time is a writ of Henry I's dating from as early as 1110. It instructs Richard de Monte to allow the abbot of Westminster ten shillings of the royal alms, 'as it is in my rolls' (*in rotulis meis*).[88] If this writ were entirely genuine, it would suggest that the word *rotulus* and the habit of referring to the royal rolls were already established in the second decade of the twelfth century. However,

[84] *Alani Prioris Cantuariensis Postea Abbatis Tewkesberiensis* ed. I. A. Giles (1846), p. 42, letter to Robert de Hardres. This may refer to a dispute between Canterbury and Lincoln, as Robert was a keeper of the vacant bishopric of Lincoln in 1184–6 (*Pipe Roll 31 Henry II*, p. 125; *32 Henry II*, p. 83; *33 Henry II*, p. 77), or alternatively to a dispute between the Hardres family and Christ Church, as suggested by W. Urry, *Canterbury under the Angevin Kings* (1967), p. 61. Henry II called Alan 'a second pope' because of his championship of ecclesiastical rights in 1184, Gervase I, p. 313.

[85] Among the 'sacramentorum latibula' of the Exchequer Fitz Neal includes 'rotulorum conscriptio', *Dialogus*, p. 26, cf. p. 126.

[86] *ibid*. p. 62. The purpose of this record 'of farms' is explained at *ibid*. p. 125 and by R. L. Poole, *The Exchequer in the Twelfth Century* (1912), p. 131.

[87] *Dictionary of Medieval Latin from British Sources* ed. R. E. Latham (1975) I, p. 216.

[88] J. Armitage Robinson, *Gilbert Crispin Abbot of Westminster* (1911), p. 149, no. 32. *RRA-N* II (1956), p. 116, no. 1053.

the text of the writ is suspect for a number of reasons. Firstly it is in favour of Westminster abbey which was a centre of forgery. Secondly it has a postscript saying, allow 'this also every year', whereas an authentic writ would probably have made this concession an integral part of the text. By the same token the phrase, 'as it is in my rolls', may be a later interpolation. The comparable certificate of acquittance for Ralf of Caen states that it is written *in rollo*, that is, in the roll of a specified year, and not *in rotulis* in general. It would have been tempting for a copyist – and this Westminster writ exists only in a copy – to insert the phrase, 'as it is in my rolls', and the postscript into the text of a genuine writ of Henry I. Westminster abbey's dilemma may well have been that Henry I had indeed made this grant, but in subsequent reigns a writ of this sort would have required the supporting evidence of the pipe rolls. A Westminster monk therefore supplied this evidence as best he could by inserting a vague reference to 'my rolls', even though Henry I may not have had any rolls at the time the writ was issued. R. L. Poole used this Westminster writ as evidence that the pipe rolls had existed since the second decade of the twelfth century, but it could be used just as well to argue the contrary.[89]

To summarize the argument so far, the pipe rolls of the Exchequer, which were created at some unknown time by Henry I's government, seem to be the prototype for royal records in roll form in England. Whether they were started in the decade 1100–1110 (as the Westminster writ implies if it is genuine) or in the decade 1120–30 (as the extant roll for 1130 might suggest) is an unresolvable problem. Either way there is no evidence of royal records in roll form before the reign of Henry I. At whatever date the Exchequer rolls were started, moreover, we should not assume that their form and purpose was generally understood until Fitz Neal revealed the 'holy mysteries' of the Exchequer in Henry II's reign.

Nevertheless records in roll form were not entirely unknown in England before 1100. The earliest roll now extant was begun in the decade preceding 1088; it records professions of obedience by suffragan bishops to the archbishop of Canterbury.[90] Likewise another Canterbury roll, informing the archbishop of elections to bishoprics, contains some membranes from the 1090s.[91] As the former of these rolls dates from Archbishop Lanfranc's pontificate, it may have originated from his interest in the reform of books and records. Until they grew in length over the years, rolls like the Canterbury ones would not have been seen as startling innovations. Rolling up a membrane of parchment was the easiest and most obvious way of storing it. Moreover, the roll had ancient origins, as it had been the usual format of writings in the Graeco-Roman world. But the layout and material of ancient and

---

[89] *The Exchequer in the Twelfth Century*, pp. 37–8.
[90] Canterbury Dean and Chapter Archives, Chartae Antiquae C.117, described by M. Richter, *Canterbury Professions*, Canterbury & York S. LXVII (1973), pp. xxvi–xxvii, and by Ker, *English MSS*, p. 17 and plate 6a.
[91] BL MS. Harley Roll A.3, described by Ker, *English MSS*, p. 17 and plate 6b.

medieval rolls differed, as the text was written in ancient rolls in columns on the longer way of the papyrus, whereas in medieval rolls it was written from the head to the tail of the parchment.

The roll was also the most convenient format for conveying a message or letter in parchment. It was customary for monasteries to send a messenger from house to house, collecting an accumulating series of obituaries forming a roll when an abbot died. A long roll of this sort, commemorating Matilda, first abbess of William the Conqueror's nunnery at Caen, was taken on an extensive tour of England soon after her death in 1113.[92] Although this roll disappeared at the French Revolution, that of Abbot Vitalis of Savigny (who died in 1122) survives and bears over 70 inscriptions from English monasteries.[93] It was perhaps an obituary roll of a comparable type that St Dunstan's biographer had in mind a century earlier when he described the saint having a vision, presaging King Edgar's death, of a man carrying a great *prolixe cartule rotella* covered all over with letters.[94] This is the earliest example of the use of the word 'roll' (*rotella* in this instance) in England. But his example also suggests that the word was unfamiliar to the biographer's readers, since he explains that the *rotella* was of *prolixe cartule*, literally meaning 'a roll of prolix little charter'. If rolls had already been common for writing purposes, it would not have been necessary to add that this one was covered with letters like a charter.

Despite the use of rolls for monastic obituaries, there was a prejudice against them which makes it surprising that the roll was adopted as the format for the most important royal records. The parchment roll was the characteristic format for the copies of the Jewish law read in synagogues and had been so since antiquity. In twelfth-century legal procedure in England the Jew was distinguished from the Christian by the fact that he took an oath 'on his roll',[95] whereas the Christian swore on the book of the Gospel. Similarly the prophets of the Old Testament were depicted in painting and sculpture holding rolls.[96] This was not an insignificant distinction, as the Bible had been written in the form of a book almost since the historical beginnings of Christianity, probably deliberately in order to distinguish it from both Jewish and pagan works in rolls.[97] In the rare instances where Christ is depicted holding a roll instead of a book in medieval manuscripts, he is usually intended to represent the God of the Old Testament. Thus the minature in the Winchester Bible of the Christ of the Gothic Majesty, holding a rolled-up scroll in his left hand and an opened one is his right, depicts God calling the prophet Isaiah; Isaiah is appropriately shown as a Jew both by his hat and by the

[92] *Rouleaux des Morts* ed. L. Delisle, Société de l'Histoire de France cxxxv (1866), pp. 177–279. This Matilda was not a daughter of William the Conqueror, as stated by Delisle.

[93] Facsimile ed. L. Delisle (1909). Ker, *English MSS*, p. 16.

[94] *Memorials of St Dunstan* ed. W. Stubbs, RS LXIII (1874), p. 46.

[95] 'super rotulum suum', e.g. Stubbs, *Charters*, p. 256.

[96] E.g. Kauffmann, *Romanesque MSS*, plates 275–6, 279–80, 285.

[97] C. H. Roberts, 'Books in the Graeco-Roman World' in *The Cambridge History of the Bible* ed. P. R. Ackroyd and C. F. Evans (1970) I, pp. 57ff.

scroll.[98] In the Bury Bible similarly the distinction between the new dispensation and the old is made in Ezechiel's vision by depicting Christ in majesty bearing a book, while Ezechiel is placed at his feet holding up a scroll.[99] Rolls bore the old law and books the new.

The faithful were reminded of the image of Christ in majesty bearing the Book of Judgment whenever they went to church, as that was how Christ was most commonly depicted in Romanesque art. William the Conqueror's book was appropriately called 'Domesday' because it reminded people of that Last Judgment.[100] Had Domesday Book been in the form of a roll, it might not have been so readily compared with holy writ. This suggestion should not be exaggerated, however, as royal rolls were themselves being compared with Scripture before the end of the twelfth century. When Fitz Neal explains that not even the king's justices may alter their rolls, once they have been delivered to the treasurer, he recalls the Gospel's warning that not one iota of the law shall pass away.[101] The Exchequer may have had the odd effect of hallowing the roll format in England.

The idea of making the pipe rolls probably originated not directly from the Jews, though that is a possibility, but from cosmopolitan arithmeticians who were familiar with Arabic practice. One suggestion is that Adelard of Bath, who introduced Arabic works on astronomy and geometry to the west, may have been an official in Henry I's Exchequer.[102] Another candidate is the royal clerk, Thurkil, who knew Hugh de Bocland, the sheriff of Essex from 1101 and perhaps earlier.[103] Thurkil's treatise on the abacus is addressed to his colleague, Simon de Rotol.[104] 'Rotol' might either be extended to 'Rotolanda', meaning 'of Rutland', or to 'Rotolis', meaning 'of the Rolls'. If the latter extension is accepted, Simon may have been the first maker or keeper of the pipe rolls. Thurkil and Simon had a common master, described only as Guillelmus R., the greatest living arithmetician; he may have been William, bishop of Syracuse in Sicily, which had just been conquered from the Arabs.[105] These scraps of information cannot satisfactorily explain the origin of the pipe rolls, but they are consistent with the hypothesis that their format was non-Christian.

The problem of origins has further complexities because the pipe rolls are in a unique format. The term *rotulus* does not describe a continuous series of membranes of parchment, which are stitched head to tail to form a length of four metres or more, like the Chancery rolls. Instead an Exchequer *rotulus* consists of two membranes only, stitched together to form a length of less than two metres.[106] Each *rotulus* comprised the

[98] fo. 131. Kauffmann, *Romanesque MSS*, plate 238.

[99] Kauffmann, *Romanesque MSS*, plate 153 or Boase, *English Art*, plate 54b.

[100] See ch. 1, n. 27 above.

[101] *Dialogus*, p. 77. Matthew ch. 5, verse 18.

[102] Poole, *The Exchequer in the Twelfth Century*, pp. 56–7. Haskins, *Studies in the History of Medieval Science*, pp. 34–5.

[103] Haskins, *ibid*. pp. 328–9.

[104] *ibid*. p. 327.   [105] *ibid*. p. 329.

[106] *Dialogus*, p. 29. For facsimiles of pipe rolls see n. 66 above.

account of a different county or bailiwick. When all the accounts for the year had been written, the different *rotuli* were piled one on top of another and secured at their heads with cords. As the lower ends are left free, referring from the face to the dorse of a particular *rotulus* is easier than on a continuous roll. Although the Exchequer had thus adopted a form of record which was easier to consult than a continuous roll, its style did not become the norm. A simplification of it, using one membrane instead of two per *rotulum* was adopted by the law courts for their plea rolls in the 1190s, but not by the Chancery in the next decade. Furthermore, when receipt rolls were introduced at the Exchequer in Henry II's reign, they were made into continuous rolls at first, as is evident from the fragments extant for Michaelmas term 1185.[107] The consequence of these haphazard developments is that in the thirteenth century the royal government made rolls in two principal formats – Exchequer style (the membranes piled on top of each other) and Chancery style (the membranes stitched head to tail in a continuous length).

These technicalities suggest that the reason why medieval England, alone in Europe, kept its records predominantly in rolls remains largely a mystery. Convenience is not a good explanation, as continuous rolls are not convenient to consult. The folded parchment forming a quire, which was the basic component of a medieval book, was as convenient as any form of roll. Nor is economy in parchment a sufficient explanation, as the pieces from which the pipe rolls were made were of exceptional size. Economy in binding costs is a possibility, but that has to be balanced against the cost of making protective covers for the rolls. Rolls had short-term advantages, which might originally have made them attractive: the separate membranes of which they were composed could be of slightly differing sizes, and they could be compiled separately by different clerks and then stitched together in appropriate order, whereas the scribe of a book had to proceed from one page of his quire to the next. As various formats of roll were used by different departments of the royal government by the time of King John, habit and precedent seem the best general explanations, although they do not explain why certain decisions were taken in the first place. Once these distinctive formats had been established, bureaucracy ensured that they remained unchanged for centuries.

In the thirteenth century other authorities followed the lead of the royal government in keeping records on rolls (see plates IX, X and XI). Sometimes they were evidently unsure about which form of royal roll to imitate. Thus among borough records the earliest guild rolls, those of Leicester (starting in 1196), are made up in Chancery style, whereas the second earliest, those of Shrewsbury (starting in 1209), are in Exchequer style;[108] the custumal of Exeter (dating from the 1230s) combines

---

[107] Ed. H. Hall (1899). These are fragments of two rolls, one measuring about 6 metres and the other 3 metres.

[108] G. H. Martin, 'The English Borough in the Thirteenth Century', *TRHS* 5th series XIII (1963), pp. 132, 135. Leicester's rolls begin before the Chancery rolls, but they may not have been made up into a roll until after 1200.

both styles.[109] Similarly the earliest part of the first bishop's register (starting between 1214 and 1217), that of Hugh of Wells, bishop of Lincoln, is in Chancery style, but one subsequent part is in Exchequer style and the *Liber Antiquus* is in book format; contemporaries probably did not think of these diverse records as forming one register.[110] By the end of the century the book format had become usual for bishop's registers, probably in order to bring them into line with continental and papal practice. Likewise the royal government itself seemed to acknowledge in the thirteenth century that rolls were not necessarily the best way to keep records. Material from rolls was copied into books, such as the remembrance books of the Exchequer, to make consultation easier.[111] Moreover, new classes of record were made into books instead of rolls; the best example are the Wardrobe books of Edward I, which contain the sort of financial details which might have gone on to the pipe rolls in Henry I's reign.[112]

Roll formats were also used for types of record other than accounts and memoranda of proceedings. A few cartularies, both monastic and lay, are in rolls, as are some monastic chronicles and narratives.[113] This practice is understandable, as such documents are akin to records. Equally understandable are those texts for which the roll format was more suitable than the book. For example, histories of the kings of England were produced in the thirteenth century in long rolls. They were perhaps intended for laymen of restricted literacy, as they depict the kings in a series of roundels with a brief commentary beneath each picture (see plate XIII).[114] When the roll is fully unfurled, the whole history of England, from its mythical foundation by the Trojans down to the reign of Edward I, is displayed as a continuous line. The most spectacular example of pictorial narrative in a roll is the life of St Guthlac of Crowland (probably dating from the late twelfth century), which depicts the life of the saint in a series of roundels without a commentary; its precise purpose is unknown.[115]

Occasionally ordinary texts appear in roll format. One pictorial history of England has on its dorse the Anglo-Norman romance, *Amadas et Ydoine*.[116] This combination is not really strange, as history and

[109] *The Anglo-Norman Custumal of Exeter* ed. J. W. Schopp (1925).

[110] *Rotuli Hugonis de Welles* ed. W. P. W. Phillimore, Canterbury & York S. I (1909) or Lincoln Record S. III (1912), I, p. iii, Cf. ch. 2 n. 93 above.

[111] See ch. 3, nn. 97–8 above.

[112] The earliest extant Wardrobe book dates from 1285–6, ed. B. F. and C. R. Byerly, *Records of the Wardrobe and Household*, HMSO (1977), pp. 1–116. An inventory in 1300 lists 18 such books, *Book of Prests*, p. 228.

[113] G. R. C. Davis, *Medieval Cartularies of Great Britain* (1958), e.g. nos. 407 (Flaxley abbey), 1188A (Ralf Basset). A chronicle associated with Thornton abbey (begun in ?1289) is in a roll, ed. T. Wright, *Feudal Manuals of English History* (1872), pp. 88–124, as is Durham cathedral priory's account of its litigation *v*, Bishop Anthony Bek, ed. R. K. Richardson, *Camden Miscellany* Camden S. 3rd series XXXIV (1924), pp. 1–58. Cf. Wattenbach, *Schriftwesen*, pp. 167–9.

[114] *Feudal Manuals* pp. ixff. Smalley, *Historians*, p. 178.

[115] *The Guthlac Roll* ed. G. Warner, Roxburghe Club (1928). Cf. ch. 8, n. 17 below.

[116] *Feudal Manuals*, p. xv.

romance were closely connected in the mind of the lay reader. More bizarre are legal and managerial textbooks in the form of continuous rolls: the Harvard Law School has a mid-thirteenth century text of *Glanvill* 293 cm long and St John's College, Cambridge, has Walter of Henley's *Husbandry* 223 cm long.[117] Here again perhaps lay land-owners, who were more familiar with records than with traditional books, did not consider it strange or inconvenient to have texts in this form. Thus one copy (dating from early in the fourteenth century) of Walter of Bibbesworth's rhyming French vocabulary, which was intended to improve the French of the gentry, is in the form of a roll 268 cm long.[118] It is unusually narrow (10 cm wide) and the tail is slotted into a length of wood, with knobs at each end, which serves as a winder. When tightly wound up, this roll can be held in the palm of the hand.

An even smaller and earlier roll (less than 8 cm wide and 56 cm long) has written on one side of it *The Song of the Barons* in French (composed in c. 1263) and on the other side the oldest secular play extant in English, the *Interludium de Clerico et Puella*.[119] Very probably this roll was made so small so that it could be carried by a wandering minstrel in his pouch as part of his repertoire. Its chance survival (until 1971 when it went missing from the British Museum) is a reminder of the thousands of little rolls of parchment, containing memoranda of all sorts, which supplied the material for more formal books. On the threshold of literacy, among knights and minstrels as distinct from monks and clerks, writings were perhaps at first more familiar and inviting in the form of rolls containing short vernacular texts than in the form of weighty Latin books. The contents of a little roll could be seen at a glance and readily grasped in the hand, whereas traditional liturgical books had been kept on lecterns or locked up in monastic sacristies.

In Spenser's *Faery Queen* Eumnestes, the sage of infinite remembrance, inhabits a ruined chamber which

> ... all was hangd about with rolls,
> And old records from ancient times derivd,
> Some made in books, some in long parchment scrolls,
> That were all worm-eaten and full of canker holes.[120]

Spenser wrote when the Middle Ages were just beginning to be gothicized and made picturesque. To the Elizabethans the twin format of English parchment documents, rolls and books, seemed as old as time itself. In fact these records took their distinctive shapes in the twelfth century. A pedantic historian or archivist might also comment that, on the whole, the real records of medieval England have been preserved in better condition than Eumnestes kept his.

[117] Harvard Law Library MS. 180. St John's College (MS. N.13, cf. *Walter of Henley*, pp. 37–8.

[118] BL MS. Sloan 809. For Walter of Bibbesworth see ch. 6, nn. 1–2.

[119] BL MS. Additional 23986. *The Political Songs of England* ed. T. Wright, Camden S 1st series VI (1839), pp. 59–63, 356–8, and ed. I. S. T. Aspin, Anglo-Norman Text S. XI (1953), pp. 12–23. Bennett & Smithers, pp. 196–200, 370–73.

[120] Bk ii, canto ix, verse 57.

Although some medieval records have been attacked by vermin, and many more have been lost or damaged by neglect, parchment has proved a remarkably durable material. This particular characteristic of it was recognized from the start by medieval scribes, whose illuminated manuscripts, like the *Book of Kells* and the *Lindisfarne Gospels*, became a talisman of Christian endurance in the Dark Ages. The initial difficulty of applying script to parchment combined with the circumstances of the time to make writing the special art of monks in Anglo-Saxon England, as elsewhere in western Europe. When documents began to be required on an unprecedented scale after the Norman Conquest, the skills of monastic scribes were adapted and extended to meet these new needs.

Surprisingly perhaps, both the traditional methods of writing and the materials, in particular parchment, showed themselves to be flexible as well as durable. It proved possible to produce parchment in varying qualities relatively cheaply and also to cut, stitch and fold it into shapes ranging from the great Winchester Bible and the pipe rolls to pocket-sized manuals for lawyers or preachers and tightly rolled royal writs no larger than a man's little finger. Similarly the cursive script, essential to secular clerks who had to write fast from dictation, was adapted from traditional book hand and not consciously invented. The price of adaptation, as contrasted with planned innovation, was a variety of styles of writing and formats of document, which were perpetuated when they settled down into bureaucratic routine. There is more history than logic in the miscellany of styles of document preserved in the Public Record Office.

On the other hand, an advantage of adapting existing practice was that the makers of medieval records had in parchment a writing medium which was better suited to long texts than the clay bricks and stone tablets of the ancient world, yet was stronger than papyrus. Moreover, the new secular documents, from Domesday Book onwards, inherited much of the respect and even awe which had been accorded to liturgical books in the monastic tradition. Some charters at first were layed out like pages of Gospel books and the finest secular legal and literary texts continued to be indistinguishable in physical appearance from other illuminated manuscripts. The growth, from the monastic *scriptorium*, of new branches and styles of writing was probably the chief reason why documents became acceptable to the laity, and upon that acceptance the future extension of literacy depended.

It is a facile speculation to assume that paper or printing, had they been readily available in 1100, would have automatically accelerated the growth of literacy faster than parchment. The initial and most difficult task was to make the laity, knights in the countryside typically, accustomed to writing. Traditionally such men respected monks, though they did not aspire to be like them, and gave them lands on their deathbeds or in time of peril. Traditionally too the monks symbolized these gifts with Gospel books and recorded them in charters. When documents produced by the king's government began to proliferate in the twelfth century, they also were accepted because, by and large, they used traditional materials and skills. The changes which were made in the technology of writing in the twelfth and thirteenth centuries went largely unnoticed by contemporaries. They were subtle and technical and have necessitated discussion in this chapter of parchments, scripts, layouts, and so on. But because known methods of writing were adapted and extended, rather than revolutionized, fundamental changes in this most conservative area of human skills were set in motion. Techniques of writing records tended to be conservative because conservation was their main purpose.

5

The preservation and use of documents

Documents do not automatically become records. Writing may be done for ephemeral purposes without any intention of keeping the documents permanently. In modern societies, where mass literacy is normal, most writings are made for purposes of immediate communication or short-term administrative convenience; when the message has been received or the obligation discharged, the piece of paper recording it is generally thrown away. Most people are literate, to a minimal standard, but relatively few documents are kept for long. The situation in the Middle Ages was the reverse of the modern one: there were fewer literates, but a larger proportion of their writings were intended to be preserved for posterity.

Medieval writing materials themselves made the scribe conscious of time. Because he was presented with the alternatives of wax or parchment as a medium, he made an initial choice between the ephemeral and the permanent. Notes written on wax tablets were necessarily transitory, whereas the fair copy on parchment was obviously durable. To write on parchment was therefore to make a lasting memorial: to commit 'bare and transient words' to script with its 'tenacious letters', as Adam of Eynsham says in the prologue to his life of St Hugh of Lincoln.[1] Modern paper, on the other hand, which is used for both notes and fair copies and is constantly disposed of, does not make the writer feel that he is producing a permanent record. Even when printing gives a modern work a physical permanence comparable with that of parchment manuscripts, the modern writer is more concerned with printing's ability to reach a wide audience in the present than with the transmission of his work, in a unique copy like a medieval manuscript, to posterity. Because parchment manuscripts were rare and special in the eleventh century and earlier, they were valued in a way which no modern literate can fully appreciate.

Monastic documents for posterity

The presupposition that documents were primarily records to be transmitted to posterity depended not only on the durability of parchment as

[1] Ed. D. L. Douie and H. Farmer (1961), p. 1.

a material, but on writing skills being so closely connected with monasticism. Before the Norman Conquest, and for a century after it, the majority of writers (in every sense of that word) were monks. In monasteries scribes had not been much concerned with using their skills for day-to-day business, the things of this world, but with making liturgical books for worship and with keeping in charters and chronicles a record, for future generations of monks, of the working of God's providence as revealed in gifts and portents. Documents were more often dedicated or addressed to God or to posterity than to individual contemporaries. Monasticism gave writers the humility or the arrogance, depending on one's point of view, to care about posterity. Their acute awareness of the passage of time is expressed in numerous chronicles. 'With the loss of books', says Orderic Vitalis, 'the deeds of the ancients pass into oblivion ... with the changing world, as hail or snow melt in the waters of a swift river swept away by the current never to return.'[2] Although these phrases are variations on a theme appropriate to a chronicler's *apologia*, they probably express a point of view which was as deeply felt as it was familiar.

As most early charters concerned gifts to monasteries, they were drafted by monks in similar terms, sometimes at length, as in this notification by William de Braose of a grant to Sele priory in the mid-twelfth century:

> Since memory is frail, and as the sage has said 'old age runs in from the first', it is necessary that things which are said or done be reinforced by the evidence of letters, so that neither length of time nor the ingenuity of posterity can obscure the notice of past events.[3]

A century later charters had become sufficiently commonplace for Bracton, the lawyer, to express the same idea more succinctly: 'Gifts are sometimes made in writings, that is in charters, for perpetual remembrance, because the life of man is but brief and in order that the gift may be more easily proved.'[4]

The fact that most monastic charters and chronicles are exclusively concerned with property rights and worldly events does not invalidate the rule that their makers had a religious purpose. Even Matthew Paris, whose work combines a broad and fascinated interest in English and European politics with a narrow and acquisitive concern for the aggrandizement of his house and his order, thought of his chronicle as an instrument of divine providence. In 1250 he decided to stop writing because 25 half-centuries had passed since the Incarnation. So he wrote an endpiece to the *Chronica Majora*, which typically combines a concern for posterity with a dedication to God and his saints: 'Here end the chronicles of Brother Matthew Paris, monk of St Albans, which he has committed to writing for the use of succeeding generations, for the love

---

[2] Orderic, bk vi, ch. 9, vol. iii, p. 284.
[3] *Oxford Facs*, no. 11. Cf. ch. 9, n. 1 below and the similar preamble to *ibid*. no. 6 (also for Sele priory) cited by Galbraith, *Studies*, p. 29.
[4] Bracton, fo. 33b, vol. ii, p. 108.

of God and the honour of St Alban, protomartyr of the English, lest age or oblivion destroy the memory of modern events.'[5] Although Matthew started writing again almost immediately, there is no reason to think that his attempted ending in 1250 was insincere. He, like other chroniclers, wrote in the face of God and was motivated by the wish to give himself and his fellow monks, who lived under the protection of St Alban, a place in the divine unfolding of events.

Monks were so worldly because they considered themselves and the property of their houses to belong to God, who would support them in their battle with the 'world', which consisted of everyone else. Writings served as a memorial of their triumphs or as a warning of their difficulties: 'Because it is certain that man's memory is frail, it is a valuable labour to put some things in writing, which can be profitable and useful to our church, so that our brethren, present and future, may be assisted in their difficulties by looking at this little book.'[6] This explanation comes from the prologue to Barnwell priory's *Liber Memorandorum*, which was compiled in the 1290s to serve as a precedent book for litigation. No monastic book could be more worldly. Yet its author, like Matthew Paris, declares his place in time – the sun is setting, the world is declining into senility, charity grows cold – and proposes to help God's servants, by which he means the canons of Barnwell, in their struggle against the cruel and wicked world, by which he means their lawsuits against their neighbours. For monks, writing had an ulterior motive; it was a providential instrument, rather than a merely convenient form of communication.

Monks would not have understood the modern demand for mass literacy. There was no point in teaching writing to people who would never have anything worth committing to the permanence of script. What was written down was carefully selected. The annalist should write 'what he thinks truest and best to be passed down to the notice of posterity', one monastic chronicle advised.[7] Similarly Gervase of Canterbury distinguished between memorable events (*memorabilia*) and those worth remembering (*memoranda*); only the latter which are really worthy of memory should be recorded.[8] So far from advocating the mass production of literates or documents, the monastic writer aimed to use records to convey to posterity a deliberately created and rigourously selected version of events. Thus Eadmer, who believed it 'to be a great thing to commit to the memory of letters the events of our times for the use of students in the future', deliberately omitted many business letters from his life of St Anselm because he considered them unworthy of more than a mention.[9] Likewise Anselm himself would not send copies of all his letters to Theodoric, the monk of Christ Church Canterbury who was collecting them, 'because I do not think it useful for

[5] Matthew Paris v, p. 197. R. Vaughan, *Matthew Paris* (1958), pp. 52–9.
[6] Ed. J. W. Clark (1907), p. 37. Cf. below nn. 131–2.
[7] *Annales Monastici* IV, p. 355. Cf. ch. 3, nn. 82–3 above.
[8] Gervase I, p. 89. Cf. ch. 3, nn. 79–81 above.
[9] *Historia*, p. 1. *Vita*, p. 32.

them to be preserved.'[10] Awareness of posterity made monks destroyers as well as preservers of writings.

The same preoccupation with posterity led to the forgery or alteration of documents. If a monastic house required a writing to support its title to some property in a lawsuit, an appropriate charter would be created. A historian today will say that such a charter is a forgery, as indeed it is, but its makers probably felt that it had been written just like their other charters and chronicles to justify the ways of God to men. As God and the patron saint wished the particular monastic house to flourish, they also wished to provide the means to fight the world with the world's weapons. Thus Eadmer was an accessory to forging papal bulls which supported Canterbury's claims to primacy over York.[11] The monks of Canterbury were very worried by the challenge from York, Eadmer explains, so they put their trust in God and discovered by divine revelation in some ancient Gospel books (which were sacred objects in themselves) about a dozen papal bulls, ranging in date from the seventh century to the tenth, which supported their cause. These Eadmer cites verbatim, because what had been found in the archives of the church was well worth commending to the memory of posterity. He adds that some even older documents had also been discovered but, as some of these were of papyrus and had grown illegible with age or were written in a script which he could not understand, he reluctantly refrained from citing them. Eadmer probably did not forge the papal bulls himself, but he added these corroborative details which made the story credible.

Monasteries experienced fortunate losses of documents as well as fortunate finds. The Crowland chronicle ascribed to Abbot Ingulf, which is itself a complex tissue of fact and forgery, records that a fire in 1091 destroyed the abbey's Anglo-Saxon royal charters and other muniments numbering nearly 400 documents.[12] Fortunately, however, Ingulf had removed several duplicates of these charters from the archive some years earlier in order to instruct the younger monks in Old English. These duplicates had therefore been preserved and upon them Crowland based its claims. This is an ingenious story, as there was indeed a fire at Crowland in 1091 which destroyed many books (as Orderic Vitalis attested at the time),[13] and it is probable that Crowland, like other great abbeys, made an effort to keep Old English alive after the Norman Conquest. Moreover, Crowland abbey did not claim that these charters were originals, but duplicates, and that explained any deficiencies in them. Similarly in its dispute with York, Canterbury claimed that it had only been left with duplicates of some documents because ancient papal bulls had been destroyed in a fire in 1067.[14]

The least credible story of a document's disappearance comes from

[10] N. F. Cantor, *Church, Kingship and Lay Investiture in England* (1958), p. 169.

[11] *Historia*, pp. 261–76. R. W. Southern, 'The Canterbury Forgeries', *EHR* LXXIII (1958), pp. 217–26. Cf. n. 35 and ch. 9, n. 72 below.

[12] *Ingulph's Chronicle* trans. H. T. Riley (1854), p. 201.

[13] Orderic, bk iv, vol. ii, p. 346. M. Chibnall (*ibid.* pp. xxv–vi) discusses the authenticity of *Ingulph's Chronicle*.

[14] Eadmer, *Historia*, p. 296.

Matthew Paris.[15] He reports that in the time of Abbot Eadmer (in
c.1010) a cache of books and rolls, written in an unfamiliar language,
were discovered in a cavity in a wall among some Roman foundations at
St Albans. Fortunately an old priest, named Unwona, was found who
could read this ancient British language. All the texts except one contained invocations to pagan Gods, such as Phoebus and Mercury, and
they were therefore burned. The remaining one turned out to be the
story of St Alban himself, which the old priest translated from British
into Latin for Eadmer and his brethren. But once the Latin translation
had been noted down, 'the original and primitive exemplar – strange to
relate – was suddenly and irretrievably reduced to dust and collapsed
annihilated.' It is entirely credible that Roman remains were found at St
Albans, and even possible that documents may have been preserved in a
wall cavity. On the other hand, the finding of an old priest with unique
knowledge of a lost language, and the initial survival of the finds when
first exposed to air, strain credulity too far. Perhaps the story started
with the discovery of some Roman remains which disintegrated when
exposed to the air.

Monks' propensity to forgery does not imply that they are unreliable
in all their statements, but only in those which particularly concern the
honour of their patron saint or the status of their house. Where there
was doubt, they were determined to establish the truth for posterity. By
truth about the past they meant what really should have happened. For a
monastic house there was a providential truth, which was higher than
the random facts from which a twentieth-century historian, motivated
by mere worldly curiosity, attempts to piece together what happened in
the past. Essentially there is no inconsistency between Eadmer of Canterbury's or Matthew Paris's religious concern for posterity and their
readiness to be accessories to forgery. The problem of forging documents
is more fully discussed in chapter 9. The fact it illustrates in the present
context is that for monks the primary purpose of writing was to inform,
or misinform, posterity. Thus the monastic approach to records was
ambivalent: documents were created and carefully conserved so that
posterity might know about the past, but they were not necessarily
allowed to accumulate by natural accretion over time nor to speak for
themselves, because the truth was too important to leave to chance.

Secular documents for daily use

Documents such as taxation lists or injunctions to officials, which were
primarily intended for administrative use at the time they were made
rather than being directed to posterity, obviously have a different function from monastic writings. The early development of such documents
in medieval England is hard to trace, partly because writing had been
used in such a different way in the monastic tradition. Administrative
documents may have been in circulation long before they were kept,

[15] *Gesta Abbatum Monasterii St Albani* ed. H. T. Riley, RS XXVIII (1867), I, pp. 26–
27.

since they would not have been thought worthy of preserving like monastic charters. Alternatively administrative documents may have developed only with the greatest difficulty, because writing was not considered an appropriate medium for mere secular ephemera. The skills and traditions of monastic scribes could not automatically be transferred to build up a bureaucracy, although they were successfully adapted and extended in our period. Neither monks nor laymen were literate, in the modern sense of using writing for day-to-day communication, at the time of the Norman Conquest.

Whether the Anglo-Saxon government had used documents in its daily business is a controversial question for historians, because the evidence is sparse. Some have suggested that numerous documents once existed, which were lost after the Norman Conquest because they were in English, whereas others argue that the scarcity of pre-Conquest administrative records implies that business documents were not in common use. All agree that the Anglo-Saxons were acutely conscious of the importance of writing as a way to make records, but that consciousness may have inhibited rather than encouraged the use of documents for ephemeral purposes. It does not follow from the fact that the Anglo-Saxon kings issued writs concerning property rights, which were preserved as title-deeds, that they also sent out written instructions concerning the daily routines of government. P. Chaplais has concluded that the use of the writ for injunctions pure and simple is a post-Conquest development, though he concedes that the injunction as a 'postscript to the notification of a grant was not entirely unknown in Anglo-Saxon times.'[16] His doubts, combined with the difficulties of accepting S. Harvey's hypothesis for the existence of a treasury archive earlier than the Domesday survey (which has been discussed in chapter 1), has led to the initial contention of this book that the Anglo-Saxon kings did not have a bureaucracy.[17]

The Domesday survey provides the first explicit evidence for a royal archive of administrative documents, as a writ of William Rufus refers to land 'which was written down in my writs, which are in my *thesauro* at Winchester'.[18] But even this evidence is ambiguous, because these 'writs' (that is, the circuit returns upon which Domesday Book was based) no longer exist and some historians have argued that references to them, like the one cited above, refer to the volumes of Domesday Book and not to a separate archive of writings. Moreover, the making of Domesday Book itself, as distinct from the Domesday survey, suggests that William the Conqueror had no intention of using an archive of administrative documents. Like scribes making monastic charters, the compilers of Domesday Book selected information from the circuit returns and other drafts to make a fair copy for the perpetual use of posterity. Whatever his intentions, William the Conqueror had created in Domesday Book a unique record in the old monastic tradition, the

[16] Chaplais, *Docs*, p. 5.
[17] See pp. 15–18 above and also n. 39 below concerning the archive in the *haligdom*.
[18] *RRA-N* I, no. 468.

Book of Judgment of Revelation, rather than a document of administrative value.[19]

The principal objection to this interpretation of Domesday Book is Fitz Neal's statement that it was kept in the treasury, along with the pipe rolls and many charters and writs, because such documents were required 'for daily use' in the Exchequer.[20] But the use of Domesday Book seems to have been principally symbolic, like the regalia, since it cannot be shown that it was frequently consulted at the time Fitz Neal was writing in c.1179. He himself was unfamiliar with its contents, as he insists that it makes no mention of 'blanch farm' (payments in assayed silver from certain counties), whereas references to such payments are quite common in Domesday Book.[21] His ignorance has puzzled editors of the *Dialogue of the Exchequer*, who have suggested as a solution that this passage about Domesday Book is an interpolation, although there is no textual evidence for that. A sufficient explanation of Fitz Neal's mistake is that neither he, nor his colleagues at the Exchequer, consulted Domesday Book at all frequently because there was scarcely any documentary continuity in administration between William the Conqueror's reign and Henry II's.

For Fitz Neal and his colleagues the pipe rolls of Henry I, rather than the Domesday survey, marked the beginning of an archive of documents which they understood and regularly consulted. One story of Fitz Neal's shows a pipe roll of Henry I being used to overule a writ of Henry II, and another remark about what is frequently to be found 'in the old annual rolls' of Henry I suggests that a number of early pipe rolls were still extant in Fitz Neal's time.[22] The whole tone of the *Dialogue of the Exchequer*, with its meticulous regard for precedent and correct form, shows how the Exchequer was dominated by bureaucratic routines by the 1170s. Yet the writings it produced were still not systematically kept as records, as many of the types of document mentioned by Fitz Neal are not extant today, nor can they be traced in the thirteenth century. The pipe rolls of Henry I themselves have been lost, apart from the roll for 1130. That roll demonstrates, moreover, that hundreds of writs were issued each year, for such ephemeral purposes as authorizing expenditure, of which no record was kept.[23] The sparse evidence available suggests that administrative documents first came into routine use in Henry I's Exchequer, rather than at the time of the Domesday survey or earlier. Turning such documents into records for posterity took even longer to develop and was far from thorough in Fitz Neal's time.

Hubert Walter seems to have been principally responsible for making the royal government as a whole, and not just the Exchequer, begin keeping records as well as issuing documents. He laid the foundations of an accumulating archival memory, first in the law courts (in the form of the feet of fines and the plea rolls) while he was chief justiciar (1193–8), and then in the Chancery (in the form of the various rolls of outgoing

[19] *Dialogus*, p. 64. Cf. ch. 1, n. 29 above.
[20] *ibid*. p. 62. Cf. nn. 79, 81 below. [21] *ibid*. p. 14.
[22] *ibid*. pp. 58, 42. [23] See ch. 2, n. 52 above.

letters) while he was chancellor (1199–1205).[24] Thenceforward the Chancery rolls are extant for almost every year. Similarly the feet of fines were successfully kept from the start, though the plea rolls proved harder to recover from the judges, because they treated them as their personal property: the best known example is Bracton's retention of the rolls of Martin of Pattishall and William de Ralegh, from which he compiled his notebook of cases for the *De Legibus*. Nevertheless by the latter half of the thirteenth century the plea rolls too were being successfully preserved, as the almost complete series from Edward I's reign demonstrate.

In Edward I's reign the era of Hubert Walter began to be recognized as a turning point in the history of keeping records. By statutes in 1275 and 1293 the date of Richard I's coronation (3 September 1189) was fixed as the legal limit of memory.[25] This meant that a litigant was not required to go any further back into the past than that date when proving a claim. Fixing an arbitrary limit for claims based on precedents was not a new device, as the date of Richard I's coronation replaced Henry II's coronation and that date had replaced Henry I's death. Up until the reign of Edward I the assumption seems to have been that memory extended back for a century at the most, that is, to the earliest time which could be remembered by the oldest living persons; any period before that was considered to be 'time out of mind'. The novelty of establishing Richard I's coronation as the new legal limit only became apparent by the end of Edward I's reign, when it was left to stand instead of being updated. In retrospect the fixed limit of 3 September 1189, which continued for the rest of the Middle Ages, marked the formal beginning of the era of artificial memory. Repeated updating was no longer urgently required, because remembrance in litigation now depended primarily on documentary evidence and not on mortal memory. It was appropriate, though at first a coincidence, that Richard I's reign was acknowledged as the point in time from which it was reasonable to require proof, as Hubert Walter's reforms had made such proof possible.

Although Hubert Walter had laid the foundation of an extensive royal archive, another century elapsed before its potential was tested. In 1291, when Edward I required historical evidence to support his claims to overlordship in Scotland, he made no attempt at first to use the royal records. Instead monasteries were ordered at short notice to search their 'chronicles, registers, and other archives, both ancient and modern, of whatever shape or date'.[26] The evidence adduced by this method turned out to be scrappy and unsatisfactory. For example, the treaty of Falaise of 1174 (by which King William the Lion submitted to Henry II) was cited from a monastic chronicle, whereas more accurate transcripts

---

[24] See pp. 48–50 above.

[25] T. F. T. Plucknett, *A Concise History of the Common Law* (5th edn, 1956), p. 719. D. W. Sutherland, *Quo Warranto Proceedings in the Reign of Edward I* (1963), pp. 226–8. Cf. ch. 1, n. 67 above.

[26] *Documents Illustrative of the History of Scotland* ed. J. Stevenson (1870) I, p. 222 (writ to the prior of Chester). Cf. E. L. G. Stones and G. G. Simpson, *Edward I and the Throne of Scotland* (1978), pp. 138ff. and the works there cited.

were to be found in both the Red Book and the Little Black Book of the Exchequer.[27]

Belatedly in the summer of 1291, after the monasteries had submitted their evidence, Edward I wrote in haste from Scotland, ordering a chest of Chancery rolls at the New Temple to be broken open and searched.[28] Two rolls of Henry III were taken out of this chest and sent to the king – the patent roll for 1254–5 and the charter roll for 1237–8. What Edward expected to find in these rolls is not specified. As they are still extant today, however, the historian can point out that in the former roll are details of Henry III's treaty with Alexander III of Scotland in 1255 and in the latter is Henry's treaty with Alexander II in 1237.[29] Since neither of these treaties would have helped Edward's case, this preliminary attempt to use the archives for historical purposes may have temporarily discouraged further research.

Nevertheless a precedent had been established and when evidence was again required in 1300 in order to justify the English case to Pope Boniface VIII and international opinion, the royal records were ordered to be searched as well as monastic sources. The instruction was vague but comprehensive – to search all the remembrances concerning the business of Scotland – and it was coupled with a similar order 'to search all the rolls and remembrances', including all the rolls of the Exchequer and Chancery, concerning the king's forest rights.[30] Whoever ordered all the rolls to be searched, 'so that nothing is left unsearched', can have had little conception of how numerous they were, or of how inadequately they were stored and filed. This search seems to have produced no new information, presumably because it proved impossible to search the archives effectively at such short notice. But despite the ineffective nature of the searches, Edward I's claims in Scotland and the need to document them had at last made the government aware of the large historical archive it had accumulated. It is probably not a coincidence that plea rolls and other legal records likewise began to be systematically listed in detail in the 1290s.[31] In 1302 a similar attempt was made to bring together the archives of the Wardrobe, 'so that we can be advised of things at all times that we want, and these books and rolls are to remain in the Wardrobe in perpetual remembrance.'[32] To keep documents for perpetual remembrance had been the purpose of archives for centuries; what was new was the demand that records should be readily available 'at all times'.

The aim of making the royal archives accessible for reference, initiated by Edward I in his last years, reached maturity in 1320 in Bishop Stapledon's great survey of the records. The prologue to Stapledon's commission deplores the way records had been carried about from place

[27] *Anglo-Scottish Relations*, p. 1.
[28] *Foedera* I, part ii, p. 757. *CClR* 1288–96, pp. 245–6.
[29] *CPatR* 1247–58, pp. 421, 426. *CChR* 1226–57, p. 236. *Anglo-Scottish Relations*, pp. 30, 38.
[30] *Calendar of Chancery Warrants*, HMSO (1927) I, p. 120. Cf. n. 156 below.
[31] *SCCKB* I, pp. cxxi–cxxii.   [32] *Book of Prests*, pp. 229–30.

to place and from person to person, and frequently mislaid, whereas the frailty of the human condition requires the acts of princes and rulers to be reduced to writings as memorials, so that kings can rule their subject people justly.[33] Although Stapledon's extensive survey of the records had little immediate effect on the conduct of government, his commission marks the point at which the crown formally recognized that its administrative documents were records for posterity. The writings of kings were a bastion against human frailty and a warning or encouragement to their successors, just as their deeds had been when recorded in monastic chronicles. The gulf between records specifically made for posterity and secular documents for mundane use had been bridged. As a consequence the English government was set on the course which has produced the largest archive to survive from medieval Europe.

To sum up, administrative documents had been in routine use since Henry I's reign, they had been extensively kept since Hubert Walter's reforms around 1200, and now in the 1300s the government subjected them to comprehensive inspection. Perhaps documents had to accumulate in considerable numbers before they could be seen as an archive with a historical purpose. Searching Domesday Book, for evidence of whether land was ancient demesne of the crown or not, had followed a similar pattern; searches had started in the 1250s and only became an established routine in Edward I's reign, although Domesday Book had been available for two centuries.[34] Making documents for administrative use, keeping them as records, and using them again for reference were three distinct stages of development which did not automatically and immediately follow from each other.

Archives and libraries

So far this chapter has considered when and why records began to be kept and used, but it has only incidentally answered questions concerning where and how they were deposited. It is worth attempting to answer such questions as precisely as possible, because the physical conditions in which documents were kept indicate contemporary attitudes towards them and also help explain why some types of document have survived better than others. It is also appropriate to consider archives and libraries together because, although all kinds of distinctions were made between different types of writings in the Middle Ages, the twofold modern division between books and records is an anachronism.

At the time of the Norman Conquest documents and books had a place among the precious objects, the hoard of treasure and relics, which a ruler or the head of a religious house aimed to pass on to his successors. Documents, books, relics of the saints and jewellery were not usually kept in places distinct from each other, because they were often

---

[33] *The Antient Kalendars and Inventories of the Exchequer* ed. F. Palgrave (1836) I, pp. 1–3.

[34] See ch. 1, nn. 37–40 above.

physically joined together and the difference between writings and other precious objects was not as obvious as it is to a modern literate. Books of the Bible – illuminated with gold leaf and precious paints, their bindings studded with gems or even with relics – were obviously treasure, both heavenly and terrestrial, rather than mere reading matter. A book as special as the *Lindisfarne Gospels*, for example, was itself a relic and a shrine, hallowed by its age and by its alleged association with St Cuthbert. Single documents like charters were sometimes bound or copied into such liturgical books for safekeeping. This practice has already been illustrated by Eadmer's story of finding in Gospel books ancient papal bulls which upheld Canterbury's claims over York.[35] Although these bulls were forged, the practice of keeping documents in books was evidently commonplace enough to sound convincing to Eadmer's readers. In the Sherborne cartulary of the mid-twelfth century liturgical texts and charters (probably forged) were made into an integrated book. 'All the secular portions were placed under the protection, as it were, of the book's sacred contents and its connexion with the altar. If anyone in the future was to be so unwise as to question the validity of any of the documents, the protection and wrath of heaven could be invoked.'[36]

As some charters were placed for safekeeping in sacred books, it comes as no surprise to find that others were put in shrines. The best known instance of this practice is the use of the Anglo-Saxon royal *haligdom* as a place for depositing charters.[37] The *haligdom* was probably the sanctuary associated with the chapel royal. Thus a Ramsey charter (dating from the 1050s) was deposited 'by the king's order in his chapel with the relics of the saints which he had there'.[38] This chapel was probably a stone building rather than a portable altar; in that case its most likely location was either at Westminster abbey or in the ancient palace of the West Saxon kings at Winchester. It has been argued that charters had been kept at Winchester, systematically filed, since the ninth century.[39] Wherever it was situated, the *haligdom* was a depository of sacred documents for posterity and not an administrative archive.

Churches and reliquaries were the obvious place to keep documents not just because they were relatively secure, being protected by stone and iron as well as by anathemas, but also because charters were themselves relics of past gifts. Moreover, since gifts to monasteries were often made to the patron saint of the church rather than to the monks themselves, it was appropriate that the charters recording such gifts

[35] See n. 11 above. The Gospel book in question has been identified by N. R. Ker with BL MS. Cotton Tiberius Aii.

[36] F. Wormald, 'The Sherborne Chartulary' in *Fritz Saxl Memorial Essays* ed. D. J. Gordon (1957), p. 109. Kauffmann, *Romanesque MSS*, no. 60.

[37] Galbraith, *Studies*, pp. 40–41.   [38] *Ramsey*, p. 172.

[39] C. Hart, 'The Codex Wintoniensis and the King's *Haligdom*', *Agricultural History Review* XVIII (1970) supplement (*Essays Presented to H. P. R. Finberg*), pp. 18–19, 20–23. But see the opposing comments of N. Brooks in *Anglo-Saxon England* ed. P. Clemoes (1974) iii, p. 228.

should be placed as close to the relics of the saint as possible, because they belonged to him. It was common practice to offer charters at an altar; thus the Guthlac roll depicts the benefactors of Crowland abbey presenting their charters at St Guthlac's shrine.[40] Similarly one of the seals of Bury St Edmunds abbey hung from the shrine of St Edmund, presumably both because it was a secure place and because the seal belonged to St Edmund in a personal sense.[41]

Together with sacred books and relics of the saints, documents came to be mixed in with cups, rings, wooden staffs, knives and any other symbolic objects which retained the memory of past events. For example in 1096 Tavistock abbey deposited in the shrine of St Rumon the ivory knife (with an explanatory note attached) by which William Rufus had given the abbot seisin of a manor;[42] likewise Spalding priory fifty years later put Thomas of Moulton's knife into its archive or *secretarium*.[43] As long as it remained customary to symbolize a conveyance of property by an object laid upon an altar, it was natural for such objects, whatever their form, to be kept with the sacred vessels and liturgical books which were similarly associated with the altar. To the modern eye an early medieval archive would have looked more like a magpie's nest than a filing system for documents. Yet however bizarre such objects might look at first sight, the sacristan could no doubt have explained the significance as a memento of each individual object. The best modern comparison might be with an old lady's handbag, which likewise might contain symbolic rings, jewellery, miscellaneous mementoes and a few letters and papers.

Each document or book had a special place of safekeeping, appropriate to its associations and function, but not all the documents or books were kept in one place. Liturgical books were often kept in the church, because that is where they were used, whereas other books were kept in the refectory for reading aloud, or in a chest or cupboard in the cloister for individual study.[44] At Lincoln cathedral in the thirteenth century the chancellor had charge of the scholastic books and saints' lives, the precentor kept the music books, the treasurer had the other liturgical books like breviaries and missals, and the provost looked after the charters and muniments.[45] There were good reasons for this arrangement, as the chancellor was associated with the school, the precentor with the choir, the treasurer with the safekeeping of sacred utensils, and the provost with the correspondence of the dean and chapter. The need for a centralized library or archive only became apparent if the number of books or documents increased to unmanageable proportions.

Furthermore, documents were scattered about on principle and not

[40] *The Guthlac Roll* ed. G. Warner, Roxburghe Club (1928), plate xviii.

[41] Jocelin, p. 2. By Jocelin's time this seal had been removed because the sacrist had used it without the authorization of the convent.

[42] *Monasticon* II, p. 497, no. v.　　　　　[43] *ibid*. III, p. 217, no. x.

[44] F. Wormald, 'The Monastic Library' in *English Library*, pp. 16–18.

[45] K. Edwards, *The English Secular Cathedrals in the Middle Ages* (2nd edn, 1967), p. 211.

just from negligence. The Anglo-Saxon practice of depositing two or three copies of an agreement in different places for greater security continued after the Norman Conquest. For example, sealed copies of Henry II's will were deposited in 1182 at Canterbury, in the Winchester treasury, and in his coffers; likewise Gerald of Wales proposed in 1202 to deposit copies of his evidence concerning the bishopric of St David's in the archives of the pope, the archbishop of Canterbury, and the bishop of St David's.[46] Similarly one reason given in 1221 for having more than one justice on the bench at a time was that each justice kept his own copy of the plea roll, whereas one roll on its own was not sufficiently secure as a record.[47] Only gradually did the crown move from the traditional notion of safety in numbers as a way to preserve its legal records to the idea of a central archive at the treasury.

To sum up, the tradition at the time of the Norman Conquest had been that documents and books were kept with other precious objects. Writings were too few and too diverse in their functions and physical formats to be treated as a special class of memento. Books and documents were not neglected, but they were kept in ways which made consultation difficult and their dispersal among various repositories meant that books belonging to an institution were not usually seen as a whole as a library, still less were documents seen as an archive.

Gradually in the twelfth and thirteenth centuries, as the number of writings increased, more specific and uniform regulations were made for their safekeeping. The initiative in this movement seems to have come from ecclesiastics and not from the royal government. The Norman Conquest encouraged monastic houses to examine their heritage in order to justify the existence of themselves and their saints to the conquerors.[48] Moreover, the reforming prelates appointed by Archbishop Lanfranc aimed to bring their churches into line with the best continental practice, and that meant reviewing and renewing their books and muniments. The Latin word *archiva* (neuter plural), meaning 'archives' in something like its modern sense of a safe and secret place for documents, was first used in England by Lanfranc in the early 1080s when ordering some letters concerning the bishop of the Orkneys to be preserved as a memorial for the future 'in the archives' of the churches of Worcester and Chester.[49] Examples of monasteries reviewing their muniments are numerous and relate to the beginnings of cartulary making, which has already been discussed.[50] V. H. Galbraith has pointed out that Heming, who completed the first cartulary, also has claims to be the earliest English archivist, as he had a new lock put on Worcester's muniment chest and repaired original documents which were torn or damaged.[51] Repairing charters was closely associated with

[46] Gervase I, p. 300. Giraldus III, pp. 230–31.
[47] *Rot. Lit. Claus.* I, p. 451.   [48] See ch. 3, n. 89 above.
[49] 'in archivis', *Patrologiae* cl (1880) col. 519, no. xii. 'Archivum' (singular) had been used earlier in the eleventh century by Aelfric to translate the English word 'boochord', *Dictionary of Medieval Latin from British Sources* ed. R. E. Latham (1975) I p. 120.
[50] See ch. 3, nn. 87–91 above.
[51] *Historical Research in Medieval England* (1951), p. 37.

replacing them, and hence with forgery. In the monastic community archivists and forgers shared a common aim in documenting a house's titles to its property.

Archives and archivists did not originate from the requirements of disinterested historical research, but from the immediate necessity to produce documents even where none existed. This monastic movement to review and modernize records continued in the twelfth and thirteenth centuries. Thus the compiler of Ramsey abbey's *Book of Benefactors* in *c.*1170 describes the 'very ancient' charters and chirographs 'which we have found in our archives', which he claims to have translated from 'barbarous' Anglo-Saxon into Latin.[52] A decade or so later the dean of St Paul's, Ralf de Diceto, made a survey of the churches owned by the cathedral and combined this with an examination of their charters; he devised a system of cross-references between his survey and the charters by using special identification symbols.[53]

The preoccupation with making lists and surveys, which had originated with the *descriptiones* of monastic estates like Abbot Samson's *kalendarium*,[54] also produced the first monastic book catalogues in the twelfth century. Strictly speaking perhaps these lists of books owned by particular houses should not be described as library catalogues, as most of them are simply inventories of possessions which do not indicate to the user where he will find a particular book. Such lists were not intended for the reader's use anyway, but for the librarian's. Nevertheless among the earliest half dozen or so English library lists extant is one from Christ Church Canterbury (dating from *c.*1170) in which a series of small letters and symbols correspond with symbols on the first leaf of each book.[55] The librarian had thus marked his books in much the same way as Ralf de Diceto marked the charters of St Paul's. Such marks did not indicate where the books or charters were placed, but they did at least show which description in a list corresponded with which document in a cupboard or chest.

A good example of an early book list is the inventory, on the fly-leaves of a work of St Augustine's, made at Rochester cathedral in 1202. It begins, unusually, with a precise date and description: 'In the year AD 1202 this is the survey of our library.'[56] The use of the term 'survey' (*scrutinium*) suggests that a comprehensive review was intended. The books are listed partly under the names of authors (Augustine, Gregory, Ambrose, Jerome, Bede) which are not in alphabetical order, partly by where certain books are placed, such as those which are 'in the precentor's chest [*archa*]', and partly under special collections comprising gifts or acquisitions from named individuals. The list comprises 241 items (according to the edited text) and is evidently more complete than an

[52] *Ramsey*, pp. 4, 65, 176. Cf. ch. 9, n. 74 below.
[53] *The Domesday of St Paul's* ed. W. H. Hale, Camden S. LXIX (1857), p. 110. Gransden, *Historical Writing*, p. 234. Cf. n. 135 below.
[54] See ch. 3, n. 53 above.
[55] Wormald, 'The Monastic Library', p. 23.
[56] Ed. W. B. Rye, *Archaeologia Cantiana* III (1860), pp. 54–61.

earlier fragment of a list on the fly-leaves of the mid-twelfth century *Textus Roffensis*.[57]

Modern libraries really started with the friars. The Dominican rule of Humbert de Romanis (dating from *c*.1260) lays down all the principal duties of a modern librarian.[58] The librarian should choose a good site for the library, secure, waterproof and well ventilated; there should be ample shelving in the book cupboard, the shelves being designated to different subjects and having explanatory notices on them; there should be a catalogue (*charta*) of the books, which should have their titles written on the spines and an inscription inside each stating the house to which the book belongs and who gifted it; the stock should be kept up to date by replacing old books and selling duplicates; the librarian should have the key of the library and open it at specified times. Books in common use, such as the Bible, papal decretals, sermons, and chronicles were to be kept in a chained reference section, whereas less used books might be borrowed by readers provided loans were recorded in writing. A general inspection of the library was to be made once or twice a year.

If these Dominican regulations are compared with those made by Archbishop Lanfranc in his constitutions for Christ Church Canterbury two centuries earlier, the change in the use of books is striking.[59] There is a librarian (*custos librorum*) in Lanfranc's constitutions and he keeps a written list of books on loan, like his Dominican counterpart; but there the similarity ceases, as the principal duty of Lanfranc's librarian is to supervise the borrowing of books once a year on the first Monday in Lent. The books were to be laid out on a carpet and each monk was issued with one book and given the year to read it. Many books of the Church Fathers were of course long and difficult; a monk who read with attention and understanding every word of St Augustine's *City of God*, for example, had achieved a great deal in a year. Nevertheless Lanfranc's constitutions indicate a different approach to reading from the Dominican rules.

The Dominicans, like modern academics, required extensive libraries in which they could glance rapidly over a whole series of books, many of very recent authorship, in order to construct a wide-ranging argument. The purpose of the library was to ensure 'that the community of friars can have ready to hand (*in promptu*)' whatever works they required.[60] Lanfranc's monks, on the other hand, were expected to ruminate on a text which had been designated to them as a sacred task. For monks in the old Benedictine tradition, books, with their precious and brightly illuminated words, were images which produced a state of mystical contemplation and understanding.[61] The difference in approach towards writing of Lanfranc's Benedictines and Humbert's Dominicans is so

[57] Ed. R. P. Coates, *Archaeologia Cantiana* VI (1866), pp. 122–8.
[58] K. W. Humphreys, *The Book Provisions of the Medieval Friars* (1964), pp. 32, 135–6.
[59] Ed. M. D. Knowles (1951), p. 19. Lanfranc's regulations derive from the Rule of St Benedict, ch. 48.
[60] Humphreys, *The Book Provisions*, p. 136.
[61] See ch. 8, nn. 69, 70 below.

fundamental that to use the same term 'literate' to describe them both is misleading. The parallel with the change of attitudes towards records is evident: at the time of the Norman Conquest documents were special objects which were treasured in shrines; whereas by 1300 Edward I, like the friars, expected them all to be available for scrutiny and comparison whenever he wanted.

In fact, however, the king's books and records were less well regulated for a long period than those either of an average Benedictine house or of the friars. To consider royal books first of all. John is the first king who can be shown to have owned and used books. This is surprising, as Henry I was *litteratus* and Henry II was the most educated king of his time; at his court there was 'school every day'.[62] Evidence about John's books comes from incidental references in the public records. An entry in the pipe roll of 1203, recording the cost of supplying 'chests and carts to take the king's books overseas' suggests that John had a library as large as any monastic house.[63] About the contents of this library, or where it was kept, there is only the sparsest information. In 1205 the king had 'a romance of the history of England' (that is, a text in French) sent him at Windsor by one of his stewards.[64] In 1208 'our book called *Plinius*' (that is, a Latin text of Pliny) was sent him from Reading abbey, where it had been deposited for safekeeing.[65] A few days earlier he had obtained from Reading abbey a copy of the Old Testament, a work by Hugh of St Victor, the Sentences of Peter Lombard and some other scholastic texts.[66] This last reference is the most interesting evidence about John's use of books, as all educated laymen of his time enjoyed history in 'romance' (in other words, in the form of vernacular stories or poems) and most *litterati* read the more obvious Latin classics like Pliny; but King John is the first king in Europe to have been interested in the theological works of the 'modern' schoolmen of the twelfth century. It is likely, however, that he required these books for a particular purpose, namely his dispute with Stephen Langton over clerical privileges; moreover, these scholastic texts probably belonged to Reading abbey rather than to the king himself.[67]

This episode showed that the king's government required a reference library, particularly for ecclesiastical business. Yet the only books possessed by John's successor, Henry III, were liturgical texts and a few romances. Henry, as a patron of artists and craftsmen rather than writers, had missals made for his and the queen's numerous chapels up and down England.[68] Queen Eleanor also used in 1250 a 'great book' in French, 'in which are contained the deeds of Antioch and of the kings',

[62] See ch. 7, n. 46 below.

[63] *Pipe Roll 5 John*, PRS new series XVI (1938), p. 139. W. L. Warren, *King John* (1961), p. 157. Concerning the number of books owned by institutions or individuals see ch. 3, nn. 107–9 above.

[64] *Rot. Lit. Claus.* I, p. 29.

[65] *ibid.* p. 108.   [66] *ibid.* p. 108.

[67] F. M. Powicke, *Stephen Langton* (1928), p. 99.

[68] At Hereford (*CLibR* 1240–5, pp. 29, 296), Nottingham (*ibid.* 1251–60, p. 11), Winchester (*ibid.* 1226–40, p. 419), Windsor *CIR* 1247–51, p. 162.

which was kept by the Knights Templar probably as part of the royal wardrobe.[69] This may be the same as Henry's 'great book of romances', garnished with silver clasps and nails, which is mentioned in 1237.[70] Such books were evidently treasured objects, rather than a library of information, and it is therefore appropriate that they should have been kept by sacristans or by the Templars.

Similarly there is no evidence of Edward I having a library. When he wished to justify his claims to overlordship in Scotland in 1291, he had to ask monasteries to consult their chronicles (as we have already seen), presumably because he had no histories of his own, even allowing for ready access to the library of Westminster abbey. Few books are to be found in Bishop Stapledon's survey of documents in 1320. In one chest a few texts were deposited along with some seals – a book called *De Regimine Principum* (On Royal Rule) bound in red leather, a 'little book' of the rules of the Knights Templar, a quire (that is, part of an unbound book) of the life of St Patrick, another quire 'in an unknown language' (Welsh), and a book of the chronicles of Roderick archbishop of Toledo.[71] These books may have belonged to Edward I. Even if they did, they have the air of miscellaneous gifts and acquisitions rather than the foundations of a library or of a personal collection. In having no library and in leaving little evidence of possessing books, the English kings were no different from other contemporary rulers. The first pope of the period who can be shown to have had a library is Edward I's contemporary, Boniface VIII, and that was dispersed after his death.[72] The explanation for the dearth of libraries is not primarily that kings were ignorant laymen, more interested in fighting and hunting than in study. Rather it is that the business of government, whether ecclesiastical or secular, only gradually became associated with book-learning and written precedents.

The royal archives

The development of the royal archives after the Norman Conquest requires special discussion because it is inconsistent and perplexing. The proliferation of documents beginning in the twelfth century, combined with the erratic movements of the kings back and forth across the Channel, caused records to be dispersed and frequently moved about, whereas they had been more safely preserved in the eleventh century. There is no clear line of progress from dispersal to centralization.

As we have already seen, some charters which served as title-deeds before the Norman Conquest were deposited in the king's *haligdom* or sanctuary, which may have had a permanent location at either Westminster or Winchester.[73] The returns of the Domesday survey were

---

[69] *ClR* 1247–51, p. 283.   [70] *CLibR* 1226–40, p. 288.

[71] *The Antient Kalendars and Inventories of the Exchequer* I, p. 106.

[72] M. Faucon, *La Librairie des Papes d'Avignon*, Bibliothèque des Écoles Francaises d'Athènes et de Rome XLIII (1886) I, pp. 3–4.

[73] See nn. 37–9 above.

likewise kept at Winchester in the reign of William Rufus 'in my *thesauro*'.[74] Whether this *thesaurus*, the 'treasure' or 'treasury' of William Rufus, was the same place as the *haligdom* of the West Saxon kings is a matter for conjecture. Certainly in the twelfth century the *thesaurus* at Winchester was developing into a permanent central archive for the government, perhaps because Winchester with its access to Southampton was a good location for the capital of the Anglo-Norman lordship. Henry I's coronation charter was deposited at Winchester by his order.[75] Similarly in 1155 Henry II ordered the bull of Adrian IV giving him jurisdiction over Ireland, together with the gold and emerald ring which the pope had sent as a symbol of investiture, to be deposited 'in the archives of Winchester', according to Gerald of Wales.[76] John of Salisbury, who had brought the papal bull and ring to Henry, confirms this story by noting that the ring was deposited *in cimiliarchio publico* for safekeeping.[77] *Cimiliarchium* had been the term used by Justinian to describe the imperial archive. John had probably therefore derived the idea of a public archive from his interest in Roman law and history, rather than from English realities. Nevertheless he was at least one influential Englishman who considered that England had a public archive in a fixed place in the middle of the twelfth century.

Later in Henry II's reign, however, as the government expanded, the use of a fixed treasury and archive at Winchester was abandoned. Instead, treasure chests were constantly moved to and fro between Winchester, London and other royal palaces, hunting lodges and fortresses.[78] The assumption has been frequently made that the treasury at Winchester was simply replaced by a similar fixed and central treasury at Westminster, but that is contradicted by the evidence. Fitz Neal's *Dialogue of the Exchequer* indicates the ambivalence of official attitudes towards the idea of one fixed place for a treasury, and hence for an archive, by the 1170s. The Pupil prompts the Master to describe the king's seal and the Book of Judgment (Domesday Book), 'the former of which, if I remember correctly, is kept in the *thesauro* and not taken out'.[79] The Master replies that the seal, Domesday Book and many other things are not taken out either. Before enlarging on this statement, he explains to the Pupil the ambiguity of the word *thesaurus*, which means both 'treasure' (such as coins, gold, silver and vestments) and 'treasury' (a place where treasure is deposited). In reply to the Pupil's implied question, 'Where is the treasury?', the Master cites chapter VI, verse 21 of St Matthew's Gospel, 'Where your treasure is, there will your heart be also.'

Speaking through the Master, Fitz Neal thus refuses to give one

[74] See n. 18 and also ch. 1, n. 35 above.
[75] According to Richard prior of Hexham (writing in c.1140), *Chronicles* ed. R. Howlett, RS LXXXII (1884) III, p. 142.
[76] 'in archivis Winton', Giraldus V, p. 316.
[77] *Metalogicon*, bk iv, ch. 42, ed. C. C. J. Webb (1929), p. 218.
[78] Galbraith, *Studies*, p. 47. R. L. Poole, *The Exchequer in the Twelfth Century* (1912), p. 72.
[79] *Dialogus*, p. 61.

geographical location to the treasury, because the king's treasure was dispersed in a number of repositories and some of it was taken about with him on his travels.[80] In the Master's words, 'plura sunt in repositoriis archis thesauri que circumferuntur.'[81] In the English version of the *Dialogus* this passage is translated, 'There are several things in the vaults of the treasury which are taken about.' However, *repositoriis archis theasauri* does not mean 'the vaults of the treasury', but 'storage chests of treasure'. *Archa* is used by Fitz Neal in the sense of a 'chest' or 'archive', not in the sense of an 'arch' or 'vault': thus the *arche* containing the Exchequer rolls are mentioned earlier in his book.[82] The Master is therefore informing the Pupil that 'several things' – among which are Domesday Book, the Exchequer rolls and numerous writs and charters – are locked up in treasure chests, which are taken about the country in accordance with the wishes of the king. For Fitz Neal there is no contradiction between his statement that Domesday Book is kept in the treasury and not taken out and his statement that it is taken about the country, because the treasury is in the king's heart; in other words, it is wherever he wants to be.

Once it is understood that *thesaurus* by the late twelfth century usually meant treasure kept in portable chests, rather than a government department or a fixed place, it becomes clear why relatively few royal records of Henry II's reign (with the exception of the pipe rolls) or earlier were successfully preserved. King John likewise had no single place for his treasure.[83] In 1215 some of his treasure chests are known to have been deposited at Reading abbey, as he recovered from there jewels, relics and 'all our rolls of our Chamber, together with our seal, and our rolls of our Exchequer'.[84] The archives in *thesauro* were evidently being 'taken about', as they had been in Fitz Neal's time a generation earlier. In addition to the records of the household and the Exchequer referred to by King John, the Chancery rolls were likewise transported from place to place by the 'portejoye' or 'serjeant of the rolls of Chancery'.[85] Some Cistercian abbeys were required in rotation to provide a strong horse to carry the rolls and books of the Chancery in the mid-thirteenth century and later.[86]

Because the royal archives had no permanent home, their safekeeping initially depended on the reliability of archivists rather than repositories. The earliest of such officials on record are William Cucuel, who had charge of the close rolls of the Chancery in 1215,[87] Roger of

[80] R. A. Brown, 'The Treasury of the Later Twelfth Century' in *Studies Presented to Sir H. Jenkinson* ed. J. Conway Davies (1957), pp. 35–49.

[81] *Dialogus*, p. 62. Cf. n. 20 above.　　　　　[82] *ibid*. p. 9.

[83] J. E. A. Jolliffe, *Angevin Kingship* (2nd edn, 1963), pp. 250–51. I have been unable to trace Jolliffe's tantalizing reference to the 'arcana regni' being kept at Corfe castle (*ibid*. p. 251, n. 9).

[84] *Rot. Lit. Pat*. I, p. 145.

[85] H. C. Maxwell-Lyte, *Historical Notes on the Use of the Great Seal* (1926), p. 293. *CPatR* 1258–66, p. 195; cf. pp. 239, 242.

[86] Maxwell-Lyte, *Historical Notes*, p. 294.

[87] Galbraith, *Studies*, p. 80. *Rot. Lit. Claus* I, p. 196. *Rot. Lit. Pat*. I, pp. 137, 199.

Whitchester, who was appointed keeper of the rolls and writs of the justices' Bench at an annual salary of £10 in 1246,[88] and John Kirkby, who held the 'office of the rolls of Chancery' at an annual salary of 20 marks in 1265 and was subsequently described as 'keeper'.[89] Unlike the 'portejoye', who was probably a mere porter, these men were royal clerks of education and status. They were archivists in the sense that they were in charge of *arche* of documents, but their archives were portable chests not permanent repositories.

Obviously, however, once documents accumulated, permanent repositories had to be found. Once a series of records like the Exchequer or Chancery rolls had piled up for fifty years or more, it became impractical and unnecessary to keep carting them all about in chests. Where the older royal records were kept in the thirteenth century has not been fully elucidated. In Henry III's reign London and Westminster replaced Winchester as the centre for storing royal treasure, but the repositories were scattered. Judging from later evidence, the Tower of London, the New Temple in London, and stores off the cloister of Westminster abbey were the chief repositories. The New Temple and Westminster abbey locations suggest that religious houses were still considered the most appropriate places to keep documents. Orders like one in 1257 to deposit plea rolls and chirographs 'in the king's treasury' throw no light on the location of this archive, although Westminster abbey is likely in this instance as legal records were subsequently kept in its chapter house.[90]

In Edward I's reign the largest archive in the kingdom was probably the New Temple in London.[91] In 1279 Roger of Seaton, chief justice of the Bench, kept his plea rolls there[92] and other memoranda show that the Chancery rolls were kept there: in 1289 a charter granting land to the king is described as being 'in a box in the chest in which the rolls of Chancery are kept at the New Temple';[93] in the summer of 1291, as we have already seen, Edward I ordered a chest at the New Temple to be broken open and a charter roll and a patent roll of Henry III were taken out of it.[94] The New Temple had also been a repository for books and documents of the Wardrobe, like the 'great book' which Queen Eleanor had brought from there in 1250, although in 1300 many recent books and rolls of the Wardrobe were deposited at St Leonard's hospital in York.[95]

The dissolution of the Knights Templar by papal decree in 1312 may have been an ancillary reason for reviewing the royal archives, as it

[88] C. A. F. Meekings, 'Roger of Whitchester', *Archaeologia Aeliana* 4th series XXXV (1957), p. 100. F. Pegues, 'The *Clericus* in the Legal Administration of Thirteenth-Century England', *EHR* LXXI (1956), pp. 546–7.

[89] *CLibR* 1260–7, p. 169. *CPatR* 1266–72, p. 475.

[90] *ClR* 1256–9, p. 281. *SCCKB* I, pp. cxxiii–iv. Similarly the treasury of the Wardrobe was in the crypt of the Chapter House when it was robbed in 1291, H. Harrod, 'On the Crypt of the Chapter House', *Archaeologia* XLIV (1873), pp. 375–6.

[91] A. Sandys, 'The Financial and Administrative Importance of the London Temple' in *Essays in Medieval History Presented to T. F. Tout* (1925), pp. 147–62.

[92] *SCCKB* I, p. clxviii.   [93] *CClR* 1288–96, p. 56.

[94] See n. 28 above.   [95] *Book of Prests*, pp. 228–9.

deprived the king of the chief custodians of his documents. Certainly in that year new cupboards for keeping the older records were installed in the Tower of London.[96] When Bishop Stapledon began his survey of the records in 1320, the White Chapel in the Tower was selected as the central repository to which all the records were brought.[97] The idea of having a central royal archive in a fixed place under the king's direct control had at last been realized, but the government let the opportunity slip and many of the records were returned to their former repositories. The records were not again brought under a single custody until the Public Records Act of 1838.

Ideally the king's government needed local archives as well as a central repository in Winchester or London. At first religious houses seem to have been used for this purpose also. Thus copies of Henry I's coronation charter were deposited in abbeys in each county, as well as being put in the Winchester treasury, according to later chronicle evidence.[98] Similarly one of the early copies of the reissue of Magna Carta was deposited at Lacock abbey by the knights of Wiltshire, presumably for safekeeping.[99] By the time of Magna Carta, however, sheriffs kept rolls themselves and must have been beginning to develop archives of their own. The earliest evidence of this arises from exceptional cases in which documents were mislaid. In 1212 a clerk of the sheriff of Gloucestershire explained to the king's justices that he had been obliged to go to London on the county's business and had left the sheriff's roll with 'Richard the priest of the castle'; when he returned, he found that the text of the roll had been altered.[100] In this instance Richard the priest was evidently acting as an unofficial, and inefficient or dishonest, archivist in the sheriff's castle. Past experience of documents in the sheriff's care being lost may have led the barons in 1258 to insist that copies of the letter, whereby Henry III undertook to submit to their council, should 'remain in the treasury' of each county.[101] Likewise in 1265 the letter publishing the terms of Henry III's peace with the barons was sent to every county, together with an order to keep it and accompanying documents safely as 'a memorial of the business' in the custody of trustworthy men chosen for the purpose.[102]

The precedent for regulating local archives and appointing commissioners to supervise them had been established in 1194 by Hubert Walter's statute for the safekeeping of Jewish bonds. It is possible that such bonds had been kept in chests in great churches before this statute, as in the anti-Jewish riot at York in 1190 the mob broke into York Minster, seized the 'muniments of debts' deposited there by the Jews and burned 'these instruments of profane avarice' in the middle of the

[96] V. H. Galbraith, 'The Tower as an Exchequer Record Office' in *Essays to T. F. Tout*, p. 232. Cf. *SCCKB* I, p. cxxiv.

[97] Galbraith, 'The Tower', pp. 232–3.

[98] R. L. Poole, 'The Publication of Great Charters by the English Kings', *EHR* XXVIII (1913), p. 445.

[99] *ibid.* pp. 451–2.   [100] *CuriaRR* VI, p. 230.

[101] *Baronial Docs*, p. 116. Cf. ch. 6, n. 93 below.

[102] *ibid.* p. 312.

church.[103] By the statute of 1194 the bonds were to be stored in future in designated centres in a communal archive (*in arca communi*) or public chest, fitted with three locks.[104] The keys were to be kept by two Jews, two Christians, and the clerk of the royal commissioners. The Jewish and Christian key-holders are the first recorded local public archivists in England and became known as 'chirographers'. Instances can readily be found in the thirteenth century of the appointment of both Jewish and Christian chirographers and of the keys being delivered to them. A chirographer was usually chosen by a jury, appointed before the justices of the Jews, and took an oath to perform his duties faithfully.[105] As an additional precaution, the contents of these archives were surveyed and enrolled from time to time.[106]

As public royal archives with official archivists and writers had thus been established in the principal towns in England by Henry III's reign, it is surprising at first sight that greater general use was not made of them. An exceptional instance from Oxford in 1227–8 shows a third copy of an agreement, made by the hospital of St John the Baptist with Geoffrey Malin and his wife, being deposited 'in the king's archive [*archa*] in Oxford'.[107] The archive meant is presumably the chest for Jewish bonds; yet neither of the parties is a Jew, nor does the business concern moneylending but a conveyance of land. From 1195 third copies of agreements (feet of fines) made before royal justices were deposited in the royal 'treasury';[108] likewise third copies of Jewish bonds were deposited in the local *arche* from at least 1205.[109] It is possible that William, the Oxford town clerk, who was the writer of this agreement in 1227–8, may also have been one of the keepers of the Jewish *archa* and recommended his archive as a safe place for retaining a third copy of this conveyance.

Had the procedure used in this Oxford conveyance become widespread, the archives of the main towns of England would have developed into centres for registering conveyances of property under the supervision of official writers and archivists. Local royal archives thus had the potential of notarial centres in imperial cities on the Italian model.[110] The potential was not realized, however, probably because the *arche* were too closely associated with the Jews and usury. In the eyes of Christians, depositing a Christian charter in a Jewish archive would have had the reverse effect of putting it in the shrine of a saint, as the charter would have been contaminated by the 'instruments of profane

[103] William of Newburgh, *Chronicles* ed. R. Howlett, RS LXXXII (1884), I, p. 322.
[104] Stubbs, *Charters*, p. 256. Cf. ch. 2, n. 77 above.
[105] *Calendar of the Plea Rolls of the Exchequer of the Jews* ed. J. M. Rigg (1905) I, p. 153 (Robert le Bret), p. 135 (Jacob Copin).
[106] *Select Pleas, Starrs and Other Records of the Exchequer of the Jews* ed. J. M. Rigg, SS XV (1901), p. 50: Simon Passelewe went 'a enrouler partye de Huches de Engleterre'.
[107] *Cartulary of the Hospital of St John Baptist, Oxford* ed. H. E. Salter, Oxford Historical S. LXVI (1914), I, p. 364 and plate iii.
[108] See ch. 2, n. 64 above.
[109] Richardson, *Jewry*, pp. 147, 264–7.
[110] Notarial practice is discussed at ch. 9, nn. 15–16, 46–50 below.

avarice' all around it. Furthermore, local *arche* may have been considered insufficiently secure despite their public supervision. In times of riots Jewish archives were burned, as happened at York in 1190 and at Bedford in the civil war between Henry III and the barons.[111]

This discussion has concentrated on the royal archives in their various forms because the king's government had the largest problems and also because, although evidence is sparse, there is sufficient to discern the outline of development. For magnates, whether ecclesiastical or lay, fewer details are available and most are of an incidental or an anecdotal type. After the king, the bishops might have been expected to accumulate business archives the fastest. Yet, just as bishops were slower than the king to make registers, their records suffered more than the king's from being carried around and having no single place of deposit in each diocese. At Rochester it was reported early in the fourteenth century that 'there never was any certain safe place appointed as a repository of muniments, but they were left about, sometimes in the cathedral church or in the manor of Halling.'[112] Some lay lords followed the king's lead and deposited documents with the Templars or at Westminster abbey.[113] Charters were also handed over to other religious persons or houses or to the village parson.[114]

Some landowners preferred to keep their own muniments, in which case they were sometimes lost or stolen. One of the earliest chirographs made before royal justices (in 1182) concerns the loss of a charter for Rochester cathedral priory by William son of Ralf of Wye.[115] The most spectacular story of a theft of charters comes from Babington in Somerset in 1201.[116] An unnamed lord was allegedly attacked in his house by a gang of eight conspirators who pulled out his tongue, broke open his chests, took out charters of Henry II, Richard I and an archbishop of Canterbury, and burned them in his face before beheading him. Whether this allegation is entirely truthful, however, is doubtful, as the accused were allowed to make a compromise and the king did not prosecute.

Retrieving information

Making documents, keeping them in archives, and subsequently using them again for reference were three distinct stages of development, as has already been argued.[117] Even when documents were successfully preserved and kept in safe yet accessible places, it might still prove difficult to find a particular item of information within a book or roll. An example has already been given of Henry III insisting to the pope in

[111] *Select Pleas, Starrs and Other Records*, p. 49.
[112] Cheney, *Chanceries*, p. 134. For bishops' registers see pp. 53–5 above
[113] A. Sandys, 'The Financial and Administrative Importance of the London Temple', p. 148, n. 6. *CuriaRR* XIII, p. 253, no. 1152 (Westminster abbey).
[114] *CuriaRR* XIII, p. 304, no. 1415 (the anchoress of Bottisham). *ibid.* XI, p. 495, no. 2499 (Southwark hospital). *ibid.* XII, p. 72, no. 382 (Clerkenwell hospital). *Berks. Eyre*, no. 304 (the parson of Inkpen).
[115] *BM Facs*, no. 63.   [116] *CuriaRR* I, p. 395.   [117] See p. 125 above.

1272 that letters patent of his being exhibited by the prior of Christ Church Canterbury at the Roman *curia* were forgeries because they could not be found in his register.[118] In fact these letters had been enrolled in the patent rolls in 1265, but the Chancery clerks were unable to find them because they thought the letters had been issued in 1270. Without an alphabetical index of names, the clerks could not search their records thoroughly.

Searches of the rolls for particular documents were usually successful only when the record was of recent origin and its date of issue was known. For example in 1250 Walter Bloweberme, a robber who had abjured the realm after triumphing in trial by combat at Winchester in 1249, was recaptured and reconvicted by referring to the Hampshire plea roll of 1249 in which his trial had been recorded.[119] Or in the London justices' visitation of 1276 the prior of Holy Trinity at Aldgate claimed from the 'record of the Chancery rolls' that he had been authorized by Henry III to close a road; the rolls were duly searched and the record found.[120] Although it was possible to find particular cases or charters in the rolls when the exact circumstances were already known, royal records could not be effectively searched in a more general way. Thus Edward I's attempt in 1300 to search all the rolls for information about Scotland produced no new information because royal records had no indexes. Similarly the pioneering attempt of baronial commissioners in 1259 to assess from the records of the Exchequer how much money had been raised by tallages during Henry III's reign was not brought to a specific conclusion, although some information may have been gathered.[121]

The government's inability to use its archives for general guidance or for precedents in making policy decisions meant in the long term that its records were of more benefit to the governed than to the crown itself. An individual property owner or the head of a monastic house who possessed a royal charter or a transcript of litigation in the king's court could use the Chancery and plea rolls to prove his title by referring to a particular enrolment. Without systemized guides to their records the king's clerks on their side had no means of finding out whether other royal documents existed which might modify or even contradict such a claim.

A good example of the king being caught in his own bureaucratic net by insisting on written proof occurred in the *quo warranto* proceedings of Edward I. The rule had been established in 1282 that the privilege of excluding royal officers from executing writs within franchises (the franchise of 'return of writs') could be upheld only by a royal charter

---

[118] See ch. 2, nn. 72–3 above.

[119] *Medieval Legal Records Edited in Memory of C. A. F. Meekings* ed. R. F. Hunnisett and J. B. Post (1978), p. 31.

[120] *The London Eyre of 1276* ed. M. Weinbaum, London Record S. XII (1976), p. 91, no. 345.

[121] *Baronial Docs*, p. 152, no. 15. A writ of a year later states that the king 'pro certo intellexit' that tallages have been excessive, *ClR* 1259–61, p. 135.

which made specific mention of the privilege.[122] This rule was reinforced by a statute in 1285 which proposed that the treasurer should make a roll of those entitled to 'return of writs'; thenceforward any sheriff who made a return to an unenrolled franchise would be punished as a disinheritor of the crown.[123] The government's insistence on recording privileges in writing is exemplified in this dispute, both in the rule that a claimant must have a royal charter and in the proposal to make an official treasury list of franchise-holders. In the real world of practical politics, however, as contrasted with the theoretical world of Edward I's legal advisers and Chancery clerks, these rules threatened the great majority of magnates because their privileges rested on unwritten acceptance and custom rather than on royal charters or treasury lists. The roll of those entitled to 'return or writs' was consequently never made.

The story did not end there, however, as a handful of ecclesiastics, who were more concerned than lay magnates to ensure that their privileges were precisely expressed in writing, obtained new charters. Among them was the abbot of Chertsey, who appeared to comply promptly with the new rules by having a charter of Richard I, which had granted 'return of writs' to his predecessor, inspected by the Chancery and enrolled on the charter rolls in 1285.[124] What the Chancery clerks did not notice was that this charter was a daring forgery, as it was a conflation of two genuine charters of Richard I for Chertsey supplemented by interpolations. The facts can be simply proved today by looking up the Chertsey charters in the index to the printed edition of the *Cartae Antiquae* rolls which were published in 1939.[125] These rolls date from Richard I's reign and should have been known to the king's clerks in 1285. But even if they were known, they would have been difficult to search without an alphabetical index. The abbot of Chertsey had presumably taken a calculated risk that the royal archives would not, or could not, be searched for a grant which was earlier than the Chancery rolls of King John.

The Chertsey case illustrates the way powerful individuals or institutions successfully used the king's bureaucratic apparatus to benefit themselves to the detriment of the crown. Ancient monasteries like Chertsey had traditionally forged charters when they required title-deeds in writing. Now that the king was keeping copies of charters on his Chancery rolls, abbots ensured that their forged documents were reinforced by inspection in the Chancery and enrolment among the royal records. The Chancery rolls, which were intended to prevent fraud, thus became a means of making forgeries official. Once the abbot of Chertsey had got the forged charter of Richard I enrolled in 1285, his title depended on that enrolment rather than on the *Cartae Antiquae*

---

[122] M. T. Clanchy, 'The Franchise of Return of Writs', *TRHS* 5th series XVII (1967), p. 71.
[123] *ibid.* pp. 73–4.
[124] *ibid.* pp. 76–7. *CChR* 1257–1300, pp. 305–6.
[125] Ed. L. Landon, PRS new series XVII (1939), pp. 65–6, nos. 118, 119. Cf. S. Painter, *Feudalism and Liberty* (1961), pp. 178–84.

rolls or his original charters of Richard I, which had presumably been destroyed in the process of making the forgery. Chertsey had acted in a similar way in 1256, when a forged charter of Edward the Confessor had been enrolled on the charter rolls of Henry III; the abbey had paid 100 marks for this 'confirmation'.[126]

Potentially the archives recording the acts of successive kings should have been a bastion against human forgetfulness and an assurance of just and efficient government, as Bishop Stapledon's commission claimed. If there had been an efficient filing system and indexes, royal clerks could have kept a check on fraudulent claims. In practice, however, the king's records had become so unwieldly by Edward I's reign that they constituted a largely unmapped territory. Particular monastic houses used them to their advantage by paying fees to have documents enrolled in much the same way as a modern company buys advertising space in a newspaper. As monasteries often kept careful records of these enrolments, they had better 'maps' of those parts of the royal archives which concerned them than any royal official had of the whole. For example, Bury St Edmunds abbey in 1281 paid 1000 marks to Edward I and made a gift of gold to the queen as well to have a new royal charter enrolled, which settled the division of property between the abbot and convent. This enrolment was noted in the Bury chronicle to be 'at the end of the Charter roll for the ninth year' of Edward I, where it can be duly found.[127]

The makers of monastic chronicles and cartularies had kept a watchful eye on the royal records since they had begun to expand in the 1200s. Many chroniclers cite official documents: the best example is Matthew Paris, who obtained transcripts of records through Alexander Swereford of the Exchequer and perhaps also through John Mansel of the Chancery.[128] Some of these documents may have been 'leaked' to Matthew by these officials so that he could give them wider currency and record them for posterity. In a sense a monastic chronicle like Matthew Paris's was an official record which was useful to the crown.[129] Some monasteries claimed that they had a right to make extracts of royal records which concerned them. Thus Dunstable priory submitted in 1276 that the prior was entitled to sit with the royal justices on the bench, and his 'enrolling clerk' with the justices' clerks, in order to copy the plea roll.[130]

The most remarkable collection of extracts from the royal records is Barnwell priory's *Liber Memorandorum*, which was composed in the 1290s, the most appropriate time to be compiling documents systematically as Edward I was beginning to do the same. The book contains the texts of nearly 90 official documents, ranging from citations from Domesday Book and the pipe rolls of John's reign to writs and plea rolls

---

[126] Clanchy, 'The Franchise of Return of Writs', p. 77.

[127] *The Chronicle of Bury St Edmunds* ed. A. Gransden (1964), p. 73.

[128] Vaughan, *Matthew Paris*, pp. 14, 17–18.

[129] See ch. 3, nn. 85, 86 above.

[130] *Annales Monastici* III, p. 272. Pegues, 'The *Clericus* in the Legal Administration', p. 554.

of Edward I. The compiler makes his purpose explicit in his extracts
from a sheriff's roll at Cambridge castle: 'It will not be necessary in
future to go to the castle to see the sheriff's roll, but rather the facts can
be seen and learned from this book.'[131] The book was a kind of cartulary
of other institutions' records concerning Barnwell. In one citation from a
Bench roll of 1288 the compiler notes that 'this record is to be found in a
certain roll on the white part [that is, on the top side of the parchment] at
the end of the roll where this sign [*signum*] is depicted.'[132] The *signum* is
a hand with outstretched index finger, which is indeed to be found in the
roll in question in the Public Record Office.[133] In this instance Barnwell
priory had evidently been allowed to mark the official roll itself, as well
as obtain a transcript of it. The Barnwell book is exceptional in containing so many extracts from royal records, but typical in its desire to keep
pace with and master the methods of the royal bureaucracy in order to
maintain the privileges gained by monks in the past. Monks had been
the specialists in written record before the king's clerks appeared on the
scene. Although they had lost this initiative by 1300, they fastened on
the royal records like leeches and drew from them the information to
sustain their privileges.

The use of a sign, like Barnwell's hand with outstretched index finger,
to mark a particular item in a document was a simple way of facilitating
the retrieval of information. Such signs are not essentially different
from the rubrics, capital letters, running titles, introductory paragraph
flourishes and other aids to the reader which are usual in medieval
manuscripts. The royal records, from Domesday Book and the pipe rolls
onwards, are particularly notable for their clear and orderly layout.[134]
Marginal abbreviations and symbols were systematically used to
extract payments due to the crown from a roll and to distinguish the
business of one county or jurisdiction from another. It is usually easy to
identify a particular item on a membrane or page of a royal document.
The medieval archivist's problem lay in not knowing which page or roll
to search in the first place.

Attempts were made from the end of the twelfth century to convert
the use of visual signs or *signa* into a system for classifying subject
matter. Ralf de Diceto, dean of St Paul's, who marked charters with
signa (as we have already seen), seems to have been the pioneer of such
systems. His elaborate explanation of the *signa* used in his chronicle
suggests that he had invented them himself and wished them to be
appreciated. He warns the reader: 'You will find certain *signa* placed in
the margin. Do not immediately conclude that this is in any way superfluous, for they are there to jog the memory more easily and are very
convenient.'[135] He then explains that, because the making of a chronicle
'always runs on infinitely', the reader needs some guide to its contents.

---

[131] *Liber Memorandorum*, p. 238. Cf. n. 6 above.
[132] *ibid*. p. 114   [133] PRO (Common Pleas) CP 40/73, m. 96.
[134] See pp. 103–4 above and pp. 227–8 below.
[135] *Radulphi de Diceto Opera Historica* ed. W. Stubbs, RS LXVIII (1876), I, p. 1. Cf. n. 53
above.

So he has devised twelve symbols (some are pictorial and some use letters of the alphabet) to indicate different subject matter, such as a sword for information about Normandy or 'PS' for persecutions of the church.[136] Matthew Paris devised a comparable system of *signa*, which he probably derived from Ralf. For example, Matthew used reversed shields in the margin to indicate the deaths of knights and reversed mitres for the deaths of bishops. For Matthew these *signa* became an artistic device in themselves: thus the reversed and broken shield and shattered sword and lance of William Marsh, who was degraded and executed for piracy and treason in 1242, epitomize his dishonourable end.[137] Matthew's contemporary, Robert Grosseteste, also devised a system of *signa* with the assistance of the Franciscan, Adam Marsh; these consisted of about 400 linear rather than pictorial signs which were used to indicate the contents of theological works by marking sections in the margins.[138] Of similar date are the *signa* indicating footnotes in Richard Hotot's estate book (see plate XV).

From the 1290s there is evidence of a system of *signa*, similar to those devised by Ralf and Matthew, being used in the royal archives to mark particular storage chests or rolls. Thus Exchequer *Liber A*, which was completed in 1294–5, used a pictogram of a man with a lance and broadsword to indicate material which was in coffer 'T' under the title 'Scotland'.[139] Likewise, when in 1296 chests of documents and treasure were sent by Edward I from Scotland to London, the chests bore identification *signa*;[140] and in 1298 a record of a serjeanty tenure in Essex is said to be 'contained in the roll *Teste de Nevill*'.[141] This is the earliest instance of the rolls of knights' fees being identified by the 'Head of Nevill', which was probably the symbol painted on the chest containing them. As there is no evidence for the use of pictorial *signa* of this type in the royal archives before the 1290s,[142] it is likely that they were introduced when Edward I's claims to overlordship in Scotland at last made the government aware that it needed some such system. As the king's clerks inspected chronicles for the Scottish business, they may have borrowed the idea directly from Ralf de Diceto.

A system of pictorial *signa*, which had worked in Diceto's chronicle because it was confined to twelve symbols and was picturesque in Matthew Paris's case, necessarily proved clumsy when extended to numerous documents and chests in the royal archives. The obvious way to classify documents and their contents in a phonetic script was by

[136] Ralf's *signa* are illustrated by Gransden, *Historical Writing*, plate vii and by Smalley, *Historians*, p. 118. Pictograms were recommended as mnemonics by Martianus Capella (cited by F. Yates, *The Art of Memory* (1966), p. 64), whose work Ralf may have known.

[137] Matthew Paris IV, p. 196. Gransden, *Historical Writing*, plate ixf.

[138] S. H. Thomson, 'Grosseteste's Topical Concordance of the Bible and the Fathers', *Speculum* IX (1934), pp. 139–44.

[139] Illustrated by E. L. G. Stones, 'The Appeal to History in Anglo-Scottish Relations', *Archives* IX (1969), plate facing p. 11.

[140] *Anglo-Scottish Relations*, p. 75.

[141] *Book of Fees* I, p. xv.   [142] Gransden, *Historical Writing*, p. 364, n. 56.

using alphabetical or numerical notations rather than pictograms. The royal archivists had begun to use individual letters of the alphabet to mark chests, like the coffer 'T' referred to above; but, at the risk of being contradicted by an exception, no English royal record from the period 1066–1307 has been found which uses an alphabetical index.

Yet the principle of using alphabetical order to classify words for reference was of great antiquity. It is found, for example, in Anglo-Saxon and Latin vocabularies dating from the eighth and tenth centuries.[143] Lists of Hebrew names with their meanings, arranged in strict alphabetical order to the third or fourth letter of each word, appear in English bibles of the thirteenth century.[144] By the end of Edward I's reign alphabetical indexes had been made to parliamentary statutes and other lawbooks. A portion of a page from such an index is illustrated at plate XIX. The layout is magnificent, the alphabetical order quite good, and the references elaborate (they use a system of Roman and Arabic numerals combined with letters of the alphabet). Nevertheless this index does not work properly, although the occasional reference in Roman numerals accords by chance with a folio number in the book. The index seems to have been made for another manuscript of similar contents but different pagination. The person who went to the trouble of appending this index to a book to which it does not refer precisely cannot have understood that indexes need to be exact in every detail if they are to work at all. Thus even when the principles of indexing by alphabetical order and numerical sequence had been laid down, it was still difficult to apply them widely in practice because the average reader did not expect to use a medieval manuscript as a source of ready reference. The owner of the lawbook illustrated at plate XIX, probably Worcester cathedral priory, was perhaps well pleased with the index as it stood.[145] For the monks of Worcester it was valuable as an object of beauty and mystery rather than utility.[146]

Instead of borrowing a primarily pictorial system of classification from traditionalist monks and their chronicles, the king's government would have done better to consult the friars, as they had the most recent experience of coping successfully with the large number of books required for their libraries, as we have already seen.[147] Because they were the latest religious order, the friars were the most up-to-date experts in the problems posed by the proliferation of literature and documents. As early as 1230 the Dominicans had compiled an alphabetical concordance of the Bible, which was the first of its kind; it was subsequently enlarged by John of Darlington, the confessor of

---

[143] *A Second Volume of Vocabularies* ed. T. Wright (1873). In general see L. W. Daly, *Contributions to a History of Alphabetization in Antiquity and the Middle Ages* (Brussels, 1967).

[144] E.g. Harvard University MS. Typ 446 (MS. from Bury St Edmunds) or BL Royal MS. 1. D. I. (MS. written by William of Devon). Such lists derive from the *Interpretationes Nominum Hebraeorum* of Remigius of Auxerre.

[145] The MS. is described by S. de Ricci, *Census of Medieval and Renaissance MSS in the USA and Canada* (1935), p. 1022.

[146] See pp. 227–8 below.   [147] See n. 58 above.

Henry III.[148] Edward I's first archbishop of Canterbury was the Dominican, Robert Kilwardby (1273–8), who had made a similar alphabetical index or concordance to the subjects discussed by the principle Church Fathers.[149]

The English Franciscans had equally ambitious schemes. They had contributed to the 400 theological symbols of Grosseteste and Adam Marsh. In addition, in the latter half of the thirteenth century the Franciscans drew up their *Registrum Anglie de Libris Doctorum et Auctorum*. This was a union catalogue of the principal books in the libraries of religious houses in England, using a numerical notation system to refer to the 183 monasteries (not just Franciscan houses) included in the register.[150] This register proved far from complete, but at least it indicates that the need for a comprehensive catalogue was understood. The Dominicans and Franciscans thus showed that they had between them the experience required to construct alphabetical indexes to particular documents and to list works scattered in numerous repositories. Moreover, some of the authors of these systems were personally known to Henry III and Edward I.

To ask why these kings made no use of such expertise, when it was readily available, is probably to expect too much too soon of the shift from memory to written record. The friars devised new guides to ancient works, like the Bible and the Church Fathers. The only equivalent document of ancient scripture for the king's government was Domesday Book and that was being consulted regularly and systematically by Edward I's reign; it had been so beautifully designed in the first place that an index was not essential. The royal records of the twelfth and thirteenth centuries, on the other hand, were too recent and too large and diverse to be seen as a whole. Their potential was not appreciated until the last years of Edward I's reign, when the dispute over Scotland compelled the king to consider events from a historical point of view. Even then he relied primarily on the evidence of monastic chronicles in preference to the royal archives. Although the difficulty of consulting his own records is a sufficient explanation for this procedure, there was probably political wisdom in it as well. If monasteries were asked to give evidence from their chronicles which had been compiled in the face of God, the king's case would be strengthened by this public process of consultation, whereas evidence which came exclusively from the royal archives could be said to be one-sided and clandestine.

Professional historians are bound to approach medieval archives in an anachronistic way. Their business is to hunt among documents for information and then rely on the evidence they find to construct an argument. Historians assume too readily that their medieval predecessors would have acted likewise. But in the world of thirteenth-century

[148] Smalley, *The Bible*, pp. 241, 333–4.

[149] D. A. Callus, 'The *Tabulae Super Originalia Patrum* of Robert Kilwardby' in *Studia Mediaevalia in Honorem Raymundi J. Martin* (Bruges, 1948), pp. 264–5, 268–9.

[150] R. M. Thomson, 'The Library of Bury St Edmunds Abbey', *Speculum* XLVII (1972), p. 620.

politics, where literate modes were relatively novel, written records were of limited value to governments. In Edward I's last years a terrible warning of what might happen to those who put their trust in written law and precedent was presented to Europe by the attack on Boniface VIII at Anagni in 1303. In a campaign of words the pope had attempted to enforce his claims of overlordship over Philip IV of France. From the point of view of traditional ecclesiastical law Boniface's various bulls, particularly *Unam Sanctam*, were well founded. Yet in the *Dispute between a Cleric and a Knight*, which was composed as counter-propaganda, the Knight says:

> I had to laugh when I heard that Lord Boniface VIII had just decreed that he is and ought to be over all governments and kingdoms. That way he can easily acquire a right for himself over anything whatever: since all he has to do is to write, and everything will be his as soon as he has written.[151]

The Knight implies that the pope could not distinguish between the theories of his chancery and *curia* and the realities of power. In reality authority depended on country-keeping knights like himself, who did not believe in the creed of writing everything down. In the *quo warranto* proceedings against the magnates, and perhaps also in his claim to overlordship in Scotland, Edward I showed that he too had been occasionally beguiled by the advice of academic lawyers with their confidence in written precedents, although by and large Edward relied on the sword rather than the pen.

Nor was it only knights and laymen who distrusted documents. In the 1180s some Parisian clerics who were going to litigate at the Roman curia were advised by the archbishop of Lyons: 'Do not confide in your decretals, for whether the pope decides for or against you, it will be said that he has decided justly.'[152] That was realistic advice, as Pope Lucius III himself admitted in 1184: 'Because of the mass of business which is referred to the Apostolic See, we cannot possibly remember the tenor of our letters and other decisions. For this reason we may be tricked into contradicting what we have written earlier.'[153] This naive and honest revelation of helplessness in the face of the mass of records, 'the inextricable wood of decretal letters',[154] would no doubt have been shared by the clerks of Edward I's Chancery vis-à-vis their letters, if they had dared to confess to such incompetence. A comparable statement, though it differs in being weary and cynical rather than naive, was made in 1279 about English official records by Roger of Seaton, who had recently retired from being chief justice of the Bench. When asked about the whereabouts of his plea rolls, he replied that they were deposited at the New Temple, but he added: 'Yet I cannot vouch for them for a number of

---

[151] B. Tierney, *The Crisis of Church and State* (1964), p. 201.

[152] J. W. Baldwin, *Masters, Princes and Merchants* (1970) I, p. 332.

[153] M. Bloch, 'The Suit of the Serfs of Rosny-Sous-Bois' in *Change in Medieval Society* ed. S. Thrupp (1964), p. 4.

[154] Duggan, *Decretals*, p. 26 (citing Stephen of Tournai).

reasons: because one thing is done and something else – more or less – is written in the rolls by the clerks, who are always failing to understand the litigants and disputants correctly.'[155] Thus in Seaton's opinion the plea rolls, which were the most formal and solemn records of the king's court, were fundamentally unreliable because the clerks who wrote them were too stupid or too careless to understand the business of the court.

The wheel had come full circle. Records had been made first of all by monasteries as an act of worship and to inform posterity of selected historical portents. Then in the twelfth century the king's government had begun to use documents in its daily business; intermittently these documents accumulated into an archive of potential written precedents. They were a treasure like the crown jewels. In the last decade of Edward I's reign ambitious, but largely unsuccessful, attempts were made to search among the royal records for precedents. 'Search all the rolls and remembrances', Edward ordered in 1300, 'search Domesday at the Exchequer at York and all the other rolls of the Exchequer and Chancery, so that nothing is left unsearched, then go to London to search all the other rolls there.'[156] In reality the authority of Edward I, or of any other king, depended more on his armies and castles than on his archives. The incalculable investment of time and skill in making records may not have been a benefit to the king's government. Or rather, lists of debts and the like were obviously useful for a year or two, but thereafter their only interest was historical. The government needed documents, but it did not necessarily require records.

Records had not originally been made for utilitarian purposes, measurable in cost-benefit terms. Rather they had been pledges to posterity and an assurance of the continuity of institutions under God's providence. Over the passage of centuries medieval royal documents have taken on the same qualities as monastic records: they have become a monument for posterity to the power and organization of the kings who persisted in making and keeping them. Whether they were profitable in the twelfth and thirteenth centuries is a question asked only by professional historians. At the time courtiers and armies, castles and palaces, gold and silk, were doubtless more potent and immediate manifestations of royal wealth and power than parchments. But now that the king's men are buried, his buildings in ruins and his treasures dispersed, the hundreds of thousands of documents survive as the best memorial to past greatness. Ironically, in attempting to make an archive for daily and practical use, the English monarchy had created one of the greatest historical monuments of all time.

[155] *SCCKB* I, p. clxviii.
[156] *Calendar of Chancery Warrants* I, p. 120. Cf. n. 30 above.

Part II

The Literate Mentality

Literacy is unique among technologies in penetrating and structuring the intellect itself, which makes it hard for scholars, whose own skills are shaped by literacy, to reconstruct the mental changes which it brings about. This difficulty has often been noticed and is most clearly put, with reference to medieval England in particular, by Maitland:

> The habit of preserving some written record of all affairs of importance is a modern one in the north and west of Europe. But it is so prevalent and so much bound up with our daily habits that we have almost forgotten how much of the world's business, even in communities by no means barbarous, has been carried on without it.[1]

Having described in the first part of this book how and when 'the habit of preserving some written record of all affairs of importance' grew up, the chapters which follow attempt to analyse the development of literate ways of thought. Because the formation of literate habits was relatively slow in England, documents from different dates can be used to pinpoint various aspects of the development. Some of these aspects are peculiar to medieval England, whereas others are common to all societies which have experienced the transition from memory to written record. Although it is difficult to reconstruct pre-literate ways of thought from historical documents, there is sufficient evidence over the two and a half centuries 1066–1307 to discern the main outlines. What is most evident is that literate habits and assumptions, comprising a literate mentality, had to take root in diverse social groups and areas of activity before literacy could grow or spread beyond a small class of clerical writers.

In medieval England all kinds of problems and prejudices had to be overcome before literate modes became acceptable to the rulers, and particularly to the knights in the counties upon whose lead further change depended. It was not, for example, a simple matter of writing down the language which was spoken, as a variety of languages and dialects were used, and Latin had a special status as the traditional language of literacy. To be *litteratus* meant to know Latin and not specifically to have the ability to read and write. The literacy of the laity

[1] P & M I, p. 25.

is the most frequently discussed aspect of medieval literacy, yet that cannot be understood until the terms are defined in their medieval contexts.

The problems just described are peculiarly medieval. Added to them are the psychological differences between learning by ear and learning by looking at script. Medieval writing was mediated to the non-literate by the persistence of the habit of reading aloud and by the preference, even among the educated, for listening to a statement rather than scrutinizing it in script. Writing had the profoundest effects on the nature of proof, as it seemed to be more durable and reliable than the spoken word. On the other hand, those who valued the traditional wisdom of remembrancers within their communities had reason to distrust it. In England at least, in matters of legal proof, compromises were made which helped written modes to become more acceptable. The growth of literacy was not a simple matter of providing more clerks and better schooling, as it penetrated the mind and demanded changes in the way people articulated their thoughts, both individually and collectively in society.

6

Languages of record

Before the formation of literate habits can be analysed the languages in use, whether oral or written, need to be described, since language is necessarily prior to literacy. After the Norman Conquest the way languages were used in England became extraordinarily complex, primarily because of the introduction of French as a spoken language and the decline of Old English as a written one. For the next two centuries, at the very time that documents came into common use, Latin, French and English had to compete with each other to establish themselves as written languages. Whether the growth of literacy was obstructed or encouraged by such competition is difficult to establish; certainly literacy cannot have remained unaffected. In addition, Hebrew was used as a language of record by the Jews who arrived in the twelfth century. These problems of diversity of language and of the differences between written and spoken language are approached in this chapter by starting with a specific example of a book which aimed to help the English gentry improve their French.

Walter of Bibbesworth's treatise

lippe   *the hare*
Vous avez la levere et le levere,
 the pount *book*
La livere et le liv(e)re,
La levere c'est ke enchost les dens,
Le levere ki boys se tent dedeins,
La livere sert de marchaundie,
Le livere nous aprent clergie.[1]

These lines come from Walter of Bibbesworth's rhyming French vocabulary with occasional English interlincations. Walter was a knight from Essex (with some interests in Hertfordshire), who participated in the county's business and served Henry III in the 1250s and 1260s.[2] He

---

[1] *Le Traité de Walter de Bibbesworth sur la langue française* ed. A. Owen (Paris, 1929), pp. 50–51, lines 61–6.

[2] Walter's career has not been thoroughly studied. There may have been two persons, father and son, of the same name. J. C. Russell, *Dictionary of Writers of Thirteenth-Century England* (1936), pp. 175–6, provides an introduction.

wrote his work for 'ma dame Dyonise de Mountechensi'.[3] There were a number of ladies called Denise de Montchensy in the thirteenth century; the one most probably known to Walter is the Lady Denise who was the wife and widow (after 1255) of Warin de Montchensy.[4] Walter explains that he wrote the book to enable Denise to teach her children the vocabulary of 'husbandry and management', which they would require when they grew up.[5]

The extract cited from Walter's work introduces all the principal problems concerning the use of languages in medieval England. Walter assumes for a start that Lady Denise can read in both English and French. He explains that he is not teaching elementary French, 'which everyone knows how to speak', but something 'not so common'.[6] By distinguishing in this extract between words of similar sound in French but different meanings in English (*la levere* 'the lip', *le levere* 'the hare', *la livere* 'the pound', *le livere* 'the book'), Walter emphasizes the need for accurate reading and grammar beyond the colloquial French 'which everyone knows'. He aims to teach good French, the king's French of the court of Henry III, and not the French of Marlborough or of Stratford-atte-Bow.[7] The existence of 'Anglo-Norman' features in the language of Walter and other English writers of French does not imply that they thought their French a different language from the French of France.

Although Lady Denise can already speak French, like everyone of her class in Walter's opinion, his work makes it clear that English is her mother tongue, as much as it is his. As Denise was the daughter of Nicholas Ansty of Hertfordshire and had been the widow of Walter Langton at the time she married Warin de Montchensy in *c.* 1235, it is likely that she was not a native French speaker.[8] The English interlineations which distinguish the masculine and feminine meanings of *levere* and *livere* would only be helpful to someone who knew English better than French. These interlineations were designed by Walter as an integral part of his work – 'You will find first the French and then the English above it', he says[9] – in order to assist those who could not have coped with improving their French entirely by his direct method. The way Walter and his readers think in English is best illustrated by his use of single English words as a starting point for building up vocabulary in French. Thus he gives the example of a handsome knight whose hair is red (*rous* in French), whose horse is red (*sor*), whose shield is red (*goules*), whose lance is red (*rouge*) and so on.[10]

For Walter and his audience English is assumed to be the mother

[3] *Le Traité*, p. 43.
[4] G. E. Cokayne, *The Complete Peerage* (2nd edn) IX (1936), pp. 421–2 (Munchensy).
[5] 'husbondrie e manaungerie,' *Le Traité*, p. 43.
[6] *ibid.* pp. 52–3, lines 82, 86.
[7] For these derogatory terms see G. E. Woodbine, 'The Language of English Law', *Speculum* XVIII (1943), p. 413.
[8] *The Complete Peerage* IX, p. 421.
[9] *Le Traité*, p. 44.
[10] *ibid.* p. 75, cited by W. Rothwell, 'The Role of French in Thirteenth-Century England', *BJRL* LVIII (1976), p. 464.

tongue, but they need to know good French as well because it is the language of the gentry, the *gentils hommes* (as Walter calls them), and of the king's court. 'For unless a man knows French, he is thought of little account' is an affirmation of another of Walter's contemporaries.[11] Because in Walter's time French was just beginning to come into common use as a written language, ambitious men and women in England required a more accurate knowledge of it than would have been necessary in the twelfth century. Walter catered for their needs by providing a practical vocabulary for those who wished to get on in society, including – as in our extract – the parts of the body ('the lip which surrounds the teeth'), hunting ('the hare which hides in the wood'), weights and measures ('the pound which is used in trade') and learning ('the book which teaches us *clergie*').

In this last reference, to the book which teaches us *clergie*, Walter reminds his audience that they will have already learned some Latin, the language of the 'clergy', as well as English and French. The difference for Walter between learning French and learning Latin is that French is initially learned colloquially by hearing and then improved by using his treatise, whereas Latin is primarily and essentially book learning. The book which teaches us *clergie* is the Latin primer, which Walter assumes his readers, including Lady Denise, are familiar with from their childhood. Latin was taught systematically by tutors, using grammar as a basis, whereas French was often more informally acquired. At the same time as Walter was writing, however, other works were being composed which treat French grammatically and proceed from Latin.[12] They presumably catered for the minority of lower class clergy who had not been exposed to French while they grew up.

Walter assumes that it is possible to teach yourself French but not Latin. Although cases can be found of Latin being learned without formal instruction, they are exceptions which prove the rule that it was difficult. Gerald of Wales has a story about a hermit, Wecheleu, whom he met near the river Wye in *c.*1193, who had acquired Latin miraculously while on a pilgrimage to Jerusalem. He only used infinitives and substantives, explaining to Gerald that 'the Lord who gave me the Latin tongue, give it not me by way of grammar and cases, but only that I might be understood and understand others.'[13] In Wales of course the language problem was even more complex than in England, as a man like Gerald needed to know some Welsh as well as Latin, French and English.

The knowledge of languages which Walter expected upper class English men and women of his day to have was some acquaintance with Latin and the book learning of the clergy, a knowledge of colloquial French which required extending and refining, and an effortless facility in English because it was the mother tongue. Walter's work underlines

[11] *Metrical Chronicle of Robert of Gloucester* ed. W. A. Wright, RS LXXXVI (1887), II, p. 544, line 7542.

[12] Rothwell, 'The Role of French', pp. 458ff.

[13] Giraldus I, p. 91.

generalizations which characterized English culture in the thirteenth century. By his time the gentry were not usually illiterate; rather, their reading ability was taken for granted, as was a little Latin. Nor were many of them native French speakers. Walter and his like were Englishmen who learned French because it was the most influential language in Europe, as it was spoken by their Plantagenet kings as well as by St Louis. Moreover, some of the English magnates, as distinct from knights like Walter, were native French speakers; the most famous example in Walter's time was Simon de Montfort. A combination of social and political pressures thus encouraged both Lady Denise and her children and knights like Walter to master languages.

Walter of Bibbesworth was not unique in being a relatively obscure knight who had a good knowledge of written and spoken French. Comparable with him is his namesake, Walter of Henley, who a generation later advised another great dowager, Isabel de Forz, and wrote his treatise on farm management, *Husbandry*, in French.[14] Both Walters were typical of the educated gentlemen of each county who acted as stewards and managers for royal and baronial enterprises. Walter of Bibbesworth was described as a 'discreet knight' of Essex in a royal writ in 1254.[15] Although such men were usually essentially English, they knew French because it was the language of management (*manaungerie*) and lordship, and they were familiar with Latin because it was the language of the schoolmen and of the older branches of the royal administration.

The variety of languages

English, French and Latin performed distinct social and intellectual functions in twelfth- and thirteenth-century England.[16] No one language could serve all the diverse purposes required because their struggle for dominance was still undecided. English appeared to have given way to Latin as the standard written language of government in the century after the Norman Conquest. But just as the renewed vigour of Latin was sweeping all before it in the latter half of the twelfth century, the time of John of Salisbury and Richard Fitz Neal, French began to flourish as a literary language. A century later, in Edward I's reign, it looked as if French might replace Latin as the commonest written language in England. Yet throughout the whole period from 1066 to 1307 English had remained the commonest spoken language and this is probably the reason why it emerged in the fourteenth century, transformed and fortified, to take its place as the principal language of literature and ultimately of record.

In addition to English, French and Latin, writings survive in Hebrew. The first Hebrew writings extant in England are notes on money-

---

[14] *Walter of Henley*, pp. 147–8.   [15] *ClR* 1253–4, p. 42.

[16] In general see P & M I, pp. 80–87; R. M. Wilson, 'English and French in England', *History* XXVIII (1943), pp. 37–60; P. Wolff, *Western Languages AD 100–1500* trans. F. Partridge (1971).

lenders' bonds. The earliest of such bonds were written in Latin with the Hebrew notes appended to them in the form of endorsements or additions on the face of the document. Thus one of the earliest Jewish bonds extant is a Latin letter patent of Aaron of Lincoln, stating that the men of Barton have paid £10 10s. at Michaelmas in 1182. To this letter is appended a note of receipt in Hebrew by Aaron's agents, which can be translated as follows:

> This my signature attests that I have received £10 10d. [*recte* 10s.] of the Barton tax at Eckel 143. And I the undersigned have received one half on behalf of Dom R. Isaac, son of Dom R. Joseph. And what I have received I have written and signed: Berechia son of R. Eliahu.[17]

The date 'Eckel 143' refers to Michaelmas (transliterated into Hebrew as 'Eckel') in the year of the foundation of the world 4800 + 143, which accords with 1182 AD.[18] Jews usually authenticated such documents with their signatures, although seals were also sometimes used. A Hebrew note of acquittance of a debt by Jacob son of Aaron, which is appended to a Latin charter dating from 1238–9, is written on the parchment tag bearing his seal.[19]

About half a dozen Hebrew writings appended to Latin documents survive from the 1180s, including two receipts and some miscellaneous notes recording the contents of bonds or the names of Jews who acquired interests in the property they concerned.[20] The latter notes were presumably made so that a Jew could readily see in his own language which bond he required when it was deposited in a chest. In the thirteenth century, up to the expulsion of the Jews in 1290, the number of such bilingual Latin-Hebrew documents increases. Moreover, from the 1260s similar documents are drawn up in French and Hebrew because French was by then competing with Latin as the language of title-deeds.[21] In addition to writings on parchment, Hebrew was also used on the wooden tallies which were kept by the Exchequer and other accountants.[22]

When Jews made written agreements with each other, as distinct from making them with Christians, they used Hebrew throughout instead of mixing Hebrew with Latin or French. The earliest English documents entirely in Hebrew survive from the 1230s.[23] Among the most evocative of such documents are: the arrangements made by three sons for the well being of their mother and sister at Norwich in 1251; correspondence to and from Rabbi David, bailiff of the Nottingham

[17] *Starrs and Jewish Charters Preserved in the BM* ed. I. Abrahams et al. (1930) I, p. 117. This is not the earliest moneylender's bond extant, as those of the Fleming, William Cade, date from the 1160s (see ch. 9, n. 23 below).

[18] *ibid.* pp. xxii–xxiii.   [19] *ibid.* plate iii facing p. 81.

[20] *ibid.* p. 119. *Shetaroth: Hebrew Deeds of English Jews before 1290* ed. M. D. Davis, Publications of the Anglo-Jewish Historical Exhibition II (1888), p. 289. Richardson, *Jewry*, p. 256. *Oxford Facs*, no. 85. *Northants. Facs*, p. 120, plate xlv.

[21] *Starrs and Jewish Charters*, pp. 12–13, 124–5.

[22] H. Jenkinson, 'Exchequer Tallies', *Archaeologia* LXII (1911), p. 378, plate li.

[23] *Shetaroth*, pp. 222–5 (Nottingham AD 1233), pp. 312–15 (Canterbury AD 1230).

Jews, in the same period; a betrothal contract made at Lincoln in 1271.[24] In the Lincoln contract part of the gift made by the future bride to the groom is a precious Massoretic Bible. It was evidently normal for both male and female English Jews to be literate in Hebrew. The men, and a notable number of women, who had business dealings with Christians had to understand Latin, French and English as well. Although the total number of Jews was small and they were mainly concentrated in towns, all large property-owners, particularly the lay barons and great monasteries, must have seen, even if they did not understand, Hebrew writings when they borrowed money. Magnates of the thirteenth century would probably have come across more writing in Hebrew than in English.

This discussion of Hebrew has been confined to legal documents because they are extant in originals and can be precisely dated. It would be a false inference, however, to conclude that medieval English Jews were only concerned with moneylending or that they used Hebrew primarily for that purpose. There was a renaissance of Hebrew in the twelfth century just as there was a renaissance of Latin. Some of the best Hebrew works were written in England, although their authors were not necessarily permanently resident there. Good examples are the *Jesod Morah* (Foundation of Reverence) and the *Iggereth haShabbath* (Sabbath Epistle) of the Spanish biblical exegete, Abraham ibn Ezra, which are stated in their texts to have been written in England in 1158.[25] Although in the *Jesod Morah* Abraham deplores his contemporaries' lack of learning, the standards he expected were as high as those of the Christian masters of the Paris schools. Original studies of Hebrew grammar and punctuation were composed by Londoners around 1200.[26] It is not too fanciful to surmise that such work was stimulated by the proliferation of documents and the precise regulations imposed on Jewish scribes by Hubert Walter in 1194. More Jews were influenced by Christian works than vice-versa because many of them spoke French or English and read Latin, whereas only a handful of Christian biblical scholars knew Hebrew, though Englishmen like Herbert of Bosham and Roger Bacon were prominent among them.[27]

This excursus on the use of Hebrew emphasizes how no one language could serve all purposes because different languages were associated with particular persons and functions. It is an anachronism to attempt to identify one language as the general language of the population. Nor is the problem resolved by assuming instead that there was complete bilingualism in English and French.[28] The statements made particularly by poets writing in French that their work is expressed in that

[24] *ibid.* pp. 43–6 (Norwich), pp. 275–7 (Nottingham), pp. 298–302 (Lincoln).

[25] C. Roth, *A History of the Jews in England* (3rd edn, 1964), p. 126.

[26] *ibid.* p. 127. As a non-Hebraist, I have benefited from the anthology by J. Jacobs, *The Jews of Angevin England* (1893).

[27] Roth, *A History of the Jews*, p. 129. Smalley, *The Bible* pp. 186ff, 329ff. P. Hyams, 'The Jewish Minority in Medieval England', *Journal of Jewish Studies* XXV (1974), p. 275, n. 19.

[28] Rothwell, 'The Role of French', p. 449 gives examples of this assumption by scholars.

language so that everyone, 'great and small' (*li grant e li mendre*), can understand should not be taken at their face value.[29] They do not mean that all classes knew French; rather, they are typical of the explanations which authors of French works had to make to justify not writing in Latin. Conversely the remark of Hue de Rotelande in *c.*1180 (in his prologue to the romance, *Ipomedon*) that, 'if the Latin is not translated, there will scarcely be anyone who understands it', is not sufficient evidence that a knowledge of Latin was rare.[30] It was a polite convention for romancers like Hue to claim that their works were based on ancient Latin books because fiction as such was unacceptable. Such explanations by authors throw little light on how widely either French or Latin were known, but they do show that the status of French as a literary language was not yet firmly established.

The relative dignity and status of the three principal languages (Latin, French and English) was a favourite subject of debate among writers at the time and has remained so with modern scholars. Latin was argued to carry greater weight than its rivals. Thus Peter of Blois apologized for a sermon, which lacked the 'dignity of eloquence', because it had been translated from a 'vulgar' tongue which preferred brevity.[31] The 'vulgar' tongue referred to here was probably Peter's native French, though it may have been English, as he admits elsewhere that he had difficulty expressing himself adequately in English.[32] Similarly in the thirteenth century the translator of a Latin sermon on Antichrist into French rhyming couplets assured his hearers that it was 'a very great thing in Latin', although it seemed so slight in French.[33]

The best known variation on this theme of rival languages is Walter Map's remark in one of his prologues that, instead of Latin epics like the *Aeneid* which celebrated the heroes of antiquity, 'only the trifling of mummers in vulgar rhymes' celebrates for his contemporaries the achievements of the Charlemagnes and Pepins.[34] Walter wrote in the last two decades of the twelfth century when the *Chanson de Roland* and other works concerning the 'Matter of France' were well known. He purports to ignore the writers of his own day, particularly the non-Latin ones, as he asks the reader: 'Is there anyone who would dare to put upon a page what is happening nowadays, or to write down even our names? Certainly if any novel orthography [*aliquis novus karacter*] were to put upon record "Henry" or "Walter", or even your own name, you would deride it and laugh at it.'[35] By calling vernacular authors 'mummers',

[29] *ibid.* p. 453 (citing Denis Piramus, line 70).

[30] *ibid.* p. 450 (citing *Ipomedon*, lines 28–9)

[31] *Patrologiae* CCVII (1855), col. 751. M. Richter, 'A Socio-Linguistic Approach to the Latin Middle Ages' in *The Materials, Sources and Methods of Ecclesiastical History*, Studies in Church History, ed. D. Baker (1975) XI, p. 76.

[32] Richter, 'A Socio-Linguistic Approach', p. 72, n. 14.

[33] Legge, *Anglo-Norman*, p. 235.

[34] 'nobis divinam Karolorum et Pepinorum nobilitatem vulgaribus ritmis sola mimorum concelebrat nugacitas,' Walter Map, bk. iv, ch. 1, p. 203.

[35] Walter Map, p. 204. I have benefited from the translation by F. Tupper and M. Bladen (1924), p. 255.

implying that they are performers in vulgar dumbshows, and by discounting the success of innovation in writing in vernacular scripts, Walter suppresses the voice of vernacular literature by ignoring its existence.

Yet Walter himself may have been teasing his Latin readers, or have been unconscious of his own inconsistencies. His question, 'Is there anyone who would dare to put upon a page what is happening nowadays?', can be readily answered by citing contemporary works in French. Thus at the time Walter was writing, Jordan Fantosme composed his verse chronicle of the war in 1173–4 between England and Scotland.[36] Like Walter's learned readers, Jordan was a graduate of Paris, a bishop's clerk and a master in the schools (at Winchester), yet he chose to write in French not Latin. Likewise in Walter's time Wace wrote (in French) the *Roman de Brut*, a history of England based on Geoffrey of Monmouth, and the *Roman de Rou*, a history of Normandy which was commissioned by Henry II.[37] Furthermore, as Walter probably knew well, other educated clerics were writing in English. *The Owl and the Nightingale*, almost certainly by Master Nicholas of Guildford, is contemporary with Walter's work and at about the same time the Worcestershire priest, Lazamon, 'studied books' and wrote his English version of the *Brut* story.[38]

In asking who would dare to write non-Latin literature, Walter Map was contributing to the debate on the relative status of languages in a characteristically facetious and ambivalent way. Gerald of Wales reports that Walter told him that *dicta* in the vernacular were more profitable than *scripta* in Latin because knowledge of Latin was declining.[39] Walter was therefore well aware that the Latinists had to make a spirited attack, if they were to compete with the trifling 'mummers' who were busy composing in 'vulgar rhymes' the greatest literature of the Middle Ages. His own *De Nugis Curialium* (*Courtiers' Trifles*) was a flashy attempt to make modern Latin literature attractive. Despite Walter, however, the classicists had already been as summarily dismissed by the greatest composer in 'vulgar rhymes', Chrétien de Troyes:

> Car de Grezois ne de Romains
> Ne dit an mes ne plus ne mains,
> D'ax est la parole remese
> Et estainte le vive brese.[40]

[For of the Greeks and Romans no one now says either much or little; their word has ceased, their bright flame is extinguished.]

---

[36] *Chronicles* ed. R. Howlett, RS LXXXII (1884), III, pp. 202–376. Cf. R. C. Johnston, 'The Historicity of Jordan Fantosme's Chronicle', *JMH* II (1976), pp. 159–68.

[37] Gransden, *Historical Writing*, pp. 202, 219.

[38] Introductions in Bennett & Smithers, nos. i and x and in R. M. Wilson, *Early Middle English Literature* (3rd edn, 1968), pp. 149–69, 205–13.

[39] Giraldus V, pp. 410–11. Gerald comments on Walter's *facetia* in this context. Cf. ch. 8, nn. 55–6 below.

[40] *Cligés*, lines 39–42, ed. A. Micha, *Les Romans de Chrétien de Troyes* (Paris, 1957) II. Cf. Curtius, *European Lit.*, p. 385.

Another of Walter's contemporaries, Jocelin of Brakelond, likewise enjoyed the languages debate and treated it humorously in his account of the election of Herbert as prior of Bury St Edmunds in 1200.[41] Herbert objected that he was insufficiently learned in Latin to preach a sermon in the monastic chapter. In reply, 'to the prejudice of the literate' (that is, the Latinists), Abbot Samson condemned rhetorical ornament and told Herbert that he could preach 'in French or better still in English'. The 'illiterate' monks were delighted and teased their 'literate' brethren with such puns as 'they have declined *musa, muse* so often that they are all bemused.' Samson himself was exceptional in steering a middle course between learning and action and in rejecting the conventional hierarchy of languages, which placed Latin at the top, French in the middle and English at the bottom. For him their different merits were not mutually exclusive. According to Jocelin, Samson was a graduate of Paris and 'was eloquent in French and Latin'.[42] In addition, he knew 'how to read literature written in English most elegantly (*elegantissime*) and he used to preach in English to the people, but in the speech of Norfolk where he was born and bred.'[43]

In this passage Jocelin emphasizes the dual status of English: there is spoken popular English (with its diverse dialects) in which Samson preaches to the people,[44] and there is written English in which he reads *elegantissime*. Jocelin thus takes it for granted that English is a language of educated men in which elegance of expression is appreciated. The literature (*scriptura*) which Samson read so elegantly was probably Anglo-Saxon; Aelfric's *Passion of St Edmund*, for example, would have been an appropriate text for an abbot of Bury to read aloud.[45] Samson may also perhaps have enjoyed twelfth-century homiletic literature in English, or even the witty legalistic debate of *The Owl and the Nightingale* (though its southern diction might have struck him as novel), as he was a fine debater in the county court.[46] Samson's trilingual mastery of Latin, French and English was probably shared by many of the energetic men who ran England in 1200, but it would not have been typical of the population as a whole. When half a century later Roger Bacon remarks that 'we speak English, French and Latin', he presumably means by 'we' his educated readers and not the masses.[47] Nor probably were the great majority bilingual either as English was their mother tongue.

Spoken and written language

The way languages were used in medieval England can be difficult to understand, because in modern received English the hiatus or

[41] Jocelin, pp. 128–30.   [42] *ibid.* pp. 44, 40.
[43] *ibid.* p. 40 (my translation).
[44] For vernacular preaching see Wilson, 'English and French in England', pp. 48–9 and M. Richter, 'Kommunikationsprobleme im Lateinischen Mittelalter', *Historische Zeitschrift* CCXXII (1976), pp. 57–8, 66–8.
[45] *Lives of Three English Saints* ed. G. I. Needham (1966).   [46] Jocelin, p. 34.
[47] *Rogeri Bacon Opera* ed. J. S. Brewer, RS XV (1859), p. 433.

disjuncture between the spoken and the written word is not usually obvious. Academic lectures are read from texts verbatim, or conversely talks are presented in writing in an informal style recalling the register in which they are spoken. Although medieval vernacular literary texts often reflect oral diction, in business documents by contrast not only the style and register but even the language itself might change in the process of transforming the spoken into the written word. A statement made in court in English or French, for example, might be written down in Latin, or conversely a Latin charter might be read out in English or French. Men like Abbot Samson evidently interchanged languages effortlessly, using whichever one was appropriate for the occasion. The fact that a statement is recorded in a certain language does not mean that it was originally made in that language. Latin had served traditionally as the common medium of literacy in a multilingual and predominantly oral society. A royal message to a sheriff in the thirteenth century might have been spoken by the king in French, written out in Latin, and then read to the recipient in English. Although this conjecture cannot be conclusively proved, because only the language of record survives, some explicit evidence of such interchangeability of languages begins to appear by the end of the thirteenth century.

A good example is the Latin notarial instrument recording the act of homage of John Balliol as king of Scots to Edward I in 1292.[48] John uttered the words of homage 'with his own mouth in the French language', but to give them full legal force they were recorded by Edward's notary, John of Caen, 'literally' (*litteralliter*). This did not mean that Balliol's words were transcribed verbatim, but that they were translated into Latin for the record. According to the notarial instrument Balliol says: 'Devenio vester homo ligeus' (I become your liegeman). By contrast, in the less solemn letters patent recording the similar acts of homage of the Robert Bruces and others in 1296, the same words are written down in French: 'Jeo devenk voster home lige'.[49] The oath of homage actually spoken on two occasions would not have differed, but the notarial instrument required the words of the king of Scots to be written down in Latin, whereas the letters patent of the earls and barons were expressed slightly less formally in French. The language of record depended on the status of the persons concerned and the nature of the document and not on the language actually spoken on the occasion.

Another example, illustrating interchangeability between French and English instead of French and Latin, is provided by the procedure for recording the *veredicta* of juries in the Kent justices' visitation of 1313–14. The jurors' answers or 'true sayings' (*veredicta*), which were presented to the court in reply to the justices' questions, were written down in a roll and, when the justices arrived, the chief clerk of the crown 'began to read the first presentments as they were entered on the roll in French'.[50] The jurors were then required to present the same answers

[48] *Anglo-Scottish Relations*, p. 63.   [49] *ibid.* p. 69.
[50] *The Eyre of Kent* ed. F. W. Maitland *et al.*, SS XXIV (1909), pp. 20–21.

orally at the bar of the court in English. If there were any deviation between the French and English versions, the jurors were liable to imprisonment. Latin was involved in this change of language as well as French and English, since early *veredicta* (the first dating from Kent in 1279) are in Latin and the first account of the procedure (dating from *c.* 1240) precisely describes how they are to be written in Latin.[51]

As Latin was involved, the following changes of language took place, if the jurors' procedure is examined in detail. First of all, the jurors were presented with the justices' questions (the 'articles of eyre' technically) in writing in either Latin or French. They replied orally, probably in English, although their answers were written down as *veredicta* by an enrolling clerk in Latin. When the justices arrived in court, the chief clerk read out the enrolled presentments or *veredicta* in French, mentally translating them from Latin as he went along. On behalf of the jurors, their foreman or spokesman then presented the same answers at the bar in English. Once the presentments, in both their French and English oral versions, were accepted by the court, they were recorded in the justices' plea rolls in Latin. Thus, between the justices' written questions being presented initially to the jurors and the final record of the plea roll, the language in use changed at least five times, although it begins and ends with writings in Latin.

This commonplace procedure has been analysed in detail because its implications are far reaching. It is obvious that the foreman of the jurors, if not his fellows, would need to be able to read French and preferably also Latin. If the oral English statement, which he presented at the bar, deviated in any detail from the written statement, the jurors faced imprisonment. The foreman may also have had this statement at the bar written out in English to ensure that there were no deviations, although it is as probable that he memorized it verbatim. The linguistic ability he required was of a high standard. To find such a man to head every jury must sometimes have been difficult. Yet that was probably not an insuperable problem, as every county had its group of 'discreet and lawful knights', like Walter of Bibbesworth, who were masters of languages and were accustomed to this sort of business.

Although by 1300 lawyers' manuals were usually written in French, it does not follow that French was the spoken language of the court, any more than Bracton's use of Latin conversation in his *De Legibus* in the 1250s implies that Latin was being spoken in the courts then.[52] There was probably no marked change in the spoken language of the courts during the thirteenth century. What did change was the language of record. From the middle of the thirteenth century, in both England and France, French became acceptable as a forensic language. Thus the earliest petitions to St Louis in 1247 are written in Latin, whereas those

---

[51] Early *veredicta* are listed by R. E. Latham and C. A. F. Meekings in *Collectanea* ed. N. J. Williams *et al.* Wilts RS XII (1956), p. 52, n. 1. Procedure in *c.*1240 is described in *SCPWW*, p. cciii. Cf. Bracton, fo. 116, vol. ii, p. 329.

[52] Woodbine, 'The Language of English Law', p. 429, n. 2.

of two decades later are in French.[53] Legal records in England were affected by the same linguistic development. Thus the Provisions of Oxford of 1258, which inaugurated the baronial revolution, are recorded in a novel mixture of Latin and French.[54] The explanation is not that there had been a sudden influx of French-speaking lawyers who displaced Latin speakers in the 1250s, nor had the barons learned to write French overnight. What had happened was that French had at last achieved literate status for legal purposes.

For the next hundred years writs, charters, petitions, memoranda and lawyers' textbooks were increasingly written in French, though Latin also continued. The fact that more French was being written down in England from the middle of the thirteenth century does not mean that more was being spoken. The relative number of documents extant in Latin, French and English is an indicator of the uses of literacy, but it bears no relation to the number of words spoken in each language at the time. If documents were the measure of speech, we would be obliged to conclude that French was not spoken at all in England in the reigns of William the Conqueror and William Rufus, whereas it had become very common two centuries later in Edward I's reign, which is absurd.

It might be objected that, as lawyers' manuals in French report court proceedings in the form of dialogues, it must be accepted that their authors presented them in the language in which they took place. At first sight such dialogues look convincing. For example, in a manual from the 1270s Hugh is accused by John of stealing a horse:

> 'Hue', fet la justice, 'avez entendu ce ke Johan ad vers vous conte?'
> ['Hugh', says the judge, 'have you heard what John recounts against you?']
> 'Sire, oyl.'
> ['Yes, sir.']
> 'Ore li respones solom ce ke vous quidez ke bon seit.'
> ['Then answer him as you think good.']
> 'Sire, pur Deu, je su un simples homs et nynt ay geres use playe de terre . . .'
> ['Sir, God knows, I am a simple man and have scarcely ever made a plea (by the law) of the land . . .'][55].

At this point the reader may begin to doubt. Hugh is a 'simple man', yet he speaks and understands French. Either we accept the unlikely proposition that poor villagers knew French, or we choose the simpler alternative that the writer of this treatise retails dialogue in French just as a monastic chronicler like Matthew Paris retails it in Latin. It is not even evident that the judge is really speaking French either. His aim is

[53] A. Harding, 'Plaints and Bills in the History of English Law', *Legal History Studies 1972* ed. D. Jenkins (1975), pp. 74–5.
[54] *Baronial Docs*, pp. 96–112.
[55] *Placita Corone* ed. J. M. Kaye, SS supplementary series IV (1966), pp. 16–17. The names of Hugh and John are muddled up in this text. For a comparable dialogue from *Court Baron* see ch. 8, n. 114 below.

to trap Hugh into confessing his guilt by cross-examining him, which would probably be most effectively done in Hugh's own language. Even in Henry III's reign the judges were native Englishmen and there is sufficient evidence to show that English was their mother tongue.[56] Like most texts, this manual is addressed to its readers. Its language, the French used for study by English students, is attuned to them and not to the real protagonists in the court.

This example does not mean that French was never really spoken in English courts, but it emphasizes that there is the same hiatus or disjuncture between spoken and written language in French records as there is in Latin ones. The formal pleadings were certainly made in French in Edward I's reign, since one lawyer's manual describes them as being 'uttered by narrators in Romance words and not in Latin ones'.[57] Nevertheless the language of the formal pleadings was not necessarily that of cross-examinations and forensic dialogue. The use of French and English in ecclesiastical courts is mentioned by William of Drogheda and in the Canterbury court in 1271, where Latin was the language of record, both French and English were used orally.[58] It is probable that the king's court did likewise. Although the Year Books, (the law reports which begin in Edward I's reign) record all conversations in the court in French, it cannot be proved that French was the language actually being spoken. In some instances, as when a 'simple man' is being cross-examined, commonsense militates against it. Moreover, the earliest of all such actual reports of a cross-examination by a judge (from the London justices' visitation of 1244), as distinct from a hypothetical dialogue like that with Hugh, is reported in Latin because that was the appropriate language of record in the 1240s.[59]

From such an instance scholars do not immediately jump to the conclusion that Latin was actually being spoken in the court, because Latin can readily be recognized by its standardized form as a language of script rather than of speech. Many early French manuscripts, on the other hand, reveal such a diversity of orthography and syntax that they give a superficial impression of having been written by naive semi-literates, who simply aimed to reproduce the spoken word as faithfully as possible. Because dialect has been used in novels since the nineteenth century to indicate *ipsissima verba*, we tend to assume that medieval writers used it likewise. In fact medieval writing in dialect arose primarily from the lack of a generally accepted standard in a vernacular, rather than from a meticulous attempt to record speech as such.

In their search for a standard, some twelfth-century vernacular writers devised consistent and individual systems of orthography from their own local dialects, whereas other works reveal a mixture of regional speech patterns. Examples of writings in consistent dialects are the

---

[56] Woodbine, 'The Language of English Law', p. 431.
[57] See ch. 8, n. 98 below.
[58] R & S, p. 278, n. 2. R. H. Helmholz, *Marriage Litigation in England* (1974), p. 119, n. 18.
[59] See ch. 3, n. 75 above.

Ormulum, which was composed and penned by its author in what was presumably his own east Midlands diction, and the *Ancrene Wisse*, which uses standard spellings even though it was penned by a number of different scribes.[60] A good example of a work revealing diverse regional speech patterns, on the other hand, is the Anglo-Norman *Romance of Horn* by Master Thomas. Its editor argues that its diversity of language is a product of Thomas's diverse personal experience, hypothetically as a child of immigrants from the Loire valley who was educated in England and at the schools of Poitiers.[61] But perhaps in this case it should not be assumed that a composer of romances, like Thomas, had either the intention or the ability to reproduce in script every nuance of his own speech, as Orm seems to have aimed to do in his eccentric *Ormulum*.

A professional medieval author, which is what Thomas appears to be, did not necessarily compose in his mother tongue, but in whichever language was appropriate to his theme and his audience. Thomas is just as likely to have been a native English speaker as a French one, as the story of Horn is English or Scandanavian in origin. Judging from the prefix 'Master', he was also a Latinist and a schoolman like his contemporary Nicholas of Guildford, the probable author of *The Owl and the Nightingale*, who composed in English. Numerous examples can be cited from the thirteenth century of clerics, like Matthew Paris and Robert Grosseteste, who composed in both Latin and French and there is at least one instance, the Franciscan Thomas of Hales, of a trilingual author who wrote in Latin, French and English.[62]

Thomas begins the *Romance of Horn* by addressing his audience: 'Seignurs, oi avez le vers del parchemin' (Gentlemen, you have heard the lines of parchment).[63] When composing his *vers del parchemin*, Thomas would aim to write in a way which was generally acceptable to the *seignurs* of his audience, rather than to reproduce the idiosyncrasies of his own diction. A sufficient explanation of the composite character of the language of the *Romance of Horn* is that this mixture of western, southwestern and Anglo-Norman French combined some of the speech traits of Thomas with those of the original scribe (to whom he probably dictated the work) and his potential audience. Among the *seignurs* of Angevin England the amalgam served up by Thomas was probably acceptable as the best French they knew. They expected their jongleurs and entertainers to have the gift of tongues. 'Scribal practice, of course, does not so much directly reflect any linguistic milieu as represent a compromise between various constraints.'[64] The relationship between spoken and written language is complex in any linguistic community; in post-Conquest England it was peculiarly so because of the variety of languages and the experimental uses of literacy.

[60] For *Ormulum* see ch. 4, n. 61 above. For *Ancrene Wisse* see *Passiun of St Juliene* ed. S. R. T. O. d'Ardenne, Early English Text S. CCXLVIII (1961), p. xxix.
[61] Ed. M. K. Pope, Anglo-Norman S. XII–XIII (1964), II, p. 122.
[62] Legge, *Anglo-Norman*, pp. 227–8. Cf. Wilson, 'English and French in England', p. 59.
[63] *The Romance of Horn* IX–X (1955), I, p. 1.
[64] C. Clark, 'People and Languages in Post-Conquest Canterbury', *JMH* II (1976), p. 24 (commenting on the trilingual *Canterbury Psalter*, cf. n. 69 below).

Chronological development

At the time of the Norman Conquest the languages in use in England, for written purposes at least, are relatively easy to identify. They were Latin and Anglo-Saxon or Old English. Both were literary languages with centuries of development behind them. Although the form of Old English used in the *Anglo-Saxon Chronicle* and royal writs had derived from West Saxon, it was not a spoken dialect but a standard literary language which extended as far as the authority of the English kings.[65] (Henceforward in this discussion this standard form of Old English will be called 'Anglo-Saxon' to distinguish it from other forms.) Like Latin on the continent of Europe, Anglo-Saxon was closely associated with monasticism and royal power. Any standardized language needs a powerful authority, whether political or cultural, behind it in order to maintain uniformity. The existence of a standard written Old English language does not imply that spoken Old English was equally uniform. The predecessors of Middle English regional dialects already existed in 1066, although they had rarely yet been committed to writing. In some parts of England written Anglo-Saxon, which was as much a royal and clerical language as Latin was, may have appeared almost as foreign and archaic to local people. Anglo-Saxon cannot be described as the popular vernacular in 1066 in contrast to Latin, as both were literary languages.

For a few years after 1066 Anglo-Saxon continued to be used in royal writs (assuming that they are authentic). Moreover, a bilingual notification dating from the 1070s, addressed by William the Conqueror's half-brother, Odo bishop of Bayeux and earl of Kent, to Archbishop Lanfranc and the sheriff of Kent, marks the transition from Anglo-Saxon to Latin in business documents.[66] This notification, which was probably written by a scribe of the beneficiary (Christ Church Canterbury) has the Latin text at the top and the Anglo-Saxon below it. Perhaps Odo wanted Latin used because it seemed absurd to address Lanfranc in a language which neither of them knew, while the Christ Church scribe favoured Anglo-Saxon because that was the traditional language of English writs. Although Canterbury produced other comparable bilingual charters in the twelfth century (see plate III), royal clerks soon wrote exclusively in Latin. This change in the written language does not imply that royal writs ceased to be proclaimed in English in the county court, but only that a text in Anglo-Saxon was no longer provided. The clerk of the court was presumably as capable of translating from Latin into the appropriate regional dialect, as he had been of making Anglo-Saxon fully comprehensible in his locality. For

[65] Bennett & Smithers, p. liv. H. Gneuss, 'The Origin of Standard Old English and Aethelwold's School at Winchester' in *Anglo-Saxon England* ed. P. Clemoes (1972) I, pp. 63–83.

[66] *Sir Christopher Hatton's Book of Seals* ed. L. C. Loyd and D. M. Stenton, Northamptonshire Record S. XV (1950), no. 431 and plate viii.

governmental purposes the language of script did not need to be the same as the language of speech.

Although Anglo-Saxon was not used after the 1070s by the king's government or by the clergy as a whole, it found defenders in the monastic antiquarian reaction which maintained English ways in the face of the Norman conquerors. Those monastic houses like Worcester and Rochester which produced the first cartularies were also among those which were most concerned to preserve a knowledge of Anglo-Saxon. Anglo-Saxon texts continued to be copied for a century after the Conquest and some works survive only in copies made in the twelfth century.[67] As we have seen in Odo of Bayeux's notification, the reaction at Canterbury took the form of producing bilingual Latin and Anglo-Saxon documents, including a manuscript of the *Anglo-Saxon Chronicle* in this form and a number of royal charters written by scribes at Christ Church (see plate III).[68]

The most remarkable product of this movement at Canterbury is the trilingual Psalter written under the direction of Eadwine in the middle of the twelfth century. The beautifully written and illustrated text gives three Latin variant versions of the Psalms in parallel, together with explanatory glosses in Latin, Anglo-Saxon and French (see plate XIV). The French gloss is the earliest French version of the Psalms extant and is written in good prose, whereas the Anglo-Saxon one is an archaic and corrupt text going back to the tenth century. In the famous full-page illustration of himself at the end of this manuscript, Eadwine describes himself as the 'prince of writers' whose fame will not die.[69] He had good reason to be proud of the calligraphy and layout of the Psalter, but not of the Anglo-Saxon gloss if that also were his. The way in which the Anglo-Saxon and French glosses are interlined could suggest that they are slightly later additions, although it is more likely that their placing indicates the relative status of the three languages in Eadwine's mind: Latin was the true language of holy writ; English and French could only be subordinate aids.[70]

The future of English as a written language was assured not by scribes like the Canterbury monks who attempted to perpetuate Anglo-Saxon, but by less conservative writers who gradually promoted various forms of spoken English to the rank of a literary language. The displacement of Anglo-Saxon as the language of government caused written English to diversify into regional dialects and simplify its noun endings, much as the collapse of Roman power had accelerated the breakaway of the Romance languages from Latin. The diversification of written English can be precisely traced and dated in one instance in the

---

[67] C. E. Wright, *English Vernacular Hands* (1960), pp. x–xi.

[68] *ibid.* p. x. The bilingual charters of Henry I and Henry II for Canterbury (written between 1107 and 1155) are listed by T. A. M. Bishop, *Scriptores Regis* (1961), nos. 95, 97, 101, 103–5, 107, 335, 344, 390–91, 399–402, 406.

[69] See ch. 4, n. 2 above.

[70] G. Shepherd, 'English Versions of the Scriptures before Wyclif' in *The Cambridge History of the Bible* ed. G. W. H. Lampe (1969) II, p. 370.

Peterborough abbey continuation of the *Anglo-Saxon Chronicle*.[71] Up to and including the year 1121 this manuscript is written in Anglo-Saxon. The annal for 1122 is written by the same scribe; but, because he no longer has an exemplar to copy from, his writing begins to show east Midlands forms. Thirty years later another scribe wrote up the annals for the years 1132–54, using spelling and script which are even further removed from the standard Anglo-Saxon of the annals before 1122. As a postscript to this development, the Peterborough manuscript has on its concluding folios a crude rhyming chronicle in French which is written around the twelfth-century text in the form of a gloss. This seems to have been done in the reign of Edward I, presumably by a monk who either could not understand the English of the original or who thought the manuscript too old-fashioned to be useful for anything except spare parchment. The Peterborough manuscript illustrates the difficulties inherent in using English as a written language in preference to Latin. If Anglo-Saxon were perpetuated, the text became archaic, yet colloquial forms with their diverse usages might be just as incomprehensible to subsequent generations.

The profound changes in how English was written down which occurred in the twelfth century do not imply that spoken English changed as dramatically. The real change was that colloquial English now affected the written language, because the old standard was no longer being maintained by a public authority. Nor does the relative reduction in the amount of English used for literary purposes imply in any way that it was ceasing to be the ordinary language of oral discourse. There is no explicit evidence that the Norman Conquest caused French to become an alternative to English as the mother tongue of the mass of the people. Numerous words of French origin ultimately entered the English language and French personal and place names became relatively common, but these changes originated from French being the language of the rulers rather than of the people. French remained the language of the influential group immediately around the king for more than two centuries, as each 'new French queen brings with her a new swarm of Frenchmen'.[72] Nor were these later immigrants often Normans; in the century after the accession of Henry II in 1154 they tended to come from the west and south: they were Angevins, Limousins, Poitevins, Provençals and so on. It has never been convincingly shown that 'Anglo-French', which has been called 'Anglo-Norman' by twentieth-century scholars for convenience, was decisively shaped by the dialect of Normandy. 'Anglo-Norman' was not a vernacular, in a dictionary's sense of being the language or dialect of the country, because 'Anglo-Normandy' never existed as one homogeneous country and it ceased altogether with King John's loss of Normandy in 1204. Yet French only became a

---

[71] *The Peterborough Chronicle 1070–1154* ed. C. Clark (2nd edn, 1970). Facsimile ed. D. Whitelock, *Early English MSS in Facsimile* IV (Copenhagen, 1954). R. N. Bailey, 'The Development of English' in *The Medieval World* ed. D. Daiches and A. Thorlby (1973), pp. 148–9.

[72] P & M I, p. 83.

common written language in England for business purposes fifty years or so later.

At all social levels except that of the king's court native French speakers seem to have been rapidly and repeatedly assimilated into the local population. The only exception to this rule are the Jews, who remained separate because of their different religion and scriptural language and not because of their French origins. The remark of Richard Fitz Neal, that English and Normans were so intermarried by his time (*c.* 1179) that they were indistinguishable, has often and rightly been cited.[73] Just as significant is the testimony of Orderic Vitalis a century earlier.[74] He was born near Shrewsbury in 1075, the eldest son of a priest from Orléans and of an English mother. Although his father was one of the counsellors of the Norman magnate, Roger II of Montgomery, Orderic learned no French from his family but only his mother tongue. Nor apparently had he ever heard French spoken in England, as he remarks that when he was sent to Normandy to be a monk at the age of ten, he felt an exile, like Joseph in Egypt, because he heard a language which he could not understand. Yet his father had been concerned about Orderic's education, as he was put into the charge of a priest, Siward, who started to teach him the ABC and Latin at the age of five. The conclusion to draw is that in Orderic's time a basic education did not include French, as it would do in Walter of Bibbesworth's time two centuries later, because French had not yet acquired sufficient prestige with its native speakers. For the Norman conquerors, Latin not French was the indispensable language of lordship and management. It was not primarily the Norman Conquest but the advance of French as an international literary and cultural language, particularly in the thirteenth century, which caused its increasing use as a written language for English records.

French could never compete with English as the mother tongue of those outside the king's court, nor at first could it compete with Latin as a written language. Nothing is extant which was written down in French in England in the period 1066–1100. Indeed very little written French exists of any sort, other than Occitan, earlier than the twelfth century. Contact with England, with its long tradition of non-Latin literature, may have helped to develop French as a written language. Thus the earliest and best manuscript (dating from the 1140s perhaps) of the *Chanson de Roland* is English, although it is not probably indigenous as its language is predominantly Francien.[75] More significant are those instances of French writing of which the earliest examples are English, notably the works of Philip de Thaon. He wrote a bestiary and lapidaries and also *Li Cumpoz*, which is a treatise in verse on how to calculate movable feast days.[76] As he gives examples of such calcula-

---

[73] *Dialogus*, p. 53.

[74] Orderic's early life is discussed by M. Chibnall, Orderic II, pp. xiii–xiv. Cf. Woodbine, 'The Language of English Law', p. 409.

[75] Bodleian Library MS. Digby 23, ed. F. Whitehead (2nd edn, 1946).

[76] Legge, *Anglo-Norman*, pp. 18–26. In general see the same author's 'La precocité de la littérature anglo-normande', *Cahiers de Civilisation Médiévale* VIII (1965), pp. 327–49.

tions and dedicates his work to Humfrey de Thaon, who was chaplain to Eudo the Steward, sheriff of Essex, it is possible to date *Li Cumpoz* to either 1102, 1113 or 1119. Any of these years is precociously early for a writing in French and the subject matter of *Li Cumpoz* is even more remarkable. Only clerics needed to know how to calculate dates and Latin was the best language in which to explain such things with the necessary precision. Philip's pioneering use of French for this purpose suggests that some clergy at least already preferred French to Latin. *Li Cumpoz* also demonstrates that French was capable of being used as early as Henry I's reign for numerical, and hence for governmental, business.

Despite *Li Cumpoz*, the practice of using French for written business purposes advanced much more slowly than its use in literary works. The earliest extant business document or charter written in French in England dates not from Henry I's reign, but from Henry II's Inquest of Sheriffs in 1170. This is a reply to the inquest and is written in an untidy semi-cursive script on a small irregularly shaped piece of parchment with no sign of a seal.[77] It is presumably a draft which was returned in mistake for the Latin fair copy. Its chance survival suggests that thousands of such informal documents once existed which were discarded when their usefulness was over. Likewise in the 1170s Jordan Fantosme describes a letter being drafted 'en Romanz' (that is, in some form of French) in the name of Henry the Young King, offering terms to William the Lion of Scotland.[78] Such documents have rarely survived because, although by the 1170s French had the status of a literary language for jongleurs, Latin was still the appropriate medium for formal documents which might be seen by posterity.

Competition from Latin was at its strongest at this time. When Richard Fitz Neal's pupil urged him in c. 1179 not to write a prolix book but to explain the workings of the Exchequer in 'common words', the ordinary language they both had in mind was Latin, not French or English; Fitz Neal describes the Latin Domesday Book similarly as being written in 'common words'.[79] Thanks to the Latin renaissance of the eleventh and twelfth centuries, which had first reached England with Archbishops Lanfranc and Anselm as an indirect consequence of the Norman Conquest, Latin became capable of serving a variety of purposes. There was the simple narrative Latin of monastic chroniclers, the ornate and antiquarian style of rhetoricians like John of Salisbury, the expressive hymns and songs of the wandering scholars, and the precise legal language of Domesday Book or Magna Carta. Twelfth-century Latin was the language of Abelard and Bernard, of Gratian and the Archpoet; so far from being dead, it was still creating new forms.

[77] H. Suggett (née Richardson), 'A Twelfth-Century Anglo-Norman Charter', *BJRL* XXIV (1940), plate facing p. 168; 'An Anglo-Norman Return to the Inquest of Sheriffs', *BJRL* XXVII (1942), pp. 179–81.

[78] 'en Romanz devise un brief, d'un anel l'enseele', *Chronicles* ed. R. Howlett, RS LXXXII (1885), III, p. 224, line 246. Cf. Galbraith, 'Literacy', p. 221, n. 44.

[79] *Dialogus*, pp. 6, 63.

Yet this new Latin was associated not so much with the monks and prelates who had been the transmitters of the Romano-Christian heritage, as with the secular *moderni* of the schools.[80] The schoolmen, the 'masters' of Paris and Bologna and then of Oxford, were a novel phenomenon of the twelfth century. Latin was their primary language, whether they were lawyers, academics or royal officials. They were responsible for ensuring that Latin could cope with the new demands made on it by the schools, city communes, religious orders, and royal lordships which took shape in the twelfth century and produced documents in unprecedented numbers. Although England was only on the periphery of this Latin renaissance, its effects were sufficient to inhibit the wide use of either English or French as a written language in the twelfth century.

Paradoxically the schoolmen, the masters of Latin, were also pioneers of writing in vernaculars. Towards the end of the twelfth century 'Maister' Nicholas of Guildford almost certainly composed *The Owl and the Nightingale*.[81] At about the same time Jordan Fantosme, of the Paris and Winchester schools, and 'Mestre' Thomas were composing histories and romances of England in French.[82] There is no real contradiction in this paradox, as the basic training of the schools was in the use of language and the techniques learned there from Latin could be applied to the more difficult task of creating styles for writing vernaculars. Often perhaps it was the most sophisticated and not the most primitive authors who experimented with vernaculars. We should not be misled by the prefatory apologies in vernacular works, or by their unusual orthography, into thinking that they were composed by the less educated.

Nevertheless, to be noticed by future generations, French had to establish itself not merely as a written medium fit for 'the trifling of mummers in vulgar rhymes' but as a language worthy of record. The earliest documents suggesting that French was beginning to attain that status in England date from 1215 – namely, a letter of Stephen Langton's, enrolled in French on the dorse of the charter rolls, and a French translation of Magna Carta.[83] The latter was copied into the cartulary of the hospital of St Giles at Pont-Audemer in Normandy, together with a contemporary letter (also in French) to the sheriff of Hampshire concerning the enforcement of the charter. These translations seem to have been made to facilitate publication of Magna Carta in the shires.

This French text of Magna Carta, which is evidently contemporary with the events at Runnymede (although the cartulary copy is a decade later), suggests that other translations of the charter into vernaculars, both French and English, once existed. As the charter was ordered (in a letter to all the king's sheriffs, foresters, gamekeepers, watermen and other bailiffs) to be read publicly, numerous copies should once have

---

[80] Clanchy, *'Moderni'*, pp. 671–88.
[81] See n. 38 above.   [82] See nn. 36, 61 above.
[83] *Rotuli Chartarum*, RC (1837), p. 209 and plate at p. xli. J. C. Holt, 'A Vernacular French Text of Magna Carta', *EHR* LXXXIX (1974), pp. 346–64.

existed.[84] To have the effect the barons wanted, these public readings were probably made in vernaculars. It is certain that readings of it later in the century were made in *patria lingua* or in English and French.[85] Such a procedure may have been taken for granted in 1215. It was no more necessary to note it specifically in the royal records than for the former British imperial government in Africa or India to specify to its own officials every native language in which government regulations were to be announced. Just as English was the official language of the British empire, Latin was the language of government and record in King John's England. His sheriffs and other officers did not need to be reminded in writing that it was not the spoken language of themselves or their people.

An English monastic scribe, who wished to record Magna Carta for posterity, would not have thought it proper to copy it in any form less solemn than the Latin in which the authentic text was written and sealed. If he heard or came across a public crier's version, in either French or English, his probable reaction would have been to reject it in preference for the Latin text. He was not aiming to record vulgar forms of French or English for the benefit of modern philologists, but to make a fair copy of the charter in its most lawful form. Why then did the Norman scribe at Pont-Audemer record Magna Carta in French? This copy seems to be a casual interpolation in the cartulary, inserted in the early 1220s. For this scribe and his fellows in Normandy, which was now under the rule of the French crown, the charter had curiosity value only, so that it did not matter if it were expressed in a form which lacked the fullest legal authority. This Norman scribe thus unwittingly preserved a text of much more interest to posterity now than the numerous identical Latin copies of Magna Carta in English monastic cartularies. Unfortunately no scribe of 1215 has yet come to light who was ignorant enough of the law of the land to think that an English version of the charter was worth copying down. Writers of English were probably too well educated for that.

Although Magna Carta was officially issued only in Latin, in the next baronial rebellion in 1258 letters patent in French and English (and Latin as well according to the Burton annalist) were sent in the king's name to every county. There were two sets of letters, dated 18 and 20 October respectively – first, an undertaking by Henry III to abide by the rulings of his new baronial council; secondly, the Ordinance of Sheriffs which proposed to investigate their misconduct.[86] No satisfactory contemporary explanation is given for issuing these letters in languages other than Latin, but it can be inferred that the reason for this unprecedented action was that Henry's sheriffs and other officials could not be relied upon to have them publicly read in the usual way because the letters were explicitly critical of their own conduct. Unlike John's

---

[84] J. C. Holt, *Magna Carta* (1965), p. 345. Cf. ch. 8, n. 42. below.
[85] See ch. 8, nn. 50, 53 below.
[86] Recent editions are *Baronial Docs*, pp. 116–23 and *English Historical Documents* III *1189–1327* ed. H. Rothwell (1975), pp. 367–70.

letters in 1215, Henry's letters in 1258 were not addressed to the sheriffs themselves but to all the king's subjects. The Burton and Dunstable annalists are mistaken to suggest that these letters were dispatched to sheriffs,[87] as the official texts deny that, as does a note in the liberate rolls which records that the letters 'are being sent throughout all our counties'.[88]

This note also records that the composer and writer of the English and French letters was Robert of Fulham, who was paid 50 shillings because this was not his usual work. He was a constable (debt collector) of the Exchequer and was subsequently its remembrancer and a justice of the Jews. Thus the writer of these non-Latin letters was not a baronial nominee from outside the administration, but a clerk who had been in the king's service before the civil war and remained so afterwards.[89] Robert is the prime example of the multilingual competence of English administrators at the time, since he must have known Latin to perform his ordinary duties and he probably understood some Hebrew too as he was a justice of the Jews. His mastery of English and French is clear from the fact that he composed and wrote the letters in both those languages. Whether his starting point was Latin or French or English is anybody's guess.

In the period before 1258 Henry III had made numerous proclamations on a variety of subjects which, if they were to be effective, cannot have been announced in the Latin forms in which they are summarized in the Chancery rolls or in Matthew Paris.[90] They were presumably proclaimed by criers in whatever vernaculars were appropriate.[91] Whether such criers translated *viva voce* from the Latin text, or whether they provided themselves with 'stage scripts' like jongleurs, is a matter for conjecture.[92] In 1258 the barons apparently distrusted the sheriffs, including their criers, and resorted instead to writing down in languages other than Latin precisely what they wanted to say. Exceptional circumstances temporarily caused both English and French to be treated as languages of record.

The barons' action implies distrust of the spoken word and a preference for the precision of writing. The non-Latin letters of 18 and 20 October were not primarily proclamations, though they have been repeatedly described as such by historians. They were letters patent which were enrolled in the Chancery rolls and were intended to serve as permanent records, not transient spoken words, in the counties. The

[87] *Annales Monastici* I, p. 453; III, p. 210.

[88] *CLibR* 1251–60, p. 440. R. F. Treharne, *The Baronial Plan of Reform* (1932), p. 120, n. 1.

[89] Robert's career can be traced in the indexed references to him in *CLibR* 1251–72, *ClR* 1254–68 and *CPatR* 1247–72.

[90] See ch. 8, nn. 37–41 below.

[91] Criers are not well documented because their art was speech, but they are referred to in 1248 (see ch. 8, n. 88 below) and in the surname 'Crier': B. Thuresson, *Middle English Occupation Terms* (Lund, 1950), p. 153.

[92] E. Auerbach, *Literary Language and its Public in Late Antiquity and in the Middle Ages* (1965), p. 288.

letter of 18 October was 'to remain in the treasury' of each county, although only Oxfordshire has retained its copy to the present day.[93] This letter's concern with written record was further emphasized by its being sent 'all in the very same words' (*al on tho ilche worden*) to each county.[94] As so few copies survive, we cannot be certain that this phrase means that a uniform orthography was adopted in every county's copy, although that is the obvious inference. If a uniform orthography were used throughout, this royal letter of 18 October 1258, the work of Robert of Fulham, marks the precocious beginning of London English as the new written standard. The letter of 20 October (the Ordinance of Sheriffs) was likewise directed primarily at readers, as it is addressed to 'all people of the county who shall see these letters', not to those who hear them proclaimed.[95] These letters reached out beyond the sheriff and the traditional non-literate procedures of the county court to the new reading public in the shires. That public consisted of knights, like Walter of Bibbesworth, who were familiar with written English and French but found Latin or *clergie* rather more difficult.

The letters in English and French of 1258, written by Robert of Fulham 'by ordinance of the magnates of our council',[96] showed that either language or a combination of them could have been used henceforward as the language of government and record. But this innovation of the barons had been no more than a temporary expedient. When they got fuller control of the administration after the battle of Lewes, Latin was restored to its former dignity as the medium of literacy. The rebels needed to invest their victory with the greatest legality possible, and that meant using Latin rather than French or English for making records. The letters patent of 14 March 1265, which publish Henry III's oath to keep peace with the barons, are comparable in their purpose with those of 18 October 1258. Like those of 1258, the letters of 1265 indicate a residual distrust of the sheriffs, as they are addressed to the whole county and not to the sheriffs specifically. But this time the letters were issued in Latin only and were ordered to be 'published' (*publicari*) in the county courts.[97] Publication presumably took the traditional form of vernacular announcements by criers working without official non-Latin texts.

The history of Henry III's non-Latin letters of 1258 forms an appropriate conclusion to this discussion. It illustrates how written language was not usually derived directly from the speech of the majority of the people but from tradition, political authority and social status. The mother tongue of ordinary discourse was normally entirely distinct from the language of script. Those who read or wrote had to master a variety of languages. They passed from English to French or Latin, and some to Hebrew as well, frequently without comment and perhaps

[93] *Royal Letters Addressed to Oxford* ed. O. Ogle (1892), p. 12. Cf. ch. 5, n. 101 above.
[94] *English Historical Documents* ed. Rothwell, p. 368.
[95] *Baronial Docs*, p. 118.
[96] *CLibR* 1251–60, p. 440.
[97] *Baronial Docs*, pp 312–15.

without effort. Knowledge and familiarity with these languages, or variants of them, depended on each individual's social status, age, domicile and personal ambitions and experience of life. Generalizations, such as that everybody was bilingual in English and French in 1200 or that only the clergy knew Latin, are pointless and misleading apart from being unprovable. Although it is impossible to reconstruct in detail the values and knowledge of men of intermediate social class, like Walter of Bibbesworth and Robert of Fulham, the evidence available suggests that in order to rule their fellow Englishmen they must have been lords of language in both speech and script.

7

Literate and illiterate

In the summer of 1297 some jurors from Norfolk came to the court of King's Bench to attest that Robert de Tony was twenty-one years of age and was therefore entitled to have his wardship terminated. Proving the age of feudal heirs by sworn testimony was a routine procedure, in which each juror attempted to recollect some memorable event which coincided with the birth of the child in question. Jurors might recall, for example, specific gifts or public events or accidents to themselves or their neighbours.[1] Thus in a case in 1304 at Skipton in Yorkshire Robert Buck, aged forty-one, remembered being at school at Clitheroc where he had been so badly beaten that he ran away and that was twenty-one years ago.[2] Such a cumbersome system was required because births were only rarely recorded in registers. This customary method of establishing the age of individuals by collective oral testimony is a good example of the medieval reliance on memory rather than written record.

The case from Norfolk in 1297 is exceptional in that the proof primarily depended not on the usual personal recollections, but on a record of the date of Robert de Tony's birth (4 April 1276), which had been written down in the chronicles of West Acre priory.[3] This record had not been made at the time of Robert's birth, as he was born in Scotland, but a year or more later when he was brought down to West Acre priory, of which the de Tony family were the founders, by his mother. She seems to have been seeking the protection of the priory on her son's behalf and had his date of birth written down there to establish that he was the lawful de Tony heir. Because the circumstances of Robert's birth could not have been known to the Norfolk jurors from personal experience in the customary way, resort had to be made to the West Acre chronicle.

The first juror, William de la Sale of Swaffham, therefore gave evidence that he had seen the chronicle and read it and was thereby certain

---

[1] S. S. Walker, 'Proof of Age of Feudal Heirs in Medieval England', *Medieval Studies* (Toronto) xxxv (1973), pp. 316–20.

[2] *Calendar of Inquisitions Post Mortem* IV, pp. 171–2, no. 239.

[3] *Placitorum Abbreviatio*, RC (1811), p. 293 (text incomplete). *Coram Rege Roll for Trinity Term 1297* ed. W. P. W. Phillimore, British Record S. Index Library xix (1897), pp. 241–3. G. E. Cokayne, *The Complete Peerage* (2nd edn) xii, part i (1953), p. 773. No chronicle of West Acre Priory is extant.

of Robert's age. Six other jurors agreed with William without exception or addition, that is, they too claimed to have read the chronicle and understood its significance. Three more likewise agreed and added ancillary recollections: Robert Corlu said his younger brother was born in the same year as Robert de Tony; John Townsend said he had a son born in the same year who was now twenty-one; John Kempe said his father had died five years after Robert had been brought down from Scotland. The eleventh juror, John Laurence, agreed with William 'with this exception, that he had not read the aforesaid chronicles because he is *laycus*'. The twelfth, Roger of Creston, attested the same. A thirteenth juror (why evidence was taken from thirteen men instead of twelve is not explained)' Thomas of Weasenham, said that he had neither seen nor read the chronicle, but he had learned of its contents from the prior. Thomas was not necessarily incapable of reading like John and Roger. He may have presented his evidence in this form simply because he had not been present on the day his fellow jurors saw the chronicle.

Thus, of the thirteen men examined, ten swore that they could read the entry in the chronicle, an eleventh may have been able to read, and two were unable to do so. The latter two were described as *layci* (laymen) presumably because they had no 'clergy' in the sense of a reading knowledge of Latin. We have already seen that Walter of Bibbesworth took it for granted in the 1250s or 1260s, the time when these Norfolk jurors were growing up, that the gentry usually had experience from childhood of the 'book which teaches us *clergie*'.[4] Those without this knowledge were 'laymen' in the modern sense of being inexpert. The other jurors were 'clergy' only in the sense of knowing some Latin. William de la Sale and his fellows were no churchmen. They were knights and freemen of the neighbourhood, approximately the social equals of the heir in question, as required in jury trial procedure.

This case therefore shows that from a random sample of thirteen gentlemen of Norfolk at the end of the thirteenth century, ten could read an entry in a chronicle, two could not, and one's ability is unrecorded. Those who swore that they had read the chronicle were presumably telling the truth, as they risked being cross-examined in the King's Bench, and they had no apparent motive for perjuring themselves since they were not claiming benefit of clergy. The statement that two of the jurors were incapable of reading, together with the unspecific testimony about Thomas of Weasenham, adds credibility to the contrasting testimony of the rest. Although evidence of proof of age was sometimes falsified, there is no reason to reject the essential facts of this testimony. Obviously no generalizations about levels of literacy can be made from a unique case. On the other hand, the evidence of this case, that the great majority of the jurors examined were capable of reading one line of Latin in a chronicle, need cause no surprise. We have already seen that the procedure for giving juries' verdicts in royal courts, which depended on documents written in Latin and perhaps also in French and English, demanded a higher level of literacy among jurors than that.[5] By 1297

---

[4] See p. 153 above.   [5] See ch. 6, nn. 50–51 above.

the two who were unable to read at this elementary level are more surprising than the ten who could do so.

Meanings of 'clericus' and 'litteratus'

The fact that most of these Norfolk gentlemen could read conflicts in appearance only with the medieval axiom that laymen are illiterate and its converse that clergy are literate. The terms cleric and lay, literate and illiterate, were used in ways which preserved intact the appearances of these fundamental axioms while acknowledging the realities of daily experience, where some clergy were ignorant and some knights knew more of books than brave deeds. Traditional roles had become confused, as Neal of Longchamp of Canterbury observed with regret in c.1192: 'In the church today there are clergy without knowledge of letters, just as there are many knights without skill and practice in arms, who for that reason are called "Holy Mary's knights" by the others.'[6] This discrepancy between theory and practice, between literature and life, did not of course mean that the ideals were immediately altered to fit the facts. On the contrary, the ideals of the learned cleric and the valorous knight became reinforced as fantasies, which had three or four centuries of vigorous life before them in literature and academic treatises.

The axiom that laymen are illiterate and its converse had originated by combining two distinct antitheses:

> *clericus: laicus*
> *litteratus: illitteratus*

The latter antithesis derived from classical Latin, where *litteratus* meant 'literate' in something like its modern sense and also (in the most classical usage of Cicero) described a person with *scientia litterarum*, meaning a 'knowledge of letters' in the sense of 'literature'.[7] The former antithesis derived from the Greek *kleros*, meaning a 'selection by lot' and hence subsequently the 'elect' of God in terms of Christian salvation, whereas *laos* meant the 'people' or crowd.[8] Gradually in the process of Christian conversion those who were specially consecrated to the service of God, the *clerici* or 'clergy', became distinct from the mass of the people, the *laici* or 'laity'. The antithesis *clericus: laicus* was thus a medieval creation, while *litteratus: illitteratus* was of Roman origin. In the half millennium 500–1000 AD the reduction in the number of learned men in the west coincided with the expansion of Christianity by the conversion of the barbarians. As a consequence *clerici* began to be associated with *litterati*, although the two concepts had originally nothing in common. This association of ideas reflected the fact that

[6] Nigellus de Longchamp dit Wireker, *Tractatus Contra Curiales et Officiales Clericos* ed. A. Boutemy, Université Libre de Bruxelles, Travaux de la Faculté de Philosophie et Lettres XVI (1959), I, p. 204.

[7] H. Grundmann, *'Litteratus-Illitteratus'*, *Archiv für Kulturgeschichte* XL (1958), p. 17.

[8] *Dictionaire du droit canonique* ed. R. Naz (1935–65) III, col. 828; VI, col. 328.

outside the Mediterranean area nearly all Latinists were churchmen and most were monks. As academic standards declined, *litteratus*, which had meant 'lettered' or 'learned' for Cicero, more often came to mean 'literate' in the sense of having a minimal ability to read Latin. Such *litterati* were still learned compared with the great majority, who had no Latin or book learning at all.

These first clerical *litterati*, whose sparse knowledge had scarcely anything in common with the Latin scholars either of ancient Rome or of the Twelfth-Century Renaissance, established a privileged status for themselves in society by despising non-Latinists as an ignorant crowd of *laici*. In reality the *clerici* were unsure of their status, as Europe was dominated not by them but by warriors with a non-literate sense of values. Charlemagne and Alfred were exceptional in wanting the nobility to be better Latinists; their examples were lauded by the clergy to encourage the others. Dark-Age Europe was far from unique in creating an élite of priests who monopolized writing, yet who were constantly aware of their impotence vis-à-vis the dominant warlords. The supposed gulf between cleric and lay, between the elect and the damned, was some compensation to the clergy, although not even Pope Gregory VII could make it a reality for long in the terrestrial world.[9]

Thus by constant repetition the pairs of antitheses, *clericus: laicus* and *litteratus: illitteratus*, were coupled in the mind. The terms of each antithesis became interchangeable and ultimately synonymous. By the twelfth century *clericus* meant *litteratus*, *laicus* meant *illitteratus*, and vice-versa. The case from Norfolk has already illustrated *laicus* being used to mean *illitteratus*. The converse (*clericus* meaning *litteratus*) was discussed in detail in the 1170s by Philip of Harvengt, who observed that a person was not called a cleric unless he was 'imbued with letters', and hence:

> A usage of speech has taken hold whereby when we see someone *litteratus*, immediately we call him *clericus*. Because he acts the part that is a cleric's, we assign him the name *ex officio*. Thus if anyone is comparing a knight who is *litteratus* with a priest who is ignorant, he will exclaim with confidence and affirm with an oath that the knight is a better *clericus* than the priest. . . . This improper usage has become so prevalent that whoever gives attention to letters, which is clerkly, is named *clericus*.[10]

Philip, like Neal de Longchamp and other writers on the state of the clergy, deplored the way real knights and clergy no longer fitted the traditional roles assigned to them. More important in the present context is his observation that a learned knight would be called a *clericus*,

[9] In general see the contributions by L. Prosdocimi and Y. Congar to *I Laici nella societas christiana dei secoli XI e XII* ed. G. Lazzati and C. D. Fonseca, Università Cattolica del Sacro Cuore (Milan, 1968), pp. 56–117.

[10] 'De Institutione Clericorum', bk. iv, ch. 110, *Patrologia* CCIII (1855), col. 816; cf. n. 31 below. P. Riché, 'Recherches sur l'instruction des laics du IX au XII siècle', *Cahiers de Civilisation Médiévale* V (1962), p. 181.

because that implies that a person described as *clericus* in a document was not necessarily a member of the clergy. Such a person is just as likely to have been an educated layman.

Philip of Harvengt's comments are best illustrated in England by Matthew Paris's obituary of Paulin Peyver or Piper, a steward of Henry III who died in 1251. He is described as *miles litteratus sive clericus militaris*, 'a literate knight or knightly clerk'.[11] Matthew thus emphasized that these terms were interchangeable in Paulin's case. Paulin was a cleric only in the learned sense, as he had numerous knights' fees and a wife and legitimate children. Similarly the Northamptonshire knight, Henry de Bray, who was born in 1269 and wrote his own cartulary, noted that his maternal grandfather, Richard lord of Harlestone, 'was called Ricardus Clericus because he was *litteratus*'.[12] The most familiar example of this usage is the nickname 'Clerk' or 'Beauclerk' given to Henry I. How learned Henry really was is a separate and controversial question; certainly he was described by Orderic Vitalis as *litteratus* and 'nurtured in natural and doctrinal science'.[13] A *clericus* in common parlance was therefore a person of some scholarly attainments, regardless of whether he was a churchman. As early as the third decade of the twelfth century a polemic of English origin, commenting on the large number of schoolmasters, asked rhetorically: 'Are there not everywhere on earth masters of the liberal arts, who are also called *clerici*?'[14] Peter the Chanter summarized the situation in around 1200: 'There are two kinds of *clerici* and in both there are good and bad, namely those who are ecclesiastics and those who are scholastics.'[15]

The use of *clericus* and *litteratus* as interchangeable terms, both meaning 'learned' or 'scholarly', is clearest in Jocelin of Brakelond's descriptions of the debates within Bury St Edmunds abbey over the election of Abbot Samson in 1182 and Prior Herbert in 1200. On each occasion the more scholarly monks argued that they must be governed by *litterati* and not by the ignorant. Their opponents teased them with a new litany, 'A bonis clericis, libera nos, Domine!' (From all good clerics, good Lord, deliver us),[16] and with puns about learning Latin grammar, 'Our good *clerici* have declined so often in the cloister that now they themselves have declined.'[17] *Clericus* was a relative term. Thus Jocelin has one monk say: 'That brother is something of a cleric [*aliquantulum clericus*], although much learning [*littere*] doth not make him mad.'[18] On another occasion Jocelin told of how Hubert Walter, the archbishop of

[11] Matthew Paris V, p. 242.

[12] *The Estate Book of Henry de Bray* ed. D. Willis, Camden S. 3rd series XXVII (1916), p. 97.

[13] Thompson, *Literacy*, p. 170, n. 40. For a contrary view see Galbraith, 'Literacy', pp. 201–2, 211–12.

[14] R. W. Southern, 'Master Vacarius and the Beginning of an English Academic Tradition' in *Medieval Learning and Literature: Essays Presented to R. W. Hunt* (1976), p. 268, n. 1, citing *Studia Anselmia* XLI (1957) p. 65. Cf. R & S, p. 270, n. 4 and n. 81 below.

[15] J. W. Baldwin, *Masters, Princes and Merchants* (1970) II, p. 51, n. 57.

[16] Jocelin, p. 12.   [17] *ibid.* p. 130.   [18] *ibid.* p. 12.

Canterbury, had to admit that Abbot Samson was a better *clericus* than he was, meaning that Samson was the better scholar.[19] The way Jocelin uses *clericus* is explained by Philip of Harvengt, who notes that when we meet a monk of humanity and charity,

> We ask him whether he is a *clericus*. We don't want to know whether he has been ordained to perform the office of the altar, but only whether he is *litteratus*. The monk will therefore reply to the question by saying that he is a *clericus* if he is *litteratus*, or conversely a *laicus* if he is *illitteratus*.[20]

It might be added that a monk who aspired to Christian humility would not call himself *litteratus*, even if he were of scholarly inclinations. Thus Adam of Eynsham, in his life of St Hugh of Lincoln, claims not to know how to satisfy the *litterati*, who will cavil at his style and simple narrative.[21] Adam is using here the hagiographer's common device of making his story appear more truthful by being naive.

As *clericus* and *litteratus* both meant learned, it followed that a person of no great book learning was a *laicus*, a 'layman', even if he were a monk or a priest. Thus Archbishop Hubert Walter was described by the chronicler of St Augustine's abbey at Canterbury as *laicus et illitteratus*.[22] Hubert was not of course a layman in the ecclesiastical sense, nor was he illiterate in any modern sense, as he was the chief justiciar and chancellor who did more than any other individual to create the royal archives. The St Augustine's abbey chronicler was using *laicus* and *illitteratus* as terms of abuse – he also called Hubert a legal *ignoramus*[23] – but he was not using these terms inaccurately. Hubert was a *laicus* in Philip of Harvengt's sense and *illitteratus* in Jocelin's, as he lacked the academic learning of Bologna or Paris. That academic snob, Gerald of Wales, alleged that Hubert's Latin was shaky and that his only school had been the Exchequer.[24]

Like *clericus, litteratus* was a relative term. Whether a particular individual was appropriately described as *litteratus* was a matter of opinion, since essentially it meant 'learned'. The same man might be *litteratus* in one assessment and *illitteratus* in another. Thus Ralf Nevill, Henry III's chancellor and bishop of Chichester, was certified by a papal legate as *litteratus* when elected dean of Lichfield in 1214, but *illitteratus* by another papal adviser in 1231 when his candidature for the archbishopric of Canterbury was rejected.[25] Conscientious churchmen considered Ralf to be a worldly administrator. Like Hubert Walter, he was no *clericus* or *litteratus* in the ideal sense of being either the elect

---

[19] *ibid.* p. 84.   [20] *Patrologiae* CCIII (1855), col. 816.
[21] Ed. D. L. Douie and H. Farmer (1961) I, p. 43.
[22] *Historiae Anglicanae Scriptores Decem* ed. R. Twysden (1652), col. 1841.
[23] 'juris ignarus', *ibid.* col. 1841.
[24] See ch. 2, nn. 82–4 above, and nn. 79–80 below.
[25] *The Great Register of Lichfield Cathedral* ed. H. E. Savage, The William Salt Archaeological S. (1924), p. 341, no. 713. Matthew Paris III, p. 207 (citing Roger of Wendover). I owe these references to Dr Jeanne Stones.

of God or a scholar. On this occasion in 1231 the successful candidate for Canterbury, St Edmund of Abingdon, was both. Hubert and Ralf were not the only distinguished churchmen and administrators to be described as *illitteratus*. To their company should be added Roger bishop of Salisbury, Henry I's chief justiciar, and the controversial Abbot Ording of Bury St Edmunds.[26] In the exalted view of John of Salisbury, who aspired to Ciceronian standards, all those who are ignorant of the Latin poets, historians, orators and mathematicians should be called *illitterati* 'even if they know letters'.[27]

John's contention is taken for granted by Walter Map when he describes a boy he had known, who was a paragon and was 'educated among us and by us'; yet 'he was not *litteratus*, which I regret, although he knew how to transcribe any series of letters whatever.'[28] Walter would have liked to have described this boy as *litteratus*, since he was one of his kinsmen, but he had to admit that nice penmanship was no substitute for scholarship. He adds that the boy left England and became a knight of Philip of Flanders (1168–91). At his learned court, where many of 'the order of laymen' knew 'letters' (according to Philip of Harvengt), this boy would presumably not have been numbered among the *milites litterati*.[29] The ability to write well comprised the technical skill of an artist and was not an integral part of the science of letters.[30] Writing is not included among the skills which cause Philip of Harvengt's knight who is *litteratus* to be described as a *clericus*. In Philip's opinion the essential abilities are to read, understand, compose by dictation, make verse and express onself in the Latin language.[31] The medieval *miles litteratus* was thus a gentleman educated in the classics; he embodied a recurrent ideal in European culture.

The way the words *clericus* and *litteratus* were used has been discussed in detail here because such examples demonstrate that neither word, when applied to an individual, can be accurately translated by its modern equivalent. A *clericus* was not necessarily either a 'cleric' or a 'clerk', although he was someone with a reputation for erudition. Likewise a person described as *litteratus* was much more than 'literate' in the modern sense. Counting the number of persons called *clericus*, or making lists of knights described as *litteratus*, provides examples of persistent and characteristic medieval ways of thinking, but it throws no light on whether such persons, whether designated cleric or lay by ecclesiastical law, were 'literate' in a twentieth-century sense of that word.

[26] William of Newburgh, *Chronicles* ed. R. Howlett, RS LXXXII (1884), i, p. 36. Jocelin, p. 11.
[27] *Policraticus*, bk vii, ch. 9, ed. C. C. J. Webb (1909) II, p. 126. Cf. Grundmann, '*Litteratus-Illitteratus*', p. 52 and Riché, 'Recherches sur l'Instruction des Laics', pp. 180–81.
[28] Walter Map, bk iv, ch. 1, p. 138. Cf. ch. 8, n. 79 below.
[29] *Patrologiae* CCIII (1855) cols 148–9. Thompson, *Literacy*, pp. 139–41.
[30] See pp. 218, 227 below.
[31] 'miles legit, intellegit, dictat, versificatur et inter clericos linguam Latinam proferens', *Patrologiae* CCIII (1855) col. 816. Cf. n. 10 above.

The question of the literacy of the laity

Discussions of medieval literacy have been bedevilled by the difficulty of distinguishing between the modern 'literate' and the medieval *litteratus*. When a knight is described as *litteratus* in a medieval source, his exceptional erudition is usually being referred to, not his capacity to read and write. Such knights were rare because good Latin scholars have always been rare among country gentry and government officials in England. A few existed even in this period. Thus shortly after the Conquest a Norman called Robert, *miles ille litteratus*, endowed St Albans abbey with an income to provide books for the church.[32] He probably had a greater interest in books than most of the monks. About a century later Gerald of Wales tells how a *miles litteratus* appeared as a ghost, demanding to play a game of capping Latin verses with a learned master, for that had been his 'social recreation' when he was alive.[33] Similarly Matthew Paris is recording his admiration for the learning and not the elementary schooling of John of Lexington, when he describes him as *miles elegans* (refined) *et facundus* (eloquent) *et litteratus*, or of Roger de Thurkelby, *miles et litteratus*.[34] John was the keeper of the royal seal, whose obituary Matthew was writing in 1257, while Roger was one of the few royal judges who possessed legal wisdom in Matthew's opinion.

The historian's initial difficulty, when discussing the literacy of the laity, is to avoid anachronisms. Medieval ideas of literacy were so different from those of today that some modern questions are meaningless. To ask, 'Were laymen illiterate?', is a tautology: of course *laici* were *illitterati* because these terms were synonyms. Faced with the question another way round, 'Were laymen literate?', a medieval schoolman might have thought that he was being invited to take part in an exercise in elementary dialectic. Asking whether laymen were literates was like asking whether evil was good or black was white. Every bachelor of arts knew that the validity of axioms such as these was not affected by individual cases of moral imperfection or greyness in this imperfect world. The axiom that *clerici* were *litterati* and its converse belonged to the same order of thinking. Contemporaries, like Philip of Harvengt or Jocelin of Brakelond, knew of numerous exceptions in their daily experience, but they saved the appearances of the rules by calling learned knights *clerici* and ignorant monks *laici*. Such axioms cannot be equated with twentieth-century historians' generalizations, which derive from an assessment of a multitude of individual cases. Scholastic axioms derived their validity not from individual experience but from universal rules, which were superior and prior to particular cases because they were part of a divine order of things. When explaining medieval ways of thought it is correct to say that all laymen were considered illiterate, yet it would be mistaken to conclude from that

[32] *Gesta Abbatum Monasterii S. Albani* ed. H. T. Riley, RS xxviii (1867), I, p. 57.
[33] Giraldus viii, p. 310. R & S, p. 273, n. 8.
[34] Matthew Paris v, pp. 610, 317.

proposition that in any particular time or place all non-churchmen were unable to read or write. Scholastic axioms differ from real cases.

Another anachronism is the assumption that the capacity to read and write is a simple and constant measure which readily applies to medieval cases. The automatic coupling of reading with writing and the close association of literacy with the language one speaks are not universal norms, but products of modern European culture. Literacy in this modern sense is so deeply implanted from childhood in every twentieth-century scholar that it is difficult to liberate oneself from its preconceptions, or to avoid thinking of it as an automatic measure of progress. Over the last two centuries medievalists have painfully learned to overcome anachronisms when discussing feudal society or scholastic philosophy. Yet, when they reach elementary education and literate skills, they tend to assume that these problems can be readily understood by applying modern criteria and experience to the medieval past. Past ideas must be analysed in their own terms before they are assessed in modern ones.

As the citations from Walter Map and Philip of Harvengt have already illustrated, reading and writing were not automatically coupled at the end of the twelfth century, nor was a minimal ability to perform these actions described as literacy. Writing was a skill distinct from reading because the use of parchment and quills made it difficult.[35] Likewise the traditional emphasis on the spoken word caused reading to be coupled more often with speaking aloud than with eyeing script.[36] Although the average medieval reader had been taught to form the letters of the alphabet with a stylus on a writing tablet, he would not necessarily have felt confident about penning a letter or a charter on parchment. Scholars and officials employed scribes, particularly for drafting formal legal documents, just as typists are employed today. To this rule there are exceptions, of which the most spectacular is the beautifully written will of Simon de Montfort, as it states in its text that it is written in the hand of his eldest son, Henry.[37] Wills were unusually personal documents, intimately associated with the family circle, because their main purpose was to ensure the testator's state of grace at death rather than the worldly disposition of his property; hence Henry was performing a special act of filial devotion in writing his father's will.

Another fundamental difference between medieval and modern approaches to literacy is that medieval assessments concentrate on cases of maximum ability, the skills of the most learned scholars (*litterati*) and the most elegant scribes, whereas modern assessors measure the diffusion of minimal skills among the masses. Consequently modern assessments of literacy have been primarily concerned with the minimal ability of persons to sign their own names and the development of

---

[35] See pp. 88, 97 above.   [36] See pp. 214–19 below.

[37] Facsimile, ed. C. Bémont, *Simon de Montfort* trans. E. F. Jacob (1930), pp. 276–8 (the will is in French and was written in 1258). M. M. Sheehan, *The Will in Medieval England*, Pontifical Institute of Medieval Studies: Studies and Texts VI (1963), pp. 260–61, nn. 128, 131.

elementary schools in which this ability is taught as the basic educational skill. In twelfth- and thirteenth-century England the ability to sign one's name was likewise considered important, but it was not directly associated either with writing or with schools. The personal signature or sign manual was not accepted by itself as a lawful symbol of authentication on a document unless the signatory were a Jew. A Christian was required either to sign with a cross, indicating that he was making a promise in the sight of Christ crucified, or more commonly he affixed to the document his *signum* or seal.[38]

In medieval England possession of a seal bearing the owner's name comes closest to the modern criterion of making the ability to sign one's own name the touchstone of literacy. Although the possessor of a seal might not be able to write, he or she was a person familiar with documents and entitled to participate in their use. Neither the medieval seal nor the modern sign manual on a document indicates that the signatory has anything more than a minimal competence in the skills of literacy. Such a person need not be *litteratus* in a medieval sense nor 'educated' in a modern one. If possession of a seal is taken as the medieval equivalent of the modern sign manual as a measure of minimal literacy, the growth of literacy (in this modern sense) can be approximately assessed. Scarcely anyone apart from rulers and bishops possessed seals in 1100, whereas by 1300 all freemen and even some serfs probably had them. Thus the statute of Exeter of 1285 expected 'bondsmen' to use them when they authenticated written evidence.[39] How far the expectations of this statute reflected actual practice is a matter for conjecture, although instances can be readily cited as early as the 1230s of smallholders and tenants owing labour services affixing their personal seals to charters.[40] The extent of minimal literacy in this sense among the peasantry by 1300 has been underestimated because historians have been reluctant to allow such competence even to the gentry.

The discrepancies between modern and medieval conceptions of what constituted literacy go deeper than differences in minimal requirements. The variety of languages in which spoken and written thoughts were formulated in medieval England made any capacity to read or write an intellectual achievment. This variety also obstructed the rapid spread of literacy, in the modern sense of the majority of people acquiring a minimal ability to read and write the language they spoke. Elementary instruction in reading and writing started from Latin because that was the traditional language of literacy and sacred Scripture. Those who wrote in vernaculars, whether in Middle English or French, were building novel and complex structures on a foundation of Latin. Neither Middle English nor French was sufficiently standardized, or well enough established as a literary language, to become the basis of elementary instruction in reading and writing until well after 1300. If a person in Edward I's reign or earlier had learned to

[38] See pp. 245–7 below.
[39] *Statutes*, p. 211. See ch. 2, n. 24 above.
[40] See ch. 2, nn. 21–2 above.

read in English or French but not in Latin, he could never have become *litteratus*, nor could he have understood the majoritiy of writings circulating in his own lifetime because these were in Latin. English and French had to have become common business and literary languages before it was practical or desirable to initiate literate skills with them.

Nevertheless by 1300 the supremacy of Latin, and the privileges of the *clerici* and *litterati* who upheld it, was increasingly being challenged, both by writings in vernaculars and by anti-clericalism. Boniface VIII introduced his bull *Clericis Laicos* in 1296, directed primarily at Edward I and Philip IV of France, with the provocative words: 'That laymen are notoriously hostile to clerics antiquity relates and recent experience manifestly demonstrates.'[41] Yet English non-churchmen were slower than their French counterparts to abandon Latin as the basis of literate skills, probably because of the competition between English and French as alternative literary languages. In general from *c.*1300, lawyers and government officials preferred French, while creative writers favoured English. Moreover, in the later Middle Ages an elementary reading knowledge of Latin became a matter of life and death for Englishmen. Any person charged with felony, who could read a prescribed verse from the Bible, was theoretically entitled to benefit of clergy and hence escaped the death penalty.[42] Now that middle-class laymen were beginning to assert themselves, they took over the old association of *clericus* with *litteratus* and turned it to their own advantage in order to save themselves from hanging. *Litteratus* was thus reduced from meaning a person of erudition to meaning a person with a minimal ability to read, albeit in Latin. A *clericus* was still a *litteratus*, but he was now neither a churchman nor a scholar: he was anyone who was literate in this minimal sense. By the middle of the fifteenth century London tradesmen are being described as *litterati*.[43] Consequently after 1300 it became relatively common to be literate. What had changed, however, was not necessarily the proportion of persons in the population who had mastered reading and writing, but the meanings of words. A *clericus* was now a common clerk and a *litteratus* was a minimal literate. The literacy of the laity had been achieved, perhaps not so much by the efforts of schoolmasters and the mysterious forces of progress, as is sometimes alleged, as by the method which Humpty Dumpty explained to Alice in *Through the Looking-Glass*: 'When *I* use a word, it means just what I choose it to mean, neither more nor less. . . . The question is which is to be master – that's all ' Verbally at least, the *laici* had mastered the *clerici* and *litterati*; and from that mastery the modern concept of literacy, meaning a minimal ability to read, was born.

[41] P. Dupuy, *Historie du differand d'entre le Pape Boniface VIII et Philippe le Bel* (1655), p. 14. G. de Lagarde, *La Naissance de l'esprit laique au déclin du Moyen Age* (1948) I, ch. 12.

[42] L. C. Gabel, *Benefit of Clergy in England in the Later Middle Ages*, Smith College Studies in History XIV (1928–9), pp. 68–78.

[43] *ibid.* pp. 82–4.

Knowledge of Latin among non-churchmen

To avoid ambiguities the question, 'Were laymen literate?', needs recasting. A more productive question to ask is, 'Did non-churchmen know any Latin?', since Latin was the foundation of literacy in England in this period. The latter question has been progressively answered in the affirmative by scholars over the past fifty years. Starting at the top of the social hierarchy, historians have demonstrated that at least an acquaintance with Latin became increasingly widespread over the two centuries 1100–1300.

Independently of each other in the 1930s, V. H. Galbraith in Britain and J. W. Thompson in California demonstrated that the kings of England from Henry I onwards were instructed in Latin and that Henry I and Henry II were even considered *litterati* by some contemporaries.[44] More importantly, Henry II showed his mastery of written instruments in a series of judgments concerning the charters of the abbeys of St Albans in 1155, Battle in 1157 and 1175, and Bury St Edmunds in 1187.[45] He evidently enjoyed presiding over legal wrangles between abbots and bishops in his court, as it gave him an opportunity to scrutinize their charters and demonstrate that he was their master in intellect and legal wisdom as well as in material power. Peter of Blois was probably not exaggerating when he states that among Henry's commonest forms of relaxation were private reading and working with a group of *clerici* to unravel some knotty question: at his court there was 'school every day'.[46] By 'school' Peter did not mean an elementary school, but a circle of learned schoolmen discussing *questiones* as they did at Paris or Oxford. From King John's reign onwards elementary instruction in Latin was taken for granted: 'Henceforth all our kings were taught letters in their youth, and their literacy, as distinct from their culture, has no particular importance.'[47]

The example set by the kings inevitably gave the baronage and gentry a motivation to learn some Latin, both to avoid looking foolish at court (where there was school every day), and to have sufficient understanding of the written demands, expressed in Latin, which began to pour from the royal Chancery and Exchequer. For these reasons H. G. Richardson and G. O. Sayles in 1963 widened the range of those who had 'a limited knowledge of Latin, a knowledge to be easily and rapidly acquired by any intelligent youth', from kings to the baronage and gentry of twelfth-century England.[48] Their conclusion concerning the baronage is cautious and unexceptionable: 'Without rashly generaliz-

[44] Galbraith's lecture to the British Academy (Galbraith, 'Literacy', pp. 201–38) was published in 1936. Thompson's *The Literacy of the Laity in the Middle Ages* (Thompson, *Literacy*, ch. 7) was completed in the same year, but was not published until 1939.

[45] *Gesta Abbatum Monasterii S. Albani* I, pp. 150–54. *Battle*, pp. 86, 164–5 and see ch. 9, n. 64 below. Jocelin, p. 51. Cf. Galbraith, 'Literacy', p. 222, n. 46.

[46] *Patrologiae* CCVII (1855), col. 198. *Becket Materials* VII, p. 573.

[47] Galbraith, 'Literacy', p. 215.

[48] R & S, p. 278 and (more generally) pp. 269–83.

ing from what may perhaps be called a handful of cases, it may fairly be said that they create a presumption that a man of noble birth will in his youth have had the opportunity of learning something of Latin letters.'[49] Richardson and Sayles also suggested that even some of the lesser knights read and wrote Latin. This suggestion is based on the written replies to Henry II's inquest into knights' fees in 1166 and his Inquest of Sheriffs in 1170. The argument is that 'the more informal documents, those that have no marks of clerkly skill' were written by the knights themselves.[50] Although the assumption that such men would or could write on parchment is contentious, the lesser conjecture that many knights read the royal writs themselves and drafted their own replies is possible.[51]

The strongest argument of Richardson and Sayles for a relatively wide acquaintance with Latin is that royal officials like sheriffs and judges, most of whom were non-churchmen, had to have a working knowledge of Latin because they performed offices 'demanding the use of written instruments'.[52] Although such officials usually employed clerks to do their writing, and to read letters aloud to them, they had to understand enough Latin to master the business in hand and not be misled by their clerks or by the litigants' lawyers. At least one of Henry II's lay sheriffs, Richard sheriff of Hampshire, wrote as well as read in Latin, as his holograph acknowledgement of a debt to William Cade is extant.[53]

The presumption that officials knew some Latin, which applies to officers of the central government by 1200, extends to manorial and village stewards, bailiffs, beadles and reeves by 1300.[54] On the basis of this evidence M. B. Parkes, in a recent contribution to the literacy of the laity question, argues that historians should allow for an 'extent of pragmatic literacy among the peasantry'.[55] His arguments are strengthened by the instances of peasants using seals and charters which have already been discussed. Parkes cites Walter Map, who took it for granted that 'serfs [*servi*], whom we call peasants [*rustici*], are eager to educate their ignominious and degenerate children in the [liberal] arts.'[56] Walter deplored this because a liberal education was appropriate only for freedom. The question had arisen one day when he and the chief justiciar, Ranulf de Glanvill, were discussing why it was that the clerical judges of Henry II were harsher than the lay ones. Walter's explanation was that the clerics did not behave like gentlemen because they were serfs in origin. Although Walter was only expressing a personal opinion, and his opinions were often perverse and ironical (Walter was a clerical justice himself), his remarks had some basis in fact.

Starting at the top of the hierarchy with kings and descending through barons and knights, historians of medieval literacy have reached the peasants at the bottom and are suggesting that even some of

[49] *ibid.* p. 273.   [50] *ibid.* p. 275.
[51] W. L. Warren, *Henry II* (1973), pp. 276–7.   [52] R & S, p. 274.
[53] Parkes, 'Literacy', p. 558, n. 20.   [54] See ch. 2, nn. 3–9 above.
[55] Parkes, 'Literacy', p. 560.   [56] Walter Map, bk i, ch. 10, p. 7.

them were acquainted with Latin. N. Orme has recently surveyed literacy (mainly in the later Middle Ages) from the top of society to the bottom as an introduction to his study of medieval schools.[57] He divides people into seven classes – clergy; kings and princes; nobility and gentry; administrators and lawyers; merchants, craftsmen, artisans; villeins; women. For the twelfth and thirteenth centuries a fourfold classification into kings and princes, nobility or baronage, gentry or knights, and peasantry (both free and unfree) is more appropriate. Neither the clergy nor women were separate social classes, as they derived their place in society from their families. Nor were administrators and lawyers yet a distinct class, as the legal profession (in a literate sense) only emerged in the late thirteenth century.

It might be thought that merchants are worth distinguishing as a group, as their families were at the forefront of education in the city states of Flanders and Northern Italy. In England, however, merchant dynasties like those of London took on the social colouring of the landed gentry and were not, in the thirteenth century anyway, a distinct 'bourgeoisie'. Knightly merchants were as educated as other knights. With lesser merchants, it is doubtful whether literacy in Latin was yet an essential skill, as they worked from memory and tally sticks. Book learning and book keeping became crucial to lesser merchants only when they ceased to travel with their wares and sat in offices instead. On the whole, that is a development of the fourteenth century rather than the twelfth, as far as England is concerned. St Godric, who mastered the *mercatoris studium* without any formal education, is probably typical of eleventh- or twelfth-century experience.[58] Financiers, on the other hand, like William Cade or Osbert Huitdeniers (Eightpence) of London, who employed the young Thomas Becket as a clerk and accountant, needed as much Latin as the judicial side of their business (writing and enforcing bonds for loans) required.[59] But financiers are not a sufficiently homogeneous group to constitute a social class, as many of them were Jews; they were literate in Hebrew and often in Latin as well.

The knowledge of the peasantry (both free and unfree), at the bottom of the social pyramid, remains to be discussed. The suggestion that some peasants were acquainted with Latin is not implausible when the role of the church in village life is considered. Theoretically at least every adult in England should have known some Latin because of its use in the liturgy. The attitude of the western church towards Latin was ambivalent. The identification of *clerici* with *litterati*, which implied that only Latinists were the elect of God, was counterbalanced by the perennial message of the Gospels insisting that Christian teaching should be conveyed to everybody, and therefore to the crowd of *laici*. Various attempts had consequently been made to translate prayers, Scripture and the church's teaching into vernacular languages. The works of

[57] N. Orme, *English Schools in the Middle Ages* (1973), ch. 1.
[58] See n. 62 below.
[59] For Cade see n. 53 above and ch. 9, n. 23 below. For Becket see Clanchy, *'Moderni'*, p. 681 and *Becket Materials* II, p. 361.

Alfred and Aelfric are obvious examples of such attempts in pre-Conquest England.

By the eleventh century an uneasy compromise seems to have been reached whereby, for the people at large, the irreducible minimum of Christian teaching – namely the Lord's Prayer and the Creed – was to be recited in Latin, while sermons, homilies and the like were expressed in the vernacular. Thus a law of Cnut enjoined every Christian to apply himself until he could at least 'understand aright and learn the *Pater Noster* and the *Credo*'.[60] Although this law does not mean that everybody is to read Latin, they are to recite these two Latin texts by heart. Hence one of the glosses accompanying this law adds that Christ himself first recited the *Pater Noster*. That Latin texts are meant and not English translations is suggested by the use of the Latin names for the texts and also by the glosses which describe the penalties for failing to learn them. If the texts had been in the vernacular, there would presumably have been no problem about learning them.

As it was, most people probably did not find this minimal amount of Latin overwhelmingly difficult because they were accustomed to using their ears to learn and furthermore they heard these texts recited whenever they went to church. Assuming that most of the population were minimally conscientious about their religious duties, we are led to the conclusion that most people could recite a little Latin. They had thus taken the first step towards literacy, as paradoxically they could speak *litteraliter*. Those who reached slightly greater competence, in other words, those who understood what they recited and could perhaps also distinguish the letters of the alphabet, would not have been altogether at a loss if they were required to sign their names with seals on Latin charters.

A conjecture of this sort, concerning the level of education of the mass of medieval people, is impossible to prove because evidence of any sort about elementary instruction, and particularly about that of ordinary people, is rare. The biographies of saints sometimes provide glimpses of childhood, but the only detailed description of an English saint of this period of undoubted peasant origins is the life of St Godric, which was written (in various versions) from his own recollections.[61] Although he features in numerous social histories, because he is the first English example of the Dick Whittington type who made his fortune as a merchant, Godric's story is worth examining again from the point of view of what sort of education he acquired.

Godric was born in Norfolk in *c.*1065 of parents who were good, though poor and ignorant. Since he had no wish to remain a peasant, but to exercise his mind, he exerted himself to study.[62] So he strove to learn to be a merchant (*mercatoris studium*), first by selling things locally,

[60] I Canute 22, ed. A. J. Robertson, *The Laws of the Kings of England from Edmund to Henry I* (1925), p. 170. Cf. n. 77 below.

[61] *Libellus de Vita et Miraculis S. Godrici* ed. J. Stevenson, Surtees S. (1845). T. A. Archer, 'Godric' in *The Dictionary of National Biography* VIII, pp. 47–9.

[62] *Libellus de Vita*, ch. 2, p. 25.

then by joining travelling chapmen and ultimately by becoming an international shipman.[63] As merchants travelled with their wares, he mastered navigation and practical maritime astronomy.[64] Business combined well with religion, as he journeyed to the shrines at Lindisfarne and St Andrews, and beyond Britain to Rome, Santiago and Jerusalem.[65] For a while he returned to Norfolk and became steward and general manager to a certain rich man.[66] Godric was a pious but not yet a bookish man, although he had known the Lord's Prayer and the Creed 'from the cradle' and he often pondered them on his journeys.[67] At about the age of forty a kinsman in Carlisle gave him a Psalter, from which he learned the Psalms most diligently, retaining them in his memory.[68] This was an abbreviated version of the Psalter, commonly called 'St Jerome's Psalter'. The book must have been quite large, as Godric permanently distorted his little finger by carrying it around, even to bed.[69] After further travels he came to Durham, where he learned more Psalms 'and afterwards he learned the whole Psalter.'[70] By staying around St Mary's church at Durham, where 'boys were learning the first elements of letters', he tenaciously applied his memory to 'hearing, reading and chanting' and thus became 'firm and certain' in the liturgy.[71] Finally he settled at Finchale, near Durham, as a hermit.

Because Godric was self-educated, both the devil and the monks of Durham adopted a patronizing attitude towards him. The twelfth-century devil shared Walter Map's opinion of serfs who had advanced in the world and called Godric a 'stinking old peasant',[72] while his chief biographer, Reginald of Durham, quite often describes him without malice as *laicus*, *illitteratus* and *idiota*.[73] Technically Reginald was correct, as Godric was not a *clericus* and *litteratus*. Nevertheless Reginald revealed his own ignorance of the effects of travel on an intelligent man, when he considered it miraculous that Godric understood 'French or Romance', even though his mother tongue was English.[74] Reginald likewise considered that it was the Holy Spirit, rather than his native wit, which enabled Godric to understand the Latin conversation of four monks from Durham, who had been sent to cross-examine him.[75] By these means Godric was able to give an impressive exposition of the Scriptures to them (in English), 'as if he were an outstanding *litteratus*'.[76] The information provided by Godric's biographers about his knowledge was not recorded for its own sake, as it was intended as evidence of his religious devotion and of those miraculous powers which were the indispensable sign of a saint. Nevertheless the various versions of the life are sufficiently circumstantial and consistent to provide a historical record of one man's self-education and rise from the mass.

[63] *ibid.* p. 25.   [64] *ibid.* ch. 4, p. 30.   [65] *ibid.* ch. 6, pp. 34, 36.
[66] *ibid.* ch. 6, p. 35.   [67] *ibid.* ch. 4, p. 28.   [68] *ibid.* ch. 9, pp. 41–2.
[69] *ibid.* ch. 92, pp. 200–201.   [70] *ibid.* ch. 16, p. 59.   [71] *ibid.* pp. 59–60.
[72] 'O rustice decrepite! O rustice stercorarie!' *ibid.* ch. 38, p. 93.
[73] *ibid.* ch. 38, p. 94; ch. 47, p. 110; ch. 87, p. 192; ch. 161, p. 306.
[74] *ibid.* ch. 94, pp. 203–4; ch. 96, p. 206.
[75] *ibid.* ch. 79, pp. 179–80.   [76] *ibid.* p. 179.

Godric's life story provides numerous correctives to the modern tendency to assume that schools are the beginning and end of education. He received his instruction in the Lord's Prayer and the Creed 'from the cradle', presumably meaning from his parents. He is therefore an example of Christian law being applied in practice, as it was the duty of every parent to teach his child the *Pater Noster* and the *Credo*.[77] Thereafter Godric was self-taught. He learned numeracy and navigation, the *mercatoris studium*, by experience. Literacy obviously presented greater problems. Godric may never have learned to write and his knowledge of Latin depended primarily on hearing and memorizing. Although he could never become *litteratus* by this method, he could evidently cope with the normal uses of Latin in ecclesiastical circles. Gerald of Wales gives an example of another hermit and traveller, Wecheleu, who had likewise miraculously learned Latin by ear.[78] The fact that such knowledge was considered miraculous suggests, however, that Latin was thought difficult to learn without formal instruction in grammar. Nevertheless even Latin was in its rudimentary stages primarily a spoken language, to which children were introduced by the church's liturgy and prayers in the home.

Although a man like Godric, who had memorized whole portions of the liturgy, could not pass as a Latinist among the *litterati*, he could probably make as good a show of Latin as some clergy. His self-taught Latin only became a problem when he wanted to be accepted as a conscientious churchman and monk. In lay society Godric's lack of a formal education had not prevented him from mastering the *mercatoris studium*, or from becoming a rich man's steward. In the latter capacity tally sticks and a trained memory were more useful than parchments, although if Godric had lived a century later, he might have found it more difficult to conduct business without writing. Yet before deciding that Godric could not have succeeded a century later, it is worth recalling that the greatest of all medieval stewards and business managers, Hubert Walter, was likewise described as *laicus et illitteratus*.[79] Like Godric, he had little or no formal schooling and was ignorant of elementary Latin grammar, if Gerald of Wales is to believed.[80] A little Latin, like a little literacy in more recent times, could get a man a long way in ordinary business, deplorable as that was in the eyes of scholars.

The acquisition of clerical education

Godric's life shows that a little Latin, and a great deal of education in the broader sense of understanding and mastering one's environment, could be acquired by a determined peasant without any formal schooling. Nevertheless those children of serfs whom Walter Map had in mind who became royal justices had probably risen through some clerical training

[77] *Wulfstan's Canons of Edgar* ed. R. Fowler, Early English Text S. CCLXVI (1972), pp. 6–7. Cf. n. 60 above.
[78] See ch. 6, n. 13 above.   [79] See n. 22 above.
[80] See ch. 2, nn. 82–4 above. Hubert mistakenly corrected Richard I's 'coram nobis' to 'coram nos', Giraldus III, p. 30.

in childhood, as Latin could only be superficially acquired by self-education. The commonness of such instruction has probably been under-estimated, both in terms of the number of children involved and of the social classes from which they came. A polemicist of the early twelfth century argued that there were numerous *clerici*, just as there were numerous royal tax collectors and officials, since highly expert school-masters existed 'not only in cities and boroughs, but even in little villages [*in villulis*]'.[81] Even if this were not exaggerated, however, the problems for a serf's family were paying for instruction and doing without the labour of the child concerned.

As a solution of these problems, the role of the church in disseminating free instruction in villages through its priests may have been as underestimated as its role in familiarizing people with Latin through the liturgy. Most scholars now agree that by the thirteenth century, when information becomes sufficiently abundant to make generalizations, parish priests were often of peasant, even servile, origins and also that the standard of learning of the priesthood was on the whole quite high.[82] The latter generalization is the more controversial, as a handful of cases of priestly ignorance have been repeatedly cited against it. The most frequently quoted report is from the dean of Salisbury's visitation of Sonning in 1222, where some of the vicar's chaplains' ignorance of Latin grammar was exposed.[83] Yet this case does not suggest that such ignorance was normal, as the incompetent chaplains were suspended or dismissed as a consequence of this visitation.

Cases of priestly ignorance, when recorded in detail in bishop's registers, indicate not that priests were generally ignorant but that reformers were requiring higher standards. Thus it has been calculated from the earliest bishop's register, that of Hugh of Wells, concerning the largest diocese, Lincoln, over a period of a quarter of a century (1209–35) that out of 1,958 institutions to benefices only 101 candidates were recorded as deficient in learning, and most of these cases arose from candidates not having completed their education; only four deficient candidates were already priests.[84] If most parish priests were of peasant origins, and if by 1230 many were sufficiently instructed, it follows that a number of persons of peasant origins had been efficiently instructed in Latin, with a view to becoming priests, even in the twelfth century.

How was the initial instruction of peasants achieved? Not often presumably through schools in towns because of the expense, either of travel or of lodging. Certainly would-be clergy lodged in town schools after they had shown sufficient ability to learn reading and elementary

[81] Cited by R. W. Southern, see n. 14 above.

[82] Gabel, *Benefit of Clergy*, p. 75 gives instances of priests of servile origin. Absentee rectors should be distinguished from the poor priests who performed their duties: G. C. Homans, *English Villagers of the Thirteenth Century* (1941) pp. 388–90. J. R. H. Moorman, *Church Life in England in the Thirteenth Century* (1945), p. 93, points out that whether one thought the priesthood sufficiently learned depended on one's point of view.

[83] *The Register of St Osmund* ed. W. H. Rich Jones, RS LXXVIII (1883), I, pp. 304ff. First publicized by G. G. Coulton, *Life in the Middle Ages* (2nd edn, 1928) II, no. 21, pp. 39–41.

[84] Orme, *English Schools*, p. 17.

Latin grammar, but their initial instruction and selection must have taken place in the villages themselves. If, as has been argued, parish priests were themselves sufficiently instructed, they could perform this function. Indeed it was required of them by canon law, reiterated in numerous manuscripts. Thus the ninth-century provision of Theodulf, bishop of Orléans, that 'priests should have schools throughout the villages [*per villas*] and teach children free of charge' was translated into English and copied into ecclesiastical compilations of the eleventh century.[85] Of course the repetition of such rules implies that some priests failed to comply. Moreover, a village priest, who was relatively poor and ignorant himself, could not have instructed many children at a time, nor have got them much beyond the ABC and the bare elements of reading Latin. Many priests probably performed these duties to a minimal level at least, as incidental references to them can be found. Thus in one of the fables attributed to Marie de France, which may be of English origin, a priest is pictured teaching a wolf the ABC.[86] The wolf is the rarity and not the priest. Among the miracles of St Edmund, recorded by Hermann in *c*.1095, is the cure of a man who had been so ill that the parish priest named Goding, immediately 'coming with his scholars', rushed to give him the last rites.[87] The elementary teaching duties of priests were so commonplace that they seem only to be mentioned in exceptional circumstances like these.

Even if the average parish priest taught only one poor boy a year, a boy for example who served him at the altar, and if only one such boy in ten proceeded beyond the ABC, nine sons of peasants in the village had acquired a little familiarity with letters and one had advanced into the lowest ranks of the clergy. Perhaps only one in ten of these boys rose to be a parish priest, and only one in a hundred became a *litteratus*, because the course grew progressively more difficult. Such speculations – and they are no more than that – suggest that each prelate and *litteratus* of peasant origin whose name has come down to history (Robert Grosseteste is the obvious example) was the one in a thousand who achieved his objective. Although it was difficult therefore for a poor boy to rise through the church, some succeeded, and the difficulties ensured that many who were disappointed in their expectations had at least learned the ABC. Famous prelates of humble origin stood at the visible apex of a pyramid of peasant education extending deep into the villages.

More specific information about peasants' sons rising through a clerical education is difficult to find, however, because childhood is rarely described and the social origins of particular persons are often a matter of subjective judgement. Either poverty or gentility may be misleadingly reported by a biographer wishing to demonstrate his subject's sanctity or success. Autobiographical information is even rarer and no

[85] *Patrologiae* CV (1864), col. 196. *Ancient Laws and Institutes of England* ed. B. Thorpe, RC (1840), p. 475, ch. 20.

[86] U. T. Holmes, *Daily Living in the Twelfth Century* (1952), p. 230.

[87] *Memorials of St Edmunds Abbey* ed. T. Arnold. RS XCVI (1890), I, p. 81.

easier to assess. Thus John of Salisbury, who may have been a peasant as his parentage is very obscure, remarks that he learned Psalms from a priest, and he was presumably first taught to read in this way.[88] Yet this instance does not indicate John's confidence in such instruction, as he only mentions it because the priest had tried to teach him sorcery as well. A clearer case of a country boy rising to be a *litteratus* is Jocelin's account of Abbot Samson, although that also illustrates the difficulties of assessing social class. Samson may even have been the model for Walter Map's remarks about Henry II's clerical judges of servile origins being harsher than the lay ones, as he 'exalted justice over mercy' according to Jocelin.[89]

Jocelin reports that, although he had heard Samson say that he had kinsmen of noble blood, 'he had no kin within a third degree, or at any rate pretended that this was so.'[90] It is possible that Samson's reticence concealed servile origins. He seems to have been brought up by his mother, who introduced him to the shrine of St Edmund at the age of nine.[91] Instead of kinsmen, Samson rewarded those 'who had treated him as their kinsmen when he was a poor cloister monk'.[92] Thus he gave benefices to the sons of the man 'of no high birth' who had preserved his patrimony, to the chaplain who sold holy water to maintain him as a student at Paris, and to the son of Master William of Diss who let him enter his school out of pure charity.[93] Whatever Samson's origins, he is certainly an example of a promising country boy who was picked out for training as a *clericus* and owed his rise primarily to ecclesiastical charity.

Samson's career also illustrates another important aspect of clerical education. He once confided to Jocelin that he would never have become a monk if he had possessed sufficient money to remain at the schools.[94] It was therefore only chance which confirmed him in his ecclesiastical vocation. Some *clerici* abandoned ecclesiastical life and traded their skills in the world, even becoming knights. This was another way in which literate education was integrated into lay society. Among the miracles of St Godric is one in which he identified one of the household knights of Bertram of Bulmer (in the middle of the twelfth century) as a *clericus* and *litteratus*, even though the knight had grown his hair to conceal his tonsure.[95] This young knight had been sent to Godric on his lord's business on a Sunday. Godric made him reveal his clerical up-bringing by compelling him to read the lesson at Mass, which he did 'not at all like a *laicus*, but rather as a *litteratus*'. So Godric gave him a good talking to, telling him that he was making unworthy use of his educa-tion in not going on to be a priest. A century later John of Gaddesden, a cleric with numerous benefices who had been the queen's chamberlain, renounced his ecclesiastical status with more ceremony. He was belted as a knight by Henry III on Christmas Day 1244 and married a lady's

[88] *Policraticus*, bk II, ch. 28, vol. ii, p. 164.
[89] Jocelin, p. 34. Cf. n. 113 below.   [90] *ibid.* p. 43.
[91] *ibid.* p. 37.   [92] *ibid.* p. 43.   [93] *ibid.* pp. 43–4.
[94] *ibid.* p. 36.   [95] *Libellus de Vita*, ch. 109, pp. 226–8.

daughter.[96] Matthew Paris reported that this gave rise to envious gossip, which he thought misplaced, as John had willingly given up all his benefices. More scandalous presumably in Matthew's view were those clerics who, instead of acknowledging their lay status, maintained spouses and illegitimate children from their benefices.

The rule of clerical celibacy, which had long been an ideal of the church, was given new force by the Gregorian reformers of the eleventh century and had come near to being the norm among the higher clergy by the thirteenth.[97] Ironically, this rule may have been the chief cause of the dissemination of clerical skills in literacy among all classes of the laity. If the Gregorian reformers had not intervened, the *clerici-litterati* might well have become a hereditary caste, like priestly scholars in some other cultures. Knowledge of Latin would then have been restricted to a self-perpetuating élite. Instead, clerical celibacy drove trained men who could not accept it back into lay society, thus disseminating literate skills, and it also made the production of future clergy depend initially and primarily on the laity. Priests found it increasingly difficult to hand on their benefices to their sons, as they were deemed illigitimate. Opportunities consequently increased for non-clerical families to get a clerical training.

A text of the mid-twelfth century, extant only in England though connected with the school of Abelard, comments that Christian families unlike Jewish ones educate one son only, 'not for God but for gain, in order that the one brother, if he be a cleric, may help his father and mother and his other brothers'; because a cleric has no heir, any acquisitions will return to the family.[98] That this selective attitude prevailed in the twelfth century, even among the nobility, is suggested by the childhood of Gerald of Wales. He was the youngest (born in c.1147) of four brothers and showed his suitability for the clergy at an early age by building sand churches and monasteries at the seaside while his brothers built castles.[99] His father was pleased and called the boy his 'bishop'. So Gerald was put in charge of his uncle, David, who was the real bishop of St David's. In due course Gerald was himself twice a candidate for the bishopric of St David's, though his election was quashed. Gerald's family had a hereditary interest in the bishopric of St David's. Clerical celibacy at least ensured that offices now passed from uncle to nephew instead of father to son, and hence initial recruitment depended on laymen like Gerald's father.

Before Gregorian reform became effective many future *clerici* must have been introduced to Latin and formal education by their own parents. Thus Orderic Vitalis's father, who was a priest, knew that Latin should be started young and had him instructed by another priest from

---

[96] Matthew Paris IV, p. 403. F. Pegues, 'The *Clericus* in the Legal Administration of Thirteenth-Century England', *EHR* LXXI (1956), pp. 556–7.

[97] C. Brooke, 'Gregorian Reform in Action: Clerical Marriage in England', *Medieval Church and Society* (1971), pp. 69–99.

[98] *Commentarius Cantabrigiensis* ed. A. Landgraf, cited by Smalley, *The Bible*, p. 78.

[99] Giraldus I, p. 21.

the age of five.[100] As hereditary priests grew rarer, the responsibility for inaugurating children in Latin became the duty of parents who were technically *laici* and *illitterati*. They thus became familiar with the problems of learning, even if they remained uninstructed themselves. As clergy were required at all social levels, ranging from a noble bishop like Gerald's uncle to peasant parish priests, an increasing number of families began to have experience of education. *Clerici* and *laici* were united in the closest kinship by celibacy, not set apart. Literacy ceased to be a high arcane mystery when a younger brother was obliged to acquire it because he had no patrimony.

Among the nobility, pious mothers who read the Psalter and lives of the saints often perhaps took an active role in educating their children, as in the uniquely documented case of Guibert de Nogent.[101] At a humbler social level in England, it may have been Samson's mother who arranged for his schooling, when she showed off her precocious son of nine at the shrine of St Edmund. A century later Walter of Bibbesworth assumes that it will be the mother, albeit a widow, Denise de Montchensy, who improves her children's French.[102] Walter assumes furthermore that both mother and children are familiar with the Latin primer, the 'book which teaches us *clergie*', because by the thirteenth century, among the nobility at least, all children both male and female were usually taught a little formal Latin and hence initiated into 'clergy'. A little *clergie* had the advantage of keeping children's options open. From inclination or necessity, boys or girls could subsequently join the 'religious', provided they had a grounding in Latin and some local influence. From the fourteenth century, moreover, a little Latin, 'benefit of clergy', was also an insurance against being hanged. Thus by 1300 conscientious or ambitious parents of all social classes had strong motives for seeing that their children were *clerici* and *litterati* in the new minimal sense of being capable of reading a verse from the Bible.

Real *litterati*, in the old sense of 'scholars', of course remained rare. Those who were totally ignorant, that is, those who could not pass a Latin reading test, were perhaps as rare. Detailed cases of failure to read are thought amusing, particularly by academics, and have therefore been repeatedly cited. Repetition gives the false impression that such cases were typical and commonplace. The description by Gerald of Wales of the abbot of St Dogmael's inability to read a papal letter, or even a missal, has already been cited.[103] But Gerald's numerous and lively descriptions of clerical ignorance are difficult to generalize from, as he even alleged that Hubert Walter was ignorant of elementary grammar.[104] Possibly that was so, yet it did not prevent Hubert mastering the royal archives. Gerald's anecdotes, like other detailed reports of illiteracy among churchmen, suggest that normal expectations were relatively high.

[100] See ch. 6, n. 74 above.
[101] *Self and Society in Medieval France* ed. J. F. Benton (1970).
[102] See ch. 6, nn. 1–5 above.
[103] Giraldus III, p. 234; see ch. 4, n. 41 above.   [104] See n. 80 above.

Total inability to read was likewise the exception and not the rule among knights by 1300. Examples of such knights are as difficult to find as their converse, the *milites litterati*. Certainly there were some, like the two jurors in the de Tony case who were described as *laici*, though the use of the word 'layman' in this context implies that *clerici* were now the norm. One example of a really ignorant and boorish knight is a certain Hugh, who was charged with rape in *c.*1300.[105] He had pleaded benefit of clergy and, when this plea was disallowed, he wished to challenge some of the jurors, which required reading out their names. At this point he had to admit that he was unable to read. But Hugh's predicament does not suggest that he was typical in being unable to read. On the contrary, it emphasizes how important it was by 1300 for a man in trouble to have sufficient *clergie* to get himself out of it. Even a century earlier in 1198 an illiterate landlord in Oxfordshire, Alan Fitz Roland, had found himself arraigned before the king's justices when he had failed to act on a writ brought against him in his court by his serfs; Alan's excuse was that he had no clerk who could read the document.[106] Thus sometimes by 1200 and invariably by 1300 a landlord, on however small a scale, needed sufficient *clergie*, in the sense of a personal knowledge of Latin, to assess, if not fully to understand, the written demands made upon him.

Educated knights

Knights who were able to read a little Latin, sufficient to get the gist of a royal writ or to understand a line in the Bible or in a chronicle, were literate in something like a modern minimal sense. By 1300, it has been argued in this chapter, such an ability was common among the gentry and may not have been rare among peasants. The conclusions to be drawn from this extension of minimal literacy are more problematical, however. In the modern world a little literacy enables a person to begin to cope with the mass of written instructions and bureaucratic demands which are a commonplace of daily experience. Further ability opens to the private reader, for recreation or self-improvement, the thousands of printed books available in his own language. A person who cannot read and write is therefore at a disadvantage in the mastery of daily life and he is also excluded from those areas of culture which depend on the printed word. These truisms are stated here only because they did not apply with equal force in the Middle Ages. A knight of the eleventh century who learned the rudiments of Latin in childhood would not have found this skill had much application in daily life, nor did it open to him the cultural heritage of his people, because Latin was a foreign language and books were not generally available.

By 1300 the situation had changed, though not radically. Bureaucratic demands in Latin were now sufficiently common to make it useful for any landowner to be able to understand them. 'Pragmatic' literacy,

---

[105] See ch. 8, n. 103 below.   [106] *CuriaRR* I, p. 46; cf. *ibid.* p. 203.

defined by Parkes as 'the literacy of one who has to read or write in the course of transacting any kind of business',[107] thus became usual. Literacy for purposes of recreation or self-improvement, the literacy of 'the cultivated reader',[108] was still not very useful, although that too was beginning to change as more was being written down in vernacular languages. The books given by the earl of Warwick to Bordesley abbey in 1306, or the various late thirteenth-century manuscripts containing treatises on accountancy and estate management, indicate the kind of literature which might be found in a nobleman's, or even a gentleman's, household by 1300.[109] On the whole, however, private reading must still have been a luxury, largely confined to retiring ladies and scholars. Books were scarce and it was ordinary good manners to share their contents among a group by reading aloud.

The increase in the number of persons who could read, at a minimal level, over the period 1066–1307 was thus a consequence of the demands of the 'pragmatic' rather than the 'cultivated' reader. That is why this book has approached literacy from record-making, instead of from the usual standpoint of an advance in culture and education. 'Documents had to precede widening literacy. . . . The gentry were not going to learn to read until documents were available and necessary.'[110] Although a little Latin had become an essential of business and a commonplace of gentlemanly education by Walter of Bibbesworth's time, it was still something alien, and even contrary, to traditional knightly culture. Hence Latin was learned from the 'book which teaches us *clergie*'. An aspiring knight of the thirteenth century did not become a cultivated gentleman primarily by being a reader, necessary as that now was. He had to master the skills of combat, hunting, hawking and chess and know the vernacular languages, law, traditional oral 'literature' and music of his people. Such knowledge was not primarily to be found in Latin books, but in speech, gesture and memory.

Clerici and *litterati* might claim that book learning was the only intellectual and noble pursuit. Yet the slightest consideration of the languages an English knight needed to know, or any knowledge of the subtelties of heraldry or hawking, suggests that knightly education was equally demanding intellectually though in a different way. This suggestion cannot be incontrovertibly proved, however, because knightly culture before the fourteenth century has been largely lost to posterity, as it was primarily oral. Lack of written record did not of course make knightly culture any less real or less demanding for contemporaries. Indeed it may have been more lively than later literate culture, because knightly culture depended on the immediacy of speech. Judging from the romances, intellect and wit were prized among knights. A knight of advanced oral education was expected to contribute towards the knowledge and entertainment of his fellows, instead of being a passive and silent recipient of book learning. The *clerici* might claim to be the elect of God, but the knights or warriors (*bellatores*) were as powerful and as

[107] Parkes, 'Literacy', p. 555.   [108] *ibid.* p. 555.
[109] See ch. 3, nn. 2, 8 above.   [110] See p. 57 above.

venerable an elite. In the extension of medieval literacy the *clerici* did not impose their culture on ignorant and passive *laici*. Rather, clerical skills were gradually absorbed, insofar as they were useful, and an amalgam was formed over generations of literate and pre-literate habits of thought.

To give substance to generalizations which may seem vague and romanticized, this chapter will conclude with a look at two small incidents concerning knights recorded by Jocelin of Brakelond. Samson's first action after being inaugurated as abbot in 1182 was to turn away all suitors except one man. This was a knight (Jocelin does not record his name), 'eloquent and expert in law' (*juris peritus*), who was retained because Samson had no experience of business in secular courts.[111] After a while Samson began to master secular law, just as he mastered canon law, and the services of this knight presumably then became less essential. According to Jocelin, everyone marvelled at Samson's new expertise and the under-sheriff, Osbert Fitz Hervey, said: 'This abbot is a debater [*disputator*]; if he goes on as he has begun, he will dazzle us all, every one of us.'[112] Soon, 'having proved himself in cases', Samson's competence in secular law was officially recognized by his being appointed a royal justice in eyre.[113]

In these two incidents (first Samson's initial appointment of the anonymous knight and then the remark of Osbert Fitz Hervey on Samson's progress) Jocelin introduces his hero and his readers to an uncharted intellectual world, for which Samson's training as a *clericus* and *litteratus* had not explicitly prepared him. As it turned out, Samson mastered this world of secular law in due course, as he mastered everyone and everything in Jocelin's opinion. Yet this was a cause for surprise. Fitz Hervey had evidently not assumed that Samson's clerical education would make him a good debater in the county court. Knights like Fitz Hervey, who mastered county business, had learned their skills which were predominantly oral by years of attendance at the court, first by listening and then by speaking. About forty years earlier in the same county court (again in a case concerning Bury St Edmunds) one of its 'proved and prudent men', Hervey de Glanvill, recalled how he had attended county and hundred courts first with his father and then as householder in his own right for over fifty years.[114] His ancient wisdom had been duly heeded on that occasion.

From knights like Osbert Fitz Hervey, who learned their business orally, the king chose most of his justices and sheriffs, and litigants chose their advocates. Such expert knights were those 'greater men of the county, who are called *buzones*, on whose nod the views of the others depend', according to Bracton.[115] The *buzones judiciorum* are recorded

[111] Jocelin, p. 24.
[112] *ibid.* p. 34.
[113] *ibid.* p. 34. Cf. n. 89 above.
[114] H. Cam, 'An East Anglian Shire-Moot of Stephen's Reign', *EHR* XXIX (1924), p. 570. Clanchy, 'Remembering', p. 174. J. C. Russell suggests that Hervey may have been the father of Ranulf de Glanvill, the justiciar, *Speculum* XLV (1970), p. 71.
[115] Bracton, fo. 115b, vol. ii, p. 326.

giving judgment in a case in 1212.[116] Samson was not the only abbot to take legal advice from knights. In 1201 the abbot of Crowland had relied on the counsel of 'the wise and discreet knight, Reynold surnamed de Argento', in his litigation with the prior of Spalding.[117] Reynold in the 1190s had been a sheriff, a justice in eyre and an attorney of the bishop of Ely among others.[118] Osbert Fitz Hervey himself served as a justice in eyre in Richard I's reign and also on the Bench at Westminster between 1192 and 1206.[119] As a judge he achieved exceptional distinction, since he is one of only seven judges (including three chief justiciars) whose opinions on points of law are referred to in manuscripts of *Glanvill*.[120]

Although knights like Fitz Hervey were experts in law (*juris periti*), their expertise was not in book learning but in oral advocacy. Skilful pleading in courts, the mastery of the spoken word, has been admired in many non-literate societies and is best exemplified in medieval Europe from those two extreme geographical points of medieval culture, the Iceland of the sagas and the crusader Kingdom of Jerusalem. From Iceland the best known example is the story in *Njal's Saga* of how Gunnar tricked the expert, Hrut, into summoning himself.[121] In the Kingdom of Jerusalem its knightly jurists (Ralf of Tiberias, John of Beirut and Balian of Sidon) were the contemporaries of Osbert Fitz Hervey and Reynold de Argento. Although their opinions were subsequently written into the law books of the Kingdom, there is no doubt that they themselves learned their art, like the English jurists of the county court, from vernacular practice and not from ecclesiastical Latin schools.[122]

It is a mistake to regard knightly jurists as amateurs and clerical ones as professionals. Both knights and clergy contributed skills which shaped the legal profession. Pleading had been developed by knights as an alternative to private warfare, both as an honourable profession and as an intellectual pastime. When Henry the Young King and his companions spent a year in England in 1175 under the guardianship of that model of chivalry, William Marshal, they did nothing 'except pleading, hunting and fighting in tournaments'.[123] Clerics were trained in a comparable, though more book centred, form of intellectual warfare by the disputations of the schools. Peter Abelard, the prototype of scholastic masters, in his autobiography saw his whole life in terms of warfare with other masters. The schools of Paris had probably taught Abbot Samson more than Osbert Fitz Hervey realized about how to be a *disputator*. In the twelfth century, when literate and pre-literate ways

[116] *CuriaRR* VI, p. 231. G. Lapsley, 'Buzones', *EHR* XLVII (1932), pp. 179ff. R & S, p. 94, n. 1; p. 183, n. 10.

[117] Stenton, *Justice*, p. 192.

[118] *Pleas before the King or his Justices* ed. D. M. Stenton, SS LXXXIII (1966) III, pp. ccxcvi–ccxcvii.

[119] *ibid.* p. cccxxx (indexed references under 'Osbert Fitz Hervey').

[120] Glanvill, pp. xliv–xlv.   [121] See ch. 8, n. 96 below.

[122] J. Riley-Smith, *The Feudal Nobility and the Kingdom of Jerusalem* (1973), pp. 123 ff.

[123] 'A nule riens fors a pleidier ou a bois ou a torneier', *L'Histoire de Guillaume le Maréchal* ed. P. Mayer, Societé de l'Histoire de France (1891–1901), lines 2393–4.

of thought were beginning to penetrate each other and interact, strong and novel institutions were formed by drawing on both traditions. Thus English common law benefited from the clerical training of scholastics like Samson and the oral lore of knights like Osbert. Whether royal judges were technically clergy or laymen seems to have had no bearing either way on their professional competence, although Walter Map thought it affected their severity. Once the judiciary becomes sufficiently documented in John's reign, it can be shown that of his fifteen regular judges (that is, those who served for ten or more terms) only four were clergy.[124] Similarly in Henry III's reign some judges, like Bracton, were clergy whereas others of equal distinction at the time, like Thurkelby, were knights.

The knights of English county courts, like knights all over Europe, were educated and cultured men regardless of whether they were literate. Perhaps by 1200, and certainly by 1300, they had usually learned enough Latin to cope with the documents which came their way. But this restricted knowledge of literacy was a pragmatic convenience, rather than a positive contribution to their intellectual education. A little Latin, learned from a relatively ignorant priest, did not educate a man in the culture of imperial or of Christian Rome, and hence it did not make him a *litteratus* in the traditional sense. Literacy became something more positive for non-churchmen only when writing recorded a substantial part of their own heritage in vernacular languages. That is a development of the later Middle Ages and not of the period 1066–1307.

Yet the twelfth and thirteenth centuries are crucially important because these are the years in which the traditional division between cleric and lay, literate and illiterate, was broken down. Gradually by all sorts of avenues a little literacy, in the sense of minimal Latin or *clergie*, became commonplace until 'benefit of clergy' came to mean the ability to read a few words of Latin. Because literacy had been identified with Latin for a thousand years, it had first to be learned by the laity in this clerical and alien form. Those old rivals, the *clerici-litterati* and the *laici-illitterati*, had to come to terms and absorb each other's thought processes before literacy could become a common vernacular habit. The extension of literacy was therefore a complex social problem in the Middle Ages and not a simple matter of providing more educational facilities. Bridges had to be built across the divide of speech and script.

[124] R. V. Turner, 'The Judges of King John: their Background and Training', *Speculum* LI (1976), p. 454.

8

Hearing and seeing

'Fundamentally letters are shapes indicating voices. Hence they represent things which they bring to mind through the windows of the eyes. Frequently they speak voicelessly the utterances of the absent.'[1] In these antitheses John of Salisbury's *Metalogicon* grapples with the basic problems of the relationship between the spoken and the written word. The difference between sounds or voices (*voces*) and things or realities (*res*) was complicated for him, writing an the mid-twelfth century, by the controversy between Nominalists and Realists, between those who argued that universals were mere names and those who claimed they were real things. This philosophical controversy is not our concern here. John's remarks are relevant because, like much of *Metalogicon*, they seem to reflect his own experience as a secretary and drafter of letters as well as exemplifying current scholastic thought.

Numerous charters of the twelfth century are addressed to 'all those seeing and hearing these letters, in the future as in the present' or to 'all who shall hear and see this charter'; these two examples come from the charters of Roger de Mowbray who died in 1188.[2] The grantor of another charter, Richard de Rollos, actually harangues his audience, 'Oh! all ye who shall have heard this and have seen!'[3] Early charters likewise quite often conclude with 'Goodbye' (*Valete*), as if the donor had just finished speaking with his audience.[4] Documents made it possible for the grantor to address posterity ('all who shall hear and see') as well as his contemporaries. In the opening words of the Winchcombe abbey cartulary, 'when the voice has perished with the man, writing still enlightens posterity.'[5] Writing shifted the spotlight away from the transitory actors witnessing a conveyance and on to the perpetual parchment

---

[1] 'Littere autem, id est figure, primo vocum indices sunt; deinde rerum, quas anime per oculorum fenestras opponunt, et frequenter absentium dicta sine voce loquuntur', *Metalogicon*, bk i, ch. 13, ed. C. C. J. Webb (1929), p. 32. John's definition, in distinguishing *voces* from *res*, sharpens that of Isidore's *Etymologies*: 'Litterae autem sunt indices rerum, signa verborum, quibus tanta vis est, ut nobis dicta absentium sine voce loquantur', bk i, ch. 3, ed. W. M. Lindsay (1911), lines 6–8.

[2] *Mowbray Charters*, nos. 92, 347. Cf. ch. 3, nn. 11–12 above.

[3] Stenton, *Feudalism*, pp. 111, 273, no. 27.

[4] E.g. *Oxford Facs*, nos. 7, 38, 54, 56, 60, 62, 72, 74.

[5] *Landboc sive Registrum de Wincehlcumba* ed. D. Royce (1892) I, p. 17.

recording it. By the thirteenth century, when charters had become more familiar to landowners, donors cease addressing their readers, as Richard de Rollos did, and likewise they no longer conclude with *Valete*. Once it was understood that charters were directed to posterity, it must have seemed foolish to say 'Goodbye' to people who had not yet been born. In place of such conversational expressions, thirteenth-century charters are more stereotyped; they are often impersonally addressed in some such form as 'Let all persons, present and future, know that I, A of B, have given X with its appurtenances to C of D.'[6]

A comparable change occurs in wills. Until the thirteenth century the will was an essentially oral act, even when it was recorded in writing. The persons present witnessed the testator making his bequests 'with his own mouth'; they 'saw, were present, and heard' the transaction.[7] By the end of the thirteenth century a man's final will no longer usually meant his wishes spoken on his deathbed, but a closed and sealed document. The witnesses no longer heard him; instead they saw his seal being placed on the document. When wills were first enrolled, as they were in London from 1258, the formula of probate still put emphasis on the witnesses who had seen and heard. But a generation later, by the 1290s, the London roll often omits the names of the witnesses, presumably because the written will was the preferred evidence.[8] The validity of the will now depended primarily upon its being in a correct documentary form and not on the verbal assurances of the witnesses. This is another illustration of the shift from memory to written record between 1100 and 1300. Wills had been made in writing by the Anglo-Saxons; the novelty lay in their being closed and sealed documents.

Symbolic objects and documents

Before conveyances were made with documents, the witnesses 'heard' the donor utter the words of the grant and 'saw' him make the transfer by a symbolic object, such as a knife or a turf from the land. William the Conqueror went one better and jokingly threatened to make one donee 'feel' the conveyance by dashing the symbolic knife through the recipient abbot's hand saying, 'That's the way land ought to be given.'[9] Such a gesture was intended to impress the event on the memory of all those present. If there were dispute subsequently, resort was had to the recollection of the witnesses. Similar rules applied to the oral 'records' of courts, which were retained (in theory at least) in the memory of those present. For example, if the record of the county court were disputed, the aggrieved litigant brought forward two witnesses who each gave evidence of what they had heard and seen. In such a case in 1212 the prior of Ware (in Hertfordshire) defended himself by 'one hearing and one

---

[6] C. A. F. Meekings analyses conveyancing forms in *Fitznell's Cartulary*, Surrey Record S. XXVI (1968), pp. cxliff. See also ch. 3, nn. 11–12 above.

[7] M. M. Sheehan, *The Will in Medieval England*, Pontifical Institute of Medieval Studies: Studies & Texts VI (1963), pp. 186–7.

[8] *ibid.* pp. 192; 188, n. 90.   [9] P & M II, p. 87, n. 4.

understanding', namely Jordan of Warew and Robert of Clopton; Robert also offered to prove the prior's allegation by battle, 'as he was present and heard this'.[10] In this case some distinction is evidently being attempted between the knowledge of the two witnesses: Jordan had heard, or at least understood, less of the preceedings than Robert. Likewise at Cheshunt (in Hertfordshire) in a seignorial court in 1220 a litigant challenged the record by 'one person hearing and another seeing'.[11] Which testimony was thought preferable in this instance, that of the person who heard or of the other who saw, is unclear. These two exceptional cases suggest that the legal commonplace of making a record by 'hearing and seeing' was not a mere formula made meaningless by repetition.

Documents changed the significance of bearing witness by hearing and seeing legal procedures, because written evidence could be heard by reading aloud or seen by inspecting the document. In John of Salisbury's definition, letters 'indicate voices' and bring things to mind 'through the windows of the eyes'. Once charters were used for conveyances, 'hearing' applied to anyone hearing the charter read out loud at any time, instead of referring only to the witnesses of the original conveyance. From there it was a short step to substitute 'reading' for 'seeing', as one of Roger de Mowbray's charters does, which is addressed to 'all his own men and to the rest, *reading* or hearing these letters'.[12] This phrase plays also with the ambiguity of the word 'letters', which in Latin (as in English) means both alphabetic symbols and missives.

A curiously worded grant for St Mary's priory at Monmouth is addressed to the donors, Richard de Cormeilles and Beatrice his wife, instead of to the recipients.[13] The charter rewards Richard and Beatrice with divine bliss because they have given the tithes of Norton-Giffard to Mary the mother of God. She is the ostensible grantor of the charter, though the document itself was presumably written by a monk of St Mary's priory which was the terrestial beneficiary. The writer's Latin is eccentric – for example he spells *uxor* (wife) as *hucxor* – but revealing in its phraseology. He includes the phrase *sicut presens breve loquitur* (as the present writing speaks), whereas ordinary usage would have *dicitur* (says) or *testatur* (attests) in place of *loquitur*. The writer also makes it clear that the named witnesses, who 'saw and heard the gift solemnly exhibited by a book upon the altar', are 'subsequent' and therefore secondary to the evidence of the writing itself. In making the writing 'speak' and in putting the pre-literate witnessing ceremony of seeing and hearing into a subsidiary role, the naïve writer of this charter has exemplified John of Salisbury's scholastic definition (which is contemporary with the charter) that letters 'speak voicelessly the utterances of the absent', the absent in this instance being the grantor, Mary the mother of God.

---

[10] *CuriaRR* VI, p. 230. See also ch. 2, nn. 104–9 above, concerning the oral 'records' of county courts.

[11] *SPC*, pp. 124–5, no. 192.

[12] *Mowbray Charters*, no. 98.   [13] *BM Facs*, no. 16.

Once property was conveyed in writing, it would have seemed logical for the charter to supersede the symbolic object, such as the knife or turf, which had formerly been used in the witnessing ceremony. As the grant to Monmouth priory shows, that object had sometimes itself been a writing – a book solemnly exhibited upon an altar. Traditionally the book used for this purpose was the text of the Gospels. For example a gift of a saltpan was made to St Peter's priory at Sele in Sussex in 1153 'by the text of the Holy Gospel upon the altar of St Peter, many persons hearing and seeing'.[14] The Gospel book was used because it was customary to reinforce oaths with it (as is still the practice in law courts); thus in Edward I's wardrobe there was kept 'a book, which is called *textus*, upon which the magnates were accustomed to swear'.[15] To replace a Gospel book by a charter in a conveyancing ceremony was a relatively small change in appearance (it was simply substituting one document for another), but a large one in substance. The charter in its text actually 'represented' (in John of Salisbury's definition) in a durable record the terms of the conveyance, whereas the Gospel book merely symbolized the solemnity of the occasion for the witnesses. The Monmouth priory charter therefore distinguishes the written grant (*breve*), which 'speaks' to the hearers, from the symbolic book (*liber*) which is 'exhibited' to the viewers.

Nevertheless, although it seemed logical to dispense with symbols and make full use of the potentialities of writing, contemporaries continued with their pre-literate habits long after charters had become common. In the rare instances where the conveyance appears to be made by the written document itself (as in the Monmouth priory charter), we should probably assume that the document is serving the ancient function of a symbolic object, rather than being considered primarily for its contents in a modern literate way. There are examples of the conveyancing document being presented on the altar like a Gospel book. In a charter of 1193 the abbot of Glastonbury states that 'the present charter was placed on the altar of St Mary by me as an offering, the clergy and people of the same vill [of Street in Somerset] standing round.'[16] In the Guthlac roll (probably dating from the late twelfth century) King Ethelbald and twelve other benefactors of Crowland abbey in Lincolnshire are depicted pressing forward with opened scrolls to lay at the altar and shrine of St Guthlac. The writing on the scrolls is specific, giving in Latin the name of each donor and the property donated, such as, 'I, Alan de Croun give you, Father Guthlac, the priory of Freiston with appurtenances.'[17] One or two of the benefactors have their mouths open, as if voicing their gifts. As some of these charters cannot be traced and may

---

[14] *Oxford Facs*, no. 9. Cf. H. Ellis, 'Observations on some Ancient Methods of Conveyance in England', *Archaeologia* XVII (1814), pp. 317–18.

[15] Chaplais, *Docs*, p. 50, n. 2.

[16] *The Great Chartulary of Glastonbury* ed. A. Watkin, Somerset Record S. LXIV (1949–50), p. 703.

[17] *The Guthlac Roll* ed. G. Warner, Roxburghe Club (1928), p. 16 and plate xviii. For this particular gift see *Monasticon* IV, p. 125.

well have been forged, the Guthlac roll could have been intended to provide a kind of documentary proof of the gifts in this peculiar form.

An explicit instance of a conveyance by the charter itself is a gift made by William of Astle in *c*.1200 to the Knights Hospitaller. The last witness is Ivo clerk of Stafford, representing the Hospitallers, 'in whose hand I, William, have made seisin with this charter in the church of Alderly'.[18] The usual rule was that a conveyance could not be made by a document alone, but depended on the recipient having 'seisin' (meaning actual possession of the property). Nevertheless the exception to this rule in William of Astle's charter may merely prove it, as the charter, conveyed from hand to hand, is a substitute for the usual object symbolizing the transaction.

The unfamiliar idea of a writing being interpreted primarily as a symbolic object, rather than as a documentary proof, is most clearly evident when the object written upon is not a parchment, but something else. Thus an ivory whip-handle found at St Albans abbey had an inscription on it stating that 'this is the gift of Gilbert de Novo Castello for four mares.'[19] The object, a whip, appropriately symbolized the gift of horses; the writing was ancillary. Similarly a knife is still preserved at Durham, which symbolized Stephen of Bulmer's agreement (perhaps made in the 1150s) with the monks of Holy Island at Lindisfarne about the chapelry of Lowick.

This knife is particularly interesting because its haft bears an inscription, which is comparable with the St Albans whip-handle and other inscribed knife hafts no longer extant.[20] Whereas the hafts of these other knives were made of ivory, Stephen's is of hard horn (perhaps a deer's) and the inscriber has had difficulty making much impression on it. He was not perhaps an experienced carver but a scribe, possibly a monk of Lindisfarne, who only had a pen knife readily available. Although the lettering of the inscription is shaky and uneven, it is conceived in a bold monastic hand. Along one side of the knife's haft is written *Signum de capella de lowic* (the sign for the chapel of Lowick) and on the other side *de capella de lowic & de decimis de lowic totius curie & totius ville* (for the chapel of Lowick and for the tithes of Lowick from the whole court and the whole vill). As well as this inscription on the haft, a parchment label is attached (written in a comparable bold monastic hand), which gives fuller details of the agreement. This label cannot be described as a charter, as it is irregular in shape and is written on both sides. A statement on its dorse helps explain the purpose of the knife. It records that Stephen of Bulmer had not come in person to make the agreement at Holy Island, but sent Lady Cecily and Aschetin, the *dapifer* or steward, in his place. Probably Aschetin brought the knife with him as a symbol of Stephen's consent. It may well have been

[18] *Cheshire Facs*, no. 13 (2).   [19] Ellis, 'Observations', p. 313.

[20] Durham Dean and Chapter Muniments, 3.1.Spec.72, illustrated very accurately by J. Raine, *The History and Antiquities of North Durham* (1852), appendix,p. 135. I am grateful to Mr M. G. Snape for assistance. Other examples of inscribed knives are given by Ellis, 'Observations', pp. 313, 315–16. See also ch. 1, n. 51 and ch. 5, nn. 42–3 above.

Stephen's own carving knife; the haft is heavy and shows signs of use and, although the blade is broken near the top, what remains of the knife still measures 13½ cm. It would thus have been an appropriate object for a steward, who probably carved at his lord's table, to bring as durable and substantial evidence that he truly represented his master.

Why go to the trouble of trying to write on a knife, when pen and parchment did the same job more efficiently? Ordinary writing materials were evidently available, as Stephen's knife has the parchment label on it as well as the inscription. The explanation may be that the parties to this agreement had more confidence in the evidence of the knife than in writing. Knives were traditional symbols for conveyances, whereas charters authenticated by seals were a relative novelty, though they should have been familiar to the monks of Lindisfarne if not to a northern knight like Stephen of Bulmer. Some contemporaries may also have thought that a knife was more durable than, and therefore preferable to, parchment and sealing wax. It was true that only the sparsest details of a conveyance could be engraved on the handle of a knife or a whip, but the tradition had been that the true facts of a transaction were engraved on the hearts and minds of the witnesses and could not be fully recorded in any form of writing however detailed. The symbolic knife would have been retained regardless of whether it had anything written on it, because it preserved the memory of the conveyance.

Only literates, who could interpret the 'shapes indicating voices' (in John of Salisbury's definition of letters), were going to be convinced that the writing was superior to the symbolic object. Such objects, the records of the non-literate, were therefore preserved along with documents. Another example is the knife by which Thomas of Moulton gave the church of Weston in Lincolnshire to Spalding priory, which was deposited in its archive (*in secretario*) according to the charter confirming the gift.[21] This latter knife is no longer preserved. To later archivists, knives and other archaic relics meant nothing unless they had inscriptions connected with them; such things were thrown away as medieval rubbish, because the language of memory which they expressed had no significance for literates.

It is possible that the seals, *signa* in Latin, attached to charters were seen by many contemporaries in a similar way as inscribed 'signs'. To students of diplomatic today seals are a method of authenticating documents which preceded the sign manual or written signature. To medieval people they may have appeared rather as visible and tangible objects symbolizing the wishes of the donor. The seal was significant even without the document. Early seals (that is, twelfth-century ones) tend to be disproportionately large – often 6 or 7 cm in diameter – compared with the writings to which they are attached (see plate I). John of Salisbury, writing on behalf of Archbishop Theobald of Canterbury about the safekeeping of seals, says that 'by the marks of a single impress the mouths of all the pontiffs may be opened or closed.'[22] Just as

---

[21] *Monasticon* III, p. 217, no. x.
[22] *Letters* ed. W. J. Millor *et al.* (1955) I, p. 109.

lctters 'speak voicelessly the utterances of the absent', seals regulate that speech. Emphasis on the spoken word remained.

The 'signs' attached to documents, whether they took the form of inscribed knives or impressed wax or even ink crosses made by the witnesses, all helped to bridge the gulf between the traditional and the literate way of recording transactions. Pre-literate customs and ceremonies persisted despite the use of documents. The doctrine of livery of seisin – the rule that a recipient must have the property duly delivered to him and enter into possession (that is, seisin) of it, whether there was a document of conveyance or not – became a fundamental principle of the common law; but there are exceptions to it, like the charter of William of Astle to the Knights Hospitaller which has already been discussed. The treatise ascribed to Bracton insists (in the first half of the thirteenth century) that 'a gift is not valid unless livery follows; for the thing given is transferred neither by homage, nor by the drawing up of charters and instruments, even though they be recited in public.' Written words were thus entirely inadequate, and even spoken ones were insufficient, without physical symbols: 'If livery is to be made of a house by itself, or of a messuage for an estate, it ought to be made by the door and its hasp or ring, by which is understood that the donee possess the whole to its boundaries.'[23] It followed also that a gift 'may be valid though no charter has been made . . . and conversely the charter may be genuine and valid and the gift incomplete.'[24] The physical symbol, the door hasp or ring in Bracton's example, continued to epitomize the whole gift better than any document.

Likewise the drafting rule became general that the past tense should be used in charters for the act of giving: 'Know that I, A of B, *have* given', not simply 'I give'. This emphasized that the ceremonial conveyance was the crucial transaction, whereas the charter was merely a subsequent confirmation of it. This rule only became firmly established in the thirteenth century. Numerous charters of the twelfth century depart from it, presumably because their more amateur draftsmen did not appreciate the relationship between written record and the passage of time. Similarly a generation or two after Bracton the need for the livery of seisin rule was not apparent to ordinary people. Some Derbyshire jurors, who had supposed in 1304 that a charter might suffice without it, were described by a second group of jurors as 'simple persons who were not cognizant with English laws and customs'.[25] The doctrine of seisin, which had once been a self-evident and commonsense rule, had become with the spread of literacy one of those technical mysteries in which the common law abounded.

The spoken versus the written word

The increasing use of documents created tension between the old methods and the new. Which was the better evidence, for example,

[23] Bracton, fos 39b–40, vol. ii, pp. 124–5.   [24] *ibid.* fo 11b, p. 50.
[25] *Calendarium Genealogicum*, RC (1865) II, p. 659. P & M II, p. 89.

seeing a parchment or hearing a man's word? How was the one to be evaluated if it conflicted with the other? A good illustration of this particular dilemma is Eadmer's account of the investiture controversy between St Anselm, archbishop of Canterbury, and Henry I.[26] Both Anselm and the king had sent envoys to Pope Paschal II; Anselm sent two monks of Canterbury, while the king sent the archbishop of York and two other bishops. The envoys returned to England in September 1101 with papal letters addressed to the king and to Anselm, prohibiting royal investiture of churches and exhorting resistance to them. When the pope's letter to Anselm had been publicly read out, Henry's envoys objected. They claimed that Paschal had given them a purely verbal message that he would treat the king leniently on the investiture question and would not excommunicate him; the pope had added that he did not wish this concession to be put in written form (*per carta inscriptionem*) because other rulers would use it as a precedent. Anselm's envoys replied that the pope had given no verbal message which conflicted in any way with his letters. To this Henry's bishops answered that Paschal had acted in one way in secret and another in public. Baldwin of Bec, Anselm's chief envoy, was outraged at this allegation and said that it was a calumny on the Holy See.

Dissension than arose in the audience. Those favouring Anselm maintained that credence should be given to 'documents signed with the pope's seal' (*scriptis sigillo pape signatis*) and not to 'the uncertainty of mere words'. The king's side replied that they preferred to rely on the word of three bishops than on 'the skins of wethers blackened with ink and weighted with a little lump of lead'. They added further venom to the argument by alleging that monks were unreliable anyway, as they should not be engaged in worldly business. Eadmer puts the controversy into dialogue form:

Anselm's monks: 'But what about the evidence of the letters?'

Henry's bishops: 'As we don't accept the evidence of monks against bishops, why should we accept that of a sheepskin?'

Anselm's monks: 'Shame on you! Are not the Gospels written down on sheepskins?'

Obviously the conflict could not be quickly resolved. In Lent 1102 Anselm set out for Rome and opened on his way another letter from the pope, in which Paschal denied that he had ever given contradictory verbal instructions to the bishops or said that he was reluctant to set a precedent in writing.[27] Who was telling the truth is of course impossible to resolve. Paschal was attempting to make peace and settle the investiture controversy by diplomacy. He may well therefore have said something off the record to the bishops which they had possibly exaggerated.

[26] *Historia*, pp. 132–40.

[27] *ibid.* pp. 149–51. Subsequently Anselm and the king came to terms, R. W. Southern, *St Anselm and his Biographer* (1963), pp. 176–9.

Like all statesmen, the pope obviously had to make a formal denial of such secret negotiations once they became public.

The substance of the story is not our concern here, but the attitudes it reveals towards documentary evidence. Papal letters, sealed with the leaden bull and bearing the symbols and monograms of curial officials, were the most impressive documents produced in medieval Europe, their only rival being Byzantine imperial letters. Yet in Eadmer's story the papal bull is disparagingly described as a sheepskin blackened with ink with a bit of lead attached to it, an extreme example of a document being treated simply as a physical object rather than for its contents. Anselm's supporters were entitled to riposte that the Gospels too were written on parchment – in other words, that Christianity was essentially the religion of a book. At Orléans in 1022 a group of heretics had been burned for disparaging the book learning of the clergy cross-examining them, which they had called human fabrications 'written on the skins of animals', whereas the heretics claimed to believe 'in the law written in the inner man by the Holy Spirit'.[28] The heretics had therefore been arguing that the true written law (*lex scripta*) was not canon law nor Justinian's code, but inspiration retained in the mind alone; real writing was not man-made script on animal parchment. Such an idea may well have derived from the Scripture itself, most probably from St Paul's Second Epistle to the Corinthians, 'written not with ink, but with the spirit of the living God . . . for the letter killeth, but the spirit giveth life.'[29] Early in the thirteenth century St Francis was to take up this theme as part of his revolt against the spiritually empty book learning of some monks: 'Those religious have been killed by the letter who are not willing to follow the spirit of the divine letter, but only desire to know words and interpret them for other men.'[30] As so often in his work, Francis blended orthodox and heretical viewpoints in an insight of his own. Literacy was not a virtue in itself. Emphasis on the word inscribed spiritually on the minds of men, as contrasted with letters written on parchment, retained its strength in the Christian message as it did in secular conveyancing ceremonies.

The argument of Henry I's envoys, that their word was better evidence than a papal bull, would not in fact have appeared as outrageous or surprising to contemporaries as Eadmer suggests in his account of the controversy with Anselm. The principle that 'oral witness deserves more credence than written evidence' was a legal commonplace. It was cited for example by Hubert Walter, archbishop of Canterbury, in a letter to Innocent III in 1200 controverting Gerald of Wales's well documented claim to be bishop-elect of St David's.[31] Gerald conceded the

---

[28] *Recueil des historiens des Gaules* ed. L. Delisle (1869–) X, p. 539. R. I. Moore, *The Birth of Popular Heresy* (1975), pp. 10–15.

[29] II *Corinthians* iii, 3, 6. Cf. Smalley, *The Bible,* ch. i ('The Letter and the Spirit').

[30] R. B. Brooke, *The Coming of the Friars* (1975), p. 126.

[31] 'testibus et non testimoniis credi oportet', Giraldus III, pp. 14, 21. H. E. Butler, *The Autobiography of Giraldus Cambrensis* (1937), pp. 168, 175–6. M. Richter, *Giraldus Cambrensis* (2nd edn, 1976), p. 109.

point in his reply to the pope, but added that he had brought both documents and witnesses. Behind this principle lay the correct assumption that numerous documents used in legal claims, from the Donation of Constantine downwards, were forgeries. Not all those who relied on the traditional use of the spoken word, rather than parchments, were necessarily therefore obscurantist conservatives. The technology of written record was insufficiently advanced to be efficient or reliable. As a consequence, documents and the spoken word are frequently both used in a way which appears otiose to a modern literate. To make a record often meant to bear oral witness, not to produce a document. For example, in the civil war of Stephen's reign Robert earl of Gloucester and Miles earl of Hereford made a treaty of friendship in writing, in the form of a sealed letter; yet both parties in this document also name witnesses, who are 'to make legal record of this agreement in court if necessary'.[32]

The rule that oral witness is preferable to documents, like the rule that seisin is superior to a charter, shows how cautiously – and perhaps reluctantly – written evidence was accepted. Much important business continued to be done by word of mouth. Bearers of letters were often given instructions which were to be conveyed *viva voce*, either because that was convenient and traditional or because the information was too secret to write down. Twice, for instance, in March 1229 Henry III sent messengers to the count of Toulouse. In their mouths, the king wrote, he had put matters which they would disclose more fully to the count, since the business (presumably concerning a truce with Louis IX) could not be committed to writing because of the dangers of the roads.[33] Similarly in the period of the baronial rebellion, when Henry was in France in 1260, he wrote to the earl of Gloucester instructing him to report on the state of the kingdom by Gilbert Fitz Hugh, the king's serjeant, who would tell the earl more fully *viva voce* about the king's situation.[34] In such negotiations the letter itself did not convey essential information but, like a modern ambassador's letter of credence, was a symbolic object replacing the messenger's ring or other *signum* which had formerly identified him as a confidential agent of his master.

Oral messages were also used to give instructions which later generations would have put in writing. For example, in 1234 John le Franceis and John Mansel were authorized by royal letters of credence to conduct inquiries concerning Jews in certain counties and give instructions to sheriffs *viva voce*.[35] An interesting but non-English case of oral delivery is the poem which the troubadour, Jaufre Rudel, lord of Blaye in the Gironde, sent to the Comte de Marche in c.1150 'without a parchment document' (*senes breu de parguamina*) by the mouth of the jongleur, Filhol.[36] The jongleur is thus being used as a kind of living letter. There is, however, a paradox in all such evidence, since historians can only know of the survival of oral ways of conveying information by extant

[32] See ch. 2, n. 104 above.   [33] *CIR* 1227–31, p. 233.
[34] *ibid*. 1259–61, p. 281.   [35] *ibid*. 1231–4, p. 586.
[36] P. Bec, *Nouvelle anthologie de la lyrique occitane* (1970), p. 179.

written evidence. Jaufre Rudel's poem, once sent without a script, is written down nonetheless.

Much business was still done by word of mouth for the obvious reason that documents were bound to be relatively rare until printing made their automatic reproduction possible. The usual way of publishing new laws and regulations was by proclamation. The following instances from the Chancery records of Henry III for 1234 are typical.[37] On 28 August the sheriff of Northumberland and some others were ordered to have it proclaimed (*clamari facias*) that pleas were to be adjourned until the coming of the eyre justices. On 29 August all sheriffs were to proclaim the regulations for supervising hundred courts in accordance with the revision of Magna Carta in 1234. On 1 September the sheriff of Norfolk and Suffolk was to proclaim throughout the two counties that no Jew was to lend money to any Christian in the king's demesne.[38] Matthew Paris suggests that Henry III pursued a policy of legislating by proclamation: in 1248 the people were harassed by diverse precepts promulgated 'by the voice of a crier' (*voce preconia*) throughout the cities of England; the king established a new fair at Westminster, for example, in this way.[39] The proclamation to which Matthew gives most attention likewise occurred in 1248, when the king 'ordered it to be proclaimed as law by the voice of a crier' that henceforward no man might castrate another for fornication except a husband in the case of his wife's adulterer.[40] The reason for this was that John le Bretun had castrated the Norfolk knight, Godfrey de Millers, for lying with his daughter.

How extensively or frequently proclamations of this sort were made is not clear. Proclamations were a quick and effective way of conveying information in crowded cities like London, but were obviously less practical in the countryside. Most references to proclamations concern cities. For example, in 1252 Henry III had it proclaimed throughout London that no one should lend money to the abbot of Westminster; or in the preceding year a proclamation had been made against the royal judge, Henry of Bath, in London and in the king's court.[41] One consequence for the historian of Henry III's government's use of the spoken word for legislation is that all trace of it is lost, unless a chronicler happened to record it or the Chancery rolls refer to it incidentally. Edward I is considered a great lawgiver partly because the legislation of his time is preserved in the statute rolls. In Henry III's reign less was written down, though a comparable amount of legislative activity probably took place.

Magna Carta became the great precedent for putting legislation into writing. Yet even it was not officially enrolled in the royal archives,

---

[37] *ClR* 1231–4, pp. 592–3.
[38] *ibid.* p. 592. C. Roth, *A History of the Jews in England* (1941), p. 53.
[39] Matthew Paris V, pp. 18, 29.
[40] 'voce preconia iussit pro lege acclamari,' *ibid.* p. 35. *CIR* 1247–51, pp. 139, 394. *CPatR* 1247–58, p. 387.
[41] Matthew Paris V, pp. 305, 223. *CPatR* 1247–58, p. 101.

although it was proclaimed extensively and repeatedly. Within a few days of King John's assent to it letters were sent to all his sheriffs, foresters, gamekeepers, watermen and other bailiffs informing them of the agreement between the king and the barons, 'as you can hear and see by our charter which we have had made thereon', which they were ordered to have read publicly throughout their bailiwicks.[42] As a result, in theory at least, everyone in England should have heard Magna Carta read out, although it is unlikely that a sufficient number of copies were available.[43] Similarly when the barons again had the upper hand in 1265, they ordered the terms of Henry III's oath to keep peace with them to be published in the full county court at least twice every year, at Easter and Michaelmas.[44] In 1300 transcripts of Magna Carta and the Charter of the Forest were delivered to every sheriff to read out 'before the people' four times a year, at Christmas and Midsummer as well as at Easter and Michaelmas.[45] Nevertheless by 1300 there had been a significant change, as considerable emphasis was now being put on seeing the document as well as hearing it. Sealed transcripts of Magna Carta were sent to all judges, sheriffs and civic officials and also to all cathedral churches.[46] A precedent for the latter had been made in 1279 when Archbishop Pecham's council at Reading had ordered a copy of Magna Carta to be posted up in every cathedral and collegiate church in a public place 'so that it can be clearly seen by the eyes of everyone entering'; in the spring of each year the old copy was to be taken down and a new fair copy substituted for it.[47]

The clergy therefore assumed that the general public could read, or would at least be impressed by seeing the Latin text of Magna Carta. The royal government likewise was sufficiently alarmed to make Pecham have all these copies removed from church doors shortly afterwards.[48] An even earlier precedent, though a fantastic one, occurs in Andrew the Chaplain's *Ars Amandi* of the later twelfth century.[49] The king of love had written out the rules of love on a parchment for a British knight. His lady then called together a court of numerous knights and their ladies, each of whom was given a written copy of the rules to take home and issue to all lovers in all parts of the world. Like Archbishop Pecham, Andrew the Chaplain probably had higher expectations of the reading ability of the public than were justified.

Public readings of documents were done in the vernacular as well as in Latin and might reach a wider audience in that way. Thus in 1300, according to the chronicler Rishanger, Magna Carta was read out at

---

[42] See ch. 6, n. 84 above.

[43] C. R. Cheney, 'The Eve of Magna Carta', *BJRL* xxxviii (1955–6), p. 340. F. Thompson, *The First Century of Magna Carta* (1925), p. 94.

[44] See ch. 6, n. 97 above.

[45] 'Articuli super Cartas', *Statutes* p. 136.

[46] *Chronicle of Bury St Edmunds* ed. A. Gransden (1964), p. 154. Similar transcripts had been authorized in 1297, Stubbs, *Charters* pp. 490–91.

[47] D. L. Douie, *Archbishop Pecham* (1925), p. 113, n. 2.

[48] *ClR* 1272–9, p. 582.

[49] Bk ii, ch. 8, trans. J. J. Parry (1941), pp. 184–6.

Westminster 'first in Latin [*litteraliter*] and then in the native tongue [*patria lingua*]'.[50] Similarly a year earlier letters of Pope Boniface VIII about the peace between England and France had been read out in Parliament 'in Latin for the literate and in the native tongue for the illiterate'.[51] Also in 1299, according to the Worcester annals, royal letters concerning a new perambulation of the forests were 'proclaimed in the city of Worcester in the mother tongue [*materna lingua*]'.[52] The 'paternal' or 'maternal' language might mean either English or French. Thus in 1254 the papal excommunication of infringers of Magna Carta was ordered to be published 'in the English [*Anglicana*] and French [*Gallicana*] tongues' whenever and wherever appropriate.[53] The use of English and French in this instance was probably a reiteration of existing practice, rather than an innovation, as it is likely that Magna Carta itself had been proclaimed throughout the land in both English and French in 1215.[54]

The distinction the chroniclers wished to emphasize in the citations above was between the language of literacy (Latin) and spoken language; they were less concerned with which vernacular was used. To pedantic Latinists vernacular simply meant the spoken language. Gerald of Wales hoped that someone would translate his work into French and claimed that Walter Map used to tell him that he (Gerald) had written much, whereas Walter had said much.[55] Although Gerald's writings (*scripta*) were more praiseworthy and durable than Walter's speeches (*dicta*), Walter had the greater profit because his *dicta* were accessible, since they were expressed in the common idiom, while Gerald's *scripta* were appreciated only by the declining few who knew Latin. In fact the distinction Gerald drew here between himself and Walter Map was misleading, as Walter also was a precocious Latinist.[56] Possibly Gerald felt that Walter had been a more successful preacher and *raconteur* in the vernacular than he was. The point of the story from our angle, regardless of whether it is true or not, is that Gerald felt that the spoken vernacular brought greater prestige than written Latin.

Listening to the word

Whatever the language, and whether the record was held solely in the bearer's memory or was committed to parchment, the medieval recipient prepared himself to listen to an utterance rather than to scrutinize a document visually as a modern literate would. This was due to a different habit of mind; it was not because the recipient was illiterate in

[50] *Willelmi Rishanger Chronica* ed H. T. Riley, RS XXVIII (1865), p. 405.
[51] *ibid.* p. 389.
[52] *Annales Monastici* IV, p. 541. For the meaning of *materna lingua* see C. Clark, 'Women's Names in Post-Conquest England', *Speculum* LIII (1978), pp. 224–5.
[53] *Annales Monastici* I (Burton Annals), p. 322.
[54] See ch. 6, nn. 84, 85 above.
[55] Giraldus V, pp. 410–11.
[56] The story is discussed from a different point of view by A. K. Bate in *Latomus* XXXI (1972), p. 862. See also ch. 6, n. 39 above.

any sense of that word. In his account of his claim to be bishop-elect of St David's Gerald of Wales describes a private audience in the pope's chamber with Innocent III in 1200, when the pope looked up a register listing all the metropolitan churches of Christendom and went through the rubrics until he found Wales.[57] But when at a subsequent private audience Gerald showed the pope a transcript of a letter of Eugenius III which Gerald had found in another papal register, Innocent handed the transcript to Cardinal Ugolino and told him to read it; 'and when it had been read and diligently heard, the pope replied that he was well pleased with it.'[58] Gerald's account of the earlier audience depicts the pope browsing through a reference book as a modern literate would do; but when at the subsequent audience the pope needs to absorb carefully the details of a letter, he has it read to him instead of scrutinizing it. Reading aloud in this case is not being done to enable everyone present to learn the contents of the letter, as the only persons at this private audience are Innocent, Gerald and Ugolino who is supporting him. Nor obviously was Innocent incapable of reading the script of papal registers. Yet he evidently found it easier to concentrate when he was listening than when he was looking; reading was still primarly oral rather than visual.

Indications of the same habit of mind appear in the 'auditing' of monetary accounts. Abbot Samson of Bury St Edmunds 'heard' the weekly account of his expenditure, yet he obviously could have consulted such a document (if the account were in documentary form at all), as his biographer Jocelin says that he inspected his *kalendarium* (his register of rents and so on) almost every day 'as though he could see therein the image of his own efficiency as in a mirror'.[59] The modern word 'audit' derives from a time when it was the habit to listen to, rather than to see, an account. Thomas of Eccleston in his description of the arrival of the Franciscan friars in England in 1224 records that when the superior heard the first annual account of the London friars and realized how little they had to show for such lavish expenditure, he threw down all the tallies and rolls and shouted 'I'm caught' and 'he never afterwards wanted to hear an account'.[60] In this instance accounts in writing existed, in the form of both wooden tallies and parchment rolls, yet the superior 'heard' them nonctheless. H. J. Chaytor points out, however, that one must be careful of colloquial speech in such an instance as this. For example modern English uses the phrase 'I have not heard from him for some time' to mean 'I have had no letter'.[61]

Similarly in law courts, 'inspecting' a document might mean hearing it read aloud. Thus in 1219 in an action of warranty of charter in Lincolnshire William of Well, the defendant, is reported in the plea roll to 'have come and claimed a hearing [*auditum*] of his father's charter'

[57] Giraldus III, p. 165. See also ch. 9, n. 94 below.
[58] *ibid.* p. 182.
[59] See ch. 3, n. 53 above.
[60] *Monumenta Franciscana* ed. J. S. Brewer, RS IV (1858), I, p. 8.
[61] *From Script to Print* (1945), p. 145.

and it was duly heard.[62] A generation later, in a similar action in Berkshire in 1248, the abbot of Beaulieu who was the defendant claimed that the plaintiff should 'show' him the charter by which he should warrant her.[63] The contrasting emphasis on hearing and seeing in these similar claims only thirty years apart may indicate a general change of attitude developing within this period, if only in the minds of the enrolling clerks; or more likely the two cases show the differing approach to documents of a knight, William of Well, and a monk, the abbot of Beaulieu.

Literary works, especially vernacular ones, were frequently explicitly addressed by the author to an audience, rather than to readers as such. Thus the nun of Barking in her French version of Ailred's life of Edward the Confessor in c. 1163 requests 'all who hear, or will ever hear, this romance of hers' not to despise it because the translation is done by a woman.[64] In the *Romance of Horn* by Master Thomas the author begins by addressing his audience: 'Gentlemen, you have heard the lines of parchment' (*Seignurs, oi avez le vers del parchemin*).[65] The parchment is evidently thought of here as a direct substitute for a jongleur; it speaks and is heard, like the charter of Richard de Cormeilles for St Mary's priory at Monmouth.[66] Likewise in the *Estoire de Waldef* (dating from c. 1190) the author refers to the *Brut* story:

> If anyone wants to know this history
> Let him read the *Brut*, he will hear it there
> [*Qui l'estoire savoir voldra*
> *Lise le Brut, illoc l'orra*].[67]

A modern literate would not say 'he will *hear* it there', but 'he will *find* it' or '*see* it there.' The emphasis in such works on hearing does not necessarily mean that their contents stem directly from oral tradition, but that reading continued to be conceived in terms of hearing rather than seeing. Until cheap printing supplied every 'reader' with his own book, the emphasis on hearing was understandable.

Latin works too were generally intended to be read aloud – hence the speeches and frequent use of dramatic dialogue in monastic chronicles. Eadmer concludes the first book of his *Life of St Anselm* with an interval, as in a play: 'But here, lest our unpolished speech [*oratio*] weary our readers or hearers by being too long drawn-out, we shall make our first halt in the work.'[68] Traditional monastic reading in particular bore little relation to a modern literate's approach to a book. *Lectio* was 'more a process of rumination than reading, directed towards savouring the divine wisdom within a book rather than finding new ideas or novel

---

[62] *Rolls of the Justices in Eyre* ed. D. M. Stenton, SS LIII (1934), p. 300, no. 630.

[63] *Berks. Eyre*, p. 150, no. 354.

[64] Legge, *Anglo-Norman*, p. 65. Other examples in H. J. Chaytor, *From Script to Print*, pp. 11–12, 144–7. In general see R. Crosby, 'Oral Delivery in the Middle Ages', *Speculum* XI (1936) pp. 90–102.

[65] See ch. 6, n. 63 above.   [66] See n. 13 above.

[67] Legge, *Anglo-Norman*, p. 143.   [68] *Vita*, p. 62.

information'.[69] The process is well illustrated by St Anselm's *Meditation on Human Redemption*: 'Taste the goodness of your redeemer . . . chew the honeycomb of his words, suck their flavour which is sweeter than honey, swallow their wholsome sweetness. Chew by thinking, suck by understanding, swallow by loving and rejoicing.'[70] Reading was a physical exertion, demanding the use not only of the eyes, but of tongue, mouth and throat. Writing was a similar act of endurance, requiring three fingers to hold the pen, two eyes to see the words, one tongue to speak them, and the whole body to labour.[71] For these reasons some monks argued that work in the *scriptorium* was an adequate substitute for manual labour.

The system of punctuating and abbreviating words in Latin works was likewise intended primarily to assist someone reading aloud, rather than a person silently scrutinizing the page. N. R. Ker cites the case of a manuscript where the Latin word *neque* (neither), which is written out in full, has been amended throughout to *neq*; he suggests that writing *neque* out in full was likely to mislead an oral reader into stressing the second syllable; writing out the word in full was an error on the scribe's part which has been duly corrected.[72] Some abbreviations were therefore intended to help pronunciation, rather than save the scribe's time when copying a book. Ideally a 'reader' was expected to look at the text as well as listen to it, but that was the exception and not the rule. In the *Life of St Margaret* of Scotland the author considered it a point worth remarking that Margaret's daughter, Matilda (Henry I's queen), 'desired not only to hear, but also to inspect continually the impress of the letters' of her mother's life.[73] A school manual, not English unfortunately and later than our period, sums up in a dialogue the medieval meaning of 'reading' (*lectio*):

'Are you a scholar, what do you read?'
'I do not read, I listen.'
'What do you hear?'
'Donatus or Alexander, or logic or music.'[74]

Donatus's *Ars Minor* and Alexander's *Doctrinale* were Latin textbooks. The term 'reading' a subject has been preserved at Oxford and Cambridge; whereas some undergraduates think that 'reading' implies studying books instead of hearing lectures, medieval students understood *lectio* primarily to mean that the master read while they listened.

Whole books were published by being read aloud. Gerald of Wales says that he published his *Topography of Ireland* in this way in c.1188

[69] C. J. Holdsworth, 'John of Ford and English Cistercian Writing', *TRHS* 5th series XI (1961), p. 124.
[70] *Opera Omnia* ed. F. S. Schmitt (1938–61) III, p. 84.
[71] A description repeated by various scribes but originating in the eighth century, Wattenbach, *Schriftwesen*, p. 495.
[72] *English MSS*, p. 51.
[73] Thompson, *Literacy*, p. 171, n. 46.
[74] F. M. Powicke, *The Christian Life in the Middle Ages* (1935), p. 88. C. H. Haskins, *Studies in Medieval Culture* (1929), p. 83.

by reading it at Oxford to different audiences on three successive days. But Gerald's action was not typical, as he boasts that 'neither has the present age seen, nor does any past age bear record of, the like in England.'[75] The normal way of disseminating scholarly works, as distinct from popular romances, was by the modern method of circulating copies. For instance Herbert of Bosham assumed in his life of Becket that his readers will be able to study Becket's correspondence, which he omits for the sake of brevity, 'because that book of letters is already in the possession of many persons and churches'.[76] If Becket is thought too exceptional an example because of his extraordinary popularity, Eadmer mentions in his appendix to St Anselm's *Life* that he intends to make a new start, because the *Life* has already 'been transcribed by many and distributed to various churches'.[77] Distributing copies did not of course rule out public readings; on the contrary, as more books became available, the practice may have grown even more widespread.

Just as reading was linked in the medieval mind with hearing rather than seeing, writing (in its modern sense of composition) was associated with dictating rather than manipulating a pen.[78] Reading and writing (in the sense of composition) were therefore both extensions of speaking and were not inseparably coupled with each other, as they are today. A person might be able to write, yet not be considered literate. As we have seen, Walter Map mentions a boy 'who was not *litteratus*, although he knew how to transcribe any series of letters whatever'.[79] Literacy involved being learned in Latin, whereas writing was the process of making a fair copy on parchment, which was the art of the scribe. Some authors (notably the great monastic historians Orderic Vitalis, William of Malmesbury and Matthew Paris)[80] did their own writing, but they are the exceptions and they distinguished that activity from composition.

Medieval distinctions are well illustrated by Eadmer. He explains that he had to conceal from St Anselm that he was 'writing' his biography. When he had begun the work 'and had had already transcribed on to parchment a great part of what I had composed [*dictaveram*] in wax', Anselm asked 'what it was I was composing and copying' (*quid dictitarem, quid scriptitarem*).[81] The process of composing on wax tablets is thus described in Latin by the word *dictitare* (literally, 'to dictate'), even though in Eadmer's case he was dictating to himself. The use of 'writing' (*scriptitare*) is confined to making the fair copy on parchment. Similarly when Orderic Vitalis wishes to say that before the time of William the Conqueror the Normans had concentrated on war rather than reading and writing, the phrase he uses is *legere vel dictare*, not *legere vel scribere*.[82] Numerous other examples of using 'dictate' where a

[75] Giraldus I, pp. 72–3.   [76] *Becket Materials* III, p. 396.
[77] *Vita*, p. 153.   [78] See pp. 97, 183 above.
[79] See p. 181 above, and n. 119 below.
[80] Their holographs are illustrated by Gransden, *Historical Writing*, plates iv, v, x.
[81] *Vita*, p. 150. Cf. ch. 4, nn. 9–12 above, concerning the practice of making drafts on wax tablets.
[82] Orderic, bk iii (prologue), vol. ii, p. 2.

modern literate would use 'write' could be given.[83] Dictating was the usual form of literary composition and the *ars dictaminis*, taught in the schools as part of rhetoric, was the skill governing it. Letter writing was thus an intellectual skill using the mouth rather than the hand. Peter of Blois, a busy secretary of state like John of Salisbury, boasted that the archbishop of Canterbury had seen him dictating to three different scribes on diverse subjects, while he dictated and wrote a fourth letter all at the one time.[84]

Reading aloud and dictating permit the non-literate to participate in the use of documents, whereas reading and writing silently exclude the illiterate. When the voice is used, the clerk or scribe becomes no more than a medium between the speaker or hearer and the document. Neither the hearer of a book nor the *dictator* of a letter needs to be a master of every detail of the scribal technique himself, just as modern managers are not required to type or to programme computers. Obviously it is helpful if the manager understands how these things are done and has some experience of them, but this expertise is not indispensable. For these reasons medieval kings and their officials, such as sheriffs in the counties, did not need to be literate in the modern sense. Lack of literacy did not mean that they were ignorant or incapable of coping with business; they were as literate as the tasks required. As the number of documents increased and habits of silent visual reading became more common, levels of literacy (in the modern sense) presumably increased also; but there is no evidence of a crisis suddenly demanding numerous literates. Because the pre-literate emphasis on the spoken word persisted, the change from oral to literate modes could occur slowly and almost imperceptibly over many generations.

The text usually quoted to show that medieval attitudes towards literacy were similar to modern ones is John of Salisbury's quotation in *Policraticus* that 'Rex illitteratus est quasi asinus coronatus' (an illiterate king is like a crowned ass).[85] In this passage John is primarily concerned that the prince should have wisdom, which is gained by reading the law of God daily. For that reason, and not for administrative requirements, the prince needs skill in letters. John concedes moreover that it is not absolutely necessary for the prince to be *litteratus*, provided he takes advice from *litterati*, that is, from priests who like Old Testament prophets will remind the prince of the law of God. 'Thus the mind of the prince may read in the tongue of the priest. For the life and tongue of priests are like the book of life before the face of the peoples.'[86] John is obviously thinking here of the spiritual, and not the worldly, value of reading. His discussion emphasizes that an illiterate prince can participate in wisdom through the medium of the priest's voice. The prince is not excluded by being illiterate: 'nor is he altogether destitute of reading

[83] Cheney, *Texts & Studies*, pp. 246–7, gives excellent examples from a letter of the Englishman, Gervase abbot of Prémontré, who died in 1228.

[84] Southern, *Medieval Humanism*, p. 119.

[85] Bk iv, ch. 6, C. C. J. Webb (1909) I, p. 255. Galbraith, 'Literacy', pp. 212–13.

[86] *Policraticus*, p. 255.

[*lectionis*] who, even though he does not read himself, hears faithfully what is read to him by others.' John thus shows that in his day non-literates could participate in literate culture; he is not arguing for the absolute necessity of rulers being literate in either the medieval sense of being learned in Latin or the modern sense of having a minimal ability to read and write. Ironically the king of England at the time, Henry II, was literate in every sense of the word; yet he was not a good king by John's definition, as he refused to listen to the lectures of priests and was responsible for the murder of Becket.

The spoken word in legal procedure

The persistent emphasis on the spoken word, despite the growing use of documents, is best illustrated by the evolution of legal procedure. The forms which had been suited to a purely oral procedure were preserved and ossified when documents were introduced. Before the thirteenth century parties were given notice to appear in law courts, not by having a writ served on them, but by an oral summons. Fitz Neal describes the summons to the county court 'by the crier's voice' and Glanvill explains in detail how the sheriff must ensure that the summoners are instructed in a public place and that the summons itself is publicly proclaimed.[87] In one list of summoners and jurors surviving from the Berkshire justices' visitation of 1248 the pair of summoners are appropriately, but exceptionally, called 'criers' (*criatores*);[88] their function was to voice the oral summons in due form. In the city of London, and in other places where population was concentrated, persons were summoned to the court of Husting not by the sound of a voice, but by a bell. If anyone claimed that he had not been duly summoned, 'the beadle has no other witness, nor ought to have, than the great bell which is rung for the folkmoot at St Paul's.'[89] Emphasis thus remained on hearing a sound, rather than seeing a document, whether the summons was made by a bell or the voice of a crier.

Nevertheless, once the rule had been established in Henry II's reign that 'no one is bound to answer for any freehold of his in his lord's court without a royal writ',[90] a document (a royal writ), instead of a voice, became the basis of legal procedure for all important land transactions in seignorial courts as well as royal ones. By Edward I's reign at the latest it had become usual for the sheriff to execute a royal writ in the first instance, not by instructing summoners orally as had been the practice in the twelfth century, but by sending a written precept to the appropriate local bailiff ordering him to execute the writ. The earliest sheriffs' precepts actually extant date from the 1240s and 1250s.[91] Yet the requirement to have oral summoners continued; by the later Middle Ages they had become fictitious persons, 'John Do' and 'Richard Ro' and the like, because their ancient function had been superseded by writing.

[87] *Dialogus*, p. 116. Glanvill, bk i, ch. 30, pp. 17–19.
[88] *Berks. Eyre*, p. 474, no. a175.   [89] Stubbs, *Charters*, p. 313.
[90] Glanvill, bk xii, ch. 25, p. 148.   [91] *Berks. Eyre*, pp. cv–cvii.

Just as summoners continued long after their usefulness had disappeared, common law procedure once the parties had come into court was likewise modelled on non-literate practices. Before the development of authenticated documents, courts were most reluctant to allow a litigant to be represented in his absence. Elaborate regulations were developed governing 'essoins' or excuses for non-appearance made by a third party. The assumption was that where possible a litigant must speak on his own behalf in court, because only words from his own mouth were authentic.[92] It is true that a few references will be found from Alfred's reign onwards to litigants having an advocate, who is described as a *forespeca* in Anglo-Saxon documents and a *perorator* in the Latin *Leges Henrici Primi*.[93] But, as the *Leges* makes clear, the advocate is not a true representative of the litigant as he may be corrected by him. The purpose of having an advocate was to allow for mistakes in the oral pleading, 'for it often happens that a person sees less in his own case than in someone else's and it is generally possible to amend in another person's mouth what may not be amended in his own.'[94] The advocate was thus a dispensable mouthpiece. His function was to make the litigant's formal claim, his 'tale' (*talu* in Anglo-Saxon), in due form.[95] The Anglo-Saxons had evidently put considerable emphasis on correct enunciation (*ryhtracu*) in their legal procedures. They may even have rivalled the Icelanders who insisted on word-for-word accuracy, as is illustrated by the passage in *Njal's Saga* where the uninitiated litigant, Gunnar, tricks the expert, Hrut, into summoning himself by pretending to admire Hrut's verbal expertise.[96]

A person similar to the *forespeca* or *perorator* reappears in thirteenth-century documents, where he is called a *narrator* in Latin or a *conteur* in Anglo-Norman. Direct links between the *forespeca* and the *narrator* or *conteur* are lacking, but as they all performed similar functions, the supposition of continuity is reasonable. The *narrator* or *conteur* made the formal claim or pleading on the litigant's behalf. The pleading was called a 'tale' (*narratio* in Latin or *conte* in French) just as it had been in Anglo-Saxon. The earliest written collection of common law pleadings, the *Brevia Placitata* dating from the mid-thirteenth century, calls them *les contes en romancees*.[97] Another early tract (date c. 1285) records that the pleadings 'are uttered by narrators in romance words and not in Latin ones'.[98] The 'narrator' was thus a 'romancer', a professional teller of tales in the vernacular, but his 'tales' were legal pleadings and not romances in the modern sense. Yet in origin the

---

[92] P & M I, pp. 211–12.

[93] The instance from Alfred's reign (concerning the litigant Helmstan) is printed by F. E. Harmer, *Select English Historical Documents* (1914), pp. 30–32. Later examples in D. Whitelock, *Anglo-Saxon Wills* (1930), references indexed under 'advocate'.

[94] *Leges Henrici Primi*, ch. 46, ed. L. J. Downer (1972), p. 156.

[95] A. J. Robertson, *Anglo-Saxon Charters* (2nd edn, 1956), pp. 366–7 explains *talu*.

[96] Trans. C. F. Bayerschmidt and L. E. Hollander (1955), p. 59.

[97] Ed. G. J. Turner, SS LXVI (1947), pp. xxxv, p. 153.

[98] 'per narratores in romanis verbis et non in latinis pronunciantur', 'Modus Componendi Brevia' *Four Thirteenth-Century Law Tracts* ed. G. E. Woodbine (1910), p. 162.

technique of the legal narrator was probably similar to that of his namesake, the Singer of Tales, studied by Milman Parry and A. B. Lord.[99] A narrator, whether of common law pleadings or of epic and romance, had originally reconstructed his tale in due form on the basis of a few remembered formulas. He was a professional oral remembrancer, very necessary before law and literature were committed to writing.

The interesting question is why narrators continued to flourish in English legal procedure once documents had become common. By the reign of Edward I a litigant required both a narrator and an attorney. The narrator was a layman, expert in oral pleadings, whereas the attorney was often a cleric and expert in written ones. The two functions remained distinct: from narrators derived the serjeants-at-law and barristers, who dominated the legal profession, while attorneys became associated with the humbler solicitors.[100] Both narrator and attorney were necessary because the narrator could not represent the litigant; that was the attorney's function, as he was appointed 'to win or lose' (*ad perdendum vel lucrandum*). Like an Anglo-Saxon advocate, the narrator spoke on the litigant's behalf in his presence; his words were not binding on the litigant, who could 'disavow' them. Behind the narrator's inability to be a true representative remained the ancient assumption that a litigant must speak on his own behalf. In fact the narrator spoke for him; but in theory at least the narrator remained no more than a spokesman, an extension of the litigant's faculty of speech.

One consequence of the litigant having to speak for himself was that the deaf and dumb seem to have had no legal rights in thirteenth-century England. Whether they were considered insane, as in Roman law, is unclear. In 1210 in a case in which one of the plaintiffs, Agnes, was a deaf mute the defendant, William de Schegetun, objected that Agnes could undertake nothing binding because she was unable to speak. When the plaintiffs' attorney asked the bench whether Agnes ought to lose her rights merely because she was a mute, the royal judges ruled that she must drop out of the case.[101] In 1224 when knights were sent to William Maufre to hear whom he wished to appoint as his attorney because he was ill, they found that he could not speak clearly owing to paralysis 'but in so far as he could speak, he appointed Reynold, his son, as his attorney.'[102] Nevertheless Reynold was not admitted by the court, because his father could not speak, and was told that he must produce his father in person.

Writing shifted the emphasis in testing truth from speech to documents and sometimes made the ancient rule that a litigant must speak on his own behalf look rather absurd. In *c*.1300 a certain Hugh was

[99] *The Singer of Tales* (1960). Clanchy, 'Remembering', p. 175.
[100] See in general H. Cohen, *A History of the English Bar and Attornatus to 1450* (1929), and in particular *SCCKB* I, pp. civ–cviii.
[101] *CuriaRR* VI, p. 13. Cf. a similar case in 1230, *ibid*. XIV, p. 31, no. 161.
[102] *ibid*. XI, p. 557, no. 2768.

charged with rape.[103] He first of all claimed benefit of clergy. When this was rejected by the judge because Hugh was married to a widow, Hugh claimed that he was a knight and should be tried by a jury of his peers. This was allowed, but Hugh then wanted to challenge some of the jurors as being prejudiced against him. The judge agreed and asked the challenges to be read out. At this point Hugh admitted that he did not know how to read and asked for his counsel. When this was refused, Hugh said to the judge: 'You have the challenges, you may read them.' The judge answered: 'No, because they must be propounded by your mouth.' When Hugh again said 'I don't know how to read them', the judge told him that he should not have claimed benefit of clergy if he were unable to read. Hugh stood silent and confused, but the judge told him not to be discomforted and that now was the time to speak. He turned to Nicholas of Leicester, Hugh's counsel, and asked: 'Do you wish to read Sir Hugh's challenges?' Nicholas replied:'Yes, my lord, if I may have his list which he has in his hands.' Having been allowed the list, Nicholas then asked: 'My lord, the challenges here are named against numerous persons, do you wish me to read them publicly?' The judge: 'No, no! You are to read them to the prisoner secretly, because they must be taken to come from his mouth.' Prompted by his counsel, Hugh duly made his challenges and was acquitted. This courtroom farce shows how by 1300 the oral procedure of challenging jurors had become in reality a written one. Hugh had to read from a list; he could not simply declare his challenges. On the other hand, the survival of oral procedure still required that he voice the challenges himself and so he had now to be able to read. In this case writing has made Hugh incapable of speaking and has reduced the voice of his counsel to a whisper.

In the long term the use of documents was bound to change the old way of pleading. Narrators survived throughout the Middle Ages, but by the fifteenth century 'counting' was no longer done orally but on paper. Cheap paper had completed the revolution begun by writing on parchment. 'But, now', regrets Roger North in the seventeenth century, 'the pleadings are all delated in paper.'[104] The forms, which the non-literate pleader had learned by listening, and the first literates by reading, are now, says North, 'better understood and learned by writing'. Nevertheless North records that a vestige of the old count survived: 'When causes, which they call real, come on, and require counting, and pleading at the bar, it is done for form, and unintelligibly; and whatever the serjeant mumbles, it is the paper book that is the text.' The use of documents had ultimately reduced the ancient art of pleading to an unintelligible mumble.

Gradually formal speech began to be learned by studying books instead of hearing the words of others. Handbooks for this purpose begin in England in the middle of the thirteenth century. An Anglo-Norman manual, *The Court Baron* composed in *c.*1265, instructs a seignorial

[103] *Year Books of 30–31 Edward I* ed. A. J. Horwood, RS XXXI (1863), pp. 530–32.
[104] *The Lives of the Norths* (1826) I, p. 30. Cf. *Novae Narrationes* ed. S. F. C. Milsom, SS LXXX (1963), p. xxvi.

steward in 'how he ought to speak' by giving a series of dialogues, like a modern conversation primer for learning a foreign language.[105] Likewise in the *Rules* of estate management, which Robert Grosseteste wrote for the countess of Lincoln in the 1240s, the lady is instructed in how to address her steward: 'Good sir, you see plainly that I have had these inquiries and enrolments made to shed light on my rights . . .' and so on.[106] A schoolman like Grosseteste probably derived the idea of writing hypothetical speeches from the *ars dictaminis* taught in the universities, where students were shown how to write letters for all occasions in this way.[107] Most English legal treatises of this sort contain the texts of oaths – a witness's oath to tell the truth, a vassal's oath of homage to his lord, a bailiff's oath to act honestly, and others; these examples are taken from *How to hold pleas and courts* composed in *c.*1272 by John of Oxford.[108] It is probable that John taught seignorial administration and elementary legal procedure at Oxford.[109] Knowledge which a century before had been passed on by word of mouth from father to son, or learned from the old wise men of the court, was now part of an academic curriculum.

Similarly the texts of speeches, which chroniclers had formerly been obliged to invent or borrow from Roman historians, were sometimes now put in writing. Thus Edward I's envoys to France in 1294 were instructed (in French in the original) as follows: 'Our messengers shall say to the king of France: "Our lord the king of England, lord of Ireland, and duke of Aquitaine, does you homage on condition . . ."'and so on.[110] A year earlier when John Balliol, king of Scots, personally protested to Edward I about his claim of overlordship, John delivered to the king and his council the text of the speech he made (in French) written on a schedule, perhaps by his own hand.[111] By far the largest collection of speeches and dialogues surviving from the reign of Edward I are the Year Books, which purport to record the actual words (translated into French or Latin) of litigants, their counsel and the judges in royal courts.[112] The case already cited of Hugh, who was unable to read his challenges, is a meagre example of a Year Book's quality of dialogue.

The makers of the Year Books appear to record actual speech, whereas the writers of handbooks for speaking in court set out hypothetical conversation as in a play. Under the heading, 'Ici comence le play de la coroune' (here begin the pleas of the crown), *The Court Baron* presents a dialogue between a steward and his bailiff.[113] (The use of 'play' in the French is a coincidence and has no connexion with 'play' in English.)

[105] *Court Baron*, p. 49.
[106] *Walter of Henley*, p. 390.
[107] C. H. Haskins, *Studies in Medieval Culture*, chs. 1, 9.
[108] *Court Baron*, pp. 77–8.
[109] Clanchy, *'Moderni'*, p. 686.
[110] P. Chaplais, 'English Diplomatic Documents' in *Study of Medieval Records*, p. 35.
[111] *Anglo-Scottish Relations*, p. 66.
[112] See ch. 3, n. 73 above.
[113] *Court Baron*, p. 62. Cf. other examples of forensic dialogue at pp. 76, 162 above.

The steward speaks first:

'Bailiff!'
'Sir!'
'Bring up the prisoners.'
'Willingly, sir. See they are here.'
'Why is this man under arrest?'
'Sir, for a mare which he took in the field in another way than he should have.'

The steward then proceeds to examine the prisoner; the dialogue vividly creates a courtroom scene. Some protagonists are even given star roles, like the naive poacher, Walter de la More, who begins his explanation (beautifully translated by Maitland) as follows:

Sir, for God's sake do not take it ill of me if I tell thee the truth, how I went the other evening along the bank of this pond and looked at the fish which were playing in the water, so beautiful and so bright, and for the great desire that I had for a tench I laid me down on the bank and just with my hands quite simply, and without any other device, I caught that tench and carried if off. . . .[114]

The poacher then tries a hard-luck story about how his wife had been ill and off her food for a month, but she had a great yearning to eat a tench. There is obviously a large element of imaginative licence in this presentation of the poacher's statement; apart from anything else, a poor peasant would have spoken in English and not in the French in which the speech is written.

Lawbooks like *The Court Baron* were not written to entertain, yet they have similarities with the use of dialogue in romances and with the earliest English drama in French.[115] The idea of each protagonist having a set part written down verbatim, which he must adhere to, was unfamiliar to the non-literate and presented actors, whether in lawcourts or on stage-sets outside churches, with common problems. In a religious drama, *Le Mystère d'Adam* (dating from c.1140), how the words are to be spoken is described in detail. M. D. Legge suggests that writing set parts may have been new; that is why the actors are instructed not to add or omit anything, to speak clearly, and to say their lines in the right order.[116]

It would be tempting to see the lawyers' Year Books and handbooks as having something in common with the jongleurs' 'stage scripts', in which the vernacular romances are thought to have been first recorded in writing.[117] Scripts, whether for jongleurs or lawyers, enabled 'a young man to see [*veer/vere*] how he ought to speak with subtlety' and 'see the

[114] *Court Baron*, pp. 54–5.
[115] Examples of dialogue in Legge, *Anglo-Norman*, pp. 92 (by Hue of Roteland), 256 (by William of Barnwell). Drama in *ibid.* pp. 311–31.
[116] *ibid.* p. 319.
[117] E. Auerbach, *Literary Language and its Public in Late Antiquity and in the Middle Ages* (1965), p. 288.

manner distinctly' (in the words of *The Court Baron*.)[118] A student now learned the rudiments of public speaking by reading, by seeing the 'shapes indicating voices' (in John of Salisbury's phrase) in a book, instead of hearing the words of his master. Yet we should not exaggerate the speed of this development; as long as writing depended on manuscripts alone, the change from oral to literate modes was gradual. Dependence on symbolic gestures and the spoken word persisted in law and literature, and throughout medieval culture, despite the growth of literacy.

Writings as works of art

Writing has the power to change the way words are perceived by the senses, because it shifts the emphasis in communicating language from hearing to seeing. The language of script can be received 'through the windows of the eyes' by silent reading, or it can be transmitted 'voicelessly', even to people not yet born, by shaping letters with the hand. In non-literate cultures the skills of eye and hand are associated primarily with craftsmanship and the visual arts, while the skills of language which depend on the transmission of sound are identified with mouth and ear. Although writing had the potential, in medieval England as elsewhere, to change the perception of language by making it visual as well as auditory, it has been argued already in this chapter that pre-literate habits of mind persisted long after documents became common. Books and letters continued to be read aloud and listened to, instead of being silently scrutinized by the eye, and authors went on thinking of composition in terms of dictation rather than of manipulating a pen. The skills of reading and writing therefore remained distinct, because reading was part of the mastery of speech whereas writing was one of the manual and visual arts.

　　Early medieval civilization shared with other ancient cultures of the world an approach to writing which was non-utilitarian. The skills of the scribe were primarily devoted not to transmitting mundane information in an economical and straightforward way, but to making illuminated manuscripts which were masterpieces of calligraphy, painting, jewellery and metalwork. In such works as the *Book of Kells* or the *Lindisfarne Gospels* the text was of secondary importance. It was there to remind the chanter of the familiar phrases of the liturgy, if he did not immediately recall them, and to serve as an act of worship in itself by catching the words of God in sacred script and displaying them on the page like butterflies in a showcase. Writing was aimed at God's eye more often than at communicating information to fellow human beings. For that reason books were kept on the altar or in a sacristy rather than in a library. Because illuminated manuscripts appealed primarily to the eye, like pictures, they could be understood almost as well by the non-literate as by the literate. To appreciate their finer points required expertise, but the knowledge needed was that of the

[118] *Court Baron*, pp. 49, 20.

artist and craftsman rather than that of the linguistically educated. As we have seen, Walter Map distinguished the good scribe, who 'knew how to transcribe any series of letters whatever', from the *litteratus*.[119] The scribe was expert in calligraphy, whereas the *litteratus* was expert in Latin.

This separation of the skills of reading and writing continued up until the invention of printing and was not immediately affected by the proliferation of documents in the twelfth and thirteenth centuries. Gutenberg himself, the inventor of printing, had not aimed to supersede the illuminated book, but to improve it and make it more readily available. The earliest book to come from his press, the 42-line Bible, is indistinguishable at first sight from an illuminated manuscript. Writings continued to be works of art, embellished in a variety of ways, as long as they were produced by hand. However humble a scrivener he was, the medieval scribe was an individual artist, who had to discipline himself to achieve anonymity and uniformity, whereas printing imposes uniformity automatically and excludes ornamentation except when it has been deliberately planned in advance.

At the very time that documents were beginning to be used in greater numbers for business purposes, in the middle of the twelfth century, some of the most elaborately written and illuminated manuscripts were produced.[120] In pride of place stands the Psalter written by Eadwine of Canterbury, which is a masterpiece of layout and calligraphy, with its three parallel versions of the Psalms in Latin, and interlinear glosses in Latin, French and Anglo-Saxon (see plate XIV). To mark his achievement, the last folio was devoted to a picture of Eadwine himself, with an inscription round the frame declaring him to be 'the prince of writers'. He differs from earlier monastic scribes, not in being an artist in calligraphy, but in drawing attention to his own merits rather than God's or a saint's, since the inscription states that Eadwine's fame will live through the centuries. Eadwine's work is clearly in the old tradition of emphasizing form in writing rather than literal meaning, as elegant design takes precedence over textual accuracy. His Anglo-Saxon text is peculiarly corrupt and his Latin has unnecessary errors. The scribe and the *litteratus* were not invariably at odds, however, as the Winchester Bible, (which is contemporary with Eadwine's Psalter) has a good text as well as magnificent calligraphy and illuminations. In the unusually purist opinion of St Hugh's Carthusians, the correctness of the text was its best feature.[121]

A rigid distinction between an artistic and a practical manuscript is often impossible to make, because a synthesis of the beautiful and the functional is a general characteristic of medieval art, as churches and castles make abundantly evident. Even the most businesslike manuscripts required some embellishment, in the form of rubrics and enlarged initials, to enable the user to find his place in the book. Thus

[119] See n. 79 above and ch. 7, nn. 28–30 above.
[120] See Kauffmann, *Romanesque MSS* and Ker, *English MSS*.
[121] See ch. 3, n. 9 above.

the larger volume of Domesday Book uses vermilion paint for three distinct types of rubrication – capital letters for the names of shires and other headings; shading for the initial letter of each paragraph and certain abbreviations; underlining for the names of places and tenants.[122] The rubrication contributes to making Domesday Book a masterpiece of functional layout, which is a form of abstract art in itself. Subsequently, however, the embellishment of the Domesday text was taken much further when multi-coloured copies were made from it: one in the twelfth century (*Herefordshire Domesday*) and another in the thirteenth (the Exchequer Breviate).[123] Unlike the original, these manuscripts are primarily ornamental. They show that Domesday Book had achieved the status of a revered text, which was worthy to be beautified and embellished like a Gospel book. The name 'Domesday', recalling the book of Revelation, had already associated it with Holy Writ.

Most manuscript books show a similar mixture of the pictorial and the functional. A representative small collection are the dozen English lawyers' manuals, containing parliamentary statutes and other texts for ready reference (dating from a decade or so on either side of 1300), which are now preserved at the Harvard Law School.[124] Lawyers' textbooks might be expected to be severely practical and economical in format. A few are, notably MS. 36 in the Harvard collection, which uses rubrics sparingly and is written rather untidily, like a plea roll, in a rapid business hand (see plate XVII). By contrast, MS. 173 has initials illuminated in blue, green and gold leaf, in addition to the usual rubrics; while MS. 12 has broad margins, pictorial initials, and other drawings illustrating the subject matter of the statutes: for example, a boar and a deer in a wood and a man shooting a deer with a longbow accompany the text of the Charter of the Forest (see plate XVIII). English canon lawyers' books of decretals of a century earlier show similar contrasts between plain working copies, presumably used by practioners and teachers, and illuminated fair copies intended for presentation or as show pieces.[125]

At the opposite poles of writings intended to catch the eye of God with their illuminations and writings intended for mundane consultation are liturgical manuscripts on the one hand and the public records (particularly legal and financial documents) on the other. Yet here also some exceptions can be found. The Sherborne cartulary of the mid-twelfth century integrates royal charters and illuminated liturgical texts into one book intended for the altar.[126] Conversely the most mundane public records are occasionally illustrated. Thus an Exchequer receipt roll for 1233 has at its head an elaborate drawing caricaturing prominent Jews of Norwich, and a plea roll for 1249 depicts trial by combat and the

---

[122] V. H. Galbraith, *Domesday Book* (1974), frontispiece. The system of rubrication is described in *Domesday Re-Bound* ed. H. Jenkinson, HMSO (1954), pp. 32–3.

[123] See ch. 1, n. 30 above.

[124] Harvard Law Library MSS 12, 33, 36, 39, 49, 56–9, 173–5.

[125] Duggan, *Decretals*, pp. 81–2, plate ii.

[126] See ch. 5, n. 36 above.

hanging of the loser.[127] Much more common throughout the public records are amateurly foliated initials and caricatured heads in profile, which seem to be doodles made by bored enrolling clerks. In a plea roll from 1249, which has a friendly-looking devil at the foot of one membrane, the clerk admitted his boredom by cancelling an enrolment and replacing it with what may have been a snatch from a French popular song, which in translation reads: 'It's my little loves that keep me cheerful and give me fun.'[128] Traditional scribal habits made rigorous formality and a total lack of personal embellishment difficult to impose. In private business documents minor embellishments are even more common, as scribes were less constrained by bureaucratic standards. For example, the earliest account roll of Crowland abbey (dating from 1258-9) is ornamented with foliations, animal heads and what seem to be facetious portraits.[129] Although to a modern eye such amateur ornament detracts from a document's dignity, the monastic writer even of an account roll may have felt obliged to give his work some embellishment to make it look authoritative.

The continuing emphasis on the visual aspects of writings, despite the increasing number of business documents (which grew more uniform and economical of materials and time in the thirteenth century), helped to bridge the gap between non-literate and literate, just as the persistence of reading aloud and listening did. Before writing became common, people were accustomed to using knives, or even Gospel books, as symbolic objects which could be transferred in the presence of witnesses as a sign that property had been duly conveyed. As has been suggested earlier in this chapter, conveyances by charter may have been made acceptable to non-literates by the seals attached to them. Like illuminated manuscripts embellished with precious stones and relics, seals were visible and tangible symbols of a donor's wishes.[130] Neither clergy nor laity would have trusted or admired documents which were writings pure and unadorned, because they would have been inadequate as symbols of a person's wishes.

To knights, who were on the threshold of literacy in the twelfth century, writing may have appeared attractive as another system of signs. Their capacity to devise and understand a complex system of pictorial signs is shown by the development of heraldry, which is contemporary with the shift from memory to written record. The first recorded rolls of arms were illustrated and written in the language of blazon in the middle of the thirteenth century, although heraldry had probably been developing visually and orally for a century before that.[131] Whether the growth of recorded heraldry and the contem-

---

[127] PRO Exchequer 401/1565, m. 1, illustrated by V. D. Lipman, *The Jews of Medieval Norwich* (1967), p. 33. Curia Regis Roll KB 26/223, illustrated by F. W. Maitland, *SPC* frontispiece.

[128] *Crown Pleas of the Wiltshire Eyre* ed. C. A. F. Meekings, WiltsRS xvi (1961), p. 25.

[129] F. Page, *The Estates of Crowland Abbey* (1934), plate v.

[130] See pp. 244-6 below.

[131] G. J. Brault, *Early Blazon* (1972), p. 8. In general see M. Pastoureau, *Les Armoires* (1976).

poraneous spread of literacy among knights are coincidental or connected developments is a matter for conjecture. Inauguration into literate ways of thought through pictorial manuscripts and visual symbols like seals may have caused knights to create an alternative system of 'shapes indicating voices' in heraldry. Traditionally 'letters' were the clergy's symbolic way of indicating their superior status, since a *clericus* was a *litteratus*. Heraldry may have originated as an alternative language of signs, which was peculiar to the knightly order and distinguished their names by symbols.

Coats of arms in England were first recorded, most appropriately, by Matthew Paris, the greatest all-round writer in the monastic tradition.[132] Throughout his work he shows that the ideal of making a synthesis of the visual and the intellectual in writing was still alive, as he composed and penned his own works and illustrated them with line drawings, maps, diagrams and more formal paintings.[133] He also devised a system of *signa*, incorporating heraldry, both as an ornament and as a finding aid in his chronicles.[134] Nor did he ignore the need for accurate texts, although like other scribal artists he considered himself entitled to make variations and embellishments of his own. Matthew Paris is exceptional in his abilities, but not in his approach to his art which treats writing as a visual skill inseparable from pictorial values.

The way manuscripts were made as splendid visual objects, rather than mundane communications, ensured that there was no irreconcilable division between writers and non-writers when documents began to be used more widely in the twelfth and thirteenth centuries. Many manuscripts continued to be lavishly embellished and all were read aloud so that the non-literate could participate in their use. There was no conscious or deliberate attempt to integrate literate and non-literate – indeed the clergy wanted to remain a class apart – but change was sufficiently slow to make gradual adaptation possible. As long as all writings were manuscripts, that is, as long as they were made exclusively by hand, old habits of mind persisted. Throughout the Middle Ages the writer remained a visual artist and the reader a specialist in the spoken word. Medieval reading (*lectio*) was primarily something heard rather than seen until the invention of printing, and writing (*scriptura*) often continued to be admired for its calligraphy rather than its textual accuracy. The laity were gradually coaxed towards literacy by ensuring that it changed the old ways of hearing and seeing as little as possible.

[132] *A Catalogue of English Medieval Rolls of Arms* ed. A. Wagner, *Aspilogia* I (1950), pp. 1–3. *The Matthew Paris Shields* ed. T. D. Tremlett, *Aspilogia* II (1967).
[133] R. Vaughan, *Matthew Paris* (1958), and see pp. 61–2 above.
[134] *ibid.* plates iv and v, and see ch. 5, n. 137 above.

9

Trusting writing

Documents did not immediately inspire trust. As with other innovations in technology, there was a long and complex period of evolution, particularly in the twelfth century in England, before methods of production were developed which proved acceptable both to traditionalists and to experts in literacy. There was no straight and simple line of progress from memory to written record. People had to be persuaded – and it was difficult to do – that documentary proof was a sufficient improvement on existing methods to merit the extra expense and mastery of novel techniques which it demanded.

A modern literate tends to assume that statements in writing, especially if they are in print, are more reliable than spoken words. This assumption is the result of schooling in reading and writing from an early age and the constant use of documents, such as bills, for even the smallest transactions. The obvious advantage to a modern literate of documentary proof is that it cannot be as easily or as readily changed as a person's word. But this advantage of writing was less obvious in medieval England, since even literates did not use documents in ways which assured their effectiveness as proof. Most charters of the twelfth century were neither dated, not autographed, nor were they copied into registers for future reference. In the earliest private charters draftsmen and scribes give the impression that, instead of sharing a common training in the drawing up of instruments, they are each making a personal and individual but necessarily amateur effort to master the complexities of documentary proof for the first time.

A charter whereby Ralf of St Audoen gave a salt-pan to Sele priory in Sussex illustrates the work of an amateur draftsman very well, even though it is dated (1153 *Anno Domini*) and autographed which is unusual.[1] The draftsman or scribe, who was probably one of the monks of Sele, begins with a justification for written record: 'Because it is appropriate that this should be brought to reach the notice of many, it is committed to the muniments of letters by provident deliberation, lest in the process of time it be destroyed by ruinous oblivion.' The gift itself was publicly symbolized not by this charter, however, but by a more

[1] *Oxford Facs*, no. 9. Cf. other Sele priory preambles at ch. 5, n. 3 above.

traditional form of writing – a Gospel book which was laid on the beneficiary's altar. The monks of Sele seem to have been determined to ratify the gift in as many ways as possible, both traditional and novel. Ralf's lord, William de Braose, made his autograph sign of the cross on the charter twice, once in the priory and again when the document was exhibited and ratified at his court in Bramber castle. Ralf also put his seal on the charter. Those who trusted the sign of the cross and those who favoured the more modern wax seal, which with its device of a knight on horseback was a symbol of feudal lordship, could therefore both be satisfied. (See plate I where a charter is authenticated in a similar way.) For those who trusted neither, lists of witnesses were specified for both transactions. As F. M. Stenton commented of a Lincolnshire charter of similar date, 'the transaction is unusually complicated, but it is probable that the expression of a grant in writing was often less important to the parties than the performance of ceremonial acts of which the charter itself makes no record.'[2] The writing was of secondary importance, and was hedged about with repetitious clauses, because less confidence was placed in it than in the oaths and public ceremonies which had traditionally sanctioned conveyances.

At first each charter tended to differ in its phraseology, because every document was felt to be an individual affirmation fixing human relationships at a certain point in time and space. Doubts about whether such stability was possible or appropriate may explain why early drafters of charters are often reluctant to state the time and place of writing and why they invoke the aid of God and his saints so frequently. The advantage to the historian today, though not to the property owner at the time, of this diversity of practice is that it provides a record, like an archaeological stratification, of how a literate mentality developed over generations. Information, which students of diplomatic have accumulated in order to date charters and identify forgeries, can be used to illustrate how attitudes to writing changed over the twelfth and thirteenth centuries. The evolution of common form is not commonplace, as it marks the stages in the gradual acceptance of literate ways of doing business.

Memory and writing

Before documents were used, the truth of an event or transaction had been established by personal statements, often made on oath, by the principals or witnesses. If the event were too far in the past for that, the oldest and wisest men were asked what they could remember about it. Numerous examples could be cited of collective oral testimony being given from memory, particularly in cases involving the proof of age of feudal heirs. The example which follows illustrates the method in answer to a less routine question. In 1127 a writ of Henry I ordered a jury to be chosen of twelve men from Dover and twelve from Sandwich to

---

[2] *Transcripts of Charters Relating to Gilbertine Houses*, Lincolnshire Record S. XVIII (1922), p. xxx.

settle a dispute between St Augustine's abbey at Canterbury and Christ Church about customs dues at the port of Sandwich. The jurors were described as 'twenty-four mature, wise seniors of many years, having good testimony'.[3] Each in turn then swore on a Gospel book in public that the tolls belonged to Christ Church, saying: this 'I have received from my ancestors, and I have seen and heard from my youth up until now, so help me God and these Holy Gospels.'

Whether in circumstances like these the jurors really told the historical truth is impossible to establish, since the past events in question were recorded only in peoples' living memories. As the jurors had publicly sworn on the Gospels that they were telling the truth, no more could be said, unless their Christian principles were to be impugned. Thus, without documents, the establishment of what passed for truth was simple and personal, since it depended on the good word of one's fellows. Remembered truth was also flexible and up to date, because no ancient custom could be proved to be older than the memory of the oldest living wise man. There was no conflict between past and present, between ancient precedents and present practice. Customary law 'quietly passes over obsolete laws, which sink into oblivion, and die peacefully, but the law itself remains young, always in the belief that it is old.'[4] Written records, on the other hand, do not die peacefully, as they retain a half life in archives and can be resurrected to inform, impress or mystify future generations.

Those who objected in the Middle Ages to the literate preference for the artificial memory of written record, instead of the living memory voiced by wise men of age and experience, were in a long tradition – had they known it – which extended back to myths about the invention of writing. According to Socrates the god who invented writing had been rebuked by the king of Egypt, Thamus, who said:

> If men learn this, it will implant forgetfulness in their souls: they will cease to exercise memory because they rely on that which is written, calling things to remembrance no longer from within themselves, but by means of external marks; what you have discovered is a recipe not for memory, but for reminder.[5]

Both to ignorant illiterates and to sophisticated Platonists written record was a dubious gift, because it seemed to kill living eloquence and trust and substitute for them a mummified semblance in the form of a piece of parchment. Henry I's partisans in the dispute with Anselm, who had called a papal bull a sheepskin 'blackened with ink and weighted with a little lump of lead', were arguing for the priority of the personal testimony of the three bishops who exercised memory over the mere 'external marks' of a writing.[6] Those medieval Christians who recalled

[3] Stenton, *Justice*, p. 118.
[4] F. Kern, *Kingship and Law in the Middle Ages* trans. S. B. Chrimes (1939), p. 179. Clanchy, 'Remembering', p. 172.
[5] Plato, *Phaedrus*, 274–5, trans. R. Hackforth (1952). Cf. Curtius, *European Lit.*, p. 304; Goody, *Literacy*, p. 50; F. Yates, *The Art of Memory* (1966), p. 52.
[6] See p. 209 above.

St Paul's warning, 'the letter killeth, but the spirit giveth life', were in a similar long tradition.[7] Likewise perhaps the Earl Warenne himself, when he allegedly produced before Edward I's judges the 'ancient and rusty sword' of his ancestors, was appealing to a sign which was superior to any letters because it lived in peoples' memories.[8]

Such objectors, moreover, had a case which was strong in substance as well as in sentiment, since numerous medieval charters were forged and the authenticity of the genuine ones was difficult to prove. Such a bewildering variety of 'external marks' had been used in idiosyncratic attempts to demonstrate the authenticity of charters that written record was highly suspicious. There were thousands of authentic charters without dates or places of issue, some of them written by scribes who seem never to have wielded a pen before (see plates I and VI).[9] Although most English charters had seals attached to them, a few were authenticated by inked crosses (some autographs and others not), or by other symbolic objects signifying the donor's wishes such as rings or knives.[10] Nearly all charters listed witnesses to the transaction, ranging in numbers from the king's unique *Teste me ipso* (witness, myself) to the 123 individuals named in an agreement in Kent in 1176.[11] It was common for a scribe to conclude his list of witnesses with some such phrase as 'and many others who would take too long to enumerate',[12] a description which was useless for future identification, although it recorded the impressiveness of the occasion at the time. Witnesses soon died anyway and some, like the saints who witness a Christ Church charter of *c*.1200, may never have lived.[13] Sometimes the scribe of the charter identifies himself as the last witness, offering a test of authenticity, but more often he does not.

In these circumstances, where practice was so varied and even eccentric, both literate and illiterate were entitled to distrust charters. Authentic looking documents might well be forged, or conversely amateur scrawls might turn out to be genuine. In addition to inconsistencies and lack of uniform scribal training, the principal difficulty was that monks, who were the traditional experts in writing, were also the greatest forgers. The more powerful and ancient the house, the more likely it was that its documents would be forged in a professional manner. Of the seals used by Christ Church Canterbury, Archdeacon Simon Langton wrote to Gregory IX in 1238: 'Holy Father, there is not a single sort of forgery that is not perpetrated in the church of Canterbury. For they have forged in gold, in lead, in wax, and in every kind of metal.'[14] Much the same, of course, could be said of the papal *curia* in an

[7] See ch. 8, nn. 28–30 above.
[8] See pp. 21–7 above.
[9] See pp. 101–2 above.
[10] For crosses see nn. 57–60 below. For other symbolic objects see ch. 1, nn. 49–54; ch. 5, nn. 42–3; ch. 8, nn. 19–21 above.
[11] Chaplais, *Docs*, p. 16. *BM Facs*, no. 57.
[12] *Mowbray Charters*, p. 17, no. 13.
[13] Galbraith, 'Literacy', p. 222.
[14] Cheney, *Texts & Studies*, p. 104. For forgery see also pp. 248–57 below.

earlier period, when it had created the Donation of Constantine and other forged decretals.

Yet in theory at least it would have been relatively easy for English medieval writers to make documents whose authenticity could normally have been proved. Although no system of safeguards could cover all cases, the great majority could certainly be guaranteed. All that was required was to follow elementary principles of Roman legal practice, which were familiar in twelfth-century Italy and throughout the *pays du droit écrit* bordering on the Mediterranean, and ensure that each document was precisely dated and written by an authorized scribe or notary. Ideally, in addition, the notary needed to register a copy of the document in a record kept by a public authority. As is well known, these elementary principles were not followed in medieval England, nor elsewhere at first in northern Europe. Although some notaries practised in England in the thirteenth century, their activities were normally restricted to a few types of ecclesiastical business. Similarly public registers of certain types of property transactions existed in England by 1200, in the Jewish *arche* and the royal feet of fines established by Hubert Walter, but there was no comprehensive system of registration.[15] Sometimes the king's government could not trace its own documents, yet alone other people's.

The reason why England did not develop a notarial system on the Roman model is generally thought to be simple and obvious: 'customary law prevailed.'[16] Although correct, this explanation is inadequate, as customary law did not prevail in other areas of bureaucratic activity because twelfth-century England had been opened to Italian and other European influences, first by the Norman Conquest and then by the Angevins. Thus the accounting system of the Exchequer, which Richard Fitz Neal thought to be largely a product of immemorial custom when he wrote his *Dialogue of the Exchequer* around 1179, had in fact been created in Henry I's reign by French (and perhaps also Arabic) arithmetical expertise. The common law itself, as articulated by Henry II's writs, owed more to deliberate legislative thought than to custom. From the latter half of the twelfth century English royal officials were sufficiently influenced by the canon and civil law schools of Bologna to know that custom by itself was inadequate. Fitz Neal himself evoked Roman law, when he credited William the Conqueror with the intention of bringing 'the conquered people under the rule of written law'.[17] Although Fitz Neal's remark has elements of anachronism when applied to William the Conqueror, it reflects the assumption of contemporary administrators in Henry II's reign that Roman *jus scriptum* could be applied to England.

Why England remained largely unaffected by the Roman notarial

---

[15] For these registries see ch. 2, nn. 64–78 above. For attempts to use them as public archives see ch. 5, nn. 107–11 above.

[16] Cheney, *Notaries* p. 6.

[17] *Dialogus*, p. 63 and ch. 1, n. 1 above. Cf. Glanvill's attitude to Roman law, nn. 82–3 below.

system, while being influenced by other continental bureaucratic procedures, is therefore a question worth pursuing further, as it goes to the roots of the non-literate's lack of understanding and consequent distrust of written modes of proof. Without documents memory had stemmed from the living wisdom of the local community whereas the dead hand of writing, the 'mortmain' of the monks and clergy, defined and extended boundaries by its 'external marks' across both time and space.

Dating documents

The difficulties experienced by English writers of the twelfth century, when confronting problems they felt to be novel, are well illustrated by their variety of approaches to dating documents ranging from those who omit the date altogether to others who use more than one system of computation on the same document. To write out the date at the head of a letter is an elementary routine for a modern literate and was relatively simple likewise for a trained medieval notary. Thus an imperial notary, Henry of Asti, wrote the date as follows on an instrument drawn up in London: 'Anno a nativitate Christi millesimo ducentesimo sexagesimo octavo, indictione undecima, die Mercurii xviii intrante mense Januraii, pontificatus domini Clementis papae iiii anno tercio.'[18] This date, Wednesday 18 January 1268 AD, is expressed in a way which is familiar to a modern European, although the papal year (the third of Clement IV) and the reference to the eleventh indiction are Roman notarial refinements which now seem superfluous. For some transactions notaries were expected to record the hour as well as the day. Thus an episcopal notification from Lincoln in 1228 specifies times of dispatch and receipt of letters, as well as verifying the sender's seal.[19] Even a common law judge, Roger of Seaton, followed notarial practice in 1279 when he acknowledged receipt of one letter from the Chancery 'at about the ninth hour' and another 'just a little after dark'.[20] These times are not more precise presumably because Seaton was estimating the hours by daylight and not by a clock.[21]

The purpose of being precise about the year, month, day and even hour at which a document was issued or received was in order to settle subsequent disputes about its authenticity by checking the time. Thus Henry III assured Gregory X in 1272 that some royal letters patent, which were being exhibited at the papal *curia*, were forgeries because 'we were not at Canterbury on that day and year'; in fact Henry was mistaken, but that is another story.[22] Dates and places of issue had the added advantage of putting documents and their makers in a temporal

[18] Cheney, *Notaries*, p. 168. *Handbook of Dates for Students of English History* ed. C. R. Cheney (1945), is a concise introduction to dating problems.
[19] *Rotuli Hugonis de Welles* ed. W. P. W. Phillimore, Canterbury & York S. I (1909) or Lincolnshire Record S. III (1912), II, pp. 145–6.
[20] *SCCKB* I, pp. clxvii (s), clxviii (t).
[21] An early example of recording time by a mechanical clock is Richard II's abdication in 1399 at 'circiter nonam pulsationem horologii', Cheney, *Notaries*, p. 137.
[22] See pp. 49, 138–9 above.

and geographical perspective, which extended over centuries if the Christian system of years of grace *Anno Domini* was used.

Despite the advantages of stating when documents were issued, most twelfth-century charters do not do so. The eight extant bonds (the earliest of their kind) of the Flemish financier, William Cade, are significant in this respect, as it might be expected that records of debts would be drafted as precisely as possible.[23] Yet none of the bonds bears a date of issue and three of them (nos. ii, v, viii) do not even specify the year in which the debt is to be paid, but only a day in relation to feast days of the church. Although the other five do specify the year, it is expressed in ways which are clumsy and could be ambiguous in the long term:

> i: After Henry, the king of England's son, espoused the daughter of the king of France [1160];
> iii: after the espousal of the king of England's son and the king's daughter;
> iv: after the king and Count Thierry of Flanders had talks together at Dover before the count went to set out for Jerusalem [1157];
> vi: after the king's great council at London [1163];
> vii: after Gilbert Foliot was received into the bishopric of London [1163].

Cade evidently did not expect his debts to be outstanding for long and so it was appropriate to date repayments in relation to current events.

More precise forms of dating begin in the last decade of the twelfth century. Royal letters are uniformly dated (by place of issue, day of the month and regnal year) from the accession of Richard I in 1189.[24] Influenced by royal rather than papal practice, English bishops begin to date their solemn *acta* with regularity from the end of the twelfth century, although their secular enfeoffments and administrative precepts went on being undated until the end of the thirteenth century.[25] Books and similar scribal work are likewise usually undated and unautographed, although there are notable exceptions like the chronicles of Matthew Paris or Domesday Book, one of whose volumes states that 'this *descriptio*' was made in 1086 AD.[26] Other than Domesday, the earliest extant English book dated by its scribe is a text of St Augustine, which is stated to have been written at the Cistercian abbey of Buildwas in 1167 AD; another book from Buildwas is similarly dated 1176 AD.[27]

Why not always give the date on a document in a precise and uniform way, if only as a routine precaution? Various explanations can be suggested for not doing so. One sometimes mentioned is that charters

---

[23] H. Jenkinson, 'A Moneylender's Bonds' in *Essays to Poole*, pp. 205–10.

[24] Chaplais, *Docs*, p. 14.

[25] Cheney, *Chanceries*, pp. 83ff.

[26] For Matthew Paris see ch. 5, n. 5 above. For Domesday Book see Galbraith, *Studies*, p. 93; *descriptio* refers to the Domesday survey as a whole rather than to the writing of this particular volume.

[27] Ker, *English MSS*, p. 21. Cheney, *Texts & Studies*, p. 331, n. 1.

were seen as mere confirmations of transactions which had already taken place, and there was therefore no point in dating them. The difficulty with this explanation is that even when a charter was written after the event, it would still have been prudent, if the draftsman really had that regard for posterity which his preamble claimed, to specify in the text the date of the transaction itself and distinguish that from the date on which the charter was written. To specify both dates was good notarial practice. Another possible explanation for omitting dates is that they were difficult to compute without printed diaries. Gervase of Canterbury describes some of the problems: when exactly was the Crucifixion (in 32, 33 or 34 AD 7)? when should the year begin – at the Annunciation (25 March), the Passion (a moveable feast), Christmas, or the Circumcision (1 January)?[28] Yet these difficulties were surmountable and since most early charters were written by monks, who were the experts in chronology, their lack of dates is still mysterious.

Other reasons for not dating documents are more profound. Until putting the date on a document became a mindless routine, dating required the scribe to express an opinion about his place in time. In relation to which persons, human or divine, and over what length of time was the date to be computed? A Jew might date his bond 'from the Creation' and think of a continuum 'from the beginning of time up to the end of the world', because the temporal order proceded without intermission.[29] For the pope, on the other hand, it was appropriate to begin a new era with the birth of Christ and to date letters *Anno Domini*, since the pope was Christ's vicar in unbroken succession from St Peter. A bishop or a monastic chronicler might likewise compute by years of grace, since bishops too were successors of the Apostles and monks had an accepted place in the Christian dispensation. Yet ecclesiastics did not date all their documents: enfeoffments and precepts were usually left undated, as has already been mentioned. In such instances omission of the date may not have been due to negligence, but to conscientiousness. Perhaps it was thought presumptuous or even blasphemous to associate worldly business with the time of Christ's incarnation. To record the year *Anno Domini* on a document was to give it a place in the chronology of Christian salvation in past, present and future time, as expounded by St Augustine in the *City of God*. Paradoxically, monks may have so rarely dated documents in the twelfth century or earlier because they were too conscious of the significance of time and of their place in posterity.

The non-religious, by contrast, had such a personal and short view of time that they too found it difficult at first to specify a numerical year on a document. Everyone knew which year was meant, the present one, and if there were doubt, some notable event could be referred to. Examples have already been given of William Cade dating his bonds in this frame of mind. The richest variety of memorable events in an early

[28] Gervase I, p. 88.
[29] Examples cited by F. A. Lincoln, *The Starra* (1939), pp. 30, 32, 57. Cf. ch. 6, nn. 17–18 above.

record appear in the guild rolls of Leicester (the earliest of their kind), which extend over the period 1196–1232.[30] The first year is specified in relation to the release from captivity in France of the earl of Leicester (in 1196) and the second 'after the death of the emperor of Germany' (Henry VI in 1197). Thereafter other events of national or international importance, such as the Interdict in John's reign or the death of William Marshal and the capture of Damietta by the crusaders (both in 1219), are interspersed with local events in Leicester, such as the dedication of St Nicholas's church (in ?1221) and the deaths or periods in office of town worthies like aldermen. Only three times are English regnal years referred to, and years *Anno Domini* are not used at all. Evidently the Leicester town clerks were uncertain of what standard to adopt for dating their rolls. By their variety of practices the rolls give an indication of how events, in Leicester and beyond, were viewed by the local community.

The earliest extant final concord made before royal justices is similarly dated not by a numerical year, but at the feast of Peter and Paul (29 June) 'after the king took the allegiance of the barons of Scotland at York'.[31] This refers to the homage done to Henry II in York Minster in August 1175 after his defeat of King William the Lion. This concord, which concerns a lawsuit in Oxford between the canons of Osney and a widow and her daughters, has no direct concern with Anglo-Scottish politics. Nevertheless it was evidently assumed that the time when Henry II formally exhibited his superiority over the Scots would be remembered for at least as long as the settlement of this lawsuit at Oxford. Whether the drafters of this concord thought that their document would last only for a generation or so, or whether conversely they thought that Henry II's triumphant ceremony in York Minster would be remembered for centuries, is impossible to establish. Probably they had not given the matter much thought either way. They dated the concord not in relation to a documented time continuum stretching over centuries, but, as a non-literate might, in relation to a recent famous event. Despite their appeals to posterity, medieval writers seem to have found it difficult to imagine that their work might survive for centuries and that a time would come when only a professional historian knew when 'the king took the allegiance of the barons of Scotland at York.'

Even when a year is given *Anno Domini* on a document, a memorable event is sometimes specified as well, as if years of grace were too alien (except to the professionally religious) to inspire personal confidence. Thus a gift by the wife of Roger de Mowbray to Fountains abbey is dated 1176 AD, 'the year in which the fortresses of Thirsk and [Kirkby] Malzeard were razed'.[32] This event likewise concerns Henry II's defeat of William the Lion, as Roger de Mowbray had been among the rebels whose castles were demolished. The Mowbrays here recalled their personal humiliation by Henry II instead of the larger submission in York

---

[30] *Records of the Borough of Leicester* ed. M. Bateson I (1899), pp. 12–35. G. H. Martin, 'The English Borough in the Thirteenth Century', *TRHS* 5th series XIII (1963), p. 133.
[31] *BM Facs*, no. 55.   [32] *Mowbray Charters*, p. 101, no. 131.

Minster. A concord made in the court of William de Ferrers is dated comparably by the fortunes of the local lord – 'the year 1192 AD, namely the year in which Earl William de Ferrers took to wife Anneis, sister of Ranulf earl of Chester'.[33] Enough has been said to show that traditionally, before documentation was properly understood, the measurement of time was related to a variety of persons and events and not to an external standard.

The novelty of dating documents, and the variety of ways in which it might be done, is best summarized by the unnecessarily elaborate datary which Ralf de Diceto gave for his survey of the manors of St Paul's cathedral. His invention of distinctive *signa* for his chronicle and the St Paul's charters suggests that he was extraordinarily sensitive to modes of documentary proof.[34] He therefore intended there to be no doubt about the year in which he made his survey. It was:

> The 1181st year AD, the 21st year of Pope Alexander III, the 27th regnal year of King Henry II of the English, the 11th regnal year of King Henry the son of the king, the 18th year that time had passed since the translation of Bishop Gilbert Foliot from Hereford to London, when this inquest was made by Ralf de Diceto, dean of London, in the first year of his deanship.[35]

Ralf thus computes the year by six different systems which he arranges hierarchically, from years *Anno Domini* through the pope and the kings down to himself at the bottom in his first energetic year of office as dean of St Paul's.

In the thirteenth century, when charters were written in tens of thousands, methods of dating become less self-conscious and more uniform. A parody of a datary in French, purporting to be written in a letter to the noble Lady Desire, sets out the commonest rules: 'Given within the four seas of England, on the eve of St John the Baptist, in the 27th year of the reign of King Edward the son of King Henry.'[36] The eve of St John the Baptist is 23 June (Midsummer's Eve) and the 27th year of Edward I's reign is 1299. Between the various possible ways of recording the year, month and day the commonest procedure adopted in England was to relate the day within each year to a feast of the church and to express the year in terms of regnal years. This compromise between church and state, which rejected years *Anno Domini* (as used in episcopal chanceries), and Roman calendar months (as used in the royal Chancery) probably seemed the most appropriate to knightly landowners. They trusted regnal years more than years *Anno Domini* because there was a more immediate point of reference in the king's coronation, which was a publicly remembered event. The growth of dating by regnal years, rather than by more personal events or by the regimes of lesser lords, also suggests that the king was becoming accepted as the head of the English community. Some knights were

[33] Stenton, *Feudalism*, p. 54, n. 3.   [34] See ch. 5, nn. 53, 135 above.
[35] *The Domesday of St Paul's* ed. W. H. Hale, Camden S. LXIX (1857), p. 109.
[36] Legge, *Anglo-Norman*, p. 342.

beginning, moreover, to learn the lengths of reigns of their kings from illustrated rolls which set them out in succession (see plate XIII).[37]

Although after 1300 many private charters still bear no date, forms of dating had become firmly established and commonplace. In general, after much preliminary hesitation, writers had got the measure of time. But because dating had evolved at the slow pace at which literate habits became acceptable, rather than being arbitrarily imposed by Roman law, English methods of dating documents remained complex and inconsistent. From a historical point of view, this variety of methods is a memorial to the formation of literate habits reflecting both feudal and Christian ways of thought. The evolution of the dating of documents is a measure of growing confidence in their usefulness as records.

Signing documents

Everyone agreed that legal documents like charters must be signed, but there was as much diversity of opinion about what constituted a valid signature as there was about what made a date appropriate. As with dating, this diversity suggests that ways were being sought which would prove acceptable both to non-literate traditionalists and to experts in records. By and large in Mediterranean Europe notarial practice was preferred for authenticating documents as for dating them. A notary provided safeguards against forgery usually by writing the document in his own hand and by appending to it his name and an individual *signum* which he drew with a pen. If dispute arose, the notary could be cross-examined or, if he were dead, reference could be made to other documents signed by him or to a register in which an exemplar of his style and *signum* was recorded.

Examples of notarially authenticated parchments can be found in England, though they are not abundant, from the latter half of the thirteenth century onwards, usually among ecclesiastical documents.[38] More exceptionally Edward I had notarized parchments drawn up in the 1290s, when he had to justify his actions in Scotland by the standards of international jurisprudence instead of English common law. For this reason John Balliol's homage in 1292, his renunciation of that homage in 1296, and his statement when Edward's prisoner in 1298 were all written up for the record by a notary, John of Caen.[39] Thus Balliol's letter renouncing his homage in 1296 was authenticated as follows:

> And I, John Arthur of Caen, notary public by authority of the Apostolic See, have written a faithful copy, word for word, in order as I have found it, of the text of the letter, and have drawn it up in the form of this public instrument with the mark of my *signum*, at the command and request of the king of England, as fuller evidence of the foregoing matters.[40]

[37] Smalley, *Historians*, p. 178. See also p. 112 above.
[38] Notaries' *signa* are illustrated by Cheney, *Notaries*, plates 1–6 and by J. S. Purvis, *Notarial Signs from the York Archiepiscopal Records* (1957).
[39] *Anglo-Scottish Relations*, pp. 64, 72, 80.   [40] *ibid.* p. 72.

This formula illustrates the main elements of authenticity in a notarial instrument. The notary states his name and authority, he pens the document in his own hand, and he authenticates it further with a distinctive *signum*.

This Roman system of authorizing notaries was a relatively simple and normally effective way of coping with the problems of authenticating documents in the Middle Ages. Not every party to a document, even if he were able to read, could be expected to sign personally with a distinctively penned signature of his own, as in modern western culture, because writing on parchment was a business for specialists. Confining signing to professional scribes had other advantages. It imposed uniform standards in the production of documents and it restricted writers to a manageable number whose credentials could be checked. A notary signed documents with his *signum* in much the same way as a master mason marked the stones he cut before they were built into a permanent fabric. Despite these advantages, qualified notaries were not much used in England.

Scribes of English charters identify themselves only in a minority of cases, and the variety of ways in which they do so suggests that there was no uniform purpose or training behind such identifications.[41] Some writers were aware, however, that their name served as an additional form of attestation, as in the following two instances from the twelfth-century Mowbray charters:

> Witness, Dom Samson d'Aubigny, by whose hand this composition was made;
> And I, John the chaplain, have written this writ [*breve*] because I was present.[42]

The declared 'maker' of another twelfth-century charter, Walter the Chaplain, appended to his attestation a curse to 'confound in eternity whoever wishes to destroy' the charter.[43] On the other hand, the scribe of another charter from the mid-twelfth century, 'Herbert the clerk who wrote this well [*bene*]', was drawing attention, like Eadwine of Canterbury, to his ability as a scribal artist rather than his importance as a witness, assuming (that is) that *bene* is not a mistranscription of *breve* (a writ).[44] Even writers of royal writs do not usually identify themselves until the latter half of the thirteenth century, when the practice began in the Chancery of the scribe writing his surname in a corner of the document.[45] For private charters it never

---

[41] J. H. Hodson, 'Medieval Charters: the Last Witness', *Journal of the Society of Archivists* v (1974), p. 71.

[42] *Mowbray Charters* p. 72, no. 97; p. 245, no. 381. In no. 97 the word 'compositio' could refer to the 'agreement' itself rather than to its 'composition'. However, J. H. Hodson, 'Medieval Charters', p. 71, n. 3 cites another example of a charter's 'compositor' naming himself.

[43] *Northants. Facs*, plate xviii.

[44] J. H. Hodson, 'Medieval Charters', p. 71, n. 2. For Eadwine 'princeps scriptorum' see ch. 4, n. 2 above.

[45] 'in quolibet brevi debet scribentis nomen inbreviari', Fleta, bk. ii, ch. 13, p. 126. Chaplais, *Docs*, p. 52.

became the rule in medieval England that the writer had to identify himself.

Some scribes seemed ambitious to follow notarial practice, but because there was no uniform training nor regulations their efforts are haphazard. For example, in an Oxford charter of 1277 the last witness is a certain Philip 'the notary' (*notarius*) and the concluding formula of the charter is embellished in a way which may have been intended to serve as his individual *signum*.[46] Yet Philip does not consistently place his name last in the charters he writes and, although he was generally known as 'the notary' (as his family charters attest), his status was probably no different from that of another professional writer of charters in Oxford at the time, Richard of Eppewelle.[47] Neither Philip nor Richard was probably a notary in any Roman sense. Similarly a century earlier a Cheshire charter appears to be 'signed' by its last witness, William Legat, as his surname is written out in capitals and his forename in full, unlike those of the other witnesses.[48] Yet William's practice is inconsistent, as in another charter his 'signature' is less prominent, though still evident, and in a third it is written no differently from that of the other witnesses.[49] Another writer, Robert Carpenter, who was not a professional scribe at all but an aspiring freeman of the Isle of Wight active in Hampshire legal business, nevertheless followed notarial practice when he gave details of his work:

> In the 49th year of the reign of King Henry son of King John and 1265 *Anno Domini*, at Whitsun, the following page was written in St Edward's chapel at Westminster and extracted from the chronicles in a small roll by the hand of Robert Carpenter of Hareslade, and he wrote this here.[50]

Robert only needed to have added a *signum* to rival the precision of a professional notary, like Henry of Asti or John of Caen.

These examples suggest that English writers had the knowledge and capacity, and some even the wish, to draw up instruments like notaries, although they were not officially accredited by public authorities. Why English common law did not develop public notaries is a complex problem, which reflects the way literate modes developed. Once documents began to proliferate, English men of business needed reliable forms of written instruments just as Italian merchants did. This need was first acknowledged by the royal government in Hubert Walter's statute of 1194, which provided for the official writing of Jewish moneylenders' bonds in designated centres. The chirographers established by this

[46] *Cartulary of the Hospital of St John Baptist* ed. H. E. Salter, Oxford Historical S. LXVI (1914), I, plate xiv.

[47] Philip's family and property: *ibid.* nos 114, 127–36. Richard of Eppewelle: *ibid.* pp. vi–vii and plates xv, xvi.

[48] *Cheshire Facs*, no. 9.

[49] *Cheshire Facs*, nos. 6, 2. Cf. J. H. Hodson, 'Medieval Charters', p. 74.

[50] N. Denholm-Young, 'Robert Carpenter and the Provisions of Westminster', *EHR* L (1935), p. 22. Cf. C. A. F. Meekings, 'More about Robert Carpenter of Hareslade', *EHR* LXXII (1957), pp. 260–69.

statute served much the same purpose as notaries. For example, in a dispute in 1218 between a Jew, Samuel son of Aaron of Colchester, and a Christian, Sewal son of William de Spineto, about a bond made by Sewal's father, Sewal denied that the seal on the chirograph was his father's. Samuel insisted that the chirograph was genuine and appealed to the testimony of both Christians and Jews, 'who know the handwriting of the clerk who was chirographer when it was made'.[51] Samuel was therefore arguing that the handwriting of bonds could be attributed to individual scribes, whose script was a better mark of authenticity than a seal; for, as Samuel also argued, a knight might have more than one seal. Although this case was adjourned and no decision is on record, it shows that notarial principles were understood, at least by Jews who were literate and preferred to ratify documents with their signatures and not with seals. Samuel's private opinion may have been that seals were mere lumps of wax, whose use typified Christian ignorance and chicanery.

A more ambitious attempt at laying down standards for authenticating bonds was made by the statute of merchants in 1285.[52] This required all merchants (excluding Jews) to have their debts recorded before the mayor of London, or before similar designated authorities in other cities and towns. The test of distinctive handwriting was acknowledged, as bonds were to be enrolled 'in the hand of one of the [town] clerks who is known' and each bond was likewise to be written by a designated clerk. Yet the statute did not require the clerk to put either his name or his scribal signature on the bond like a notary. By 1285 English legal practice was probably too accustomed to seals to replace them by notarial *signa*. Nevertheless the possibility of forging seals was recognized by the statute, as royal seals were to be made in two interlocking parts, one part to be kept by the mayor and the other part by the authorized clerk. The statute of merchants thus came close to the essentials of notarial practice, while avoiding the name: bonds were to be written by authorized writers, enrolled in official registers and authenticated by a *signum* (in the form of a special seal) in the writer's charge. If these rules had been enforced and extended from money bonds to all written conveyances of property, England would have had official writers and registries on a scale superior to any in Europe.

The symbolism of seals and crosses

The reasons why England did not develop a uniform scribal system for authenticating documents seem to centre round the use of seals. Although medieval seals varied considerably in size, materials and design, they had two essential elements – a device or pictorial symbol in

[51] *Calendar of the Plea Rolls of the Exchequer of the Jews* ed. J. M. Rigg I (1905), p. 7, cf. p. 14. For another case involving distinctive handwriting see n. 97 below. For chirographers see p. 137 above.

[52] *Statutes*, p. 99 (amending the statute of Acton Burnell of 1283). See also ch. 2, n. 29 above.

the centre, such as a knight on horseback or a king seated in majesty (see plates I and V), and a legend or inscription around the circumference bearing the sealer's name. In combining a device or *signum* with the signatory's name, a seal was no different from a notarial form of authentication. Moreover, in one way a seal was more efficient than a notary's manual *signum*, as every seal in wax from the same matrix was identical.

In some ways sealing was as significant a step towards extending literacy as Gutenberg's subsequent invention of printing, which likewise depended on the mastery of metal engraving and casting. Because seals reproduced script, they enabled people to sign their names in an acceptable form without labour or skill. In the century *c.*1180–*c.*1280 the use of seals extended down the social scale from princes and barons through the gentry to smallholders and even serfs, as we have already seen.[53] In effect every possessor of a seal could be his own notary, as it enabled him to authenticate documents with his individual *signum* and name, even if he were unable to manipulate a pen. Like the practice of reading documents aloud, seals helped to bridge the gap between the literate and the non-literate. For the possessor of a seal the scribe who wrote the document, like the clerk who read it aloud, was a mere intermediary, an artisan of script. Perhaps English scribes were not required to identify themselves, nor to put their *signa* on the documents they wrote, because writers were of little significance. Instead, the donor and witnesses themselves authenticated the documents with their own *signa* in the ready-made form of seals.

Seals had the added advantage of appearing majestically old-fashioned to traditionalists (although seals in their medieval form were really an innovation), as they had originally been the prerogative of kings and princes. It had long been customary to symbolize a conveyance of property with a symbolic object, which was personally associated with the donor. Similarly a messenger might be given a finger ring, which the recipient could recognize as belonging to the sender. Once conveyances began to be made or messages to be sent in greater numbers, some method of reproducing authenticating objects was required, if the custom were to continue. From this point of view, seals in wax were standardized and massproduced symbolic objects.

Seals perpetuated pre-literate custom in an automated and literate form and thus prevented documentary proof from being followed through to the ultimate point of dispensing with symbolic objects altogether. To those who were not familiar with documents, seals looked as if they had a better chance of surviving the rigours of time than a piece of parchment, although in fact this opinion was mistaken. The seal was a relic, which could be seen and touched in order to obtain from it that authentic view and feel of a donor's wishes which no writing could adequately convey. Many early seals were made from Graeco-Roman gem stones, which were valued as talismans associating their medieval

---

[53] See pp. 35–6 and p. 184 above.

users with the great and mysterious men of antiquity.[54] The seal was also a more convincing sign than a notary's *signum* because the notary was a mere hired scrivener, whereas the seal emanated from the donor himself as its matrix was kept either on his person or among his treasure. Hence phrases soon became commonplace in charters explaining that the seal gave dignity and strength to the document. The two examples which follow are typical of thousands:

> And so that this gift of mine may be permanent, stable and unshaken, I have esteemed it worthy to be strengthened with my seal.
> And so that this gift and grant of mine and confirmation of my charter may last in perpetuity, I have reinforced the present writing with the impress of my seal.[55]

Although such phrases soon become common form, their variety suggests that abstract documentary proof without the physical reinforcement of symbolic objects was widely and deeply felt to be inadequate.

Competing with the seal, as a sign of authenticity convincing to non-literates, was the cross. Although many crosses on charters were made by the signatories themselves, the cross was valued not primarily as a distinctive autograph, since it was easy to forge, but because it was the most sacred of symbols. In some twelfth-century charters it is evidently preferred to a seal, or considered no less important. Charters are quite common which bear a cross, either that of a signatory or as a symbol on its own, together with a seal (see plate I).[56] The purpose of the cross is made explicit in a charter of Hugh earl of Chester, who died in 1101:

> I, Earl Hugh, and my barons have confirmed all these things before Archbishop Anselm not only by my seal but also by the seal of Almighty God, that is the sign of the Holy Cross, so that each of us makes a sign in the form of a cross with his own hand as evidence for posterity.[57]

The purpose of signing with a cross was not necessarily therefore because the signatory was illiterate, but because of its symbolism. The sacredness of the cross was evoked by the sign, whether it was made on the parchment or across the head and shoulders with the hand. As William the Conqueror declared in one charter, 'I hand over this testament dedicated with the sign of the Holy Cross.'[58] Historically minded

[54] A. B. Tonnochy, *Catalogue of British Seal Dies in the British Museum* (1952), p. xviii. G. Henderson, 'Romance and Politics on Some Medieval English Seals', *Art History* I (1978), p. 27.

[55] *Luffield Priory Charters* ed. G. R. Elvey, part i, Buckinghamshire Record S. xv (1968) or Northamptonshire Record S. xxii (1968), p. 98, no. 98; p. 75, no. 72.

[56] *BM Facs*, no. 16. *Oxford Facs*, no. 9.

[57] *Monasticon* ii, p. 386.

[58] Orderic, bk. vi, ch. 5, vol. iii, p. 238. Galbraith, 'Literacy', pp. 217–21 provides an introduction to signing with a cross.

monks were aware that seals, compared with the cross, were a recent secular innovation. Thus the Ramsey chronicler attributed the introduction of these 'two-faced images' to the growth of malice and cunning, while Matthew Paris compared unfavourably the new fashion of appending a seal to a document with the old custom of marking charters with golden crosses drawn by the hands of kings.[59] The St Albans' charter which Matthew had in mind, however, allegedly signed by King Offa, was probably a forgery as Anglo-Saxon charters were not autographed by their signatories.

As crosses were sometimes used by William the Conqueror and his Normans in the eleventh century (see plate I) and by prelates throughout the twelfth, for example in the professions of obedience to the archbishops of Canterbury,[60] it is at first sight surprising that seals came to be preferred, since they derived no divine sanction from their form. Papal documents set an example in continuing to use an elaborated form of the cross (the *rota*) as part of the personal signature of the pope, although it is true that they were reinforced by a seal (the *bulla*) as well. Thus Hugh the Chanter describes a privilege for York being signed by the pope and cardinals in 1120 and he reports a debate about the need for *bullae* in 1123.[61] The English kings of the twelfth century, on the other hand, dispensed with autographs and came to rely primarily on seals for authenticating documents at the very time that they were growing personally more literate and more generally aware of the canonical procedures being established in Mediterranean Europe.

One explanation for this paradox may be that seals were better suited to non-literates, because they were visible and tangible objects, as has already been argued. The papacy issued documents primarily for clerics who could read, whereas the English government at first was sending out writs to local officials who were only on the threshold of literacy. Another possibility is that Henry I's government became so busy that it preferred seals to any form of monogram made with a pen because sealing was an automatic process. Although the papacy actually produced more documents than the English government, they tended to be charters and privileges which were sought by and paid for by the beneficiaries. The papal *curia* was consequently prepared to have a large staff authenticating documents by hand as well as with the *bulla*. Henry I's Exchequer, by contrast, from which English bureaucracy developed, used writing chiefly for its own administrative purposes. It needed to authenticate thousands of written instructions to local officials each year. Like printing, sealing reproduced script in a repeatable series, and hence it was well suited to the proliferation of documents by the royal bureaucracy. The tenfold increase in the weight of sealing wax

[59] *Ramsey*, p. 65. *Gesta Abbatum Monasterii S. Albani* ed. H. T. Riley, RS XXVIII (1867), I, p. 151.

[60] *Canterbury Professions* ed. M. Richter, Canterbury & York S. LXVII (1973), pp. 30 ff. Bishops' charters, however, are usually authenticated by seals, Cheney, *Chanceries*, pp. 46–7.

[61] *The History of the Church of York* ed. C. H. Johnson (1961), pp. 90, 115. Papal signatures are discussed by Cheney, *Texts & Studies*, pp. 52ff.

used by the Chancery in Henry III's reign alone is an indication of the accelerating pace.[62]

Sealing was the first step towards the automation of writing. Although the writing process itself was not automated until the invention of printing, sealing resolved the problem which was prior to that of reproducing books for the literate public. Before being offered printed books, the public had to be persuaded of the authenticity of writing itself. Sealing resolved this problem in terms which were acceptable both to chanceries and to non-literates. The seal was the harbinger of literacy, as it was the device which brought literate modes even into remote villages, particularly in the form of taxation demands from the Exchequer sealed with the hated green wax. Sealing was a labour-saving technology, both at the exalted level of the royal Chancery and at the humble level of the peasant who could sign his name with his seal without being able to write. In the formation of a literate mentality seals were indeed 'two-faced images': they looked back to charms and memorized symbolic objects and forward to the automation of writing.

Forging documents

Although it has long been known that many early medieval documents (particularly monastic charters) are forgeries, the connexion between forgery and the growth of literacy has not been extensively explored. In England the greatest period for forging documents was the century after the Norman Conquest, when the old houses of Black monks had to convince the incomers of their ancient dignities and privileges. 'No document coming from such centres of proved fabrication as Westminster, Evesham, Winchester cathedral, Chertsey and Malmesbury should be accepted at its face value without close examination.'[63] This list of monasteries is cited by F. M. Stenton in his summary of the critical work of W. H. Stevenson at the beginning of this century. Many more centres of proved fabrication could now be added to this list, such as Christ Church and St Augustine's abbey at Canterbury and Gloucester and Ramsey abbeys. Nor was the Norman Conquest the root cause of the problem, since houses founded after the Conquest, notably Battle abbey, likewise forged audacious title-deeds.[64] Even the estimate made by C. N. L. Brooke, that about 17 out of 30 pre-Conquest monastic houses 'tolerated forgery on a fair scale', may be an under-assessment.[65] Recent research may ultimately lead to the conclusion that in England in the century after the Norman Conquest forgery of charters was the rule rather than the exception.

The extent of forgeries can be approximately gauged by the following figures, which estimate the number of authentic documents extant in

[62] See pp. 43, 58–9 above.
[63] F. M. Stenton, *The Latin Charters of the Anglo-Saxon Period* (1955), p. 11.
[64] The forgeries were made for Battle's lawsuit *v.* Chichester in 1154–7: *Battle*, pp. 71–104. H. W. C. Davis, 'The Chronicle of Battle Abbey', *EHR* XXIX (1914), pp. 431–3. E. Searle, *Lordship and Community: Battle Abbey and its Banlieu* (1974), pp. 29ff.
[65] *Gilbert Foliot and his Letters* (1965), pp. 128–9.

the name of Edward the Confessor (1042–66).[66] In the greatest monastic houses documents of his were specially valued because William the Conqueror claimed to be his lawful successor.

Charters of Edward the Confessor

Total extant	164	100
Authentic	64	39%
Undecided	56	34%
Spurious	44	27%

These figures are subject to every kind of qualification because opinions will always differ about what makes a document authentic. Many of the problematical charters about which scholars are undecided may never be satisfactorily resolved. Allowing, however, for all such qualifications and for the possibility that Edward the Confessor's writs were forged more than those of any other king, the conclusion to draw is that most documents extant in his name are of doubtful authenticity. Medieval forgeries are extraordinarily difficult to evaluate because a document like a charter of Edward the Confessor may be spurious, in the sense that it was written after his death, and yet be accurate in the essentials of the information it records. Forged charters were often based on earlier authentic documents or on good oral traditions. The purpose of forgery was to produce a record in a form which was acceptable, particularly in courts of law, at the time it was made. Forgery was necessary because contemporaries had no historical sense. A good oral tradition or an authentic charter of an early Anglo-Saxon king might be rejected by a court of law because it seemed strange, whereas a forged charter would be acceptable because it suited contemporary notions of what an ancient charter should be like.

Forgers recreated the past in an acceptable literate form. They are best understood not as occasional deviants on the peripheries of legal practice, but as experts entrenched at the centre of literary and intellectual culture in the twelfth century. The most influential historical writer of the century, Geoffrey of Monmouth, probably invented most of the *History of the Kings of Britain* (written in c.1136), although scholarly opinion will always differ about that.[67] Similarly, in order to give verisimilitude to the Arthurian legend which Geoffrey had made popular, Glastonbury abbey in 1191 exhumed the bodies of King Arthur and Queen Guinevere. Here again, scholars differ as to whether this was a deliberately staged forgery or a genuine discovery of ancient tombs.[68] Judging by some other forgeries of the time, the Glastonbury monks would certainly have been capable of creating such an ambitious

[66] The figures have been estimated by me from P. H. Sawyer, *Anglo-Saxon Charters* (1968), pp. 298–343.

[67] C. N. L. Brooke, 'Geoffrey of Monmouth as a Historian' in *Church and Government in the Middle Ages* ed. C. N. L. Brooke *et al.* (1976), is a recent introduction.

[68] A. Gransden, 'The Growth of Glastonbury Traditions and Legends', *Journal of Ecclesiastical History* XXVII (1976), p. 352, reasserts that the exhumation was 'bogus, a spectacle put on for the credulous public', whereas L. Alcock, *Arthur's Britain* (1971), pp. 73–80 argues that the exhumation has authentic features.

deception. Forgery succeeded because it was ordered or condoned by the greatest scholars, prelates and administrators. Walter abbot of Battle, who was responsible for the Battle forgeries, was the brother of Richard de Lucy, Henry II's chief justiciar, and Walter presumably acted with his brother's knowledge.[69] The former head of Henry I's writing office, Robert de Sigillo, seems to have been responsible for forging a royal charter for Reading abbey after he became a monk there.[70] Among scholars responsible for forgeries were Osbert de Clare, prior of Westminster, who created charters of Edward the Confessor in Stephen's reign, and Gilbert Foliot, who was an accessory to forgery when abbot of Gloucester.[71]

Those monastic writers, who are most insistent in the prologues to their works on the importance of telling the truth, are often those who were involved in fabricating charters. Thus Eadmer of Canterbury, who affirmed 'that it is a shocking thing for anyone knowingly to write what is false in sacred histories, for the soul of the writer is slain every time they are read or listened to', was an accessory to the Canterbury forgeries in 1121–2.[72] Similarly 'it is hard to exonerate William of Malmesbury from the charge of knowingly including forged material in his history', despite his precocious concern with evaluating evidence.[73] In general, twelfth-century writers protest too much about their veracity to inspire confidence. For example, the compiler of Ramsey abbey's *Book of Benefactors* insists that his purpose is to translate charters from Old English into Latin, so that the Normans will understand them, and also to retain the record of oral gifts in the memory of writing 'so that all falsehood and controversy may be removed'.[74] Yet two of the royal charters he cites were certainly forged, although it is possible that the compiler himself was ignorant of this.[75]

The distinction between fact and fiction was sometimes so finely drawn by twelfth-century writers as to be impossible to see. Occasionally authors may have misled themselves as well as their readers. Not only monastic chroniclers but literary historians, like Geoffrey of Monmouth, and composers of vernacular romances insisted that their works derived from ancient books. Thus the Anglo-Norman poet, Hue de Rotelande (writing in *c*.1180), assures his audience that his story of *Ipomedon* comes from a Latin text, although he is surprised that 'those wise clerks who understand many languages have not put it in memory.'[76] Hue's audience were presumably intended to appreciate the irony of referring to the authority of a Latin text which probably did not exist. Likewise in *Ipomedon* Hue is able to describe for his secular audience

[69] See n. 64 above.　　　[70] See n. 81 below.

[71] For Osbert see P. Chaplais, 'The Original Charters of Herbert and Gervase Abbots of Westminster' in *MM for Stenton*, pp. 91–5. For Gilbert see Morey and Brooke, *Gilbert Foliot*, pp. 124–7.

[72] Eadmer, *Vita*, p. 149. See also ch. 5, nn. 11, 35 above.

[73] Gransden, *Historical Writing*, pp. 177–8.

[74] *Ramsey*, pp. 161, 243. See also ch. 5, n. 52 above.

[75] Sawyer, *Anglo-Saxon Charters*, nos. 798, 1109.

[76] Ed. E. Köbling (Breslau, 1889), lines 21–4. Legge, *Anglo-Norman*, p. 95.

the writer's craft with greater frankness than a self-righteous monk like Eadmer can:

> Now understand this very well, my lords,
> Hue says that he never tells a lie in it,
> Well, hardly ever, and then not much;
> No one can keep himself entirely from it.[77]

To a modern reader Hue do Rotlande is a composer of creative literature, a writer of fiction or romance, who therefore has no need to excuse himself for telling untruths to his audience. Hue himself, however, apparently felt that some explanation was required, perhaps because poetic licence or unadorned fiction was difficult for his 'lords' to accept, particularly when authors were just developing into writers on their own account instead of being reciters of traditional tales. Unlike Hue, a monastic chronicler or composer of charters is expected by a modern reader to record the literal truth, and furthermore the chronicler will often assure the reader in his prologue that this is precisely what he intends to do. Nevertheless the distinction between fact and fiction in writing, which leads the modern reader to think of Walter abbot of Battle or Osbert de Clare as forgers and Hue de Rotelande as an entertaining romancer, would not have been as sharp to medieval people, although they were very conscious of the moral difference between truth and falsehood and of the penalties, both material and spiritual, for fabricating seals or documents.

The fundamental difficulty was that literate criteria for making or criticizing documents had not usually been applied in the first place. Even the English royal government, which was a pioneer of chancery procedure, did not constistently date its charters until Richard I's reign and began to keep regular copies of them only in John's reign. Nor was keeping registers of documents much use unless they could readily be referred to. We have already seen that neither Henry III's government nor Edward I's had foolproof means of searching their own rolls; Edward I's Chancery was deceived by a forged charter of Richard I even though an authentic copy was in the government's possession.[78] Up to Henry II's reign the old practice had continued of the royal seal being affixed to documents written by the beneficiaries' scribes (see plate III), although gradually this practice became the exception rather than the rule.[79] From the king's point of view, the procedure whereby a royal officer fixed the royal *signum* to a writing made by the beneficiary was essentially oral and manual rather than literate. The document was presumably read out loud to the king or his delegate, perhaps only in a translated and summarized form, and then authenticated by the touch of the seal. In these circumstances the difference between a document which had received the royal touch and one which had not, between 'authentic' and 'forged' by modern criteria, was a fine one.

[77] *ibid.* lines 7173–6. Legge, *Anglo-Norman*, p. 94.
[78] Searches of the rolls are discussed above at ch. 2, nn. 70–73 and ch. 5, nn. 118–21. Chertsey abbey deceived Edward I with a charter of Richard I: see ch. 5, nn. 124–5 above.
[79] See ch. 2, nn. 47–8 above.

Often documents were produced in duplicate or triplicate for greater security, and occasionally alternative texts seem to have been prepared by the beneficiary, probably in the hope that the seal would be affixed to the more advantageous one. This hypothesis seems the most plausible explanation for the existence of two parallel charters in King Stephen's name, both dated Christmas Day (1139) and written by the same scribe, who had probably been a clerk of Roger bishop of Salisbury, the chief justiciar.[80] As Roger had just died, the purpose of the charters was presumably to ensure that Salisbury cathedral retained the property they concerned. Both charters quitclaim royal rights in lands and churches, which Roger had given to Salisbury, but the second charter adds that King Stephen had given 10 pounds worth of his own demesne lands as well; the place in which this demesne lies is left blank. H. A. Cronne, who published these two charters (though with a different explanation), has drawn attention also to a charter in King Stephen's name for Reading abbey, which is written by a known royal scribe although it bears a forged seal.[81] He suggests that Robert de Sigillo, who had been the master of Henry I's *scriptorium* and had become a monk at Reading, may have been behind this forgery. These instances show that documents might be unauthentic even when they were written by official scribes. Indeed, to think of writs produced by the royal Chancery as official and other documents bearing the royal seal as unofficial is an anachronism until the last decade of the twelfth century. Without defined standards of authenticity, there could be no definite criteria for distinguishing forgeries from authentic documents.

The apparently careless attitude of even the king's government towards its written *acta* was not a product merely of incompetent administration, nor of the special circumstances of Stephen's reign when so many forgeries seem to have been made. Stricter procedures were not followed because written record itself was unfamiliar and abnormal outside a small circle of royal officers and old monastic houses. Despite the growth of the Exchequer and the proliferation of writs, the emphasis in royal government remained largely oral until Henry II's reign at least. Henry himself was an energetic legislator, yet even his decrees were not written down in authoritative and officially authentic statutes. They seem to have been promulgated orally and then noted haphazardly by chroniclers. There was no *Liber Augustalis* of the common law. This lack of a *jus scriptum* so troubled the author of *Glanvill* (writing at the very end of Henry II's reign), who wished to harmonize his knowledge of English and Roman law, that he felt obliged to begin by arguing that it is not absurd to speak of English 'laws' even though they are unwritten because 'what pleases the prince has the force of law.'[82] With this nod towards Roman principle, the author then hopes that it will not be considered presumptuous on his part, 'but rather very useful for most people and highly necessary to aid the memory', if he commits at least the commonest rules of the king's court to writing.[83]

---

[80] *RRA-N* IV (1969), p. 6 and plates xlviii, xlix.
[81] *ibid.* pp. 5–6 and plate x.   [82] Glanvill, p. 2.   [83] *ibid.* p. 3.

Like the author of *Glanvill*, monastic charter makers and chroniclers had to set about filling the gaps and correcting the anomalies in written record which kings and other past benefactors appeared to have negligently left. It was the responsibility of the beneficiaries and not of the donor to see that adequate documents were supplied. In the non-literate past people had been accustomed to the flexibility of speech and memory and they applied similar criteria at first to written record. A charter was inaccurate and should be corrected if it failed to give the beneficiary a privilege which the author had obviously intended it to have, had he still been alive to express his wishes. Writing, or the lack of it, should not be allowed to annul or invalidate previous pious gifts. From this point of view 'forgery' is an inappropriate term to apply to renewals of evidence which were intended to ensure that a monastic house was adequately provided with charters to defend its patrons and saints against rivals. Even a charter which a modern critic would consider perfectly genuine did not record the complete and precise wishes of the donor himself, as these had been expressed orally and physically by oaths and symbolic gestures at a public ceremony in the presence of witnesses and not by any form of writing. The charter could not record the donor's exact words, because it was written in Latin, and furthermore it was often expressed in the past tense – 'Know that I, A of B, have given . . .' – which made it clear that it was an afterthought.[84]

In these circumstances the distinction between a 'genuine' and a 'forged' charter depended on what interval of time between giving and writing, and what mark of approval by the donor, was generally considered allowable. To a modern critic a charter of Edward the Confessor, if written by Osbert de Clare seventy years or more after the king's death and sealed with a new seal, is a forgery. To Osbert, on the other hand, who composed a life of the Confessor and was pressing for his recognition as a saint, Edward was immortalized by his sanctity and still lived in the church where his relics were preserved. In his capacity as prior of Westminster, Osbert may have thought that writing a charter in the dead king's name was essentially no different from writing on behalf of a contemporary ruler. Osbert was fulfilling Edward's pious intentions and assuring him his place in heaven by restoring the evidence of his endowments. Discussing Osbert's work, Brooke comments:

> There had been forgery in England before the Conquest, and it may even be the accidents of survival which lead us to suppose the twelfth century to be its golden age. Yet there is clearly a sense in which the spread of literacy and of written instruments of land tenure made the eleventh and twelfth centuries, in a special sense, *the period of the shift from oral to written testimony*. The opportunities, the temptations, and the urgent calls of duty in such a period were quite exceptional.[85]

[84] See p. 208 above.
[85] 'Approaches to Medieval Forgery', *Medieval Church and Society* (1971), p. 115 (my emphasis).

Galbraith, referring to 'this slow evolution from oral to written government', made a comparable observation twenty years earlier: 'Written evidence was still the exception rather than the rule, and, as a novelty, was apt to be accepted without very close scrutiny. It is scarcely surprising, then, to find that the twelfth century was the golden age of forgery.'[86] The forgery or renewal of documents was essentially a product of the movement from memory to written record and is best understood in that context.

In theory it would have been as easy to eliminate forgeries as to produce charters which were uniformly dated and signed. Reliable cirteria for detecting forgeries had been developed by canon lawyers in Italy, just as Roman law prescribed rules for the production of notarially authenticated instruments. The *summa* (dating from the last quarter of the twelfth century) of the best canonical authority on forgeries, Huguccio, was known in England. He recommended that, where there was doubt about the authenticity of a decretal, resort should be had first of all to the papal registers.[87] If the document were not found there, other tests should be applied regarding the style and substance of the text and the physical characteristics of the parchment, the *bulla* and its attaching thread. In short, the document should be examined as a whole from as many aspects as possible. These were sound rules, which were subsequently promulgated generally by Innocent III, who had been Huguccio's pupil at Bologna.[88]

Nevertheless the gulf between theory and practice was enormous, because these rules were as difficult to enforce as those governing the drawing up of written instruments. When discussing forgery, the English canonist glossators were obliged to ignore Huguccio's advice to resort first of all to registers, presumably because there were no systematic registers of English ecclesiastical documents. Instead, they recommended testing forgeries by the customary oral method of swearing oaths and producing witnesses.[89] In other words, the validity of documents was primarily assessed by the pre-literate wager of law and not by tests using writing.

Similarly Innocent III himself, when he came to practice as distinct from laying down rules, could be as easily deceived by a forged papal bull as anyone else. Thomas of Marlborough, abbot of Evesham (1229–36), gives a first-hand account of how Evesham forgers deceived Innocent and his cardinals in a case in the Roman *curia* in 1205.[90] Thomas was at that time Evesham's principal advocate in its claim to be exempt from the jurisdiction of the bishop of Worcester. Among other documents adduced as evidence by Thomas were two bulls in the name of Constantine I, who had been pope from 708 to 715. Worcester counter-claimed that these documents were forgeries 'in parchment and

---

[86] *Studies*, pp. 48–9.   [87] Duggan, *Decretals*, p. 41, n. 1.
[88] *ibid.* p. 41, n. 2. Brooke, 'Approaches to Medieval Forgery', p. 108, n. 18.
[89] Duggan, *Decretals*, p. 42.
[90] *Chronicon Abbatiae de Evesham* ed. W. D. Macray, RS xxix (1863), pp. 160–61. R. L. Poole, *Lectures on the History of the Papal Chancery* (1915), pp. 147–9.

script, thread and *bulla*' and stated that privileges of Constantine I were entirely unknown in England.[91] So the bulls were handed to the pope, who 'felt them with his own hands and pulled on the *bulla* and the parchment to see if he could separate the *bulla* from the thread, and he examined them most diligently.' He then passed them round the circle of cardinals, while Thomas admits to being worried about the outcome. However, when the bulls were passed back to the pope, he held the documents up and magisterially pronounced: 'Privileges of this sort, which are unknown to you, are well known to us, and they cannot be forged. These are genuine.' Although Thomas perhaps exaggerated the forthrightness of Innocent's opinion, there is no reason to doubt the substance of his story. The papal judgment in Evesham's favour encouraged Thomas to copy the bulls of Constantine I, which had released Evesham from the 'Egyptian slavery' of Worcester, into his chronicle for future reference.[92] The copies demonstrate that the bulls were undoubtedly forged and, as Thomas 'improved' Evesham's chronicle as well to suit the dispute with Worcester,[93] it is likely that he had played a major part in deceiving the pope.

This case suggests that, although by 1200 the papal *curia* had developed rules for detecting forgeries of recent decretals, it had no effective means of checking documents which claimed to be hundreds of years old. By fingering the parchment and pulling the thread, Innocent III was applying elementary physical tests and not the canons of careful textual criticism which would have revealed the bulls to be forgeries. But it would be anachronistic to expect even Innocent III to have shown a sharper awareness or a deeper understanding of the development of papal documents than he did in this case. Scientific historical criticism was first applied to early papal documents by Renaissance humanists of the fifteenth century and it revealed that the pope's own title-deeds, the Donation of Constantine, were themselves forgeries. Of course Innocent III was highly educated and learned in law, yet he and his cardinals were not accustomed to the careful scrutiny of documents.[94] Their training in the schools had been predominantly oral in character and caused them to prefer touch, speech and hearing to intensive literate study.

Moreover, neither the papal *curia* nor lesser courts had anything to gain by scrutinizing forged charters with strict regularity. Decisions had to be reached in cases even when both parties produced forged documents. Conventions seem to have existed among the higher clergy within which forgery, while not being openly approved of or acknowledged, was at least tolerated. Every ruler in Europe, from the pope downwards, had suspect title-deeds if historically authentic writ-

[91] 'nam carta et stylus, filum et bulla', *Chronicon Abbatiae de Evesham*, p. 160. For variations on this phrase see Duggan, *Decretals*, p. 41, n. 2.

[92] *Chronicon Abbatiae de Evesham*, pp. 171–3.

[93] Gransden, *Historical Writing*, pp. 112, 519.

[94] Gerald of Wales shows Innocent III scrutinizing a register in an exceptional instance, Poole, *Lectures on the History of the Papal Chancery*, pp. 150–51, 194–6. But Gerald's story also shows that Innocent was more accustomed to listening to a text than to reading it for himself: see ch. 8, nn. 57–8 above.

ings were to become the yardstick of authority. Medieval criticism of charters was quite sophisticated compared with general standards of historical criticism. The fictions or half-truths of Geoffrey of Monmouth and other creators of political myths were often accepted as historically reliable. Thus Geoffrey's *History of the Kings of Britain* was used by Edward I (though admittedly as an afterthought) in his letter to Boniface VIII in 1301, setting out the precedents for English overlordship in Scotland going back to the days of the prophets, Eli and Samuel, and the fall of Troy.[95] Nor in their reply did the Scots deny the historicity of such myths, but only the English interpretation of the evidence.[96] Although by 1300 governments and owners of property had begun to use documents on a scale unprecedented since the fall of the Roman empire, they still approached the past through hearsay and myth.

This is not to suggest that literate standards of documentation were unknown, but rather that they could not be uniformly or readily applied to particular cases, because literate ways of doing business were still too novel. In exceptional cases, where the opposing parties were unequally matched and unprotected by clerical conventions, forgery could be systematically revealed. Thus Galbraith has described a case in 1220 in the Jewish Exchequer where a bond attributed to the prior of Dunstable was shown to be a forgery on numerous counts – its unusual form of date, ungrammatical Latin, unauthorized handwriting, false chronology and peculiar physical condition (it had been washed and whitened).[97] Nevertheless it is a mistake to conclude that this case shows how skilful the English courts had become in the detection of forgery, as these points of criticism were made not by the court but by the plaintiff, Master Richard de Morins, the prior of Dunstable, who was a canonist and a graduate of Bologna.[98] He was able for once to put legal theory into practice because his opponent was a Jew and the bond was evidently an amateur forgery. Had Richard been facing an opponent of his own expertise and status, like Thomas of Marlborough, he might have found that his allegations of forgery received no more sympathetic a hearing than Innocent III had given to Worcester in its plea against Evesham. Successful forgery was the business of monks and *magistri*; amateurs, still less Jews, were ill advised to try it.

The Dunstable case, like the exceptional instances (which have already been discussed) of documents being dated with simplicity and consistency or of English scribes authenticating charters with the precision of Roman notaries, shows that principles of good documentary procedure were known to experts. The problem lay in putting academic theory into general practice. Illiterate magnates were just as likely to distrust genuine charters as to be suspicious of forged ones. Not even the

---

[95] *Anglo-Scottish Relations*, pp. 97ff. Cf. also Edward I's references to arms and armour in this letter, ch. 1, nn. 61–4 above.

[96] *ibid.* pp. 113ff.

[97] Galbraith, *Studies*, pp. 51–2. *Select Pleas etc. of the Exchequer of the Jews* ed. J. M. Rigg, SS xv (1901), pp. 4–5. *Annales Monastici* iii, p. 66. (These references amend Galbraith's.)

[98] Cheney, *Texts & Studies*, p. 221.

greatest experts, like Innocent III or Edward I's Chancery officials, could be relied upon to detect forgeries. The monks who had the temerity or desperation to deceive them must have learned that forgery was the best course, provided it was competently done.

In this bewildering world, where holy men forged documents and writers of fiction were concerned to tell the literal truth, it may seem surprising that written record ever got a good name at all or established itself as a reliable form of communication. Perhaps it did so not for the practical and progressive reasons which a modern literate would expect, but because of the prestige which writing had acquired in the centuries before the Norman Conquest from its use by monks in liturgical books. The Gospel book placed on the altar had been used as a symbol of conveyance by laymen long before they became accustomed to charters. Although it is true that monks were commonly forgers, they compensated for this by imbuing script with sacred associations. All writers of the twelfth century – whether forgers, romancers, or simple scribes – drew on this rich reserve of awe and faith.

Faith was needed because most twelfth-century documents, whether forged or not, were not trustworthy in the strict sense of that word, as they did not state precisely when they had been written nor were they penned by authorized and professionally trained scribes. Effective precautions against fraud were not taken because they demanded extensive professionalism and because writings seem to have been thought of at first as subsidiary aids to traditional memorizing procedures and not as replacements of them. A new technology usually adapts itself at first to an existing one, camouflaging itself in the old forms and not immediately realizing its potential. By the thirteenth century documentary proof had become more familiar and routine. Nevertheless throughout the Middle Ages many common forms of document, particularly charters for conveyances of property, retained in their physical format and set phraseology numerous reminders that they had been developed in an earlier period when more reliance had been put on living memory than on parchment.

10

Practical literacy

The theme of this book has been the growth of literacy for practical purposes. Laymen became more literate in order to cope with written business, initially in England with writs from the royal government demanding information or money. Knights involved in county business, and even peasants who acted as manorial reeves, needed to be able to read the warrants presented to them and to keep records themselves in order to make adequate answers. According to the *Anglo-Saxon Chronicle* William the Conqueror in the Domesday survey had made a list of every ox and cow and pig in the land;[1] two centuries later bailiffs were recommended to record in writing in the autumn of the year each tool and horseshoe and everything that remained on the manor, great and small.[2] Although these schemes were too ambitious and can never have reached the point of listing every person, animal and thing in up-to-date inventories, the idea of such lists was a continuing aspiration between William the Conqueror's Domesday Book and the series of inquests undertaken by Edward I's government which culminated – and collapsed under their own weight – in the *quo warranto* proceedings.

The first part of this book, 'The Making of Records', has described the proliferation of business documents and the development of skills to produce them and of archives to make them of lasting use. Judging by documents now extant, the output of the royal government increased more than tenfold in the century spanning the reigns of William the Conqueror and Henry II (see the graph at p. 44). In the thirteenth century this geometric progression continued, with the royal Chancery using 3·63 lb of sealing wax per week in the late 1220s and 31·9 lb by the late 1260s (see the table at p. 43).

Such increases necessitated the creation of a bureaucracy, which can be seen in embryo in Fitz Neal's *Dialogue of the Exchequer* (written in c.1179). During the years 1193–1205 when Hubert Walter dominated the royal administration, written record was effectively extended to nearly every sphere of government, both central and local. Hubert Walter's achievement was to put theory into practice. It is possible that Chancery rolls, plea rolls, feet of fines, Jewish *arche* and the rest had been thought of before he appeared on the scene; but he first gave them

[1] See ch. 1, n. 26 above.   [2] See ch. 2, n. 6 above.

continuing life. His influence on county and village record-making was as important as his effectiveness at the centre, although local records took another century before they were established as a norm. By Edward I's reign serfs possessed seals to sign their names and they recorded their property transactions in writing. Thus the *nativi* – the natives, naifs, villeins or serfs – who had thought Domesday Book to be the Last Judgment (according to Fitz Neal in the twelfth century)[3] had charters of their own (the *Cartae Nativorum*) by the 1300s.[4]

The types of writing which were done became increasingly more practical. The sacred Scriptures, which had dominated literate culture before 1066, still stood in pride of place of course, but they were surrounded and overlaid from the twelfth century onwards by the glosses and summaries of the schoolmen. The scholastic *summa*, 'a concise encyclopedia of instances',[5] was intended as a shortcut through the mass of words for the 'many who are in a hurry and the many who are unlearned'.[6] The written statements of individuals likewise became more immediately practical in purpose and format. Although solemn charters (which had often been written by monastic beneficiaries after the event) were still produced, less portentous and more sophisticated forms of document increased in numbers. Sealed chirographs in particular emphasized the equal status of the two contracting parties and required both of them, together with their witnesses, to participate with their seals in the making of the written instrument. Similarly in the late twelfth century letters, in the modern sense of missives sent by one individual to convey confidential information to another, came into more general use. Previously letters had usually been either writs patent, which were open declarations or title-deeds, or 'literature' composed by rhetoricians and preachers.[7]

Gradually too the idea of accumulating memoranda for future reference became established, first with the pipe and plea rolls of the king's court and then with comparable documents produced by bishops, barons and boroughs. By the 1260s the countess of Leicester, and presumably other great housekeepers also, were keeping diaries of their daily expenditure (see plate XI).[8] At a similar date records begin in the Year Books which purport to record evey word spoken by learned counsel and judges in royal courts.[9] Even the art of speech itself was taught in books of hypothetical dialogues (like the *Court Baron*) for students of law and estate management.[10]

The traditions and techniques of monastic writing, which had been created to produce illuminated liturgical manuscripts, had to be adapted to the utilitarian demands made on them by secular writs and rolls. It was relatively easy to economize on materials by omitting coloured inks and using thinner and smaller pieces of parchment. Although most business documents continued to have enlarged initial

[3] See ch. 1, n. 27 above.
[4] See ch. 2, nn. 18–21 above.
[5] See ch. 3, n. 114 above.
[6] See ch. 3, n. 118 above.
[7] See ch. 3, nn. 31–5 above.
[8] See pp. 71–2 above.
[9] See ch. 3, n. 73 above.
[10] See ch. 8, n. 113 above.

letters and some still had rubrics and even illustrations (see plate XVIII), they were generally on a far less lavish scale than Gospel books.[11] Even the Scriptures themselves were presented in cheaper and more access-ible formats. Orm, who wrote his Gospel homilies or *Ormulum* with his own hand in *c.*1200, seems to have cared little about its untidy and unprofessional appearance.[12] As an Augustinian canon he exemplified the new ideal of simplicity in spreading the Gospel, instead of treasur-ing it in precious manuscripts as the Black monks did. Illuminated manuscripts themselves began to be produced in more economical formats so that they could be put in the pocket or held in the hands while at prayer.[13] Likewise students' and lawyers' textbooks of the thirteenth century use smaller and more economical formats (see plate XVI).[14]

Even more pressing than the need to economize on parchment and pigments was the need to save the scribe's time, as the application of his skill was the most expensive element in the production of documents. To meet this need secular scribes learned to write faster in cursive hands instead of the traditional monastic book hands. Contrary to former paleographical teaching, cursive script is not evidence of special train-ing in chanceries but of 'a common pressure of urgent business'.[15] Hence in the thirteenth century cursive scripts began to be used for writing books as well as writs and rolls (see plate XVII). The new pressures of secular business, as contrasted with the studied calm of the monastic tradition, are most strikingly conveyed in the contrast between royal writs in cursive hands and liturgical manuscripts in book hands (com-pare plates IV and XIV). The royal administration even automated writ-ing, at least to the point of producing stereotyped documents (like common law writs) and of authenticating them with a seal instead of with the king's sign manual. The seal was the forerunner of printing, as it reproduced script from a metal exemplar in a repeatable series.[16]

Speeding up the production of documents was easier than organizing archives and reference systems to make good use of them. There was nothing new about keeping precious writings in treasuries or reli-quaries. The novelty lay in getting into the habit of referring to a book or archive for information instead of seeking oral testimony. Domesday Book seems scarcely ever to have been consulted in the century after it was made; only in Edward I's reign did regular consultation begin.[17] Gradually Edward I's government began to realize that it possessed an archive of information which could be used in disputes with opponents. As late as 1290 when the king first called for historical information about the claims of the English crown in Scotland, resort was made to the monasteries, as the traditional remembrancers and chroniclers, and not the royal archives.[18] A year later, however, Edward I hurriedly sent a message from Scotland, ordering a chest of Chancery rolls to be broken

[11] See ch. 8, nn. 124–9 above.   [12] See ch. 4, n. 61 above.
[13] See ch. 4, n. 75 above.   [14] See ch. 4, n. 73 above.
[15] See ch. 4, n. 51 above.   [16] See pp. 245–8 above.
[17] See ch. 1, n. 39 above.   [18] See ch. 5, n. 26 above.

open and searched, and thus inaugurated systematic searches of the archives.[19]

The reasons for not regularly consulting records hitherto had been mixed. Even when officials had learned that documentary evidence could be more advantageous than oral testimony (which was not invariably the case of course), archives and the collections of documents within them had to be arranged in ways which made consultation possible. Edward I's instructions in 1300 to search all the rolls and remembrances 'so that nothing is left unsearched' was absurd, when chests of documents were scattered in a variety of repositories and their contents unlisted.[20] The surveys of the records in Edward I's last years, which culminated in Bishop Stapledon's array in 1320, mark the point at which the royal government at last recognized the usefulness of its archives. Archives had become a department of government instead of a treasury of relics. Libraries likewise, owing to the initiative of the friars, began to be arranged systematically so that readers could have books 'ready to hand' (*in promptu*),[21] just as Edward I wanted his archives available 'at all times'.[22] Hurriedly extracting information from quantities of books was a different kind of literate activity from meditating on a single text for a year, as the Black monks had done in the old Benedictine tradition.[23]

In establishing literacy as a practical convenience, much in the inheritance of the past had to be overcome. The second part of this book, 'The Literate Mentality', has indicated some of the problems. Most fundamental was the problem of language itself. After the Norman Conquest written Old English became an archaic language like Latin, with which it had competed for so long. Neither English nor Norman administrators could use the language of everyday speech in business documents, because they did not share a common language and also because written English and French were still in a fluid stage of development. Both languages, moreover, were for long overshadowed and beguiled by the ancient dignity of Latin. In these circumstances the linguistic skill required of a local man doing a practical task, like a foreman of a jury or a knight collecting testimony for the county court, was unusually demanding. In the thirteenth century such a man needed to speak English and French and to read in English, French and Latin.[24] In this multilingual society people switched languages often probably without comment. The practice of writing documents in a particular language for the record, usually Latin (or French by 1300), does not mean that Latin (or French) was necessarily the language in which the business was done.[25] By and large the knights of thirteenth-century England, and their families too, probably had a wider and deeper knowledge of language than those historians who have adopted a patronizing tone towards them because they were not highly literate.

[19] See ch. 5, n. 28 above.
[20] See ch. 5, n. 156 above.
[21] See ch. 5, n. 60 above.
[22] See ch. 5, n. 32 above.
[23] See ch. 5, n. 59 and ch. 8, n. 69 above.
[24] See p. 161 above.
[25] See ch. 6, n. 52 above.

The variety of languages in use made the acquisition of literacy difficult both to acquire and to define. Traditionally a person who was *litteratus* had been learned in Latin literature and of a clerkly disposition. Such a *litteratus* had little in common with the average modern literate, who has learned to read and write his own language for pragmatic purposes. It is probably not a coincidence that the royal officials who pioneered the use of writing in government – Roger bishop of Salisbury (Henry I's chief justiciar), Hubert Walter (Richard I's chief justiciar and King John's chancellor), Ralf Nevill (Henry III's chancellor) – were all described as *illitterati* by contemporaries.[26] What was meant was that they were administrators, rather than good churchmen or scholars. According to Gerald of Wales at least, Hubert Walter's school had been the Exchequer and not the university.[27]

The question, 'Were laymen literate?', cannot be answered directly from contemporary sources because it is a contradiction in medieval terms. A layman (*laicus*) was unclerkly by definition, whereas a literate (*litteratus*) was clerkly even if he were a knight.[28] Leaving these scholastic subtleties to one side, it is probable that a minimal knowledge of Latin among the population at large has been underestimated. A little Latin was the broad but shallow foundation from which men of peasant origin rose to be clerics and it was also indispensable for literacy in vernacular forms. Gradually 'clergy' in common parlance came to mean a little Latin instead of meaning an estate of the church. From the fourteenth century a person who knew a little Latin had 'benefit of clergy'.[29]

This minimal knowledge of Latin did not make a person educated in any real sense, but it was of practical use. It could save a man accused of felony from being hanged and it gave him sufficient knowledge to cope with government business. Thus in a case in 1297 ten jurors were able to read the entry of Robert de Tony's birth in a monastic chronicle and those who were unable to do so were described as *laici*, meaning that they were non-readers rather than 'laymen' in a more general sense.[30] Such minimal skill did not make a man either *litteratus* or educated in the traditional sense. Knights had been educated in the skills of language long before they were required by the growth of documentation to learn a little Latin or 'clergy'. Traditionally they had learned to speak well and to give counsel to clergy as much as to kings. Thus the judges who shaped the English common law in the twelfth and thirteenth centuries were drawn indifferently from knights and clergy.[31] For laymen literacy was a practical convenience long before it became an education. Although the Scriptures might teach religion, wisdom in the worldly sense did not depend on writings.

Because writing was only an ancillary aid at first for laymen, it did not immediately sweep away traditional non-literate ways of doing business. Reliance upon symbolic objects and 'livery of seisin' in con-

---

[26] See ch. 7, nn. 25–6 above.   [27] See ch. 2, n. 82 above.
[28] See ch. 7, n. 10 above.   [29] See ch. 7, n. 42 above.
[30] See ch. 7, n. 3 above.   [31] See ch. 7, n. 124 above.

veyances of property persisted.[32] Writing was converted into the spoken word by the habitual practice of reading aloud and of listening to or making an 'audit' of a statement, rather than scrutinizing its text on parchment.[33] Clerks and scribes themselves were slow to comprehend the full potentialities of documentary proof, as their inconsistencies in dating and signing documents demonstrate.[34] Writing was distrusted and for good reason, as numerous books and charters of the twelfth century in particular were forgeries. Paradoxically the continuance of non-utilitarian and primarily visual forms of writing, especially in liturgical manuscripts, may have helped to persuade the laity that literacy was valuable because of its long association with sacred Scripture. Writers of the twelfth and thirteenth centuries – whether they were composers or copyists of texts, or clerks making business documents – drew on the reserves of awe and faith with which monks had imbued writing in the half millennium before 1066.

The growth of literacy for practical purposes, which has been the theme of this book, was not necessarily an inevitable process. Emphasis on practical literacy is a commonplace of twentieth-century culture because we have inherited the values of the utilitarians. In nineteenth-century Europe and North America mass literacy was promoted by governments for the first time in the history of the world in order to ensure that populations could cope with the growing written demands of daily life – in railway trains, factories, conscript armies and so on. Opponents of government policy were worried that schools might succeed in educating people to a point where there would be a surplus of scholars and critics who might undermine the social hierarchy. Such fears were allayed by reformers emphasizing elementary practical literacy and numeracy (the three Rs of reading, writing and arithmetic) rather than a liberal education in the classical tradition, which remained as much the preserve of an élite of *litterati* in 1900 as it had been in 1200. The twentieth-century assumption that literacy is primarily utilitarian in purpose and character is a product of recent history and not an invariable norm.

Although practical or utilitarian literacy only became a mass movement in Europe in the nineteenth century, this book has argued that it had its origins in the twelfth and thirteenth centuries in the shift from memory to written record. That change might alternatively be described as a shift from sacred script to practical literacy. In Anglo-Saxon England, and generally in early medieval Europe, writing had been primarily associated with monasticism, sacred Scripture and the liberal arts of antiquity. Only in the twelfth century did the number of documents, and the number of persons who understood them, begin to increase at a fast rate under the pressures of emerging bureaucracy. Practical business was the foundation of this new literacy.

The old literacy of the village had no implication for the art of government and politics and the transmission of manual skills. . . . The

[32] See ch. 8, nn. 23–4 above.
[33] See ch. 8, nn. 58–68 above.   [34] See ch. 9 *passim*.

recording of disputes, collection of village statistics, transmission of government orders to villagers are tasks that require literacy, but this is a feature of the new literacy.' This contrast between old and new uses of literacy is not made by a medieval historian, but by an anthropologist, S. J. Tambiah, in a study of the uses of writing in a village in Thailand.[35] In the village temple Buddhist monks have been skilled in writing from time out of mind and they have been in direct contact with the people of the village, from whom their numbers are drawn and to whose community many of them return to marry. Writing has been used (in three scripts) by a variety of specialists in the village – monks, lay officiants, physician, astrologer and folk-opera entertainers.[36] Nevertheless, although a fair number of people in the village have been acquainted with writing in one form or another perhaps for centuries, literate skills were not applied to pragmatic purposes until the Thai government began to promote the 'new' or practical literacy under European influence.

The recording of disputes, collection of village statistics, transmission of government orders to villagers are essentially the uses to which literacy was applied in England by William the Conqueror in his Domesday survey. Thereafter his successors, because they were foreigners ruling in a tradition of conquest, bombarded local officials with one inquest after another. Landlords, clerical and lay, followed suit. From that momentous new start – *Doomsday* to the 'natives' and a Roman triumph of *jus scriptum* to court functionaries like Fitz Neal – documents proliferated and accumulated in archives until lay literacy became the basis of the culture which produced our own.

Writing takes many forms and has been used for diverse purposes in different societies. Ashanti warriors covered their war-coats with written charms to ward off bullets.[37] Likewise medieval knights had their swords inscribed with prayers or mysterious letters[38] and Richard the Engineer (who may have been one of the architects of Durham cathedral in the twelfth century) carried around with him numerous names of Christ and extracts from the Gospels on slips of parchment, which he kept in a small silken bag with some relics of St Cuthbert.[39] Warriors and builders were in perilous professions where they needed charmed lives. Technologies are created or adapted to suit the requirements of different societies. The Tibetans used rotary motion solely for prayer wheels and their monks used block printing to make charms and to write invocations on the surface of the water to acquire merit.[40] In early medieval Europe the skills of scribes were likewise primarily applied to

[35] 'Literacy in a Buddhist Village in North-East Thailand' in Goody, *Literacy*, p. 122, cf. p. 93. A comparable situation is described by Goody, 'Restricted Literacy in Northern Ghana', *ibid*. pp. 216ff.

[36] *ibid*. pp. 128–9.

[37] Goody, *Literacy*, p. 202.

[38] R. E. Oakeshott, *The Archaeology of Weapons* (1960), plates 6d and 7b.

[39] *Reginaldi Monachi Dunelmensis Libellus* ed. J. Raine, Surtees S. I (1835), ch. xlvii, pp. 94–7 and ch. liv, pp. 111–12.

[40] Goody, *Literacy*, p. 16 (citing R. B. Ekvall).

acts of worship through the production of liturgical manuscripts like the *Lindisfarne Gospels*. Gradually, however, despite Christianity being a religion of a book and medieval culture being shaped by monks, writing on parchment was adapted and applied to mundane purposes of government, property-owning and commerce. The beginnings of this growth of practical literacy, of depending for daily business on written record instead of the living memory, have been the subject of this book.

Plates

Plate I: Charter and seal of Ilbert de Lacy

This charter of one of the Norman conquerors records the gift of the manor (*mansio*) of Tingwick (*tinduicz*) in Buckinghamshire to the abbey of La Sainte Trinité du Mont at Rouen. It is authenticated by the crosses, presumably autographs, of King William Rufus, Ilbert and Hawise (*Haduidis*) his wife. In addition to these *signa*, Ilbert's seal used to be attached to the charter (at the hole below Hawise's cross). This SIGIL-LUM ILBERTI DE LACEO, in brown wax with the obverse blank, is one of the earliest knightly seals in existence. The apparently long pointed nose of Ilbert on the seal may in fact be the nasal piece of a helmet of the type depicted in the Bayeux Tapestry. The writer of the charter, perhaps a monk at Rouen, seems unaccustomed to producing this sort of document. He is inconsistent in his spacing and size of script and eccentric in his spelling, for example *Wiliel-mi* for King 'William'. Also his *m*'s and *n*'s with initial descenders and his tall embellished *s*'s are peculiar. The concluding words & *decimam de Fraite villa* ('and the tithe of Freteval') look as if they have been added by someone else, possibly with the donor's approval. The writing upside down at the bottom is an archivist's finding aid, dating probably from the fourteenth century.

Winchester College Muniments 11334. Reduced in size. Date *c*.1090 (*VCH Bucks*. I, p. 212). Transcript: *Archaeological Journal* IV (1847), pp. 249–51. Comment: W. E. Wightman, *The Lacy Family in England and Normandy* (1966), pp. 11, 56–7, 60.

Notum sit omnibus xpianis tam uiuentib; quam futuris qd ego hubt' de laceio

uisa cu hadeuide uxore mea do in elemosine tantuer sce kyn' mir' de

uaoite rotomagensi. grauia s'alicet cu aqua q' ppinal q' sileut omnib; q;

ad ipam grasiorem terenerab; p' anima mea atq; diu ui'g Willi'

im regii q' amitiab; parentum q' amicos meos. ueepior

q' uxoris mee. filia mea hugonis. q' eo qd et ipse

supradictus filius mi' in loco requiesceu' q' decimam de

fraite uilla

S' Willmi regis

S' h. Alba

S'
herludis
uxoris eia

Plate II: Early writ of Henry I

This plate shows the typical form of a royal letter patent, penned on thin parchment in the assured hand of a king's scribe. The narrow tag at the bottom of the document served as a tie to secure the writ when it was folded up. On the broader tag in the middle was fixed the king's seal: the burn mark, made by the hot wax, can be seen. The text is neatly and economically written on ruled lines. It grants Bernard abbot of Ramsey the right to tax his own knights (*vavasores*) and to recover the lands which his deposed predecessor, Abbot Aldwin, had alienated. The writ is addressed to the lords of the region – Robert bishop of Lincoln, Simon the earl (of Huntingdon) and Roger the sheriff. Although this document looks as if it were a letter sending information to the addressees, that is not its real purpose. The first of the addressees, Bishop Robert, already knew what it said, as he is also named as the first witness. The purpose of this writing was not primarily to convey information but to provide Abbot Bernard with evidence that the king supported his cause. Essentially this document is a title-deed.

BL Add. Charter 33642. Actual size. Date 1103 (*RRA-N* II, p. 33, no. 650). Transcript: *Ramsey*, p. 220. The handwriting is identified as that of Scribe I by T. A. M. Bishop, *Scriptores Regis* (1961), p. 52, no. 316.

Henr· rex Angl· Rob· epo· lincolie· ⁊ Simon comiti· ⁊ Rob· vicecomiti de Warewic· ⁊ omnib;

vicecomitib; ⁊ ministris de Warewicsir salutem· Sciatis qd volo ⁊ facio

ut ille Bernard de Normannia habeat ⁊ honorifice habeat· ⁊ teneat omnes terras suas· ⁊ facio nolo que ei

de homine suo teneant pie regis ad Warwic· sicut fuit· Et precipio ut ipse administret terras suas ⁊ nauastra

sicut ad pficaui gestu habent uadiauerit aliorum· sicut regni mei· administret ei· Et facio ut ipse amplius

obsescrat que de Albur debet nec excambium· de bona· fi· Et habeat ad ipsae honore· sicut alias ne

gestu· nel ⁊ nemini inde Apli respondeat· T· Rob· epo· linc· ⁊ Walt· cancell· ap̃· Wodest·

⁊ obtas pentecostes·

Plate III: Bilingual writ of Henry I

By contrast with the writ illustrated in plate II, this one was probably written not by a king's scribe but by a monk of Canterbury. Its ostensible purpose is to confirm to Archbishop Anselm and to the monks of Christ Church their ancient rights of sac and soc, toll and team, etc. The text is in both Latin and English (the English starts at line 8). As much of the Latin text consists of English formulas (*on strande & streame, on wudu & felde*, etc., line 3), the bilingualism is largely superfluous. These alliterative formulas derive from the oral recitations of remembrancers. Canterbury's bilingual writs seem to be an attempt to put this traditional lore, superficially Latinized, into a written form acceptable to the Norman government. The reasons for thinking that this writ is not a product of the royal Chancery are that the seal is eccentrically attached on the left-hand side (where the tag projects), the parchment is too thick, and the style of script is book hand. A note on another exemplar of this writ states that it was originally produced in quadruplicate. It is thus a throwback to pre-Conquest practice, when great monastic houses wrote out for themselves copies of title-deeds in the king's name and then got the royal seal affixed to them.

BL Campbell Charter xxix. 5. Reduced in size. Date c.1107 (*RRA-N* II, p. 72, no. 840). Transcript: *Journal of the British Archaelogical Association* XXIX (1873), p. 242. Comment: *BM Facs*, no. 6.

h. dei gra rex anglor. epis. comitib. ptib. iusteciar. ceterisq. fidelib. suis fidelib. franc. 7 anglis. monib. comitatib. 7 indb. archiepis. iusstcar. 7 monach. 7 omnib. fidelib. suis...

Plate IV: Writ of King Stephen

This writ is an unusually early example of cursive script. The writing is controlled and professional but rushed. It suggests the urgent pressure of business which caused the king's scribes to write as fast as they could. T. A. M. Bishop considers this 'the most fluent of twelfth-century Chancery hands' (*Scriptores Regis*, plate xxia). The change of style can be readily seen by comparing this hand with that of Henry I's scribe in plate I and with the book hands in plates III and v. Nevertheless the way the letters are formed in this writ of King Stephen is not a fundamental departure from the minuscule of Henry I's scribes. The differences stem from the need to write fast rather than from special training. This writ is addressed to Henry of Essex and Adam of Belnai and all the king's officers in Essex. It acquits William Fitz Robert of a forfeiture. Like the writ benefiting Bernard abbot of Ramsey (see plate II), this one would have been obtained and kept by William, the beneficiary, and shown by him to the king's officers in Essex when and if evidence was demanded of Stephen's judgment on his behalf. The document is in the form of a letter patent, which can be opened and closed repeatedly, as illustrated in plate II.

BL Add. Charter 28319. Actual size. Date 1135–41. Transcript: *RRA-N* III, p. 120, no. 318. Other facsimiles of this hand are shown in *RRA-N* IV, plates xvii and xviii.

Sj. rex Inust. h. de effessr. z A. de belnac. z omib; hoib; suis. sd effic...
clamo secu W... At hoc fauisfaciut. inde iplaciat... fuit. ec effauzast...
sug de Barsestun. ita qd am inde ger ficr. nec inde ampli fir iplacitauaus...
fi anust z luce fuerit firdn. istauea are sug. ec barsestun. z. Etc la
ec...Af Westm.

Plate V: Charter and seal of William del Turp

This charter is typical of many non-royal documents produced in the latter half of the twelfth century. Written on ruled lines in a firm book hand, its purpose is to serve as proof for the future that the beneficiary, Simon son of Robert, holds his land (2 bovates in *Eden'*) by hereditary right and honourably as a free tenant quit from any servile conditions. The grantor, William, is obscure; but he has a fine knightly seal and Robert de Turp, presumably a descendant, held half a knight's fee in Edenhall in Cumberland in 1235–6 (*Book of Fees* I, p. 553). Most early charters record gifts to religious houses and were written by the monks who benefited from them (see plate I), whereas this one benefits a lay tenant. Simon may have obtained it as a precaution at the time he came into his inheritance. The writing could be that of the first of the named witnesses, Ralf the priest (*Rad' p[re]sbit[er]*). Whoever the scribe was, he has produced an elegant and professional piece of work – consistent in its layout and script, and generous in its use of parchment – which contrasts with the charter of William Benedict which follows (see plate VI).

Harvard Law Library MS. 87, 2. 012. 5. Reduced in size. No certain date (? last quarter of the twelfth century).

Willrs delturi p oïb; uidentib; 7audienr̄ɓ; has lır̃as sal᷑. Scıatıs me dedisse 7 p̃cessisse 7 p̃senti

karta n̄sirmasse Simoni filio Rob̃ti 7 heredib; suis duas bouatas tr̃e in edeñ q̃s pat̃ suus Rob̃s

de me tenuit. scilicet ut Simon 7 heredes siu teneant eas ĩ feudo 7 hereditate de me 7

heredib; meis libe 7 q̃ete 7 honorifice in tosuis 7 pascuis 7 uiis 7 semitis 7 exituis; 7 oïb;

libtatib; . faciendo p eis libum forense suum duar̃ bouatas in edeñ ɓ̃ ũtq; Simon 7

heredes eı̃ ɓ p̃dictis duab; bouatis ab oïb; aluis sutuis 7 n̄suetudinib; libi 7 q̃eti. Testes. Rad̃

psb̃r. Higrellus. Ioh̃s ɓ cadredesacs 7 adã fileı̃. Walt̃s ɓ elletun̄. Rob̃ ɓ poinull. Rob̃ ɓ heselde

Walt̃us ɓ querendun̄. Alexd̃ ɓ herdwic. Walt̃us fr̃ Simonis. Gamel ɓ cadredesacs.

Plate VI: Charters of William Benedict and Walter Deyville

These two little charters, both dating from the first half of the thirteenth century, contrast with each other and with the preceding one (see plate V), although all three serve a common purpose in providing written evidence that their beneficiaries hold by hereditary right as free tenants. The top charter is untidily written in uncouth script (possibly that of the first witness, John the chaplain of Irnham), whereas the lower one is in a tiny and assured cursive hand similar to that of royal writs of the period. This contrast may reflect the different rank of the persons concerned. Walter Deyville (*Daivill'*), the grantor of the lower charter, was lord of Stoke in Coventry and the beneficiary, Walter son of Terry of Coventry, likewise came from a known family (*Warwickshire Feet of Fines*, Dugdale S. xi (1932), p. 17, no. 83). The grantor of the top charter, on the other hand, William Benedict of Boleby (*Boleb'*) in Lincolnshire is obscure and so is the beneficiary, Henry son of Thomas of Hawthorpe (*Huvartorp'*). Henry was perhaps a smallholder of relatively low status, comparable with the fenland peasants of the *Carte Nativorum* (see chapter 2, nn. 18–19 above). Despite these differences, both charters concern small properties: William's grants 4 strips in an open field and Walter's grants a croft. Both charters therefore show how documentary evidence was increasingly used in the thirteenth century, even for small properties and even by peasants.

Harvard Law Library MS. 87, 2. 012. 4 and 2. 013. 8. Both actual size. The seals are not illustrated because they are damaged; William's is a floral seal (befitting a peasant), whereas Walter's is armorial.

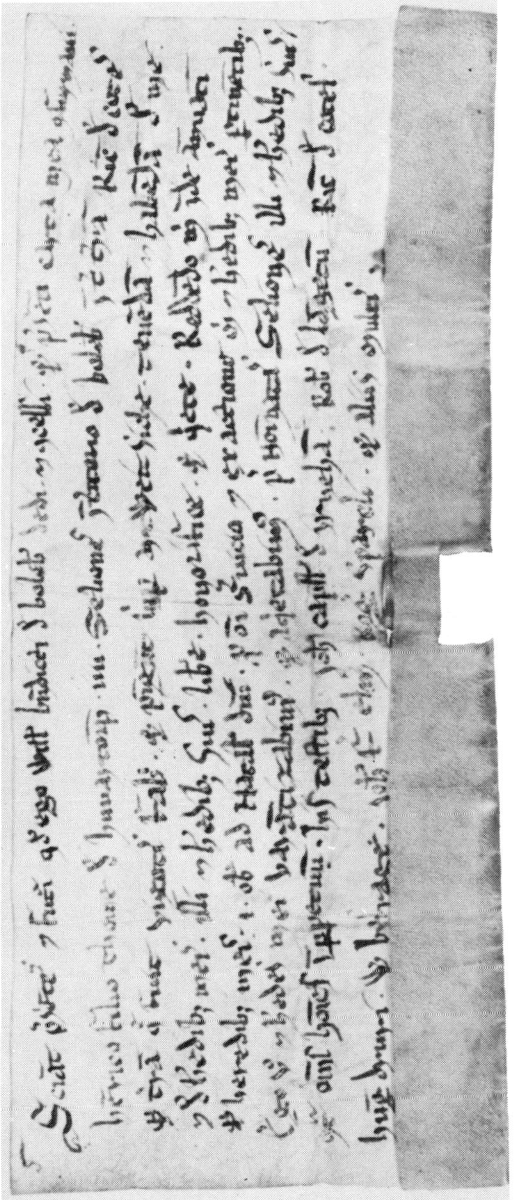

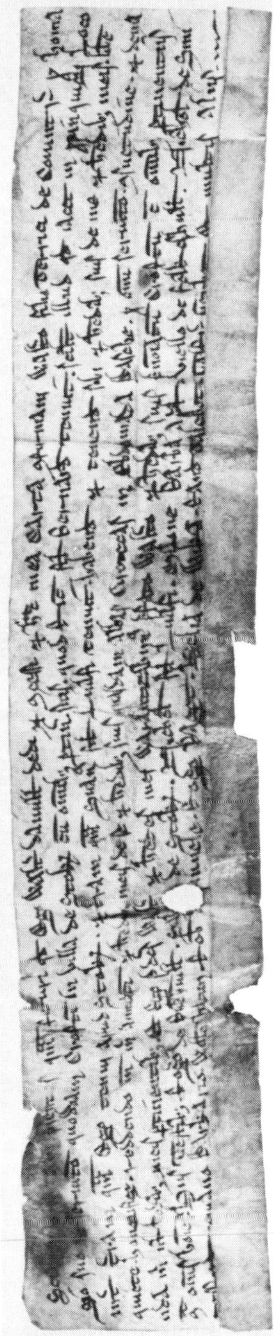

Plate VII: Agreement between Colchester abbey and the burgesses

This plate illustrates a precisely dated piece of writing and the typical format of a chirograph. The date is given in the first line as the 39th year of King Henry son of King John on Sunday after the feast of St Edmund (22 November 1254). In an agreement by chirograph each party received a matching copy of the document authenticated by the seals of the other party (see page 65 above). Thus at the top of this document can be seen where the word CYROGRAPHUM has been cut across by a wavy line to match its counterpart. This is Colchester abbey's copy, as it bore the seals of the 12 burgesses of Colchester who are named in lines 2 and 3 (there are 12 slits for seals, although only 5 survive). The document is written in a formal cursive or business hand,

comparable with the cursive book hands illustrated at plates XVI and XVII, either by a monk of Colchester or by a clerk of the town. The agreement concerns hunting rights: the abbey is to have free warren 'on the left side of the path which leads by the stile (*scalario*, line 5) next to the house which was Hamo de Campo's,' while the burgesses 'can lawfully hunt hare, fox and cat' (*leporem, wlpem & catum*, line 11) on the right. Putting this agreement in writing was evidently intended to prevent disputes in future; yet the terms of the settlement are conceived for the present only, as posterity might soon forget which house had been Hamo de Campo's.

Harvard Law Library MS. 87, 2. 254. Reduced in size.

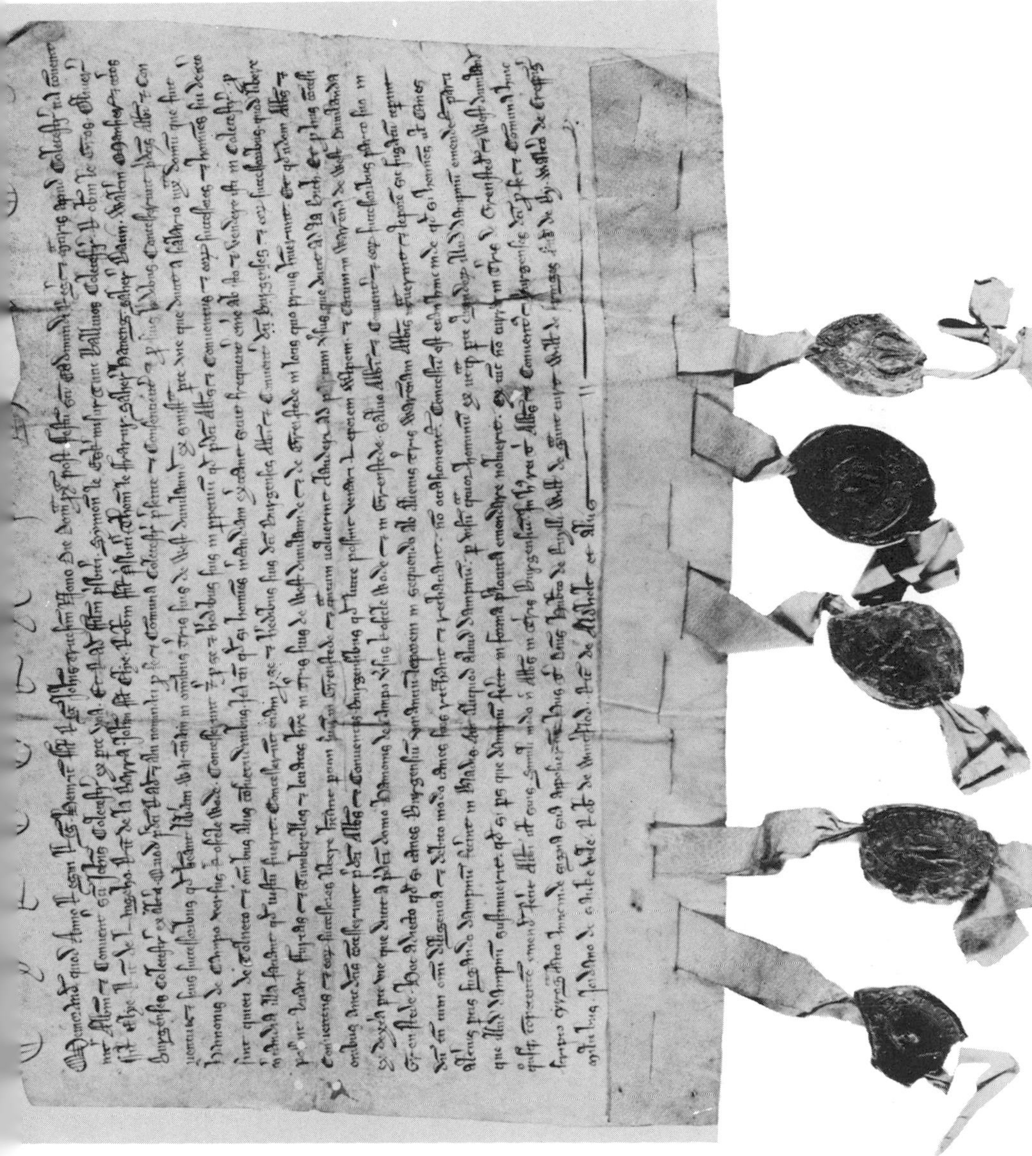

Plate VIII: Tally sticks of Robert of Glamorgan

These tallies were issued by the Exchequer to Robert of Glamorgan, sheriff of Surrey and Sussex, as receipts for payments into the treasury in the financial year 1293–4. Like a chirograph (see plate VII), a tally stick was a bipartite record. When completed it was split down its length; the larger part (the stock) was issued as a receipt, while the smaller part (the foil) was kept by the Exchequer. The sticks in the photograph are all different depths and shapes. Thus the stick at the top, with a pair of deep triangular notches at the right-hand end, is a receipt for 2 × £20. The next stick has a single triangular notch (for £20) on the lower side and 7 × £1 and 8 × 1 shilling notches on the upper side. On the third stick 19 × 1 shilling notches are visible and on the bottom stick there are 8 narrow notches (for 1 penny each) on the upper side and a single notch for 1 shilling on the lower side. From the 1290s onwards writing was also put on tallies to help identify them. Thus the sticks illustrated all bear the sheriff's name and county, the regnal year and term, and details of what the payments are for. These notes are not all visible in the photograph because they are written on different sides of the sticks. As the photograph shows, tallies were an intricate but robust form of record, which could not be readily replaced until the invention of carbon copying.

PRO E. 402/2. Actual size. Illustrated by M. H. Mills, *The Pipe Roll for 1295*, Surrey Record S. VII (1924), p. x. See also chapter 4, nn. 28–9 above.

Plate IX: Wallingford's first roll of tradesmen

This short roll lists people by trades, recording how much each person owes for the year to practise his trade in the town. The portion illustrated lists, under headings in the left-hand margin, the glovers (*Wantieres*) and mercers (*Merecatiarii*) or general traders. Other portions list butchers, carpenters, hosiers, smiths, weavers, etc. After each person's name is entered the sum due from him, followed by details of payment. For example the second enrolment in the list of glovers states that from Roger the Clothier *(D[e] Rog[er]þ Parme[n]tario)* 16 pence *(xvi. d.)* are due. To the right of this sum follow receipts by instalments in three distinct hands: received 4 pence *(r. iiij. d.)*: received 6 pence; received 6 pence, *quit*. The roll thus served both as a list of traders and as a record of receipts for licences.

The royal Exchequer had kept rolls of receipts since Henry II's reign, but this is the first example of such a record from a town. Possibly the clerks who wrote it had worked for the government, as the roll is dated by the regnal year (11 Henry III, that is, 1226–7) and Wallingford was usually held by a royal nominee or kinsman. The parchment is thin, causing the enrolments on the dorse to show through on the right-hand side.

Berkshire Record Office W/FC 1. Portion of the face of the roll, which is headed *Rotulus de pactionariis in Walingeford*. Actual size. Comment: N. M. Herbert, *The Borough of Wallingford* (unpublished PhD thesis, Reading 1971). See also page 73 above.

Plate X: Wallingford's second roll of tradesmen

This roll contrasts in appearance with its predecessor (see plate IX). The portion shown lists the glovers and mercers, as in the previous roll. But the names are written more boldly and lines are ruled to separate the enrolments and to make vertical columns. The receipts are likewise more clearly set out, so that there is no mistake about which sum refers to which person. The roll is dated 14 Henry III (that is 1229–30) at its head. The clerk who designed it also wrote Wallingford's roll of rents (W/FT 1) for the preceding year, which is laid out in the same way. In each case the receipts are entered in a different hand from the names. It will be noticed that the names appear in much the same order in both rolls of tradesmen (see plate IX), although some of the assessments differ and there are four extra names (one of which is cancelled) concluding the list of glovers

in the second roll. The order seems to be one of precedence or seniority rather than financial means. The greater formality of this second roll, compared with its predecessor, suggests that the Wallingford clerks were now thinking in terms of rolls being permanent records rather than casual memoranda supplementing receipts on wooden tallies. A tradesman who saw his name engrossed, as if in a liturgical book, and his payments accumulating from left to right on the parchment until they culminated with his acquittance in the right-hand margin, should have been impressed by the dignity of written record.

Berkshire Record Office W/FC 2. Portion of the face of the roll. Actual size.

Wauricies.

- Dᵉ Hostre le vostler.
- Dᵉ Rogers le parmnur.
- Dᵉ Huchot moghun.
- Dᵉ hugou le Waure.
- Dᵉ thoŋ le Waure.
- Dᵉ thoma le taillur.
- Dᵉ Michiel le heaue.
- Dᵉ Michant Vourel.
- Dᵉ Jesse plahnue.
- Dᵉ Wills suffe pennir.
- Dᵉ henr Roe.
- Dᵉ Godefrid de Windesor.
- Dᵉ Wills balenan.
- Dᵉ martin le Peler.
- Dᵉ henr parmentar.
- Dᵉ edmund le Waure.
- Dᵉ Vincent le Waure.
- Dᵉ Helie drauapapet.

Hostlani.

- Dᵉ Wills Gauf.
- Dᵉ Stephano de clopkot.
- Dᵉ henr de Windesor.
- Dᵉ Hue le baker.
- Dᵉ Wilfrns.

Plate XI: Household roll of Eleanor de Montfort

This roll records Eleanor's daily expenditure and itinerary during the last months of Simon de Montfort's life. The portion illustrated concerns the week 19–26 February 1265, when Eleanor proceeded southwards from Wallingford to Odiham via Reading. Each day is enrolled separately, sometimes by a different clerk. Thus the first three enrolments illustrated appear to be in different hands. The entry for Saturday, marked *Rading'* (that is, at Reading) in the margin, is typical. It notes expenditure on bread, wine, beer and cups, which is followed by kitchen expenses on herrings, fresh fish, peas and dishes. Finally comes the expenditure of the marshalcy on hay for 65 horses, oats, bedding straw (*litere*), charcoal (*carbonibus*, possibly coal), barley and blacksmithing. To conclude the enrolment the day's expenditure is totalled, amounting in this instance to 44 shillings and 6½ pence. Each day's expenditure could thus be seen at a glance by running the eye down the sums on the right-hand side of the roll. The initiator of detailed accounts like these was the king's government. As Eleanor was Henry III's sister, she would probably have been familiar with written accounts from childhood.

BL Add. MS. 8877. Reduced in size. Transcript: *Manners and Household Expenses of England*, Roxburghe Club LVII (1841), pp. 3–5. Comment: M. W. Labarge, *A Baronial Household of the Thirteenth Century* (1965), pp. 189–201. See also pages 71–2 above.

¶ Die Jouis ebdo die prox post dorm añim p com z dieb; panis .ij. qr. z di. de Abindon. frum' .iiij. qrd. p alb. in stampo. cepit p̃c. Coquina. alleer .vij. de iustāpo castr' Piscis .com̃ .j. d. Pis alb. .xvij. d. o. Sope .ij. d. Alleo .xij. d. Salsa .iij. s. .j. d. Maresc' fenum p .l.x.j. equis .iiij. s. iij. bus. de Rading castr'.

Com̃ xxvij. s. x. d. o.

p cont z pisc̃.

¶ Vigil' de coquina. panis .ij. qr. .ij. bus. de Abindon. panis ex empt .xij. d. .xviij. iiij. qrd. uñ dns ep̃us de Bādm'. At sacc' Gossis dñe agnere .j. sacc' edt. Sallo .xij. de iustāp' Pisas .iiij. s. xj. d. ff fenum ad Reg̃ .xij. equos ducend .iiij. qr. .v. bus. p Ruscel .iiij. d. z gagus lb. Almers .xij. d. o.

Com̃ s. s. x. d. o.

¶ Die sab' sequenti apud Rading. p com̃. Vñofs. contūm' edt. de genco fo'ci z alus. panis de istampo. ij. bus. de Abindone. Panis de empt .iij. s. xj. d. .xiiij. s. cxd. de iustāp' de Balingefford. Coquin' empt .iij. s. iiij. d. Oth .xij. d. Coquina alleer .iiij. s. Piscis .com̃ s. xj. d. Pis. o. d. Elsa. xj. d. Maresc' fenum p .lx. equis .ij. s. .viij. d. Anona ex empt. v. qr. .v. s. xj. d. p̃ qr. .xxiij. d. Litere de Abb in castumbz. .v. d. In busa. xj. d. o. Forge. s. Com̃ xlvij. s. xj. d. o.

¶ Die Dñica p cont z pisc̃ apud Oeth. panis .ij. qr̃. z di. de iustāp' .xviij. ij. sacc̃ z di. Ep̃ xij. galones ducend z xij galones. x. s. xj. d. Coquin. iij. alleer. Piscis ex empt .xvij. s. Copheth. z .iiij. equos. fenu de iustāp' castr' ducend .x. qr̃. de iustāp'.

Com̃ xxix. s. xvj. d.

¶ p coquin' z equis adductis de Balingefford usq; Oeth'. xxvj. s. iv. d.
Com̃ xxvij. s. iv. d.

¶ Die Lune p cont. panis .j. qr̃ z di de istāp'. xviij. ij. sacc̃ j. Eag̃m. ij. multo brad. z. qrd. opd. xiij. z di. Anone Coquin. iiij. alleer. piscis ex empt. xvij. s. Copheth. xxij. iij. equos. fenu iustāp'. ducend. ij. qr̃ z p bus.

Com̃ xxij. s.

¶ Die marcis p cont. panis .j. qr̃. z di de istāp'. xviij. ij. sacc̃. z .j. Eag̃m. equis p̃ nc̃ .ijd. Coquin. iiij. alleer. Piscis ex empt. xvij. s. v. d. Copheth. fenu []iiij. equis ducend .j. qr̃ xij. bus. z di. de iustāp'.

Com̃ xxj. s. iv. d.

¶ Die martis p cont. z alleo de Winbrox. panis .j. qr̃ z di. de istāp'. xviij. ij. sacc̃ z di. equis p̃ nc̃. Coquin. iiij. alleer. Piscis ex empt. x. s. xj. d. Pisis. xv. d. prd. xxvij. d. Waynes .ij. d. o. Sope. xij. d. o. Pomd. iiij. d. o Copheth fenu de iustāp' p̃ Ab. xxxiiij. equos. ducend .ij. qr̃. de iustāp'. Forge. xij. d.

Com̃ xxvj. s. v. d. o.

¶ Die Jouis p cont z pisc̃. panis .j. qr̃. z .j. bus. xviij. ij. sacc̃ z di. dūs fuit Coquin. Coquin iiij. alleer. de iustāp' Piscis ex empt. iiij. s. ij. d. fenu aqua. iiij. d. Copheth. fenu de iustāp' Ab. xxv. equos. ducend .ij. qr̃. .j. bus. de iustāp'. busa empt apud Balingefford ad coquin' no coputat̃. xij. d.

Com̃ x. d. ij. d.

¶ Arreār' .ff. ij. auroc̃is captuar'. Com̃ capt' i Clongar. xxxv. com̃. ibt traba' de Cistoll uscz carling ep̃' Ab. s. j.d. de q piscz. ordicat' plene z misa apt carling' uald' capta'a fuit apt adhuit. tristāuo capta' Ab .jd. p̃ poc piscis demisf fno ext. p̃c ij. pocis piscis. forg' ij. d.

Com̃ v[l]ij. s. vjd.

Plate XII: Peter of Poitiers dictating to a scribe

As Peter explains in the prologue to his *Compendium* or *Tabula Historie* reproduced here, he devised a time chart which overcame the 'prolixity of sacred history' by encouraging students to learn with their eyes through simple diagrams. The figure in the central roundel is God as Christ in Majesty. In the roundels at his feet are Adam and Eve and from them stems the genealogical tree of man's history. The author is himself depicted in the roundel on the left at the top. He holds open a book while dictating to the scribe on the right. The matter being dictated is presumably the text of the prologue which is set between them. The book (represented as open pages with ruled blank lines) on the author's lectern must be one of the prolix histories which Peter aimed to simplify. The scribe turns towards the author in order to catch his words. In this contorted posture he dips his quill into an extravagantly large inkhorn, while holding a penknife of comparable dimensions in his left hand. He is bald but not clearly tonsured like the author, as a scribe was not necessarily of clerical status. Dangling over his lectern is the blank membrane of parchment on which he is about to write. Peter's text was designed to form a continuous roll displaying man's unfolding history from Adam to Christ.

Harvard University, Houghton Library fMS. Typ 216. Reduced in size (actual size of roll 354 cm × 35 cm). Date c. 1210. Comment: P. S. Moore, *The Works of Peter of Poitiers* (1936); *Supplement to the Census of Medieval and Renaissance MSS in the USA and Canada* ed. W. H. Bond (1962), p. 271. See also page 97 above.

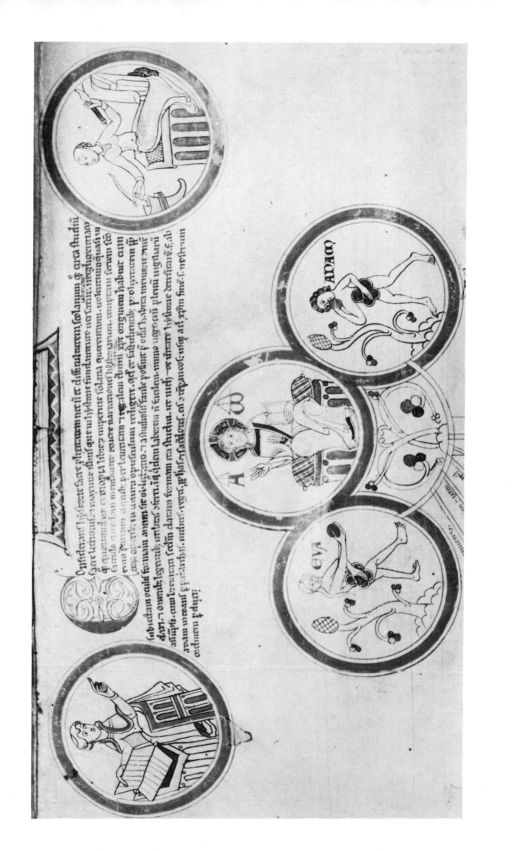

Plate XIII: Genealogical history of England

Just as biblical history was presented in a sequence of diagrams by Peter of Poitiers (see plate XII), so the roll format was used from the middle of the thirteenth century to schematize the history of England. This plate shows the portion depicting William the Conqueror (*Willam Bastard*) from a genealogical history of the kings of England down to Edward I. William sits in state, like Christ in Majesty (see plate XII) and like the image on the king's seal. The text in French on the left records that William conquered England from Harold, reigned 12 years, died in his 59th year in 1087, and had been crowned by the archbishop of York on Christmas Day 1067 (1066 by modern reckoning). From William stem his nine children – Robert *Cortehuse* duke of Normandy, William *le Rous* (Rufus), Richard (who died in c.1075), Henry I, Ela (or Adela) duchess (or countess) of Blois, Cecily abbess of Caen, Constance countess of Brittany, and two unnamed daughters. The countesses wear coronets and the abbess a nun's veil. This pictorial scheme with captions thus provides an elementary but precise chronology of the rulers of England, together with an explanation of their relationship to each other. The design attracts the eye, like Peter of Poitiers's (see plate XII), and it can be understood by someone of restricted literacy. A knightly family possessing a roll of this sort therefore had the means to master chronology, which had hitherto been the preserve of monks.

Harvard University, Houghton Library MS. Typ 11. Reduced in size (actual size of roll 403 cm × 26 cm). Date c.1300. See also chapter 4, n. 114 above.

Plate XIV: The Canterbury or Eadwine Psalter

This masterpiece of calligraphic design was made at Canterbury under the direction of Eadwine, 'the prince of writers'. The layout makes it possible to show all on one page the three versions of St Jerome's Latin text of the Psalms, side by side in parallel columns, together with Latin glosses and Anglo-Saxon and French translations. The main text, the 'Gallican', is in the largest script towards the left of the page. Its marginal and interlinear glosses, in miniature abbreviated script, comprise a commentary derived from the Church Fathers. For example in the margin to the left of the capital Q is written: *Dilexi l[egem]q[u]i dilig[it]q[uo]d iub[et] d[ominu]s* ('I loved the law who love what the Lord commands'). Similarly to the right of the Q, immediately above *dilexi* ('I loved') is interlined: *non timui* ('I did not fear'). The pair of slimmer columns on the right

of the page show the 'Roman' and 'Hebrew' variant texts. Between the lines of the 'Roman' text is the Anglo-Saxon translation, written in a style derived from insular minuscules, and between the lines of the 'Hebrew' is the French translation.

Trinity College Cambridge MS. R.17.1. Lower portion of fo. 219b: Psalm 118 (*QUOMODO dilexi legem tuam, Domine*), that is, Psalm 119, verses 97–100, in the Authorised Version. Actual size. Date *c.*1147 (Kauffmann, *Romanesque MSS*, p. 97). Facsimile ed. M. R. James (1935). Comment and bibliography: C. Clark, 'People and Languages in Post-Conquest Canterbury', *JMH* II (1976), pp. 1–7, 23, 26, 30–32. See also page 166 above.

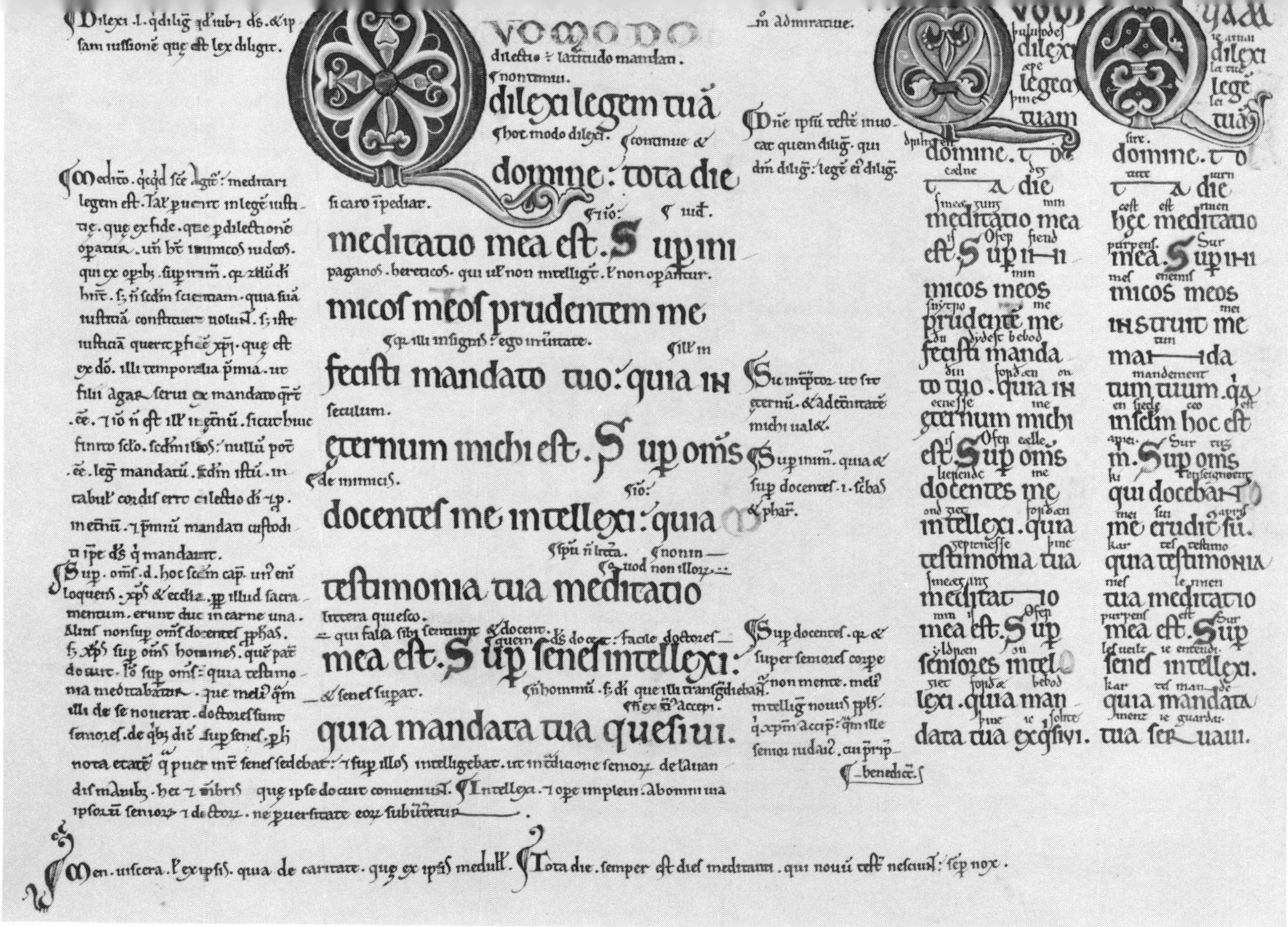

QUOMODO

dilige legem tuam

DOMINE: tota die

meditatio mea est. Super inimi-

cos meos prudentem me

fecisti mandato tuo: quia in

eternum michi est. Super omnis

docentes me intellexi: quia

testimonia tua meditatio

mea est. Super senes intel-

lexi: quia mandata tua quesivi.

Plate XV: Estate book of Richard Hotot

Richard was a minor landowner in Northamptonshire and Bedfordshire. His book contains a family chronicle, details of his properties and copies of Magna Carta and the Charter of the Forest. The opening folios are generously laid out and illuminated in green (showing up as a lighter tone in the photograph) with red embellishment, which gives it a bucolic air. The page illustrated is headed on the left: *Redditus et f[ir]me de Torveye ad festum s[anc]ti Micael* ('Rents and farms from Turvey at Michaelmas'). Beneath are listed the tenants' names and their rents: *De Will[elm]o Martell iii d.*, and so on. The writing looks like the work of trained clerks, comparable with those who wrote Wallingford's lists of dues at about the same date (see plates IX and X). A noticeable peculiarity are the symbols or *signa* preceding most of the names. These tally, though in a different order, with the footnotes specifying each tenant's property in smaller script. Thus the symbol preceding William Martel's name indicates that his rent is *pro dimidia v[ir]gata* ('for a half virgate'). Although some of these symbols look like Arabic numerals, the sequence is too random for that. More probably, these *signa* were invented by the scribe. Richard's book is consequently not only among the first to have been made for a layman, but among the first to use footnotes.

BL Add. MS 54228, fo. 6b. Reduced in size (actual size 28 cm × 18 cm). Date 1220 × 1250. Comment: E. King, 'Large and Small Landowners', *Past and Present* XLVII (1970), pp. 39–43. See also pp. 80, 143 above.

De natiue hoīb3 de torueye

	e Wīlło marcel ·	iiij d
	e radulfo chico	viij d
	e robeo gern̄	iij d
	e Wīllo fił ade	ix d
	e rogo filio simon̄	vj d
	e Walteo le packere	iiij d
	e ric̃ de laleye	iij d
	e hem̃ fił lleffan̄	ij d
	e rad de nordho	iij ob
	e auguere lechatt	iiij d
	e ...	v d
	e hug le coteꝪ	vj d
	e gauffrido de bosco	iiij d
	e Wīllo le macon	iiij d
	e amicia cannaꝪ	j d
	e abbate de sc̃o iacobo	j d
	e l̃ fiƚ fił rad	ij d
	e Wīllo le packere	j d
	e michot de gaticheu	iiij d
	e rob̃eo mandalle	iiij d
	e l̃ w̃ hưet	ij d
	e ada preꝪ	iij d
	e ada fił w̃a	ij d
	e hem̃ ner de ga	iij d
	e bauto petal	vij d
	e gilbeo bayhel	iij ob
	e onlsent	iiij d
	e rcolot ourcet	iij d
	e Wīlls de ticheyn̄	j d

Plate XVI: Pocket book of statutes

This is an example of a book which is small enough to carry in the pocket of a robe. As it is shown actual size and fully open, its compactness when closed can be appreciated. The growth of formal legislation in Edward I's reign, culminating in the confirmations of Magna Carta in the 1290s, encouraged the production of handbooks of parliamentary statutes (usually starting with Magna Carta) in various shapes and sizes. Thus the text illustrated here on the right-hand page is the beginning of the statute of Merton of 1235 (headed *Mertone*) and that on the left is the ecclesiastical condemnation issued in 1297 of infringers of Magna Carta (headed *Sentencia sup[er] cartas*). As is usual in manuscript books, the two sentences written boldly at the bottom of the left-hand page point out where one text ends and another begins: *Explic[it] sente[n]c[ia]lata s[upe]r cartas* ('Here ends the sentence imposed on the charters') and *Incipiunt p[ro]visiones de M[er]tone* ('Here begin the provisions of Merton'). This book was probably written shortly after 1297, perhaps for a practising lawyer and presumably by a professional scribe. Manuscripts like this, which emphasize the text rather than scribal ornament, were often written in a distinctive type of cursive script which is analyzed and described as 'Anglicana' by M. B. Parkes, *English Cursive Book Hands* (1969), plate 4.

Harvard Law Library MS. 175.

Plate XVII: Larger book of statutes

This manuscript was presumably made for a practising lawyer who was primarily concerned with its content rather than its appearance. It is written in a faster cursive script than the pocket book just illustrated (see plate XVI) and pays less regard to pleasing layout. Thus the letter 'p' at line 11 on the left has never been completed by the rubricator, by contrast with the similar 'p' on the right-hand page of the pocket book (see plate XVI). There are also cancellations and interlineations, which are acceptable in plea rolls but not usually in books: for example *d[o]m[ini]* is crossed out in line 11, because it is written twice, and an ampersand is interlined at line 13. The texts on this page are the end of the Charter of the Forest (Stubbs, *Charters*, pp. 347–8) and the beginning of the statute of Merton (*Statutes*, pp. 1–2). The symbols in the margin on the right point out where each clause of the statute of Merton begins, so that a user of the book can readily find his place. Similarly the headlines (*de foresta/M[er]ton*) indicate the contents of the page. Although such an untidy looking book might have disgusted a monk trained in a traditional *scriptorium*, it is a professional piece of work nonetheless. Lawyers, who were accustomed to working with the plea rolls and writs of the royal courts, would probably have found it easier to read than something in book hand like the page which follows (see plate XVIII).

Harvard Law Library MS. 36. Actual size. Date *c*. 1300.

EXPLICIT CARTA DE FORESTA INCIPIT PROVISIO DE MERTON

Plate XVIII: Illustrated book of statutes

Unlike the books just illustrated (see plates XVI and XVII), this one seems to have been made for someone who primarily wanted a manuscript which was pleasing to look at, even if it were a lawbook. The owner may have been a prelate or lay baron building up a treasured private library. The two columns, precisely ruled both horizontally and vertically, and the generous margins contrast with the cramped layout of the page in the preceding illustration (see plate XVII). Moreover, the text is written in book hand, which gives the page a more settled and liturgical appearance than the urgent cursive script of the preceding one. Originally this book had no headlines (the heading *Stat. de Merton* is a later addition), which suggests that the reader was not intended to flick rapidly through it. But it does use rubrics (they show up in a lighter tone in the photograph) and illuminated capital letters (E in the left column and C in the right) introduce each statute. The line drawings in the margins, which illustrate the subject matter of the statutes, are exceptional. The one on the left, showing a man with a longbow shooting at a deer, is placed alongside Edward I's ordinance of 1306 against trespassers in forests. Similarly the drawing on the right, showing a widow with her hand pointing towards a French text of the statute of Merton, is appropriate because its first chapters concern the rights of dowagers. Illustrations like these could therefore help a reader to find his place, but they are not used consistently in this way throughout the book.

Harvard Law Library MS. 12. Reduced in size (actual size 34 cm × 24 cm). Date *c.*1307.

lens g[ue]tonis [et] confirmonis [et] celes ple te
nour des p[re]sentes lettres renoulons vol
lans [et] g[ra]ntans p[ur] no[us] [et] p[ur] nos hens qe lau[n]te
dit chse en tout [et] en chescon de ceos articls
fermem[en]t [et] san[s] blemissem[en]t seient gar
dez si aucons articles en cele chse contre
uns p[ur]ueu[n]t deshes en eos neie[n]t este
gardez ceos testmoynes [et]c. done p[ur] vn[e]
meyn a Westm[inster] le xxviij· iour de Mar[s]
lan de n[ost]re regne vint [et] vime·

¶ Ici comence les addition sur la chse de forest·

E Dward p[ur] la g[ra]ce de dieu roy deng[le]
seign[ur] dulaund duc de Aquin[e] A tou[s]
ces loaanz salu[s]· ¶ En p[re]mes vo
lomsno[us] qe trespas fait de si auant en
nos forestes de vert [et] de venesó[n] les fo
resters enqi baillie[s] ceaus trespas se
ront fes les p[re]sent[es] Ap[er]tem[en]t [et] a[u]ta[n]t
mymot [et] qe chiges deuant foresters ver
ders regardours Agistours [et] les autre[s]
ministres de la foreste les drem[er]s seit
fait solenpnem[en]t p[ur] a[n]ent [et] accord de
tous [et] en consel de tou[s] lor seau[s] [et] si autre
mane seit set le[ur] le[n]dite[n]t p[ur] mil· Et
si a neigne qel nul des a[ua]ntdis foresters
verders re[g]ardours Agistours ou autres
ministres p[ur]uen[ge] ou seit desturbe p[ur] ma
lice ou p[ur] autre mane p[ur] qu il ne puisse
venir a sc[ha]umymot me[r]uent[e]u[s]e la iustice
ou son lieu tient vnet autre en son lieu
issint qe le[n]dite[n]t se face p[ur] tout· Et qe
le ministres qe seint mys· seront mys
si com adeste a costume Auant ces houre[s]
issint toutes vyes q[ue] les verders seient mys
p[ur] election [et] p[ur] br[e]f· Et vet le roy q[ue] tout ceus
ministr[es] a[ua]ntdis seient h[er]es de aisses [et]
iures [et] des enq[ue]stes issint q[ua]l ne seient mys
desormes en countre ne de lois· Et si [n]ul
son charge seit troue de nul q[ue] se p[ur]test
eu[m] ministre de la foreste seient ouste[r] [et] en
p[ri]sonez p[ur] la discret[i]on de la iustice· [et] si ceus
q[ue]les a[ua]nt mys seient ainsi p[un]ni[s] a la
volente le roy· En droit de ceus q[ue] en te[m]p[s]
qe la foreste n[o]s este desla[fo]reste h[er]e t[r]ouy[s]

de ven ou de veneson p[ur] ce qe lp roy g[ue]sta
le de forestement com[en]t qil nele fer my[e]
de sa vn[e] v[o]lu[n]te si vit le roy q[ue] les tresp[s]
seient p[ur] donez fors p[er] tresp[s] fe[r] en ce q[ue]
demora en forest iss[i]nt tout[es] v[y]es qe les la
yes [et] les fosse[s] fe[r] en lez le mene te[m]ps g[ui]re
lassise de la foreste seient a latru[s] [et] de tut of
tez [et] ameu[n]ses Et les arentem[en]z le roy
de morge[n]t solom lassise de foreste· Et vet
le roy qe les lors cowpe[z] en forest[e] seient
oustre[z] [et] remue[z] de ce q[ue]st en estaunt de mer
ge en foreste· [et] le verder face g[ui]re al sea
tour solom le afferaunt de la p[ri]zo[n] qer en
estaunt en la foreste [et] qi auia este en si ven
du en le mene te[m]ps [et] solom ce qe en auap[s]·
Et vet le roy q[ue] la iustice de la foreste ou
son lieu tient ensemblem[en]t oue le tresor
er eyent p[ur]er de pu[n]ire su[n]s [et] rau[n]sons de
ceus qe sont eudite[z] des trespas fe[r] sau[n]s
eyre entendre· Et vet le roy qe ceu[x] qe
auoient c[om]e de pasture en les forestes deust
la puuale fe[r]e [et] qe si[n]t p[ur]u[s] reuu[n]s enforeste
qi ou[n]t este destou[r]ue[z] de loir c[om]e puuale ei
ent c[om]e de pasture en les forestes dez or mes
sauv[s] largem[en]t [et] auv[s] fuelem[en]t com il so
loient auer A[ua]nt la puuale fe[r]e en te[s]
mony[n]age de qele chse auo[n]s fer nos lettres
patentes. temoyne moy mesmes a Westm[inster]
le vint [et] sime iour de may lan de n[ost]re reg
ne xxxviij· Ici comen[c]e le st[at]ut de Mer toun

C Es sut les pueances de M[er]ton fete[s]
en le an del coronem[en]t le roy he[n]
ri fiz le roy iohan· xx· a M[er]ton· ¶ P[ur]
ueu est en la court le roy le[n]de may[n]
de seint vincent en lau del coronem[en]t
le roy henri fiz le roy iohan· xx· a M[er]toun
deuant Erceuesches Eueskes Countes [et]
barons [et] la communate du royaume p[ur]
le coronemse le roy [et] la roine Elpano
re q[ui] p[ur] tous furt mandez com est p[u]ueu
del comun p[ur]fit del Royaume solom les ar
ticles en cel roule escrites iss[i] est p[u]ueu [et]
g[ra]unte Auribute[n] des Erceuesse[s] Eueskes
Co[u]tes [et] barons A[ua]nt nome[s] eu[n] de mene

Plate XIX: Alphabetical index

This is a portion of a folio from a large lawbook made in the 1290s. The book contains Bracton's treatise together with statutes and some other texts. The index refers both to Bracton and the statutes (Magna Carta is mentioned, for example, under the heading *scutagium* on the left). As the illustration shows, the index is arranged in columns with subject headings in approximate alphabetical order. Thus subjects beginning with *S* appear on the left and those beginning with *T* in the centre, but the sequence is not strictly alphabetical within these columns. On the right *W* (*Warentu[m]* 'warranty'), *U* (*Utlagaria*, 'outlawry') and *V* (*Vent[er]i[n]spiend[us]*, 'womb inspection') are all treated as one letter for alphabetical purposes. The references following the subject headings are elaborate. For example after *Submersus* ('drowning') in the bottom left-hand corner is written *xli*. ('41' in Roman numerals) *3*. ('3' in Arabic numerals) *f*. (the letter 'f'). The Roman numerals should refer to folios, the Arabic ones to numbered articles or chapters, and the letters to subsections. In practice, however, this index fails to work consistently. Although it sometimes refers to the correct folio number in Roman numerals, the Arabic ones and the letters have no equivalents throughout the text. The index was evidently made not for this particular manuscript but for another one of similar contents. It works only by chance. The reasons for giving this book an elaborate yet unreliable index are discussed at page 144 above.

Harvard Law Library MS. 1. Unnumbered preliminary folio. Actual size of complete folio 40 cm × 26 cm.

Index

Medieval persons are indexed by forename and modern persons by surname.

Simon of Senlis
  earl of Huntingdon, plate II
  steward of Ralf Nevill, 68
Simon Passelewe, 137
Simon son of Robert, plate V
Simpson, G. G., 123
Siward, a priest, 168
Smalley, B., 86, 104, 112, 143, 145, 156, 195, 210, 241
Smith, D., 54
Smithers, G. V., 113, 158, 165
Socrates, 97, 233
Somerset, 138, 205
Sonning, visitation of, 192
Southampton, 25, 133
Southern, R. W., 15, 40, 43, 80, 86, 119, 179, 192, 209, 219
Spalding priory, 127, 200, 207
speech
  instruction in, 223–6
  mastery of by knightly advocates, 199–200
  spoken word, 68, 183, 204, 220–26
  text of written down, 224
  see also oral skills
spelling *see* orthography
Spenser's *Faery Queen*, 113
spigurnel *see* sealing
Staffordshire, 50
standardization of forms, 17, 62, 64, 69, 87, 105, 260
  formularies, 85
  see also format; orthography
Stapledon's survey of records, 124–5, 132, 136, 141, 261
statistics of record production *see* numbers
statutes
  diocesan, 74–5
  parliamentary, 62, 85–6, 105, 123, 140, 212, 228, 244, plates XVI–XVIII
  see also Exeter; Forest Charter; Magna Carta; merchants; Merton; *quo warranto*
Stenton, D. M., 69, 83, 165, 200, 216, 233
Stenton, F. M., 38, 55, 64, 66, 202, 232, 240, 248
Stephen, king, 44, 46, 56, 66, 79, 211, 252, plate IV
Stephen Langton, archbishop of Canterbury, 75, 131, 170
Stephen of Bulmer, 25, 206–7
Stephen of Tournai, 146
Stevenson, J., 123, 189
Stevenson, W. H., 248
stewards *see* seignorial administration
Stewart-Brown, R., 75, 77
Stiennon, J., 88
Stoke priory, 55

Stone, E., 71
Stones, E. L. G., 6, 79, 123, 143
Stones, J., 180
Stranks, C. J., 24
Stubbs, W., 21, 50, 51, 92, 109, 137, 142, 213, 220
students *see* schoolmen; schools
Suffolk, 95, 212
Suggett, H., 169
summa, 84–6, 104, 254, 259
Summerson, H. R. T., 32
Surrey, 19, 65, plate VIII
surveys & rentals, 6, 51–2, 72–4, 103, 129, 240
  see also bishops (*matricula*); *descriptio*; Domesday Book; exchequer remembrance books; seignorial administration; Stapledon's survey
Sussex, 32, 55, 68, 205, 231, plate VIII
Sutherland, D. W., 22–3, 27, 123
swords
  Conyers falchion, 25–6
  of Earl Warenne, 21–7, 234
  inscribed, 264
symbolic objects of conveyance, 23–5, 37, 127, 133, 203–8, 229, 245–8, 262
  see also sealing; *signum*
Symeon of Durham, 24

tablets for writing *see* wax
tabulation *see* format & layout
Talbot, C. H., 92, 105
tale *see* advocacy; minstrels
tally sticks, 32, 63, 72, 88, 95–6, 155, 188, 191, 215, plate VIII
Tambiah, S. J., 264
Tavistock abbey, 127
taxation records, 51, 73, 139
  see also exchequer
television, 8
Templar knights, 73, 132, 135, 138
  New Temple *see* archives (royal)
Testa de Nevill, 143
testimonials, 32, 67–8
testimony *see* oral testimony; witnesses
textus, book called, 205
  see also script
Thailand, 264
Theobald archbishop of Canterbury, 61, 207
Theobald brother of Hubert Walter, 48
Theodoric monk of Christ Church, 118
Theodulf bishop of Orléans, 193
Thierry count of Flanders, 237
Thomas, A. H., 92
Thomas Aquinas, St, 84–5
Thomas, author of *Romance of Horn*, 164, 170, 216